Globalization and Growth

Case Studies in National Economic Strategies

Globalization and Growth

Case Studies in National Economic Strategies

Richard H. K. Vietor
Harvard Business School

Robert E. Kennedy
Harvard Business School

Harcourt College Publishers

Fort Worth   Philadelphia   San Diego   New York   Orlando   Austin   San Antonio
Toronto   Montreal   London   Sydney   Tokyo

Publisher   Mike Roche
Acquisitions Editor   John Weimeister
Market Strategist   Beverly Dunn
Developmental Editor   Jana Pitts
Project Editor   Christy Goldfinch
Art Director   David Beard
Production Manager   Lois West

ISBN: 0-03-031969-2

Library of Congress Catalog Card Number: 00-103224

Address for Domestic Orders
Harcourt, Inc., 6277 Sea Harbor Drive, Orlando, FL 32887-6777
800-782-4479

Address for International Orders
International Customer Service
Harcourt, Inc., 6277 Sea Harbor Drive, Orlando, FL 32887-6777
407-345-3800
(fax) 407-345-4060
(e-mail) hbintl@harcourtbrace.com

Address for Editorial Correspondence
Harcourt, Inc., 301 Commerce Street, Suite 3700, Fort Worth, TX 76102

Web Site Address
http://www.hbcollege.com

Printed in the United States of America

0 1 2 3 4 5 6 7 8 9   066   9 8 7 6 5 4 3 2 1

Harcourt College Publishers

Globalization is the historic process of economic integration that has occurred since World War II. Trade in goods and service, investments in equity and debt, tourism, development of intellectual property, and financial transactions have become thoroughly internationalized. Thus it is more important than ever to understand the political economic strategies for development deployed in major areas of the world.

The cases in this book were developed for use in teaching international political economy at the Harvard Business School. They represent the major developmental trajectories that have defined the recent history of economic growth. These cases empirically describe the strategies of China, India, Japan, Mexico, South Africa, Poland and the Czech Republic, Europe, and the United States. As a group, these countries represent more than half the world's population and nearly two-thirds of its domestic product.

The cases are as much political and institutional as economic. This is intentional. At Harvard, we teach an analytical methodology for managers called "country analysis." This is a method of identifying the economic performance, social and political context, and national development strategy of a country (or region) and of assessing the strategy in terms of its effects on performance and its fit with context. Once mastered, this form of analysis allows mangers to assess international environments and issues themselves and confidently draw conclusions about the near-term future. We believe that all business and governmental managers should be able to perform this sort of analysis.

Richard Vietor is the Senator John Heinz Professor of Environmental Management at the Harvard Graduate School of Business Administration, where he teaches courses on regulation of business, the environment, and the international political economy. He received a B.A. in economics from Union College (1967), an M.A. in history from Hofstra University (1971), and a Ph.D. in history from the University of Pittsburgh (1975).

Before coming to the Business School in 1978, Professor Vietor held faculty appointments at Virginia Polytechnic Institute and the University of Missouri at Columbia. He is the recipient of a National Endowment for the Humanities Fellowship and Harvard's Newcomen Fellowship. In 1981, he received the Newcomen Award in business history. He was appointed Professor in 1984 and is chairman of the Business, Government, and Competition Area at the Business School. In 1993–94, he served as president of the Business History Conference.

Professor Vietor's research on business and government policy has been published in numerous journals and books. Recently, he has contributed chapters to *America versus Japan* (1986), *Wallstreet and Regulation* (1987), *Future Competition in Telecommunications* (1989), and *Beyond Free Trade* (1993). His books include *Environmental Politics and the Coal Coalition* (1980), *Energy Policy in America since 1945* (1984), *Telecommunications in Transition* (1986), *Strategic Management in the Regulated Environment* (1989), *Contrived Competition: Regulation and Deregulation in America* (1994), and *Business Management and the Natural Environment* (1996).

Robert Kennedy is an Assistant Professor of Business Administration at the Harvard Business School. He teaches an elective course, New Opportunities in Emerging Markets, and two courses in the first-year foundations sequence, Creating Modern Capitalism and The Economics of Markets. Kennedy has also taught the required course Business, Government and the International Economy (BGIE) and in various executive education programs. He holds B.A. degrees in economics and political science from Stanford, an M.S. in management from M.I.T., and a Ph.D. in business economics from Harvard.

Prior to his appointment to the Harvard faculty in 1995, Professor Kennedy worked in more than a dozen countries as a management consultant and a venture capitalist. His consulting experience focused on international corporate strategy, which, in many cases, involved cross-border mergers and acquisitions. His venture capital experience was primarily in eastern Europe. He has also worked as an operations manager at the Chase Manhattan Bank and as a marketing manager at Microsoft Corporation.

Professor Kennedy's research focuses on business strategy and industrial dynamics in emerging economies. Recent publications use an industrial organization framework to analyze how industry structure changes following economic liberalization and how these changes affect business strategy. Previous research focused on the competitive effects of firm failure.

CONTENTS

India's currency, the rupee, falls to 44 rupee/dollar. The European Central Bank lowers interest rates half of one percent. Fuji Bank, Dai-Ichi Kangyo and the Industrial Bank of Japan plan to merge. Hoping for WTO membership, China negotiates the terms of its entry with the United States. Mexico's President Zedillo stands firmly behind NAFTA. Each of these seemingly diverse events is part of a globalization process that increasingly and unceasingly shapes the conditions of national economic development.

This casebook presents eight cases of national economic strategies that represent the major development trajectories in this era of globalization. The cases are used in the MBA curriculum and in executive programs at the Harvard Business School to teach the issues and problems in economic development today. This is an applied, empirical approach to learning about macroeconomic management, economic development, international trade, and cross border flows of goods, services and capital. The country cases provide both description and data on a particular situation. The class discussion covers both concepts and decision points, with the intention of helping students to develop useful frameworks for analyzing political-economic conditions and possibly acting on that understanding.

The book begins with a brief introduction that defines globalization, describes the important trajectories of economic development, and summarizes our "country analysis" methodology. The rest of the book contains eight chapters, each a country case: (1) China, (2) India, (3) Japan, (4) Mexico, (5) South Africa, (6) Poland and Czechoslovakia, (7) the European Union, and (8) the United States. As a group, these countries represent about half the world's population and two-thirds of its gross domestic product.

Globalization is a historic process of economic integration that has occurred since World War II. Globalization is characterized by increased flows of goods, services, communications, and capital across national borders. The process was hastened by significant advances in transportation and communication technologies, as well as several rounds of trade liberalization. Since the 1950s, the volume of international trade has grown at more than twice the rate of GDP.

Cross-border capital flows have grown even faster, with both positive and negative effects. Capital flows have done much to finance growth in developing countries and to allow multinational enterprises to create global production and distribution systems. Bu they also caused the breakdown of the Bretton Woods System of fixed exchange rates in the early 1970s, ushering in an era of extreme currency volatility.

More recently, a series of regional treaties such as the European Union, the North American Free Trade Agreement, and the Asian Free Trade Agreement have led to even closer integration and a new set of challenges.

The global economy has experienced a vast transformation in the last half-century. Barring unforeseen circumstances, globalization will likely continue. This book aims to help the reader understand the effects of this continuing transformation.

Development trajectories are sets of economic, political, and social policies that sweep countries forward for years or decades before bending, often sharply, in some new direction. To some extent, a country can influence its trajectory through its choice of policies. But a country's trajectory is also influenced by other factors, such as culture, resources, and institutions. We have selected six trajectories for this book. The list is not comprehensive, but we believe it is representative of the most important developments in the global economy in the late-20th century.

Asian High Growth is the trajectory that has most affected the greatest number of people in the past 40 years. Japan pioneered this model between 1953 and 1971, growing 10.1 percent in real terms annually. Korea, Taiwan, Hong Kong, and Singapore emulated pieces of the model and achieved extraordinary growth. India, by contrast, relied on an import substitution strategy with far less success until 1991, when it changed trajectories and began to grow faster. China was a late developer and has pursued a somewhat distinct strategy.

Debt Crisis and Recovery is the far less successful trajectory that befell much of Latin America and Africa in the past 25 years. Some thirty-seven countries began to borrow heavily in the mid-1970s in order to jump-start growth after the first OPEC oil shock. This strategy worked for a few years. But a second oil shock after the Iranian Revolution led to more borrowing and skyrocketing interest rates. Then, in August 1982, Mexico went belly up! President Lopez Jose Portillo announced that the country could not service its $82 billion foreign debt. Over the next few months, Brazil, Argentina, Venezuela, and many other countries in the region were forced to ask for help.

These debt problems led to IMF intervention, debt restructuring, and a program of domestic structural reforms and external liberalization, all designed to restart growth. We have chosen Mexico as the example of this trajectory. The case explores Mexico's 1982 crisis, its efforts to recover during the de la Madrid administration, and its policies under President Salinas. Following wide acclaim in the early 1990s, currency and banking imbalances led to another currency crisis in December 1994. That, too, is typical of the trajectory.

Southern Africa's Renaissance is a third trajectory. After decades of slow or negative growth, sub-Saharan Africa began growing again in the 1990s. Poorly managed countries have begun replacing dictators, privatizing assets, reducing trade barriers, balancing budgets, and controlling inflation. The spark plug for this renewed growth has been South Africa, newly confident and engaged after emerging from decades of apartheid. South Africa accounts for 21% of Africa's GDP, and has a standard of living much higher than its neighbors. As such, it is the leading candidate to drive growth in the region. But before that happens, the new black-majority government must solve difficult social problems and make its economy grow. Thus, this case reflects well a new growth trajectory, albeit shaky in its early stages.

Trajectory four is the *collapse of communism in East Europe and the Soviet Union*. This collapse, finalized between 1989 and 1992, has changed the economic future for almost 600 million people. The process of restructuring, however, has been immense. Policymakers in the region were forced to confront a much broader range of issues than their counterparts in other countries. It was not simply a matter of freeing prices, lowering trade barriers, and encouraging foreign direct investment. The entire institutional foundation of these economies had to be reconstructed, often from the ground up. The case on Poland and Czechoslovakia compares the situation, and potential reform strategies, in the two countries. The case highlights the interdependencies between politics and economics, and how different elements of reform interact with each other.

The fifth trajectory is *economic integration in Europe*. Europe has been pursuing integration since 1951, when it removed trade barriers in iron and coal. In 1956, six countries created the European Community, with a goal of removing all internal trade barriers by 1969. That goal, accomplished a year early, lead to the first tentative steps toward monetary integration in 1978. The Single Europe Act in 1985 aimed to create a single market, with free movement of people, goods, and capital. At Maastricht in 1991, 12 European nations agreed to pursue monetary union, which 11 members accomplished in 1999. Now, other countries are contemplating the monetary union, or joining the community itself.

Our sixth and final trajectory is the *United States' decent into deficits and debt*. By 1992, the fiscal deficit reached $290 billion, with a trade deficit of $110 billion. Average real hourly wage for factory workers had been declining since 1973. The case explores U.S. economic policy in the 1990s, which has led to elimination of the fiscal deficit and a stabilization of hourly wages. However, the savings rate has tuned negative and the trade deficit remains immense.

Country analysis is a framework for studying countries' economic strategies. First developed at the Harvard Business School in the late 1970s, the approach combines elements of business strategy and Alfred Chandler's work linking strategy and structure. When used as a tool to understand country performance, the framework organizes information into three groups: performance, context, and strategy. Performance generally includes economic outcomes, such as growth, inflation, unemployment, etc. Context includes important social and political conditions, institutions, natural resources and population, industry structure, law, government, etc. Finally, strategy represents the goals and policies of the nation state. These include fiscal and monetary policy, trade policy, and various structural policies such as privatization, foreign direct investment, price controls, industrial policy, etc.

Once the relevant and important data are organized under these headings, the analysis shifts to understanding how the various elements fit together. For example, how does culture or demography affect a country's strategy? How does geography determine which strategies are viable? Or, how does strategy affect performance?

The cases in this textbook include a number of fairly standard indicators of economic performance. Among these are the national income accounts, balance of payments accounts, inflation and unemployment, fiscal balances, monetary measures (money supply and interest rates), exchange rates, and often productivity and unit labor costs. What other data are presented depend on the case: data on resource extraction, foreign direct investment, banking data, debt, oil production and prices, tax details, tariff details, environmental performance, wage rates, etc.

Even more important is the salient context. In China, the absence of the rule of law is crucial. In India, contracts are in English and are typically negotiated by lawyers. In Japan, the system of permanent employment and the structure of keiretsu groups is crucial to the country's past success and its present difficulties. In Mexico and South Africa, unequal income distribution is an important political reality. In Europe, price variations say much about unfulfilled integration.

Among the important ideas and concepts students should try to derive from these cases are **strategy, structural adjustment, institutional reform, foreign direct investment,** and **economic growth.** In several of the cases, countries are struggling to develop a viable economic development strategy or to change strategies to go forward. Students should think about the feasibility of these choices, in terms both of implementation and of effectiveness for the new millennium. Several countries are trying to adjust their economic structures to fit better with the new terms of trade in global commerce. In every case, implementing the strategy requires institutional reform, either fixing state-owned enterprises in China, streamlining bureaucracies in Japan, privatizing banks in the Czech Republic, or reforming social security in the USA.

We often ask our students, and encourage the reader to think about, whether multinational firms should invest in the country being considered. That is, are the political circumstances conducive to investment? Is the investment secure? Is the government secure? Will economic growth, inflation and exchange rate stability allow the manager to build a strong business? Is the market growing? Are wages low enough and stable enough to make this a competitive export platform? Are incomes high enough to provide enough local customers? Is the regulatory environment stable? Are contracts secure? Above all, can one expect to make money in this environment?

These are some of the important ideas you should bear in mind as you work through these cases. We hope they provide a better understanding of how countries are responding to globalization, and how globalization is changing the business environment.

Gradual Transition from a Planned Economy

Since its revolution in 1949, China has experienced 50 years of economic and political turmoil. This case focuses on China's development strategy since 1978 and the challenges the country faces at the end of the century. Although China's economic transformation has been astounding, continued rapid growth is by no means assured.

Gaining some understanding of China is important for several reasons. First, it is the world's most populous country, with more than 1.3 billion people. It also has a huge economy when measured according to purchasing power, the third largest in the world. Finally, China's strategy has been unique. It borrowed from its high-growth Asian neighbors, but the policies are not neatly categorized into standard development frameworks.

The case is organized into four broad sections, the first two of which are introductory. The first section provides a very brief introduction to China's history, dating to 2200 BC. The second section discusses the Mao era, during which the country experienced a series of abrupt and arbitrary economic and political transformations.

The third section, which is the heart of the case, discusses the market-oriented economic reforms put in place by Deng Xiaoping following Mao's death. Unlike economic reforms implemented in Europe, Eastern Europe, or Latin America, Deng had no grand design. His reforms were experimental and sequential, took place at the margin, and generally bubbled up from the provinces.

The final section of the case discusses a series of challenges facing China as the century ends. These include the reform of state-owned enterprises; rising unemployment; financial-sector reform; relations between the provinces and the central government; pressure for political liberalization and human rights; the process of globalization while being kept outside the World Trade Organization; and widespread environmental devastation.

This is a challenging case. China development strategy is not always logical or consistent. Likewise, the challenges that the country faces are complex, and in many cases, efforts to address one problem make the others worse. Despite these challenges, China's performance has been so extraordinary and it occupies such a central place in the world economy that global managers must grapple with these issues.

CASE STUDY CHINA: FACING THE 21ST CENTURY

As 1997 drew to a close, economic czar Zhu Rongji considered the economic and political challenges that China would face in the next decade. It had been a tumultuous year. Long-time paramount leader Deng Xiaoping had died in February, trade tensions with the United States escalated when the United States blocked China's membership in the World Trade Organization (WTO), and a series of currency crises in Asia threatened regional recession and the competitiveness of Chinese exports. Perhaps most important, there was widespread concern that China's vigorous growth was threatened by several long-neglected issues. Should China alter its development strategy, especially in light of the leadership change?

Since Deng had initiated China's program of economic reform in 1978, China had experienced a stunning transformation. GDP had grown at a 9.5% annual rate, per capita income had more than quadrupled, foreign direct investment had boomed, and trade had increased from 10% to 45% of GDP-making China the world's seventh-largest exporter.[1] Although per capita GDP was still only $600 when measured at official exchange rates, China's economy had become the world's third largest when adjusted for purchasing power.[2] Most observers were awed by the magnitude of the transformation; the World Bank referred to the reforms as "spectacularly successful."[3]

Deng's death had settled a long-simmering dispute over succession for the top positions of the Communist party and the country. After seven years of grooming, President Jiang Zemin, Zhu's patron and a cautious reformer, had emerged as the top leader. Zhu was currently number three in the hierarchy and was expected to become the prime minister when the current prime minister, Li Peng, retired in March 1998.

Deng's death and the political ascendancy of the reformers provided an opportunity to reassess China's economic strategy. Deng's primary goals had been political stability and rapid economic growth. But the focus on short-term growth had left many issues unaddressed. Losses at state-owned enterprises and banks were growing, posing a potential threat to China's fiscal health. Trade tensions with the United States were increasing on both political and economic fronts. The Communist party's political legitimacy was threatened by corruption and a shift of power to the provinces. Pollution was a growing danger to public health. Finally, and perhaps most threatening in the long run, China's market institutions remained underdeveloped.

As economic czar, Zhu was charged with addressing these issues. He was inclined to think strategically, but radical action would be difficult. Nearly everyone agreed that China had great economic potential, but that potential might remain unrealized unless Zhu found a way to address the factors that threatened long-term growth.

Historical Background

Dynastic China

China claims one of the longest histories of any civilization, dating from at least 2200 BC, when farming clans began to form in the Yellow River valley. Central government first arose in approximately 1120 BC, when the Zhou clan established control over the Yellow River valley. The Zhou ruled the region until 480 BC, when China splintered during the Warring States period (480 BC–221 BC). During this period, Confucius, one of China's greatest philosopher-sages, tried to convince the rulers of the virtues

Professor Robert E. Kennedy and Research Associate Katherine Marquis prepared this case as the basis for class discussion rather than to illustrate either effective or ineffective handling of an administrative situation. We are grateful for substantial input from Professor Yasheng Huang and Research Associate Teresita Ramos.

of order and the ways of maintaining it. China's first emperor, Qin Shi Huang, unified the country in 221 BC, creating its first dynasty. Qin is credited with laying the foundation for the birth of the Chinese state. He standardized the Chinese currency, weights and measures, and the written language. He also created a national army and established a centralized political apparatus that ruled much of China's present territory. Qin died in 210 BC, and his empire quickly disintegrated. Following Qin, China was ruled by a series of dynasties that all used the imperial system he created. Confucianism became the official state ideology under the Han dynasty (206 BC–AD 220).

Three basic pillars sustained China's imperial system. The first was the emperor, who sat at the pinnacle of power and enjoyed the "Mandate of Heaven." This mandate gave the emperor the divine right to rule but was contingent upon good conduct. Chinese history contains many examples of peasants rising against an emperor whose conduct was perceived as a sign that he had lost the mandate of heaven. The second pillar was the imperial bureaucracy. The Chinese invented the art of bureaucracy, along with sophisticated procedures to reward, monitor, and control these bureaucrats. The bureaucracy was selected using arduous, multitiered and multiyear civil service examinations, which were quite well developed by the seventh century.[a] The third pillar was Confucianism, a philosophy that stressed three bonds: between subject and ruler, between son and father, and between husband and wife. The idea was that rulers should govern their countries as patriarchs governed a family. This moralistic approach had a profound impact on the development of Chinese political institutions and has influenced China through modern times. Because it viewed the rulers as moral beings, Confucianism downplayed the need to create institutions to "check and balance" the ambition of rulers. Confucianism's view of society as a network of relationships also led to the practice of *guanxi*, the cultivation of relationships to help make one's way in the world, which was still important in contemporary China.

Dynastic China has been credited with some of the world's greatest technological inventions. The Chinese invented paper, printing, the compass, iron casting, mechanical clocks, and gunpowder, in each case centuries before these items were introduced in the West. In addition to its technological lead, imperial China seemed to have many of the ingredients required for rapid development. The currency was unified, production was quite specialized, and the cities housed great markets. Thus, China's subsequent economic stagnation was one of the great paradoxes of economic history. As historian R. H. Tawney commented, Chinese peasants "ploughed with iron when Europe used wood, and continued to plough with it when Europe used steel."[4]

China's last dynasty, the Qing (1644–1911), collapsed under both internal and external forces. Probably the single most important internal factor was the unprecedented population growth between the mid-18th and mid-19th centuries, when China's population increased from 143 million to 423 million. This growth strained food supplies and led to widespread malnutrition. In addition, the dynasty refused to allow the bureaucracy to grow along with the population. This increased the competition for coveted civil service positions, leading to bribery and corruption that ultimately undermined the imperial examination system.[5]

A second important factor was Western penetration of China starting in the 19th century. The first opium war with the British (1839–1842) led to the Treaty of Nanking, signed in 1842. The treaty forced China to open five port cities to British trade, ceded Hong Kong to the British, established extraterritoriality (where foreign

---

[a] There were three rounds of qualifying examinations: one at the county level, one at the prefectural level, and then the qualifying examination itself. The actual examination then was offered at three levels—in the provincial capitals, in Beijing, and then at the imperial palace. Typically, a man started preparing for these examinations at the age of seven and, if successful, finished all of them around the age of 35.

[b] The Qing emperors were ethnically Manchu, a tribe that had traditionally been on the fringe of Chinese civilization and outside China proper. For that reason, the manchu dynasty was never fully accepted by the Han Chinese—the ethnically dominant racial group—even though the Manchus were completely absorbed into Chinese culture.

nationals were exempted from Chinese law), and surrendered substantial economic sovereignty to foreigners. The treaties undermined the legitimacy of the Qing emperor and inspired Chinese nationalism against the Manchu regime.[b] The dynasty was overthrown in 1911 by the army in the hinterland city of Wuchang. Given the enormity of the event, the mutiny was relatively small, involving only a few thousand soldiers and was largely nonviolent.

The Republican Era

After the demise of the Qing, the country descended into chaos. Regional warlords established fiefdoms throughout the country and the central government became inoperative. Throughout the 1910s, the warlords fought among themselves while Chinese intellectuals debated what direction the country should move. This changed abruptly when the Versailles Peace Conference, which brought World War I to a close, awarded German holdings in China's Shangdong province to Japan instead of returning them to China. Students in Beijing rioted, burning down government buildings and assaulting the Japanese ambassador. The riots soon spread and brought the country to a standstill. The riots, which came to be known as the "May Fourth Incident," introduced a new form of violent "mass politics" to China.[6]

Two broad political efforts emerged from the May Fourth Movement: the Guomindang (GMD), a nationalist party that had been founded by anti-imperial revolutionaries; and the Chinese Communist Party (CCP), founded by leftist students, academics, and other urban intellectuals. In the early 1920s, the GMD gained control of several southern provinces, most notably Guangdong. The CCP had a following in the cities but did not control any provinces. Both groups had close ties to the Soviet Union, which convinced them to join forces in 1924 in an effort to reunify the country.

GMD/CCP cooperation ended in 1927 when GMD leader Chiang Kai-shek launched a surprise attack that killed nearly 90% of the CCP's members. The surviving Communists fled to the rural areas in the south and began building support among the peasantry. Between 1927 and 1934, the CCP rebuilt itself as a rural party. It was during this period that Mao Zedong, a young peasant from the central province of Hunan, developed his thinking on four crucial issues: land reform, how to develop and sustain political activity among peasants, how to govern territory under the CCP's control, and how to use military force effectively in the countryside. In 1927, Mao wrote that peasants' "political activity tends to rise up like a storm that unleashes tremendous violence and passion, but then quickly exhausts itself."[7] This view shaped Mao's political thinking until his death and did much to change modern China.

The Communists were eventually forced to move north in the fantastic "Long March" from Jiangxi to Shaanxi, a year-long trek that took them through vast reaches of inhospitable terrain. More than 80% of the marchers died, and for decades, participation in the Long March was a powerful legitimizing force for surviving political leaders.

External events again intruded when Japan invaded China in 1931. The Japanese occupation prompted a second alliance between the GMD and CCP that lasted until the early 1940s. The CCP remained in the northern provinces while the GMD retreated to China's southwest. When the Allied Forces defeated Japan, the United States recognized the GMD as the legitimate government of China and airlifted GMD officials to China's leading cities. Chiang launched another effort to exterminate the CCP in the winter of 1946, prompting a full-scale civil war. By late 1949, the CCP had routed the GMD, which fled to Taiwan. On October 1, 1949, Mao stood atop the Tiananmen "Gate of Heavenly Peace" and proclaimed the formation of the People's Republic of China.

---

[c] In 1820, China had been the world's largest economy, with a 30% share of world GDP. By 1950, its share had fallen to only 7%. A. Maddison, *Monitoring the World Economy* (Paris: OECD, 1995). Elsewhere, Maddison (1991) estimates that China's per-capita GDP declined from $500 in 1400 to $454 in 1950, measured in constant 1985 prices.

The Maoist Era

When the CCP came to power, China had been in decline for nearly a century, and by one estimate, since 1400.[c] Between 1949 and his death in 1976, Mao directed a radical transformation of the country. He appears to have been driven by two goals: achieving a peasant-led socialist revolution and rapid economic development. As his focus shifted from one goal to the other, policy followed, often abruptly. The Maoist period can be divided into four eras: political consolidation and economic reconstruction (1949–1957); the Great Leap Forward (1958–1960); economic recovery (1961–1965); and the Cultural Revolution (1966–1976).

After expelling the GMD to Taiwan, Mao moved quickly to establish political control and rebuild the economy. He deployed the People's Liberation Army throughout the country and set up provincial governments under CCP control. He also targeted potential opponents with mass political campaigns. These included land reform (which targeted land-owners and rich peasants), the "Suppression of Counter-revolutionaries" campaign (former GMD officials), the "Thought Reform of Intellectuals" campaign (non-CCP intellectuals), and the "Anti-Rightist" campaign (intellectuals and some party officials). These campaigns employed the techniques Mao had developed in the countryside, including mass action, violence, and forced public "confessions." During the period of consolidation, the CCP looked to the Soviet Union for guidance on how to rebuild the economy. Thus, the first five-year plan (1953–1957) emphasized central planning, capital accumulation, and investment in heavy industry. The strategy led to GDP growth of nearly nine percent[d] and by 1957 Mao had consolidated his power.

Mao became increasingly disillusioned with Soviet guidance in the late 1950s and sought to establish a distinctive Chinese approach to development. He was particularly incensed by a 1956 speech in which Soviet Premier Nikita Khrushchev attacked Joseph Stalin's legacy, cautioning against granting too much power to a willful leader. As Mao searched for another approach, he became convinced that mass action by the peasantry would allow China to leap over the normal stages of economic development. This led to a program referred to as the "Great Leap Forward." Land that had been distributed to peasants was reclaimed and granted to rural communes. Communes were directed to mobilize peasants in order to increase agricultural production, build rural infrastructure, and establish an industrial base in the countryside—with a special emphasis on steel production. Ambitious targets were set and initial reports from the countryside were promising. More than a million "backyard" iron smelters were constructed in the first year and the state statistical bureau claimed that the production of food and cotton doubled. But the gains were largely fictitious. Local officials, eager to report that the masses had responded enthusiastically to the program, falsified production figures. Most steel was of such low quality that it could not be used. But this was not apparent to the planners, who instructed the communes to shift more labor from farming to industry. Agricultural output plummeted and 20 million–30 million people—mostly the elderly and people in poor health—starved to death. Kenneth Lieberthal, a well-known political scientist, observed that the Great Leap was "in the final analysis, a tremendous, willful leap away from reality."[8]

As the extent of the Great Leap disaster became clear,[e] Mao quietly shifted strategies. He withdrew from day-to-day decision making and recalled the country's well-trained bureaucracy. Mao's longtime lieutenant, Deng Xiaoping, was asked to stabilize the economy. Deng quickly reversed much of the Great Leap—breaking communes into smaller units, reorganizing economic reporting, bringing back technical experts,

[d] During the first five-year plan, national income grew at an 8.9% annual rate and agricultural output grew by 3.8%. Fairbank, p. 358. Maddison (1991) estimates that this growth was due almost entirely to capital accumulation. The capital stock grew at an annual rate of 9.2% between 1950 and 1973, while total factor productivity grew by only 0.49%.

[e] Estimates put the GDP decline at more than 30%, approximately the same decline experienced in the United States during the Great Depression. See Fairbank and Reischauer, *China: Tradition and Transformation*, p. 500.

and forcing peasants to return to farming. The economy quickly recovered and, by 1965, output had returned to pre–Great Leap levels.

Mao apparently found it difficult to remain in the background. He grew increasingly suspicious of the government bureaucracy and of intellectuals in the CCP, who he suspected were exploiting the countryside, just as the imperial elites had done. Mao launched a stunning attack on the establishment in 1966, declaring a Cultural Revolution to "destroy the old and establish the new." His goal was to rekindle the spirit of the Long March, throwing China into a state of permanent revolution. Mao encouraged youthful Red Guards to destroy the "four olds" (e.g., old ideas, old culture, old customs, and old habits). In practice, this meant widespread beatings, denunciations, and mob-instigated "trials." Red Guards roamed the country attacking establishment elites, including government officials, managers, intellectuals, and former members of the bourgeois class. Even high government officials were not immune; Mao denounced Deng Xiaoping, and he was "sent down" to the countryside. Deng's son was permanently disabled when he was thrown out of a window by Red Guards.

China turned inward during this period. All ambassadors were recalled from abroad, and students attacked the British, Soviet, and Indonesian embassies. Mao eventually realized that the Cultural Revolution had spun out of control and ordered the army to reestablish control in 1969. The violence continued sporadically, especially in the countryside. When Mao began to experience health problems in the early 1970s, political infighting between "moderates" (headed by Zhou Enlai) and "radicals" (led by Mao's wife, Jiang Qing) took center stage. Deng was rehabilitated in 1973 and became the leading moderate when Zhou died in January 1976. Mao died on September 9, 1976. After a two-year struggle between the rival camps, Deng emerged as the paramount leader in mid-1978.

Institutions of Social Control

The CCP exercised a tremendous degree of control over the Chinese population, primarily though four layers of administration: the central government, provinces, local authorities (either counties or cities), and "units" (*danwei*). Although the economy was centrally planned, it was less rigidly hierarchical than in the Soviet Union. The central government set broad goals but allowed the provinces and local authorities a high degree of autonomy regarding how to reach these goals. Political control was tight, however, and the locus of this control was the unit. All citizens were required to belong to a unit. For most, the unit was their employer; for students it was their school; and for farmers, their commune. The *danwei* were multipurpose bodies. They were responsible for providing housing, primary and secondary schooling, pensions, and ration coupons for food, clothing, and furniture. The units also administered birth control programs, approved marriages and divorces, and resolved personal disputes. The key to the unit's importance was that few individuals were given permission to transfer from one unit to another. Workers were guaranteed lifetime employment but were not free to switch jobs or move to another city. Each unit, even within cities, was an isolated political and social organization, with little communication between members of different units.

The Era of Economic Reform

Compared with the upheaval China had experienced since 1949, the situation that Deng inherited in 1978 was relatively stable. The moderate faction of the CCP had gained control of the party but did not enjoy the unchecked power that Mao had possessed. Political interactions between the reformers and hard-liners would dictate the pace and thrusts of the reform effort throughout the 1980s. Deng was wary of political manipulation and mass upheaval and shifted away from ideological exhortations, using material incentives instead. His strategy involved two simple principles: "reform measures were legitimate if they promoted rapid economic growth and if they did not weaken the Party's control of the political system [and]; everything else was subject to compromise."[9] Deng was known for his pragmatism, perhaps best summed up in his slogan "Who cares if a cat is black or white, as long as it catches mice." In practice, this meant both the marketization and internationalization of the economy. Deng also moved to depoliticize society, creating a sphere of private activity beyond the reach of politics. But political reform was relative. There would be no move toward democracy and the CCP would retain its monopoly on power.

While the economy had stabilized, Deng still faced a great challenge. China territory was nearly identical to that of the United States, but it had four times the population and just one-quarter of the arable land with which to feed them.[10] Eighty-two percent of the population lived in rural areas, but rural incomes had been stagnant for more than a decade. The Great Leap and Cultural Revolution had inflicted lasting damage on the economy,[f] and more than 60% of the population lived on less than one dollar a day, the international poverty line. There was no rule of law in the Western sense.[11] Famine was an ever-present concern—mass starvation had occurred just 15 years before and population growth had outstripped grain production since the early 1950s.[12] Still, China did have several factors working in its favor. Its workforce was skilled and disciplined. Millions of overseas Chinese were willing to trade with and invest in China. And China's neighbors in Asia had demonstrated the potential for high growth.

One of Deng's first steps was to tighten controls on population growth. The country had long been the most populous in the world, and opinion among the leadership was divided about whether this was a national asset or liability. Mao had considered a large population an asset, as "every person added two more hands to work." During the first 20 years of the People's Republic, no effort was made to restrict births, and the birth rate was consistently above 30 per thousand population. Zhou Enlai had come to believe that controlling population growth was a precondition for economic development and had initiated a two-child policy in 1971—with the goal of reducing the birth rate to 20 per thousand by 1980. The campaign's slogan was "late, sparse, and few."[13] Zhou's policy had limited success, as the birth rate declined to 23 per thousand by 1975. Deng launched a one-child policy in 1978. Women were required to obtain permission to have more than one child, with monitoring and enforcement provided by the units. A variety of rewards and punishments was used to enforce the policy, including subsidies, social sanctions, destruction of property, and occasionally, forced abortions. The program was fairly successful in the cities, where the average number of children declined to one per family. The program was, however, fiercely resisted in the countryside where the average number of children was still 2.3 per family. In an effort to maintain social peace, the government relaxed the one-child policy where resistance was greatest. Ethnic minorities were exempted, and most counties granted permission for a second child if the first was a girl.

While Deng was clearly responsible for the economic reforms initiated since 1978, only a few policies were imposed from the center. Beijing, with the support of the Peoples Liberation Army, was responsible for maintaining political stability. Further, the high savings rate and exchange rate policy were also due to central government policies. Most other reforms bubbled up from below. Deng created space for experimentation and local officials responded enthusiastically. Successful innovations

---

[f] One study estimates that the damage done by the GLF and Cultural Revolution had reduced China's 1978 GDP by at least 50%. G. Chow and Y. Kwan, 1996, "Estimating Economic Effects of the Political Movements in China," *Journal of Comparative Economics* 23 (2): 192–208.

were duplicated and eventually endorsed by the central government; unsuccessful experiments were discarded. The reforms can be divided into four broad categories. These were rural reform, trade and investment reform, SOE/urban reform, and institutional reform.

Reform in the Countryside

The first wave of reforms took place in the countryside. In 1978, most peasants still lived in rural communes and were instructed to produce fixed quantities of agricultural products to meet the plan. In some areas, local officials had begun to allow peasants to retain production above their contracted amount and often looked the other way when this production was sold on local markets. Prompted by officials in drought-ravaged provinces, Deng undertook several measures to increase crop production and raise rural incomes. He instructed local officials to increase procurement prices for central plan quotas and to allow above-quota output to be freely sold.[14] This created a "dual price" system, in which a fixed amount of output was delivered to meet the plan and all incremental output was sold at market-determined prices. Deng also increased state investment in agriculture and relaxed restrictions on interprovincial trade in agricultural products.[15]

A related innovation was the "Household Responsibility System." Although officially prohibited by the central government, many communes began to lease plots of land to individual households. As payment, the family was responsible for managing production and delivering a fixed quota of output to the commune. The system shifted control of production decisions from communes to households, and thus led to very different behavior. The Household Responsibility System spread quickly after 1979. In 1981, when the central government officially approved the system, 45% of rural households were already participating. By 1983, the system had spread to 98% of farming households.

The reforms had an immediate impact and production of all types jumped sharply. The most rapid gains in agricultural output occurred between 1978 and 1984, when grain yields grew at a 5.7% rate, the production of oilseeds doubled, and cotton output tripled.[16] Pork, beef, and mutton production all grew by at least 80%.[17] After 1984, growth slowed to its long-term average of about 2%.

The changes in the countryside led to a virtuous cycle. Increased production and procurement prices raised rural incomes and led to a sharp increase in savings.[g] Higher incomes created demand for consumer goods that were in short supply. To meet this demand, local governments began to direct savings into collectively owned firms, known as "Township and Village Enterprises," many of which were actually established during the Great Leap Forward to promote rural industrialization.[h] Increases in agricultural productivity freed up surplus labor in the countryside.[i] Industrial output in the countryside boomed. By the time the central government officially approved rural industrial development in 1984, Township and Village Enterprises' share of industrial output had grown from 22% to 30%. It grew to 36% in 1988, and has stayed at about that level since. Throughout the 1980s, TVE output grew at an average rate of 30% a year.[18] By 1995, 23 million TVEs employed 129 million people.[19]

---

[g] The annual rural household income increased from 133.6 yuan in 1978 to 397.6 yuan in 1985. Gross savings by rural households increased from 55.7 billion yuan to 438.1bn between 1978 and 1984. China Statistical Bureau.

[h] Most TVEs were owned by rural *danwei* (units) and enjoyed much more freedom than SOEs. They could generally produce anything they chose, within geographic limits, and retained their own earnings. After the disastrous experience during the Great Leap Forward, most TVEs produced agricultural equiment and simple manufactured products.

[i] By the mid-1980s, more than 100 million adults had given up farming and were working in villages and townships across China. Lieberthal, p. 148.

Trade and Investment Reforms

China's self-imposed isolation during the Cultural Revolution had come at a time when other Asian economies were taking off. Hong Kong, Japan, Singapore, South Korea, and Taiwan had all combined technology imports with export promotion to drive rapid growth. Deng believed a similar strategy would work for China, but the country had a long way to go. The economy was extremely isolated, with a trade to GDP ratio of only 10% and no stock of foreign direct investment. Internationalization was also needed for less philosophical reasons. Reform in the countryside had led to strong demand for imports, primarily fertilizer and capital equipment, and foreign exchange reserves had fallen dangerously low. Despite these factors, internationalization proved to be quite controversial. Hard-liners resisted because of worries about foreign influence.

As with other elements of Deng's reforms, events quickly overtook the planners' deliberations and reform proceeded along three distinct paths. The first was piecemeal trade reform, which started in 1979 and continued through the mid-1990s. Prior to 1979, all trade had flowed through 12 foreign trade corporations (FTCs). After that, local officials started to license their own FTCs and allowed local firms to bypass central government FTCs. By 1988, the number of registered FTCs had grown to 5,075. In addition, the number of domestic firms with foreign trade rights mushroomed, reaching nearly 10,000 in the mid-1990s.[20] In the early 1980s, the central government also began a slow reduction in import tariffs, but many nontariff barriers remained.[21]

The liberalization of foreign direct investment (FDI) was much more controversial than trade reform. Neighboring high-growth countries had pursued different strategies with regard to FDI. Foreign direct investment had played an important role in Hong Kong and Singapore, but little role in Japan and South Korea. FDI troubled hard-liners because it involved much closer foreign ties than simple trade. To the hardliners, foreign investment implied foreign control of Chinese assets and a dilution of the socialist character of the economy. Given China's history, this was an especially sensitive issue. A compromise was reached in which foreign investment would be restricted to just a few geographic areas, thereby isolating foreigners' influence while the costs and benefits of FDI could be studied. Four coastal cities were designated Special Economic Zones in 1980 and granted permission to experiment with new institutions, such as tax rates and approval procedures for foreign investment.[j] Enterprises operating in the Special Economic Zones were exempted from the central plan, labor regulations, and many taxes.[k]

A third set of reforms involved foreign currency. The inflation-adjusted (i.e., "real") value of the yuan was steadily lowered, starting in 1980 and continuing through 1993. Several microeconomic reforms were also implemented. Until the mid-1980s, foreign currency transactions were tightly regulated. All capital transactions required central bank approval, while the treatment of trade transactions varied according to firm ownership. Enterprises with foreign capital that were located in Special Economic Zones were generally allowed to retain foreign currency and to

---

[j] Three SEZs were located in Guangdong province (Shenzhen, across from Hong Kong's New Territories; Zhuhai, next to the Portugese colony of Macao; and Shantou, in the northern part of the province). The fourth (Xiamin) was located in Fujan province, near Taiwan.

[k] The most ambitious of the SEZs was Shenzhen, a small town on the border of Hong Kong's New Territories. The location was chosen to take advantage of the Hong Kong economy, which was beginning to transfer labor-intensive industry offshore. Shenzhen had almost no industrial base, but the local government moved quickly to upgrade the infrastructure and create a friendly legal environment. The results were immediate and astonishing. Industrial output grew at an annual rate of 56% between 1979 and 1983 and increased to 100% in both 1983 and 1984. In 1984, 14 more SEZs were opened along the coast and in major cities. One persistent problem during the early years of investment until 1986 was the issue of currency conversion, but foreign trade continued to increase in the second half of the decade after the expansion of the SEZ experiment. Joint Economic Committee, 1986, *China's Economy Looks toward the Year 2000* (Washington, DC: U.S. Government Printing Office), p. 355.

import and export freely. Domestic firms required regulatory approval and foreign-currency allowances to import and were forced to turn over all export earnings to the state banking system. In the mid-1980s, the government introduced a complex system in which domestic firms could retain a portion of the foreign exchange they generated. In 1986, the government introduced a dual exchange rate system on which domestic firms could buy and sell limited amounts of foreign currency (this is discussed in greater detail below).

The reforms led to a dramatic transformation of China's links to the outside world. Merchandise exports grew from $11 billion in 1978 to $24 billion in 1984, a 14% growth rate. By 1996, exports had reached $154 billion. During this same period, exports increased from 4.9% to 18% of GDP. The response to liberalization of FDI was much slower. Foreign direct investment flows grew from $57 million in 1980 to $2.7 billion in 1990. It exploded after 1993, jumping from $7.2 billion in 1992 to $42 billion in 1996. Since 1993, China has been the world's largest developing-country recipient of FDI. In the mid-1990s, large trade surpluses and inbound-capital flows put upward pressure on the yuan and led to a rapid accumulation of foreign reserves.

The reforms led to some severe distortions, however. Naughton concluded that by 1987, China had established, in essence, two separate trading regimes. One was an export-processing regime. Although it was extremely open, access was controlled: most domestic firms were excluded, while most foreign-invested firms could participate. The other was the traditional, but increasingly reformed, [domestic] Chinese regime, which is basically an import-substitution regime.[22]

Much of the export-processing regime revolved around simple, labor-intensive assembly. In this system, components were imported duty-free, an enterprise in China assembled them, and the goods were then re-exported. In many cases, the Chinese firm simply provided assembly work on a contract basis—it never took title to the imported materials. The export-processing regime was fairly small until the early 1990s, never accounting for as much as 10% of total Chinese exports. But as inbound-FDI increased and economic growth in the Special Economic Zones reached a fever pitch in the mid-1990s, foreign invested enterprises' share of exports increased rapidly, reaching 31% in 1995, and more than 40% for the first six months of 1996 [see **Exhibit 1.9**]. Exports from the rest of the economy had grown but at a much slower pace.

State-Owned Enterprise Reform

The reforms in the countryside and the Special Economic Zones fueled sharp increases in production and incomes, but they also increased pressure on state-owned enterprises—the backbone of the urban economy. The SOEs had been nurtured under central planning and accounted for 78% of industrial output and 19% of total employment in 1978 (vs. 72% of employment in agriculture). SOEs in key sectors (such as heavy industry, mineral extraction, energy production, and banking) reported to the central government. Others reported to provincial or local governments. Enterprises purchased inputs and sold their output at state-determined prices, produced to a quota, and turned all of their profits over to the state, which also covered operating losses. As of 1978, SOEs were also the primary source of government revenues—they paid income taxes equal to 19% of GDP and remitted profits equal to an additional 19% of GDP.[23] Like most SOEs elsewhere, state-owned enterprises in China were considered overstaffed, inefficient, and poorly managed. The World Bank estimates that manufacturing productivity in SOEs declined at an annual rate of 1.2% from 1978 to 1983.[24] SOEs were, however, the primary conduit for social services in urban areas. They provided housing, education, health care, and lifetime employment for their workers. In many cases children inherited their parents' jobs. This system was known as the "iron rice bowl."

In the early 1980s, some local officials began to experiment with an ad hoc "Management Responsibility System," a counterpart to the Household Responsibility System used in agriculture. New freedoms were negotiated on a firm-by-firm basis and fell into three categories: increased autonomy over production and investment decisions, the right to retain a portion of profits, and the right to sell above-plan output at market prices. By 1984, profit retention and production autonomy were in widespread use, but formal permission to produce above the plan was still rare [see **Exhibit 1.10**]. In October 1984, the central government formally approved these practices, which then spread quickly. Price controls for (above-plan) final goods were loosened starting in 1980, and dual-track prices were introduced for intermediate goods in 1985.

Unlike the rural and trade reforms, initiatives designed to improve the performance of SOEs had limited success. SOEs' share of industrial output continued to fall, from 78% in 1978 to 55% in 1990. Despite this drop in their share of output, SOEs' share of total employment showed only a small decline, from 19% to 18%. As non-state firms gained competitiveness, SOEs' monopoly positions were eroded and their combined contributions to the central government fell sharply (from 38% of GDP in 1978 to only 3.6% in 1990).[1] About two-thirds of SOEs lost money in 1992 and government subsidies to loss-making enterprises increased from 2.0% of GDP in 1985 to 3.1% in 1990.[25] The data are mixed about whether productivity in SOEs increased following the reforms, but most analysts agree that productivity growth in SOEs lagged that in TVEs and the private sector.[26]

While the Management Responsibility System did little to improve SOE performance, it provided opportunities for corruption. Enterprise directors used their personal relationships (*guanxi*[m]) with local and national leaders to negotiate prices for industrial inputs. Directors often used their lowest-quality inputs for goods bound for the state and focused their efforts and resources on above-plan production. The dual-price system created the opportunity to earn high profits by diverting plan-output to the unregulated market. Because state-delivery quotas were negotiated, SOE managers had an incentive to bribe local officials. International surveys rated China as one of the most corrupt countries in the world.

Institutional Reform

In addition to the rural, trade, and urban reforms, China implemented a series of institutional reforms between 1978 and 1995. Four were particularly important: increased provincial autonomy, fiscal reform, financial-sector reform, and currency reforms.

As part of Deng's impulse toward experimentation, the central government granted provincial governments increased autonomy with regard to taxation and industrial development in 1984. Local governments were granted significant tax collection authority in what was known as the "tax contract system." Under this system, the local government collected taxes and turned over a tax quota to the central government, retaining a high proportion of any above-quota tax revenue. Provincial authorities used this freedom to allocate funds to local SOEs and TVEs. The new system led to a sharp decline in central government revenue, which fell from 9.6% to only 6.0% of GDP between 1986 and 1992. The central leadership viewed this development with alarm as the fiscal contraction at the center eroded the government's ability to stabilize the economy and to effect income transfers across regions.

---

[l] This figure, although accurate, overstates the extent of SOE's relative decline. Taxes as a share of GDP were declining sharply during this period, and the central government's share of total tax revenues was also declining (see exhibits). Both of these issues are discussed below.

[m] Guanxi was an integral part of Chinese culture and business. Some viewed guanxi as a social lubricant that helped to establish trust and reciprocity. Others viewed it as mere corruption.

In 1994, the central government implemented an extensive tax reform. It established a National Tax Service that was responsible for direct collection of national taxes, making central tax collection largely independent of local officials. The 1994 reform also reduced the number of taxes from 32 to 18 and introduced a value-added tax. Finally, it moved the system toward more uniform treatment for domestic and foreign-invested firms. Prior to reform, income tax rates had varied by ownership type and because of bargaining between firms and various tax collection authorities. After the reforms there was a single income tax applied to all domestic firms, and the government announced that it planned to unify the tax treatment of foreign-invested firms.[27] The new system reversed fiscal contraction, and the central government's share of consolidated revenue rose dramatically from 22% in 1993 to 50% in 1996.[28]

The dispersal of economic power to the provinces also had an adverse effect on the conduct of monetary policy. Because local governments often appointed the directors of regional branches of the People's Bank of China, they could pressure local branches to overextend credit and to direct loans to politically favored projects, rather than to those that were economically viable or which the central government wished to support.[n] This led to excessive credit expansion and a rising share of bad loans. In response, the central government moved to strengthen the monetary functions of the People's Bank of China. In 1995, the central government established a new Central Bank Law that prohibited overdrafts to government agencies and recentralized monetary control in the central bank.

Although the main thrust of institutional reforms in the 1990s was to recentralize fiscal and monetary controls, there had also been a quiet move away from China's rigid political centralization. During the Maoist period, the commune system served both economic and political functions such as tax collection and enforcing population controls. As the commune system was dismantled, the reformist leaders began to fear that a political vacuum was forming in the countryside. To fill this void, reformist leaders began to introduce competitive elections for village-level officials in the late-1980s. By the mid-1990s, four-fifths of Chinese villages had held at least one such election. Studies show that village elections improved governance. For example, in areas where village elections were held, there was more compliance with tax collection and population controls.[29]

The final set of institutional reforms involved currency convertibility. Prior to 1986, the yuan was largely inconvertible. Domestic exporters were allowed to retain only a small percentage of their export earnings,[o] and importers had to petition the Bank of China for currency. In an effort to decentralize decision making while still retaining some control, the central government introduced a dual exchange rate system. Under this system, the central bank fixed the official exchange rate but allowed limited free exchange on a parallel "swap market." The exchange rate on the swap market was set by market forces and was generally much lower than the official rate. Domestic enterprises were forced to turn over the bulk of their foreign receipts to the central bank at the official rate but could trade a small portion on the swap markets. Enterprises with foreign capital were allowed to trade all their export receipts. The treatment of domestic enterprises served as a tax on domestic exports while subsidizing imports.[30]

In 1994, the authorities abolished the dual exchange rate and merged the market and official rates at the market rate. This amounted to an effective devaluation of the yuan by about 50%. The action gave a large boost to Chinese exports. The merchandise trade balance was in surplus every year from 1993, rising to $18.1 billion in 1995. With the exception of 1993, the current account was in surplus every year since 1990. These surpluses, combined with large FDI inflows, led to a huge buildup of foreign exchange reserves.[31]

---

[n] The local influences on money creation came out when the central government needed to print money to meet the credit shortfalls created by the actions of these local governments.

[o] Special allowances were made for foreign producers operating in SEZs.

Economic Strategy in the Mid-1990s

China's ninth five-year plan (1996–2000) outlined the country's economic strategy at the end of the century. It established a goal of 8% GDP growth and noted the necessity of completing two fundamental transitions: from a traditional, planned economy to a "socialist-market economy," and from extensive growth (based on increases in inputs) to intensive growth (driven by improvements in efficiency).

The plan consisted of five (sometimes contradictory) initiatives. The first was to continue the fight against inflation through fiscal and monetary restraint. Inflation had peaked at 24% in 1994 but had fallen to 3% by 1997. Second, the reform of state-owned enterprises was to be refocused and accelerated. The effort was narrowed to the 1,000 largest state-owned firms. Smaller firms were to be privatized or shut down.

The third initiative involved strengthening China's integration with the international economy. To achieve its growth objectives, China needed unfettered access to international export and capital markets. But tensions created by China's import restrictions, rapid growth in exports, and the large bilateral trade surplus with the United States had led to China's exclusion from the newly formed World Trade Organization. WTO membership would have guaranteed access to export markets. Without it, China would be forced to rely on bilateral negotiations.

The fourth initiative was designed to increase productivity growth. Science and technology funding was increased, and the central government announced that it would focus industrial policy on five "pillar" industries. These industries (machinery, electronics, petrochemicals, automobiles, and construction) were to receive increased investment appropriations and special protection from international competition. Proposals to protect these industries had led to some of the sharpest conflicts with China's trading partners. Finally, the plan reiterated the need for economic and political stability.

Challenges on the Eve of a New Millennium

China experienced a stunning transformation in the Deng era. Although highest in the coastal provinces, growth was widespread. If China's 30 provinces had been counted as individual economies, the 20 fastest-growing economies in the world between 1978 and 1995 would have been Chinese.[32] The share of the labor force employed in agriculture declined from 71% to 50%, a shift that took 59 years in Japan. China's economic transformation was matched by improvements in social indicators. The birth rate fell by 25%. Infant mortality declined from 85 per 1,000 births in 1975 to 45 in 1990—compared with 127 for India and 111 for Indonesia, both measured in 1990.[33] Various estimates put the number of people who were lifted above absolute poverty in the 1980s at around 100 million.

Despite these impressive achievements, Zhu faced a series of unresolved issues that threatened to derail future growth. SOE losses were mounting and rising unemployment threatened social stability. The banking system was in danger of collapse. Relations between the central government and the provinces remained tense. Further integration with the world trading system was threatened by China's exclusion from the WTO. And unchecked development had caused serious environmental damage.

SOE Reform

Despite vigorous reform efforts since 1984, the financial performance of SOEs continued to deteriorate. As TVEs, private firms, and foreign-invested enterprises flourished in the 1990s, state-owned enterprises had been in steady retreat. By 1994, SOEs produced the majority of output in just nine sectors.[p] These sectors were protected by

---

[p] Sectors dominated by SOEs include resource extraction, utilities (water, power, and gas supply), tobacco, machinery, petrochemicals, automobiles, and construction.

regulatory or technological barriers to entry and thus provided a safe harbor for struggling state firms. In 1996, half of SOEs were losing money, and the government estimated that 30% were effectively bankrupt.

In 1996, Vice-Premier Zhu expressed pessimism about SOE performance: "The current problems of SOEs are excessive investments in fixed assets with very low rates of returns and a low sales-to-production ratio, giving rise to mounting inventories. The end result is that the state has to inject an increasing amount of working capital through the banking sector into the state enterprises."[34]

The politics of SOE reform had always been much more difficult than the economics of reform. The SOEs were considered the backbone of socialism, thus making an explicit privatization policy difficult. Surveys suggested that about one-third of the 100 million SOE workers could be laid off with no effect on output, but liquidating insolvent SOEs could easily lead to political and social instability.

Beginning in 1994, the Chinese government adopted a three-pronged new approach toward SOEs, summarized in the slogan, "Grasping the big ones and letting go of the small ones." The first prong was to preserve government control of the largest SOEs, while attempting to reform these enterprises by combining them into Chaebol-type conglomerates and by altering their governance structures.[35] The second prong was to permit outright privatization of the small SOEs controlled by local governments.[q] The third prong was to allow bankruptcies and mergers of the truly nonperforming SOEs. In September 1997, at the 15th Party Congress, the Chinese leadership formally affirmed this policy.

Unemployment

China's intense focus on rapid growth was driven by the need to create jobs for the country's vast population. Even with a highly effective birth-control program in place, China's population continued to increase by approximately 14 million people per year—equivalent to adding another Texas or Australia annually. In addition to this natural population growth, several factors heightened the need to create jobs. Large numbers of workers continued to leave farming. Chinese experts predicted that as many as 180 million working-age adults would be under- or unemployed in rural areas by 2005.[36] Further, there was vast overemployment in the state-sector. Finally, the reforms since 1978 had loosened political control of the population. As the power of the units (*danwei*) declined, many workers left their home counties, creating an estimated 100 million "floating workers" who moved from city to city seeking temporary employment.

The Financial Sector

The poor financial performance of SOEs was reflected in the deteriorating finances of the financial sector. In the late 1980s, in an effort to contain fiscal deficits, the central government directed state banks to cover SOE losses with loans. By the mid-1990s, SOEs absorbed more than 70% of the loans granted by state banks. The Chinese government estimated that loans at state banks equal to 8%–10% of GDP would have to be written off, but international analysts put the figure much higher—at 25% to 35%. By contrast, the costs associated with the savings and loan crisis in the United States amounted to only 2% of GDP.[37]

To deal with this issue, the political and policy functions of Chinese banks were separated from their commercial functions. Three new policy banks were established in 1994 for the purpose of policy lending. This allowed other banks, primarily the four

---

[q] Because of the ideological sensitivity of the issue, the Chinese government does not use the term *privatization* explicitly. Instead, euphemisms such as *ownership change* and *nonpublic ownership* are used to refer to what functionally is a privatization process.

large state banks, to specialize in commercial lending activities.[r] Over time, the commercial banks were to transfer their policy-lending portfolio to the policy banks.[38]

In addition, the authorities opened two stock exchanges in Shanghai and Shenzhen and allowed the establishment of nonbank financial institutions to engage in limited financial intermediation. Several foreign banks opened representative offices, although their operations were strictly limited.

Provincial-Center and Province-Province Tensions

The moves toward fiscal recentralization helped to stabilize the central government's fiscal situation, but significant tensions remained. The income gap between the booming coastal provinces and the interior regions continued to grow [see **Exhibit 1.14**], and the central government's attempts to transfer resources to poorer regions were resisted by the wealthier provinces. As coastal provinces became fiscally self-sufficient, the central government's influence over them was sharply curtailed. Senior officials in Guangdong have noted that central austerity efforts have little effect on them, because they were net contributors to the central budget.[39]

The rich coastal provinces had nearly independent industrial policies—they provided tax breaks to investors, built infrastructure, and subsidized key sectors. Many provinces had erected trade barriers against neighboring provinces, and the transportation infrastructure often petered out at provincial borders. Despite China's huge size, little regional specialization had occurred. Alwyn Young, who analyzed trade patterns and interregional variation in production patterns, concluded that, instead of specializing, most provinces attempted to enter the same industries. This led to excessive industrial duplication, large opportunity costs, and growing regional tensions.[40]

Political Liberalization and Human Rights

China's economic reforms had not been matched by political liberalization. While many villages had held contested elections for local positions, the CCP maintained its monopoly on all provincial and national positions. There was disagreement among economists and political scientists about whether sustained economic growth required political freedom.[s] The CCP clearly believed it was not.

Grassroots calls for democracy and local autonomy led to several incidents that heightened tensions with other countries. Two events in 1989 brought these issues to a head. In March of that year, demonstrations protesting China's control of Tibet led to PLA intervention and the imposition of martial law in the region. Two months later, tanks were used to clear democracy demonstrators from Tiananmen Square, leading to several hundred deaths.[t] These incidents, as well as other disagreements over human rights—such as the use of prison labor and forced sterilizations—led to periodic calls for economic sanctions against China. These issues were raised annually when the United States Congress reviewed China's most-favored-nation status.

Economic Integration

China's economic strategy depended on continued access to international markets, but its trading partners had become increasingly concerned about their levels of access to the Chinese market. China's exporters could be assured of continued access to foreign

---

[r] The policy banks are the State Development Bank, the Agricultural Development Bank, and the Export-Import Bank. The four main state banks are the Industrial and Commercial Bank, the Agricultural Bank, the Bank of China, and the People's Construction Bank.

[s] Some economists suggested that political freedom was a luxury good—that is, one for which demand grew rapidly as living standards rose.

[t] There remains much disagreement about the number of deaths that occurred in Tiananmen Square. The Chinese government denies that any students died. *The New York Times* cites "a minimum of several hundred killed." *The Times* continues: "It is possible that the true number of deaths might be 1,500 or more." *The New York Times*, June 6, 1989, p. A1.

markets only if China joined the World Trade Organization and conformed to its fair trade principles. But the United States had blocked China's ascension to the WTO because of a dispute about the pace of import liberalization. The United States promised to veto China's entry to the WTO until it agreed to join as a "developed country." China was unwilling to join without "developing country" status. "Developed" countries were expected to meet WTO standards quickly, while "developing" countries were allowed an extended transition period, as well as an exemption for "concessions that are inconsistent with their development, financial, and trade needs."[41]

China's status upon entry to the WTO would determine the pace of further import liberalization, particularly in "pillar" industries and those dominated by SOEs. Abrupt import liberalization would place further pressure on SOEs and state-owned banks, perhaps further complicating the reform process.

In spite of the WTO dispute, China had undertaken several policies designed to encourage closer integration with the world economy. The yuan was fully convertible for current account transactions, although not for capital account operations. The government had implemented a series of tariff reductions, with the average tariff level declining from 40% in 1991 to 23% in 1996. The government announced that it planned further reductions, to 15%, by 1998. Nontariff barriers had been reduced—the number of items with import quotas was cut from 660 to 384 in 1996—but still covered a large portion of trade, including many agricultural products, machinery, and electronic products. Finally, the central government had cut back on import tariff rebates and VAT rebates for exports by enterprises with foreign capital.[u]

The dispute over China's WTO entry was exacerbated by a disagreement over the size of the U.S.–China bilateral balance. The United States reported a $39.5 billion deficit with China in 1996, while China claimed its surplus was only $10.5 billion.[v] The primary source of conflict was over how to account for the value of goods that passed through Hong Kong. When calculating the bilateral trade balance, the United States attributed to China the full value of all goods shipped through Hong Kong. China counted only the value of goods leaving China whose final destination was known when they left the country. At heart, the dispute centered around how to account for the value added to these goods in Hong Kong. One group of economists put the true bilateral imbalance at $16 billion—$22 billion for 1995 (compared with the U.S. estimate of $33.7 billion and the Chinese claim of $8.6 billion).[42]

The Environment

Rapid economic growth had led to extensive environmental damage in China. The country's air and water were among the most polluted in the world, especially in urban areas. In addition to aesthetic losses, the economic costs of pollution were extremely high. The World Bank estimated that the total economic costs of pollution were between 3% and 8% of GDP and that more than 20% of deaths in China were pollution-related.[43]

At least three factors contributed to the high levels of pollution in China. First, energy use had grown rapidly, and nearly 80% of China's energy was generated using

---

[u] Both measures have produced an outcry among foreign companies. Although the tax equalization is meant to level the playing field, foreigners believe that domestic firms have many other advantages including lower land rentals and lower prices for many essentials. Lower tax burdens are viewed as offsetting these disadvantages on the part of foreign-invested enterprises (FIEs). The scrapping of the tariff exemptions is expected to increase the business costs for the FIEs. The US–China Business Council estimates that the business cost will rise by 28%. "How and Why to Survive Chinese Tax Torture," *The Economist* (1995): 63–64.

[v] If the U.S. figure is correct, then China has the second highest bilateral surplus with the United States (after Japan's $59 billion). If the Chinese figure is correct, China's surplus with the United States would be lower than those of Japan, Canada, Mexico, Germany, and Taiwan.

coal—a pollution-intensive energy source. Second, rapid urbanization had overtaxed waste disposal systems and exposed high numbers of people to pollutants. More than 200 million people had moved to urban areas since 1978, but the waste infrastructure had not kept pace. Seventy-seven percent of industrial waste was treated, compared with only 7% of municipal waste.[44] Third, deforestation and the loss of arable land had reduced the environment's ability to absorb pollution. Deforestation averaged 0.7% per year in the 1980s, and approximately 0.35% of farmland was lost each year to urbanization and construction. Total cropland in China declined from 105 million hectares in 1961 to only 96 million in 1990, while the population doubled.

Despite high levels of pollution, several positive trends had emerged. Growth in the emission of major pollutants grew more slowly than GDP, and the government indicated that it would raise energy prices and invest in pollution control.[45] Still, the magnitude of the required investment was disputed. China spent approximately 0.6% of GDP on environmental control and planned to increase this to 0.85%.[w] The World Bank recommended that China invest at least 3.1% of GDP in pollution abatement— as compared with 2.2% in the United States. World Bank economists estimated that these investments would lead to benefits totaling 8.8% of GDP.

Whither China?

In late 1997, the Asian financial crisis highlighted the severity of the issues facing China. Starting with several bank defaults in Thailand, the crisis had spread quickly to Malaysia, Indonesia, the Philippines, and South Korea. Each was forced to close insolvent financial institutions, devalue its currency, and ask the International Monetary Fund for assistance. The Asian crisis was of great concern for two reasons. It revealed weaknesses in the "Asian" development model China had been pursuing. In addition, the large devaluation by China's neighbors threatened its export markets, potentially cutting into export growth just as domestic demand was slowing.

Zhu had recently received his year-end economic projections for 1997. The good news was that GDP had increased by 8.8%, while inflation had declined to less than 3%. But these figures masked several troubling developments. Foreign investment had grown only 3%, retail sales had slowed, and inventories had piled up.

Although China's growth rate since 1978 was extraordinary, the structural impediments to reform were becoming more severe. It was not difficult to design isolated policies to address SOE restructuring, job creation, relations with the provinces, international trade relations, or the environment. The difficulty arose when the individual policies came into conflict.

Could China continue to muddle through—relying on incremental reform, spontaneous innovation in the provinces, and annual U.S. approval of MFN? Or was it time for a fundamental rethink of China's strategy, perhaps leading to faster and more comprehensive reform?

---

[w] The Chinese government estimates that higher expenditures are needed and that it would take at least 1.5% of GDP just to control environmental degradation. *World Resources: A Guide to the Global Environment*, World Resources Institutes, 1994, p. 62.

EXHIBIT 1.1   MAP OF CHINA

EXHIBIT 1.2	NATIONAL INCOME ACCOUNTS (BILLIONS OF YUAN AT CURRENT PRICES)

Year	1978	1982	1986	1990	1991	1992	1993	1994	1995	1996
Private Consumption	204.4	320.9	522.9	911.3	1,031.6	1,246.0	1,568.2	2,123.0	2,634.3	3,257.9
Investment	119.0	157.5	419.8	644.4	751.7	963.6	1,499.8	1,859.2	2,278.7	2,686.7
Government Consumption	26.3	43.8	85.2	225.2	283.0	349.2	450.0	598.6	697.3	759.2
Exports	17.2	40.5	79.0	297.0	382.8	468.4	524.2	1,043.3	1,242.7	na
Imports	–17.9	–32.5	–77.8	–255.2	–339.6	–444.4	–594.0	–997.0	–1,078.3	na
Net Exports										145.9
GDP[a]	349.1	530.2	1,029.1	1,854.8	2,161.8	2,663.8	3,463.4	4,662.2	5,826.1	6,849.8
Real GDP Growth (%)	na	9.0	8.8	8.3	13.5	14.2	13.4	11.2	10.7	9.7
Govt. Consumption as % of GDP	7.5	8.3	8.3	12.1	13.1	13.1	13.0	12.8	12.0	11.6
Gross Savings as % of GDP	36.5	28.2	34.7	37.4	na	37.2	40.3	43.6	41.0	42.9
Inflation (%)	1.9	2.1	8.9	3.1	3.5	6.3	14.6	24.2	16.9	8.3

SOURCE: World Bank, IMF. Chinese Statistical Yearbook.
na: Data not available.
[a] GDP as reported by the Chinese government includes the value of subsidies paid to agriculture, industry, and the service sector in addition to the factor costs of production.

EXHIBIT 1.3	GROSS OUTPUT VALUE BY SECTOR AND OWNERSHIP[A] (BILLIONS OF YUAN AT CURRENT PRICES)

Year	1978	1982	1986	1990	1992	1994	1995	1996
Total	**563.4**	**829.4**	**1,520.7**	**3,158.6**	**4,615.0**	**9,266.0**	**11,223.4**	**12,302**
Agriculture	139.7	248.3	401.3	766.2	908.5	1,575.0	2,034.1	2,342
Industry, of which	423.7	581.1	1,119.4	2,392.4	3,706.6	7,690.9	9,189.4	9,959
State-owned	328.9	432.6	697.1	1,306.4	1,782.4	2,620.1	3,122.0	2,838
Collective-owned	94.8	144.2	375.1	852.3	1,410.1	3,143.4	3,362.3	3,924
Individual-owned	na	0.3	30.9	129.0	250.7	885.3	1,182.1	1,544
Other	na	3.9	16.3	104.8	263.4	1,042.1	1,523.1	1,653
Agriculture as % of Total	24.8	29.9	26.4	24.3	19.7	17.0	18.1	19
SOEs as % of Total Industrial Output	77.6	74.4	62.3	54.6	48.1	34.1	34.0	28
COEs as % of Industrial Output[b]	22.4	24.8	33.5	35.6	38.0	40.9	36.6	39
COEs as % of Total Agricultural and Industrial Output[b]	16.8	17.4	24.7	27.0	30.6	33.9	30.0	31

SOURCE: Chinese Statistical Yearbook.
[a] These figures exceed the GDP figures because they report Gross Output Value, not value added, by sector. Gross Output Value for a sector is equal to the sum of output value (list price multiplied by quantity produced) for each enterprise in the sector. This methodology leads to double counting of intermediate goods. The government does not provide the data required to calculate value added by sector.
[b] COEs are collectively owned enterprises. The category includes Township and Village Enterprises, Urban Enterprises, and Cooperative Enterprises.
na: Data not available.

EXHIBIT 1.4 CONSOLIDATED GOVERNMENT REVENUE AND EXPENDITURES (BILLIONS OF YUAN AT CURRENT PRICES)

Year	1970	1975	1980	1985	1989	1990	1991	1992	1993	1994	1995	1996
Revenue from Enterprises[a]	37.9	40.0	43.5	63.9	64.6	68.2	70.2	68.4	63.1	60.9	75.9	82.2
Industrial and Commercial Taxes	24.2	35.8	51.0	109.7	176.0	185.8	198.1	224.4	319.4	391.4	458.9	527.0
Tariffs	0.7	1.5	3.3	20.5	18.1	15.9	18.7	21.2	25.6	27.2	29.1	30.1
Other	3.3	4.1	18.0	56.8	67.2	81.4	78.7	78.6	67.5	78.6	92.8	135.0
Total Revenues	**66.1**	**81.4**	**115.8**	**250.9**	**325.9**	**351.3**	**365.7**	**392.6**	**475.6**	**558.1**	**656.7**	**774.3**
Construction	39.3	48.2	71.5	112.8	129.2	136.8	142.8	161.3	183.5	239.3	285.5	na
Culture and Education	5.2	10.3	19.9	40.8	66.8	73.8	884.9	97.0	117.8	150.2	175.6	na
National Defense	14.5	14.2	19.4	19.2	25.1	29.0	33.0	37.8	42.6	55.1	63.7	na
Government Administration	3.2	4.2	7.6	17.1	38.6	41.4	41.4	46.3	63.4	847	99.7	na
Subsidies to SOEs				50.7	59.8	57.8	51.0	44.4	41.1	36.6	32.7	na
Other	2.7	5.1	4.4	10.5	22.6	27.3	36.4	31.8	56.9	49.9	57.8	na
Expenditures[b]	**64.9**	**82.0**	**122.8**	**251.1**	**342.1**	**366.1**	**389.5**	**418.6**	**505.3**	**615.8**	**715.0**	**827.4**
Deficit/Surplus	**1.2**	**-0.6**	**-7.0**	**-0.2**	**-16.2**	**-14.8**	**-23.8**	**-26.0**	**-29.7**	**-57.7**	**-58.3**	**-53.1**
Surplus/Deficit as % of GDP			-1.5	0.0	-1.0	-0.8	-1.1	-1.0	-0.9	-1.2	-1.0	-0.8
Central Govt. Revenue as % of Total Rev.	28	12	25	31	25	28	26	25	20	52	50	47
Central Govt. Spending as % of Total Spending	59	50	54	32	26	27	28	28	26	29	28	na

SOURCE: Chinese Statistical Yearbook.

a Includes profit remissions and income taxes from SOEs.

b Excludes interest payments on government debt. This means that expenses and the deficit are understated. The Chinese government reports only consolidated principal and interest payments.

na: Data not available.

EXHIBIT 1.5   BALANCE OF PAYMENTS[a] (MILLIONS OF US DOLLARS)

Year	1978	1980	1982	1984	1986	1988	1990	1991	1992	1993	1994	1995	1996
Merchandise exports		18,188	21,125	23,905	25,756	41,054	51,519	58,919	69,568	75,659	102,561	128,110	151,077
Merchandise imports		−18,294	−16,876	−23,891	−34,896	−46,369	−42,354	−50,176	−64,385	−86,313	−95,271	−110,060	−131,542
Trade balance		**−106**	**4,249**	**14**	**−9,140**	**−5,315**	**9,165**	**8,743**	**5,183**	**−10,654**	**7,290**	**18,050**	**19,535**
Net services		241	488	−46	1,551	1,220	1,451	2,784	−225	−868	302	−6,093	−1,984
Net factor payments		195	451	1,620	176	−126	1,107	914	288	−1,259	−1,019	−11,774	−12,437
Net transfers		570	486	442	379	419	274	831	1,155	1,172	335	1,435	2,130
Current account		**900**	**5,674**	**2,030**	**−7,034**	**−3,802**	**11,997**	**13,272**	**6,401**	**−11,609**	**6,908**	**1,618**	**7,243**
Capital account items													
Net FDI		57	386	1,124	1,425	2,344	2,657	3,453	7,156	23,115	31,787	33,849	38,066
Net portfolio flows		na	21	−1,638	1,568	876	−241	235	−57	3,049	3,543	631	1,744
Mon. and bank transactions		−290	−69	−489	2,951	3,913	839	4,344	−7,433	−2,690	2,685	4,035	156
Errors and omissions		na	293	−889	−958	−957	−3,205	−6,767	−8,211	−10,096	−9,100	−17,822	−15,504
Overall balance		**561**	**6,305**	**138**	**−2,048**	**2,374**	**12,047**	**14,537**	**−2,060**	**1,769**	**30,453**	**22,469**	**31,705**
Current acct. balance, % of GDP		0.3	2.1	0.7	−2.4	−0.9	3.1	3.3	1.3	−1.9	1.3	0.2	0.9
Avg. exchange rate (yuan/$)	1.68	1.50	1.89	2.32	3.45	3.72	4.78	5.32	5.51	5.76	8.62	8.35	8.31
Real exchange rate (Inflation adjusted, 1978 = 100)[b]	100	96	68	54	39	43	37	32	32	34	28	31	33
Foreign currency and gold reserves	na	3,116	11,840	17,801	11,994	19,135	30,209	44,308	21,230	22,999	53,560	76,037	107,676
Total foreign debt	na	4,504	na	na	na	42,439	55,301	60,259	72,428	85,928	100,457	118,090	na
Inflation (CPI, %)	1.9	2.6	2.1	11.6	8.9	16.3	3.1	3.5	6.3	14.6	24.2	16.9	8.3
Credit growth (%)	11.2	18.4	10.4	31.6	34.1	18.9	23.3	20.0	22.3	42.1	23.8	22.8	na

SOURCE: IMF, *Balance of Payments Statistics Yearbook* and *International Finance Statistics Yearbook*. 1980 information from World Bank, *World Tables*, 1991, as reported in China: The Great Awakening, Harvard Case Study, no. 9-794-019.

[a] The trade figures in this table differ from those that follow because of differences in the way China and the IMF account for goods transshipped through Hong Kong. This table is based on IMF data. The tables that follow are based on Chinese government data.

[b] Measured against the U.S. dollar. A decline in the index indicates a *depreciation* of the yuan.

na: Data not available.

EXHIBIT 1.6   EXPORTS BY DESTINATION

	Exports (millions of U.S. dollars)							Exports (as percentage of total)						
	1978	1980	1985	1990	1992	1994	1996	1978	1980	1985	1990	1992	1994	1996
Total	9,955	18,099	27,327	62,091	84,940	121,047	151,197							
Hong Kong	2,533	4,354	7,148	27,163	37,511	32,365	32,904	25.4	24.1	26.2	43.7	44.2	26.7	21.8
Japan	1,719	4,032	6,091	9,210	11,699	21,490	30,888	17.3	22.3	22.3	14.8	13.8	17.8	20.4
Taiwan	na	na	na	320	697	2,242	2,804	na	na	na	0.5	0.8	1.9	1.9
Other Asia	479	1,734	1,493	4,076	6,740	11,462	16,959	4.8	9.6	5.5	6.6	7.9	9.5	11.2
United States	271	983	2,336	5,314	8,599	21,421	26,731	2.7	5.4	8.5	8.6	10.1	17.7	17.7
Germany	330	771	746	2,062	2,447	4,762	5,852	3.3	4.3	2.7	3.3	2.9	3.9	3.9
Other EU	843	1,543	1,537	4,213	5,557	10,656	14,016	8.5	8.5	5.6	6.8	6.5	8.8	9.2
Other	3,780	4,682	7,976	9,733	11,690	16,649	21,043	38.0	25.8	29.2	15.7	13.8	13.8	13.9

SOURCE: Direction of Trade Statistics Yearbook.

na: Data not available.

| EXHIBIT 1.7 | TRADE BALANCE WITH SELECTED COUNTRIES^A (MILLIONS OF U.S. DOLLARS) |

	1978	1980	1985	1990	1992	1994	1996
Total	**–1,140**	**–1,900**	**–1,490**	**8,740**	**4,350**	**5,400**	**12,200**
Hong Kong	2,458	3,784	2,386	12,598	16,972	22,877	25,065
Japan	–1,386	–1,137	–9,087	1,554	–1,987	–4,829	1,698
Taiwan	na	na	na	–1,934	–5,193	–11,842	–13,382
Other Asia	93	808	–600	1,173	200	–1,340	–4,108
United States	–450	–2,847	–2,863	–1,277	–304	7,444	10,552
Germany	–700	–562	–1,701	–918	–1,576	–2,374	–1,473
Other EU	–97	132	–2,167	–1,954	–1,283	–812	1,458

[a] Chinese trade statistics vary from some of its trading partners, particularly the industrial countries. See the text for a short discussion of the disagreement with the United States on this issue.

na: Data not available.

SOURCE: Direction of Trade Statistics Yearbook.

| EXHIBIT 1.8 | UTILIZATION OF FOREIGN CAPITAL^A (BILLIONS OF U.S. DOLLARS) |

	1979–1983	1984	1985	1986	1987	1988	1989	1990	1991	1992	1993	1994	1995	1996
Foreign loans	11.8	1.3	2.7	5.0	5.8	6.5	6.3	6.5	6.9	7.9	11.2	9.3	10.3	12.6
Foreign direct investment	1.9	1.6	1.7	2.0	2.3	3.2	3.4	3.5	4.4	11.0	27.5	33.8	37.5	41.7
Other foreign investments	0.9	0.2	0.3	0.4	0.3	0.6	0.4	0.3	0.3	0.3	0.3	0.2	0.3	0.4
Total	**14.5**	**3.1**	**4.7**	**7.3**	**8.4**	**10.3**	**10.1**	**10.3**	**11.6**	**19.2**	**39.0**	**44.3**	**48.1**	**54.7**

SOURCE: Chinese Statistical Yearbook.
[a] This table reports total *inbound* FDI. The balance of payments (Exhibit 1.5) reports *net* FDI.

EXHIBIT 1.9A	EXPORTS BY ENTERPRISES WITH FOREIGN CAPITAL (%)

Year	Exports	Share in Total Exports
1985	0.3	1.1
1986	0.6	1.9
1987	1.2	3.1
1988	2.5	5.2
1989	4.9	9.4
1990	7.8	12.6
1991	12.0	16.8
1992	17.4	20.4
1993	25.2	25.8
1994	34.7	28.7
1995	46.9	31.5
1996 (first six months)	26.2	40.8

SOURCE: China, SSB; China, General Administration of Customs, China Customs Statistics, as reported in Barry Naughton, "China's Emergence and Prospects as a Trading Nation," *Brookings Papers on Economic Activity* 2 (1996), p. 299.

EXHIBIT 1.9B	PRINCIPAL IMPORTS AND EXPORTS FOR CHINA (1996)

Principal Exports $ billion		Principal Imports $ billion	
Clothing and Textiles	37.1	Machinery and Elect Equip.	54.8
Machinery and Elect. Equip	35.3	Chemicals	18.1
Foodstuffs	11.6	Textiles	12.0
Chemicals	8.9	Iron and Steel	7.2
Footwear	7.1	Mineral Fuels	6.9
Mineral Fuels	5.9		

SOURCE: Economist Intellegence Unit: Country Report: China, 3rd Quarter 1997.

EXHIBIT 1.10	DECENTRALIZATION OF DECISION MAKING IN STATE-OWNED FIRMS									
	1980	**1981**	**1982**	**1983**	**1984**	**1985**	**1986**	**1987**	**1988**	**1989**
Marginal retention rate (%)[a]	11	12	11	14	17	17	19	23	26	27
Autonomy in production decisions (% firms)	7	8	10	14	25	35	40	53	64	67
Management responsibility system (% firms)	0	0	0	1	2	4	8	42	83	88
New management appointed after 1980 (% firms)	9	9	15	25	40	40	61	75	85	94

SOURCE: The World Bank, *China 2020: Development Challenges in the Next Century*, 1992.
Note: Based on a 1991 retrospective sample survey of state enterprises.
[a]Portion of profits that could be retained if profits exceeded the base level.

EXHIBIT 1.11	POPULATION

	Total Population (millions)	**Urban Population as % of Total**	**Rural Population as % of Total**	**Population Growth Rate (%)**
1975	924.2	17.3	82.7	1.57
1980	987.0	19.4	80.6	1.19
1986	1,075.0	24.5	75.5	1.55
1988	1,110.2	25.8	74.2	1.58
1990	1,143.3	26.4	73.6	1.44
1991	1,158.2	26.4	73.6	1.30
1992	1,171.7	27.6	72.4	1.16
1993	1,185.1	28.1	71.9	1.15
1994	1,198.5	28.6	71.4	1.12
1995	1,211.2	29.0	71.0	1.05
2000[a]	1,255.1	na	na	0.93
2010[a]	1,348.0	na	na	0.70
2020[a]	1,434.3	na	na	0.60
2030[a]	1,500.6	na	na	0.39

SOURCE: Chinese Statistical Yearbook. World Bank, *World Population Projections*.
[a] Projections.
na: Data not available.

EXHIBIT 1.12   INDICATORS OF ECONOMIC DEVELOPMENT

Country	Population in 1995 (millions)	Population Density (people/km²)	GNP per Capita ($, 1995)	Average GDP Growth (1990–95)	External Debt as % of GDP (1995)	Trade as % of GDP	Labor Force in Agriculture (%, 1990)	Population Below $1/day (%, 1985 prices)	Average Inflation (%, 1990–95)
Asia									
China	1,200.2	125	620	12.8	17.2	40	74	29.4	9.3
India	929.4	282	340	4.6	28.2	27	64	52.5	9.8
Indonesia	193.3	101	980	7.6	56.9	53	57	14.5	8.8
Korea	44.9	454	9,700	7.2		67	18	na	6.7
Malaysia	20.1	61	3,890	8.7	42.6	194	27	5.6	3.3
Philippines	68.6	229	1,050	2.3	51.5	80	45	27.5	9.8
Thailand	58.2	113	2,740	8.4	34.9	90	64	0.1	5.0
Vietnam	73.5	221	240	8.3	130.2	83	72	na	88.3
Other Developing Countries									
Chile	14.2	19	4,160	7.3	43.4	54	19	15.0	17.9
Poland	38.6	123	2,790	2.4	36.1	53	27	6.8	91.8
Russia 1	48.2	9	2,240	–9.8	37.6	44	14	1.1	148.9
South Africa	41.5	35	3,160	0.6	na	44	14	23.7	13.9
Developed Countries									
Canada	29.6	31	9,380	1.8		71	3	na	2.9
Japan	125.2	331	39,640	1.0		17	7	na	1.4
Germany	81.9	230	27,510	na		46	4	na	na
United Kingdom	58.5	238	18,700	1.4		57	2	na	5.1
United States	263.1	28	26,980	2.6		24	3	na	3.2

SOURCE: World Bank, World Development Indicators, 1997.
na: Data not available.

EXHIBIT 1.13   INDICATORS OF SOCIAL DEVELOPMENT

Country	Life Expectancy at Birth (years)	Fertility Rate (1995)[a]	Adult Illiteracy Rate (% males)	Adult Illiteracy Rate (% females)	Labor Force (millions, 1995)	Annual Deforestation[b] (1,000 km²)	Average Annual Deforestation[b] (%, 1989–90)	Population with Safe Access to Water (%)	Malnutrition (% under age 5)
Asia									
China	69	1.9	10	27	709	8.8	0.7	83	17
India	62	3.2	35	62	398	3.4	.6	63	63
Indonesia	64	2.7	10	22	89	12.1	1.1	63	39
Korea	72	1.8	1	na	22	0.1	0.1	89	na
Malaysia	71	3.4	11	22	8	4.0	2.1	90	23
Philippines	66	3.7	5	6	28	3.2	3.4	84	30
Thailand	69	1.8	4	8	34	5.2	3.5	81	13
Vietnam	68	3.1	4	9	37	1.4	1.5	38	45
Other Developing Countries									
Chile	72	2.3	5	5	6	-0.1	-0.1	96	1
Poland	70	1.6	na		19	-0.1	-0.1	na	na
Russia	65	1.4	na		77	15.5	0.2	na	na
South Africa	64	3.9	18	18	16	-0.4	-0.8	na	na
Developed Countries									
Canada	78	1.7	na	na	15	-47.1	-1.1	100	na
Japan	80	1.5	na	na	66	0	0	na	3
Germany	76	1.2	na	na	40	-0.5	-0.4	na	na
United Kingdom	77	1.7	na	na	29	-0.2	-1.1	na	na
United States	77	2.1	na	na	133	3.2	0.1	90	na

SOURCE: World Bank, World Development Indicators, 1997.

[a] Fertility rate is the number of children that would be born to a woman if she were to live to the end of her childbearing years.

[b] Annual deforestation refers to the permanent conversion of natural forest area to other uses as a percentage of forested land. Includes shifting cultivation, permanent agriculture, ranching, or infrastructure development. These areas do not include areas logged but intended for regeneration or areas degraded by human or natural disasters. Negative numbers indicate an increase in forest area.

na: Data not available.

| EXHIBIT 1.14A | INCOME INEQUALITY: NET INCOME OF RURAL HOUSEHOLDS IN SELECTED PROVINCES (YUAN/CAPITA, CURRENT PRICES) |

Province	GDP or National Income per Capita[a]			Index (all China = 100)		
	1978	1985	1995	1978	1985	1995
All China Total	133.57	397.6	1,577.7	100	100	100
Selected High-Income Provinces						
Beijing	224.8	775.1	3,223.7	168.3	195.0	204.3
Shanghai	290.0	805.9	4,245.6	217.1	202.7	269.1
Jiangsu	152.1	492.6	2,456.9	113.9	123.9	155.7
Zhejiang	na	548.6	2,966.2	na	138.0	188.0
Guangdong	182.3	495.3	2,699.2	136.5	124.6	171.1
Selected Low-Income Provinces						
Yunnan	123.9	338.3	1,011.0	92.8	85.1	64.1
Shaanxi	133	295.3	962.8	99.6	74.3	61.0
Gansu	98.4	255.2	880.3	73.7	64.2	55.8
Qinghai	na	343.0	1,029.8	na	86.3	65.3
Ningxia	115.9	321.2	998.7	86.8	80.8	63.3
Standard Deviation from Index— Calculated using all 30 Provinces				35.2	32.2	49.3

SOURCE: Chinese Statistical Yearbook.

[a] 1978 column reports national income per capita; 1985 and 1995 report GDP per capita.

na: Data not available.

| EXHIBIT 1.14B | INCOME INEQUALITY: RURAL AND URBAN GDP PER HEAD (YUAN, CURRENT PRICES) |

	1978	1980	1985	1990	1992	1994	1995	1996
Rural household income	133.6	191.3	397.6	686.3	784.0	1,221.0	1,577.7	1,926.1
Urban household income	316.0	439.4	685.3	1,387.3	1,826.1	3,179.2	3,892.9	4,377.2
Rural income as % of urban income	42.3	43.5	58.0	49.5	42.9	38.4	40.5	44.0

SOURCE: Chinese Statistical Yearbook.

1 Sachs and Woo, "Understanding China's Economic Performance," NBER working paper 5935, 1977.

2 "How Big Is Asia?" *The Economist*, February 7, 1998, p. 72; *International Financial Statistics Yearbook.*

3 *China 2020: Development Challenges in the New Century* (The World Bank, 1997), p. ix.

4 A. Eckstein, *China's Economic Revolution* (Cambridge, UK: Cambridge University Press, 1981).

5 John King Fairbank, *The Great Chinese Revolution, 1800–1985* (New York: Harper & Row, 1987).

6 Kenneth Lieberthal, *Governing China* (New York: W. W. Norton and Company, 1995).

7 Lieberthal, p. 45.

8 Lieberthal, p. 102.

9 Quoted from John Bryan Starr, *Understanding China* (New York: Hill and Wang, 1997), p. 79.

10 Starr, p. 19.

11 Lieberthal, *Governing China*, p. 150.

12 Grain yields had grown at a 1.8% annual rate between 1952 and 1978. Population had grown at a 2.0% rate. Bruce L. Reynolds, ed., *Chinese Economic Policy* (New York: Paragon House, 1988), p. 214.

13 Starr, *Understanding China.*

14 Procurement prices for quota—production increased an average of 17%. Above-quota production could be sold for 30%–50% more than the new quota prices. J. Y. Lin, "Rural Reforms and Agricultural Growth in China," *American Economic Review* 82 (1): 34–51.

15 Michael Ying-Mao Kau and Susan H. Marsh, eds., *China in the Era of Deng Xiaoping: A Decade of Reform* (Armonk: M.E. Sharpe, Inc., 1993), p. 107.

16 World Bank, China 2020.

17 Kau and Marsh, *China in the Era of Deng Xiaoping*, p. 106.

18 *The Economist*, China Survey, November 28, 1992, p. 12.

19 *China Statistical Yearbook*, 1997.

20 Naughton, "China's Emergence as a Trading Nation," Brookings Papers on Economic Activity, 1996, pp. 273–344.

21 Naughton, p. 297.

22 Naughton, 1996, p. 298.

23 Sachs and Woo, "Understanding China's Economic Performance," p. 27.

24 Kau and Marsh, *China in the Era of Deng Xiaoping*, p. 108.

25 World Bank, *China 2020*, Tables 19–22.

26 Ibid.

27 World Bank, 1995, #1697, pp. 61–63.

28 The tax figures are from State Statistical Bureau. *Zhongguo tongji nianjian 1997 [China Statistical Yearbook 1997]*. Beijing: Zhongguo tongji chubanshe, 1997.

29 Yasheng Huang, 1995, #1128.

30 Walter Tseng, et al., *Economic Reform in China: A New Phase* (Washington, DC: The International Monetary Fund, 1994), pp. 5–6.

31 "Emerging Market Indicators." *The Economist* (1997), p. 108.

32 World Bank, *China 2020*, p. 3.

33 Infant mortality is measured as deaths before age five. "China's Growth Path to the 21st Century: Recommendations from the World Bank," *Transition* 8.5 (1997), pp. 5–7.

34 *People's Daily*, Overseas Edition, March 11, 1996. Quoted from Sachs and Woo, "Understanding China's Economic Performance," 1997.

35 See "China and the Chaebol." *The Economist* (1997), pp. 97–98.

36 Lieberthal, *Governing China*, p. 245.

37 *The Economist*, March 8, 1997, "Survey China: The Death of Gradualism," p. S16.

38 See *The Chinese Economy: Fighting Inflation, Deepening Reforms* (Washington, DC: The World Bank, 1996) for a detailed discussion.

39 Country Profile: China, *Economist Intelligence Unit*, 1996–1997, page 30.

40 Alwyn Young, "The Razor's Edge: Distortions and Incremental Reform in the People's Republic of China," University of Chicago working paper.

41 Office of the United States Trade Representative, "A Summary of the Final Act of the Uruguay Round," via the Internet, @ http://www.wto.org/wto/ursum_wpf.html.

42 R. Feenstra, W. Hai, W. Woo, J. Sachs, and S. Yao, "The U.S.–China Bilateral Trade Balance: Its Size and Determinants." Research presented at the UNDP-HIID Conference on China's integration with the World Economy.

43 World Bank, *Clear Water, Blue Skies*, 1997.

44 World Bank, *Clear Water, Blue Skies*, p. 12.

45 World Bank, *Clear Water, Blue Skies*, p. 9.

Import Substitution to Washington Concensus

India is the world's largest democracy and its second most populous country. This case introduces this vast country and explores its economic strategy during two distinct eras—the import substitution period (from 1947 to 1991) and the liberalization era (since 1991).

Following a short introduction, the case explores India's early development strategy, which was based on import substitution. The strategy involved government regulation of international trade and investment, public control of key sectors, central allocation of investment, and extensive regulation of nearly all aspects of business (including plant location, capacity expansion, layoffs, and many prices). The measures were designed to prevent "unnecessary competition" and ensure social peace, but they came at a high economic cost. During the 1960s, 1970s, and 1980s, many Asian countries consistently grew at rates averaging 6-10%. India's real growth averaged only 3.5% a year, and in the late-1980s, per capita GDP was still only $300.

Following a balance of payments crisis in 1991, Prime Minister P.V. Narasimha Rao implemented a classic "Washington Consensus" reform program. This type of program has been widely prescribed by the World Bank and International Monetary Fund for developing countries that have experienced crises. The case describes India's program, which was fairly standard. The program involved

- fiscal and monetary tightening designed to ensure macroeconomic stabilization;

- external liberalization, including tariff reductions, elimination of quotas, and devaluation;

- announcement of an extensive privatization program;

- financial sector reform, including licensing of private banks and capital markets promotion; and

- microeconomic deregulation.

The final section of the case then explores the how the program has worked. After an initial slump, GDP growth rose and inflation fell, the fiscal deficit stabilized, and trade flows increased rapidly. More disappointing, however, FDI-inflows were well below projected levels, and regional inequality rose. Most FDI accumulated in just a few rich states.

Five years after the program was implemented, the ruling Congress Party was swept from office. The case concludes with the newly appointed finance minister considering his options. Should he push forward with more reforms? Retreat on a few high-profile issues in the hope of gaining maneuvering room for less visible reforms? Or was classic liberalization simply too controversial for a society fractured by ethnic, language, and religious barriers?

Chidambaram's Dilemma

In June 1996, newly appointed Finance Minister Palaniappan Chidambaram considered the future of India's economic reforms. Following five turbulent years of economic reform efforts, the ruling Congress Party had recently lost its majority in the federal parliament. H. D. Deve Gowda, the leader of a small regional party, had managed to form a coalition government, but few political observers thought the coalition would last more than a few months. Gowda appointed Chidambaram finance minister and gave him just two weeks to set the future course of reform.

For more than 40 years, India pursued a strategy of self-reliance and import substitution-but economic performance was disappointing. By the late 1980s, GDP per capita was only $300, and the country had fallen far behind its Asian neighbors. When, in 1991, a combination of political turmoil and several economic shocks precipitated an economic crisis, then Prime Minister P. V. Narasimha Rao responded with a sweeping economic reform program. The 1991 reforms were somewhat successful, but extremely controversial. Regional and class disparities widened; unions strongly opposed any reform of labor laws; and business executives in previously protected industries resisted new competition.

After five years in power, both Rao and his reform program had lost momentum. Controversy over economic reforms and a series of corruption scandals led to the Congress Party's worst-ever election defeat in the 1996 elections. The Bharatiya Janata Party (BJP)-a Hindu-nationalist party that opposed reforms-captured the most parliamentary seats but was unable to form a coalition government. A 13-party coalition group-the United Front-led by Gowda, formed a government with the reluctant support of the Congress Party (Rao's party). Most political observers doubted Gowda's ability to reconcile the coalition's conflicting interests and predicted the coalition would last only a few months.

Chidambaram—a Harvard Business School graduate who served as the commerce minister in the outgoing national government-was considered a leading advocate for reform, although he was keenly aware of the political costs involved. He considered three scenarios for future reform. First, he could accelerate reforms, hoping that anti-reform pressures had been dissipated by the election. A second possibility was to halt the more controversial reforms, such as privatization and foreign investment in "strategic" sectors, while working to consolidate political support for the less controversial ones. A third possibility was to return to India's traditional import-substitution strategy. Perhaps a country as diverse and divided as India could not cope with the turmoil of economic liberalization.

Overview of India

Physical Characteristics

Consisting of over 3.2 million square kilometers, India was the heart of the Indian subcontinent. The country bordered Pakistan, Bhutan, and Bangladesh and was separated from China and Nepal by the Himalayas. The west coast was on the Arabian Sea, and the more populated east coast was on the Bay of Bengal. Given its size and

Professor Robert E. Kennedy and Research Associate Teresita Ramos prepared this case as the basis for class discussion rather than to illustrate either effective or ineffective handling of an administrative situation. Some portions are drawn from research performed by Ashish Dhawan and Sarat Sethi (MBAs 1997), and from the case "India (A)" by Max Weston and Waleed Iskandar (MBAs 1993).

Copyright (c) 1998 by the President and Fellows of Harvard College. Harvard Business School case #798-065.

population, the country was not well endowed with natural resources, except for deposits of coal, iron ore, and bauxite in the east.

In the mid-1990s, approximately 52% of the country's land was used for agriculture, and two-thirds of the population depended on agriculture for their livelihoods. Most farms were not irrigated, so food production was heavily dependent upon the south-west monsoon, which delivered 80% of India's annual rainfall between June and mid-September. Such dependence on the sometimes volatile weather led to extensive government involvement in the agricultural sector.

Demographic and Social Characteristics

India's population was approximately 940 million in 1995. Annual population growth had fallen from 2.3% in the 1960s to slightly under 2% in the 1990s. Still, population has been forecast to exceed one billion by the year 2000, and India would likely overtake China as the world's most populous country by 2030. Fifty-two percent of the population lived on less than $1 per day—the international poverty line. The literacy rate remained below 50%, and only 14% of the population had access to sanitation. Approximately 29% of the population lived in urban areas in 1991—an increase of 3.6% since 1960 [see **Exhibit 2.5** for comparative social and economic indicators].

India has always been characterized by division and diversity. Its citizens observe many religions, speak dozens of languages, and are classified into approximately 900 subcastes. Religious and caste tensions have often erupted into violence. The population spoke more than 45 major dialects—24 of which were each spoken by more than a million people. Hindi, spoken by less than one-third of the population, has been considered the national language. Only 10% of the population speaks English, the official language of business and government. Hindus and Muslims are the largest religious groups, comprising 83% and 11% of the population, respectively.

A Brief Political History

Prior to the arrival of foreign conquerors, India was ruled by Hindu principalities for over 2,000 years. Muslim invaders arrived in 988 and extended their control over northern India throughout the next two centuries, culminating in the second Battle of Tarain in 1193. After Muslim rule ended with the death of the last emperor in 1707, British, French, Danish, and Dutch trading companies established increasing control over everyday life. By the 1760s, the British East India Company (BEIC) had gained the upper hand. BEIC controlled all British–Indian trade and administered the country on behalf of the British crown. By the late 1700s, the outlines of the system—known as the *Raj*—by which Britain would rule India were clearly visible. For the next 180 years, India exported raw materials and imported British manufactures.

In 1813, the British Parliament opened trade with India to all British subjects, and the BEIC shifted its focus from commerce to administration. The BEIC retained its administrative responsibilities until 1858 when, following a bloody mutiny, its charter was dissolved and the crown assumed direct control.

By the turn of the century, both nationalist sentiments and religious tensions were rising. The Indian National Congress (INC) was the leading Hindu political organization, while the Muslim League (ML) represented the Muslim minority. In 1935, three-way discussions between the British, the INC, and the ML led to the *Government of India Act*, which introduced limited self-government. Following the Second World War, and in the face of massive peaceful protests led by Mahatma Gandhi and Jawaharlal Nehru, Britain announced that it would withdraw from India—transferring power preferably to one government but not hesitating to establish two countries if the INC and the ML could not agree to terms. On June 3, 1947, the parties announced a plan for partition of India into two independent nations—India, consisting of the primarily Hindu states, and Pakistan, made up of the predominantly Muslim states in the northeast and northwest of the country. On August 15, 1947, the British Indian Empire ceased to exist. The process of partition, which unfolded over the next several months, involved the migration of 10 million to 15 million people, religious violence in the Punjab and Bengal regions, and an undeclared war between the two new nations in October 1947. India and Pakistan clashed again in 1965 and 1971. During the third dispute, East Pakistan declared independence and became Bangladesh.

Structurally, the central government established in 1947 strongly reflected its British origin: a bicameral parliament with legislative powers, a cabinet led by a prime minister with executive powers, a large central bureaucracy, and an independent judiciary. Each of the 22 states adopted a similar parliamentary structure. In addition to their usual social and community responsibilities, the states were granted exclusive power to tax agricultural income and land and to regulate the ownership of property. The central government was thus denied access to an extremely large tax base and the means to transform an inefficient agricultural system.

Mahatma Gandhi accepted no role in the newly established government, choosing instead to preach nonviolence in the partitian-ravaged states of Bengal and Bihar. On January 30, 1948, Gandhi was assassinated by an orthodox Hindu fanatic.

In direct elections to federal and state governments in 1947, the Congress Party emerged as the dominant political group. Nehru was elected prime minister and held that post until his death in 1964, when he was succeeded by another Congress leader, Lal Bahadur Shastri. When Shastri died in 1966, Nehru's daughter, Indira Ghandi, became prime minister. Following an economic crisis and severe political infighting, the Congress Party split in 1969, with Mrs. Gandhi bringing most Congress MPs into a new "leftish" coalition—the Congress (I) Party. Mrs. Gandhi ruled until 1977, when, following a declared State of Emergency, an opposition coalition, lead by the Janata Party, gained control of the federal government.[1]

In 1980, the Congress Party and Indira Gandhi returned to power. After clashes between the Indian army and militant Sikh leaders in Punjab, Mrs. Gandhi was assassinated by her Sikh bodyguards in 1984. Her son, Rajiv Gandhi, was elected prime minister and served until December 1989 when, for the second time since independence, the Congress Party lost the general election and a minority government was formed by Gandhi's former finance minister, V. P. Singh. Singh's minority government included the Janata Dal Party, the Bharatiya Janata Party (BJP), a Hindu nationalist party, and the Communist party.

Regional and religious strife continued, and another election was called for May 1991. During that election campaign, Rajiv Gandhi was assassinated by a Tamil suicide bomber. The Congress Party went on to win the election and Narasimha Rao was selected as prime minister.

Rajiv's assassination ended an extraordinary era in India's history. The Nehru/Gandhi family had established a family dynasty, ruling India for 37 of 44 years since independence. Jawaharlal Nehru, Indira Gandhi, and Rajiv Gandhi had dominated Indian politics during their respective eras, even during the brief periods when no family member occupied the prime minister's office. Rajiv's death, and the end of this dynastic era, left a tremendous vacuum at the center of India's political system.

Economic Strategy and Performance: 1947–1991

Economic development had been debated within the Congress Party even before independence. The debate revolved around two distinct visions, each associated with one of the heroes of the independence movement. Mahatma Gandhi's vision was of village-based economic development, with an emphasis on the development of agriculture and traditional cottage industries. He was wary of large-scale industrialization because he believed that it would displace labor, increase foreign dependence, concentrate wealth, and disrupt the village-based social system he regarded as ideal.

The second vision, advocated by Nehru and many leading industrialists, focused on industrialization through large, centrally directed investments. Nehru was, in many ways, typical of the Indian bureaucracy. He was a British-educated socialist with a general distrust of business but great admiration for the Soviet planning system. He was impressed with the Soviets' ability to achieve rapid growth in an underdeveloped country, and especially by their ability to do so while remaining largely isolated from foreign influence, investment, trade, and aid.

The debate was resolved in favor of central control after a planning commission was established with Nehru as chairman. In 1951, the commission instituted the first of nine five-year plans. Although the commission had enormous potential power, the first plan was fairly cautious, emphasizing fiscal conservatism and increased savings rates. Over the next few decades, however, several economic crises provoked the commission's administrative tendencies, causing economic policy to shift away from market coordination and toward centralized control mechanisms.

A Strategy of Import Substitution

As India's economic strategy evolved over the next three decades, a curious mix of macroeconomic stability and microeconomic rigidity emerged. The government maintained tight control of the economy through four complementary policies: extensive regulation of international trade and investment; public control of "key sectors"; central control of domestic investment; and the "licensing Raj."

Regulation of International Trade and Investment After a balance of payments crisis in 1957, the planning commission moved to limit the outflow of foreign currency and encourage domestic production of goods India had traditionally imported. The explicit objective was to become self-sufficient in the manufacture of all products. In order to limit foreign currency outflows, the commission instituted detailed controls over both foreign exchange transactions and imports. Foreign exchange was allocated according to perceived priority. Debt repayments were deemed highest priority, followed by capital goods, raw materials, and consumer goods—which were rarely approved.

These tight import controls succeeded in reducing foreign exchange outflows, but they also created economic and bureaucratic inefficiencies for any firm engaged in international commerce. Most Indian firms were forced to purchase domestic inputs, even when foreign alternatives were cheaper and of higher quality. Small firms found they were unable to negotiate the maze of regulations, while larger industrial groups and state-sector firms invested significant resources into working around them.

India's policies toward foreign direct investment and technology licensing varied. After the balance of payments crisis in 1957, the central government encouraged joint ventures with multinational firms as an effective source of foreign currency. As a result, foreign collaboration increased dramatically between 1957 and 1970. By the early 1970s, however, dividends, profit repatriation, and technology licensing fees associated with these joint ventures exceeded investment inflows. When the 1973 OPEC oil price shock led to another balance of payments crisis, the government responded by placing a 40% limit on foreign equity ownership. This forced many foreign firms to liquidate their investments on unfavorable terms, and many firms left the country. After the second oil shock in the late 1970s, and yet another balance of payments crisis, India again reversed itself and relaxed restrictions on foreign investment, but few firms returned.

By the 1980s, India's economy was essentially closed—with trade to GDP ratio of only 15%—among the lowest in the world.[a]

---

[a] The trade to GDP ratio is equal to (exports + imports)/GDP. In 1987, exports were 210 billion rupees (6.3%), imports were 296 billion rupees (8.9%), and GDP was 3,326 billion rupees.

Public Control of Key Sectors   In 1948, the first *Industrial Policy Resolution* (IPR) had given the government exclusive authority to operate infrastructure industries such as railroads, the telephone system, and the post office. The second IPR, in 1956, extended this control to 12 additional high-priority sectors, including mining, oil, steel, and heavy equipment. The IPRs led to several waves of nationalizations, including most commercial banks, the entire life insurance industry, and large firms in manufacturing and processed material industries such as fertilizer, mining, steel, chemicals, and oil.

The public sector's dominance steadily increased through the 1980s, by which time the government owned nearly half of India's industrial assets. This occurred despite the fact that the economic performance of state-sector firms was dismal [see **Exhibit 2.11**]. One estimate put the return on investment from public-sector investment between 1976 and 1986 at 3% to 5%, compared with 17% to 23% for private-sector investment. Despite high rates of investment, India's growth was hampered by poor infrastructure—power shortages, poor roads, clogged ports, and a shortage of railroad cars.[b]

Central Allocation of Investment   Because the financial sector was state-owned and foreign capital effectively prohibited, the government exerted tremendous control over investment throughout the economy. The Planning Commission established investment policies for state-owned firms directly. It influenced the private sector through its control of the banks and tight regulation of industrial expansion (see below).

Although the state sector's share of total economic output was not high, the state accounted for approximately 50% of investment and had a major presence through public ownership and employment in the finance, energy, capital goods and heavy industry, and infrastructure sectors [see **Exhibit 2.10**].

The License Raj   Tight government regulation and licensing were the final component of India's economic strategy. The bureaucracy controlled nearly all aspects of business, including approval of all capacity expansions, permission to enter or exit lines of business, and many prices. These controls applied to both state-owned and private firms.

Capacity licensing was designed to prevent duplication and "unnecessary competition." Firms could not expand capacity without bureaucratic approval. In many cases, approval was granted only when a firm agreed to other actions, such as dedicating a portion of production to exports; locating plants in less-developed regions; or purchasing machinery and raw materials from domestic suppliers. The approval process for capacity expansion typically took two to four years.

The central government also controlled the prices of many services and goods, including essentials such as coal, steel, pharmaceuticals, edible oils, and sugar. The prices of raw materials and intermediate goods were controlled to limit inflation and ensure the profitability of public-sector units. Finally, transportation costs were regulated as a way to subsidize development in less-developed regions.

The bureaucracy also intervened when a company was in financial difficulty. "Sick unit" regulations prevented firms from going bankrupt. Laying off workers required specific approval, which was rarely granted. Instead, the government provided subsidies through state-owned banks. With no way to exit, firms could not dispose of non-

---

[b] Perhaps the most glaring example was provided by the State Electricity Boards (SEBs), where annual losses on revenue account exceeded Rs. 5 billion ($1.5 billion)—equivalent to a negative 13.5% return of fixed assets. Operational indices of efficiency were extremely low, and transmission and distribution losses averaged 21%–23%, compared with an international average of less than 10%. In the state of Andhra Pradesh, the SEB had 5,000 megawatts of installed capacity and 80,000 employees, 150 times as many as would be employed in an American utility of similar size. (*The Economist*, January 21, 1995, p. S20).

performing assets so that they might be reallocated to more efficient uses. In 1980, there were 90,000 sick units, mostly public-sector companies.

Most elements of India's industrial policy biased development toward capital-intensive industries, but other regulations reserved certain activities for the "small-scale" sector. India had a high proportion of employment in very large units,[c] but other industries were completely reserved for small enterprises. Small-scale enterprises enjoyed a wide range of incentives, including subsidized loans, preference in public procurement, exclusive product reservations, and tax exemptions.[d]

Corruption

The dominance of the public sector and the vast scope of regulation strongly influenced the business environment and provided ample opportunity for corruption. A government-sponsored report in 1985 found "widespread corruption and abuse of all forms of public discretionary authority." It continued:

> The use of discretionary authority to extract or levy illegal tolls has spread far beyond the area of economic controls. Particularly at the lower levels of the state apparatus it has become quite common for illegal payments to be demanded in return for regular public services such as the registration of a document, the repair of a telephone, the issuance of a tax-assessment order, the admission of a student to an educational institution, or decisions on postings and transfers in the public services.[2]

Robert Wade, a British economist, has written about a well-developed "market for public office." He found that government jobs change hands for as much as 10 to 15 times their annual salary. Wade also found evidence of institutionalized bidding systems throughout the public sector for engineering jobs, various police stations, state electricity boards, hospitals, and public administration.

Economic Performance: 1950–1990

Despite an often intense focus on development, economic performance between 1950 and 1990 was unremarkable or, as The Economist described it, a "barely qualified economic failure."[3] India pursued a planned approach to development that combined stable macroeconomic management with active state ownership in key sectors and extensive regulation of private business activity. GDP grew slowly but steadily, trailing its neighbors in Asia. Under Nehru, GDP growth averaged 3.5% per year. By contrast, its East Asia neighbors experienced 5% to 6% growth rates. Inflation was generally subdued, and fiscal and balance of payments imbalances seldom reached crisis proportions. Some progress was achieved in improving social indicators, but, as with growth, India trailed its neighbors [see **Exhibit 2.5**].[4]

After taking office in 1984, Rajiv Gandhi introduced measures to reform the economy and reduce corruption. His government loosened import and capacity licensing requirements, eased entry restrictions in sensitive sectors, and invited foreign investors to return. These reforms led to an acceleration of economic activity, as both GDP growth and trade increased. There were pronounced increases in public investment in the energy and infrastructure sectors (coal, petroleum, electricity, and

---

[c] In 1976, 48% of employment and 65% of capital were in units with more than 1,000 employees.

[d] The World Bank has suggested that these policies distort firms' business strategies and, in many cases, reduce their ability to compete in international markets. A study of India's textile sector concluded that the costs of these regulations were extremely high. For example, after large textile mills were not allowed to increase their production of cotton cloth, they expanded into synthetics, which were heavily taxed to protect the cotton industry. Soon, both the cotton and synthetic industries were uncompetitive.

railways) and, to a lesser extent, in manufacturing. The investment to GDP ratio increased by about 2% in the mid-1980s, while manufacturing production grew by 10%. There was also an upward inflationary trend, although it did not reach dangerous levels.[5]

Unfortunately, these promising trends reversed within a few years. With ethnic and caste tensions rising and corruption scandals plaguing the Congress Party, growth again slowed. A controversy over the Babri Masjid mosque in Ayodhya (in the western state of Uttar Pradesh) served as a divisive rallying point for both Hindus and Muslims. When a group of Hindu nationalists tried to tear down the mosque, which was situated on the presumed birthplace of the Hindu god Lord Ram, a riot ensued. Police fired on the Hindus, causing a nationwide spasm of Hindu–Muslim violence. At the same time, politics were becoming increasingly caste-based. The Congress Party had traditionally united the various castes under its banner. This changed when several smaller parties began to base their campaigns on "compensatory discrimination," or quotas, in government employment and university admissions.

For the second time since independence, the Congress Party was defeated in a national election in 1989. Political turmoil again overwhelmed the economic reform process, and the economy lurched toward crisis. The disintegration of the Soviet Union led to an abrupt decline in exports,[e] and reduced remittances from workers abroad exacerbated India's already burgeoning current account deficit. In January 1991, the government introduced new import controls and raised both personal and corporate tax rates.

Rao's Reform Program: 1991–1996

The May 1991 elections were the bloodiest since independence. In addition to Rajiv Gandhi's assassination, more than 200 people were killed during the two days of voting. Even though the Congress Party trailed the Hindu nationalist-BJP after the first day's voting, the reaction to Gandhi's assassination boosted the party's performance and allowed Congress to win 240 of 511 seats. The party formed a minority government led by Narasimha Rao, a 70-year-old compromise candidate. When the government took office in June 1991, GDP had stalled, a current account crisis was developing, and foreign exchange reserves, at less than $2 billion, covered barely two weeks of imports. India's ability to pay for essential imports, to finance its external debt, and to halt capital flight was disappearing. To make matters worse, a $1.8 billion International Monetary Fund (IMF) loan had been exhausted, and the IMF was unwilling to provide further stabilization funding without fundamental economic reforms. Rao faced a full-blown economic crisis, with only a tenuous political foundation upon which to rally support for reform.

Rao's Policies

Rao and Finance Minister Manmohan Singh acted quickly. They reopened negotiations with the IMF but gained flexibility by airlifting 25 tons of gold (worth approximately $300 million) to the Bank of England. The gold was to be used as collateral for an emergency loan if Rao and Singh could not reach an agreement with the IMF. Over the next few months, they introduced an aggressive program of reform designed to stabilize the economy while radically transforming its microeconomic underpinnings. The program, introduced in July 1991, promised to "unshackle the Indian industrial economy from the cobwebs of bureaucracy." The program closely resembled the "Washington consensus" reforms espoused by international development agencies. It

---

[e] Total exports to the former Soviet Union fell from more than $3 billion in 1990 to less than $270 million in 1993. "Getting Down to Business," *Far Eastern Economic Review*, July 14, 1994, p. 18.

included (1) fiscal and monetary tightening; (2) the overhaul of foreign trade and investment regulations; (3) reduced state control of industry; (4) financial sector liberalization and decreased central control of investment; and (5) the elimination of many microeconomic regulations such as capacity and import licensing.

First came the foundation of the program—macroeconomic stabilization—which included both fiscal tightening and reform of monetary policy. To reduce the budget deficit, subsidies to public-sector units were slashed; the tax base was broadened while tax rates were reduced; and the inefficient patchwork of excise taxes was overhauled, changing them into a value-added tax. The implementation of monetary policy was transformed when the treasury agreed to phase out the practice of financing the fiscal deficit by having the central bank print money.

Second, the program overhauled the regulations governing international trade and investment. The rupee was devalued 22% in dollar terms and (by 1994 was) made fully convertible for current account transactions. Most import licensing restrictions were eliminated. Tariffs were lowered and simplified: between 1990 and 1993, the maximum rate fell from 350% to 65%, while the import-weighted average fell from 87% to 33%.

The government simplified the rules and procedures governing foreign direct investment in an effort to attract foreign capital. The 40% ceiling on foreign ownership was removed, and foreign investment approvals of up to 51% of equity were granted automatically, subject only to a registration procedure with the Reserve Bank of India. Strategic sectors (such as power, mining, telecommunications, and pharmaceuticals) were opened to foreign investment.

Third, the government announced that the role of the public sector would be reduced to "essential infrastructure goods and services." Public-sector monopolies over power, telecommunications, domestic aviation, and petroleum were to be opened to private competition. A Divestment Commission was established to devise a long-term privatization plan, although Rao insisted that the government would retain 51% ownership in "divested" companies. In addition, legislation was introduced to allow the government to restructure or close down chronically loss-making enterprises.

Fourth, the government embarked on a far-reaching reform process covering the banking and insurance industries, as well as the capital markets. These reforms were designed to reduce the government's role in capital allocation while improving capital efficiency. For the first time, public sector enterprises were permitted to form joint ventures and raise outside equity capital to finance their expansion plans. Private banks were to be licensed, and the government established a commission to study deregulation of the insurance industry. Within a year, ten private banks had been licensed and eight foreign banks were granted permission to open branches in India. Interest rates on both deposits and loans were partially deregulated.

The capital markets also were strengthened by the establishment of disclosure rules, licensing of foreign institutional investors and private-sector mutual funds, and the establishment of a market regulator—the Securities and Exchange Board. Controls governing takeovers were also loosened. The Takeover Act of 1994 removed many barriers to mergers and acquisitions and established protections for public shareholders.

Finally, a number of concrete steps were taken to reduce the regulation of microeconomic activity. Capacity licensing was abolished for all but a select list of hazardous and environmentally sensitive industries. The list of industries reserved for the public sector was reduced from 17 to 6, and limited private sector participation was permitted in the industries on the reserve list.

The Impact of Rao's Reforms

After the 1991 reforms were announced, virtually all opposition parties denounced reform as an IMF plot and claimed it would produce a "lost decade," as in Africa and

Latin America in the 1980s.[6] The immediate impact of the program was a sharp fall in growth, as fiscal and monetary tightening took hold. This downturn was short-lived, however. Starting in 1992, trade rose sharply, and both FDI and domestic investment increased. By 1994, a broad-based economic recovery was in progress.

Although the economic effect of the reform program was positive, it remained quite controversial. The coalition opposing liberalization—public-sector unions, less-developed states, the government bureaucracy, and many industrial conglomerates—supported politicians who promised to slow down—or reverse—reforms. This anti-reform backlash contributed to the Congress Party's rout in the 1996 elections.[7]

Despite improved economic performance in the 1990s, India remained a desperately poor country. Its GDP was smaller than Belgium's. Only 2.3% of the population enjoyed household incomes above 78,000 rupees (about $2,500). Sixty-three percent of children under five were malnourished, and less than a third of the population had access to sanitation. The literacy rate hovered around 50%. Although the population was nearly one billion, the country had only six million telephones and 35 million television sets.[8]

Aggregate Growth and Inflation By 1997, GDP growth had recovered strongly—averaging 5.4% between 1992 and 1996. The manufacturing sector grew at a 6.5% annual rate, while services increased 6.4% and agriculture 3.2% [see Exhibit 2.2b].[9] Some observers suggested that economic growth might reach 8% or 9% if the government implemented further free-market reforms, including labor market deregulation and reform of "sick unit" regulations.[10]

Strong GDP growth was accompanied by several other encouraging developments. Inflation declined from 14% in 1991 to 9.7% in 1996. And the money supply was within target, despite growing Reserve Bank lending to the government.

Fiscal and Monetary Changes The fiscal deficit declined somewhat after 1991, although it was still high compared with that of other countries in the region. The deficit declined from 8.4% to 5.3% of GDP in 1995/1996. A large part of this decline occurred in the first two years, and fiscal deficits had hovered around 6% since then.

The fiscal improvement was accomplished largely through control of spending. Central government expenditures declined from 19.1% of GDP in the 1990/1991 fiscal year to 16.5% in 1995/1996. More than half of this decline was due to a reduction in capital spending. The government also implemented a significant tax reform in 1994. Maximum corporate tax rates were reduced from 57.5% to 46%; the top individual rate was reduced from 45% to 40%; and indirect taxes were rationalized—broadening the base and lowering the rates on many items. The tax reforms reduced central government revenues from 11.4% of GDP to only 10.5%.

Rao also announced a privatization program aimed at weaning public-sector units from government subsidies. But proposals to sell off small amounts of equity in state corporations met with fierce resistance and the divestment program fell well short of expectations. Labor groups allied with opposition political parties and succeeded in scaling back the program.[11] By 1995, less than 3% of the government's holdings had been privatized or sold. Of the enterprises that had been "privatized," an average of only 15% of the shares had made their way into public hands.[12]

The agreement between the finance minister and the RBI (central bank) to limit monetization of the fiscal deficit was successful. Money supply growth has declined, easing inflationary pressures. The shift from printing money to credit market financing bore a fiscal cost, however. Interest payments grew rapidly, reaching 600 billion rupees ($19 billion) in 1996.

Trade and Foreign Direct Investment Rao's 1991 victory had been won on the promise of reforms aimed at weaning India away from Nehru's ideology of "economic self-reliance." Rao's policies had encouraged both trade and investment links to the world economy. Between 1991 and 1995, India's trade to GDP ratio increased from 15.5% to 19.8%. The rupee declined a total of 56% between 1991 and 1996, helping to boost exports and hold down the growth of imports. The current account deficit declined from 3.1% in 1990 to 1.6% in 1995.

Portfolio and equity capital inflows also grew rapidly. Portfolio capital inflows totaled more than $9 billion between 1993 and 1996, with positive net capital flows in every month since foreign institutional investors were permitted to invest in equity and credit markets in 1992. Direct investment grew from only $300 million in 1992 to $1.9 billion in 1995 and an estimated $2.8 billion in 1996. By comparison, China attracted more than $40 billion in FDI during 1995 alone.[13] The improvement in the trade balance and capital inflows led to rapidly growing foreign currency reserves. Reserves reached $20.8 billion in 1995 and were more than $17 billion in mid-1996.

Although the level of foreign direct investment fell well short of the government's goals (it had hoped for $10 billion by 1996), FDI was still quite controversial. Some politicians had used FDI to incite political turmoil.[14] Several bitter disputes arose involving foreign investments into food-related and infrastructural industries. Pepsi-Co's food-processing investments in Punjab state and a Kentucky Fried Chicken franchise in New Delhi became political flashpoints. Likewise, repeated renegotiations between the Indian government and Enron over the $2.8 billion Dabhol power project raised questions about property rights and the validity of contracts in India. These disputes damaged India's image in the eyes of foreign investors, especially in the United States.

Financial Sector Reforms   While reforms in the banking system and capital markets appeared successful, liberalization in the insurance sector lagged. Despite repeated promises to allow private firms and foreign investors into the insurance industry, reform was continually postponed due to resistance by incumbents.

The assets intermediated by the capital markets increased eightfold, to Rs. 5,210 billion ($165 billion) between 1990 and 1996. Market capitalization quadrupled and trading volumes tripled.[f] In 1993, Indian companies were granted permission to raise money outside the country, and between 1993 and 1996, 61 companies raised a total of $4 billion abroad.

The fixed investment to GDP ratio fell sharply between 1991 and 1993, from 16.5% to 11%. Much of the decline was the result of weak domestic demand and persistent uncertainty. This "investment pause" seemed to be over by 1996. A surge of imports, particularly capital goods, pointed to an investment recovery starting in 1994. By 1995, the fixed investment to GDP ratio had reached 18%.[g]

Regional Trends   The income gap between wealthy and poor states grew, and estimates were that the disparity in state growth rates would continue for at least a decade. Wealthy states such as Maharashtra and Gujarat had prospered under reform—achieving growth rates of nearly 10%—while West Bengal and the populous states of the North (Bihar, Uttar Pradesh, Madhya Pradesh, and Rajasthan) continued to fall behind. This caused great concern among politicians, because these states accounted for almost 40% of India's population. [See **Exhibit 2.7** for data on the states.]

One factor that contributed to the widening gap was the loosening of federal regulations on plant location. When the central government stepped back, state governments began to compete among themselves to attract foreign investors. The rich states enjoyed several advantages in this competition: attractive locations for expatriates, superior infrastructure, and better ability to afford tax incentives. For example,

---

[f] Market capitalization grew from 1,110 billion rupees in 1991 to 4,473 billion in 1995.

[g] Fixed investment excludes changes in inventories. Ajai Chopra, et al., "India: Economic Reform and Growth," Washington, DC: International Monetary Fund Occasional Paper, December 1995, p. 24.

Maharashtra had invested in the development of a financial cluster in Bombay, as well as in industrial zones in Nagpur, Pune, and Aurangabad. Both investments were successful; much of the financial services industry had moved from Calcutta, and manufacturing FDI had flowed disproportionately to the state.[15]

The majority of foreign investment had gone to just a few states—primarily Maharashtra and Gujarat. As of 1994, figures on planned (not realized) foreign investment put Gujarat (1,260 rupees per capita) and Maharashtra (760) far ahead of poorer states such as Uttar Pradesh (160) and Bihar (55).[16] This had occurred despite the fact that the costs of doing business were much higher in these states.[17]

Political Backlash

> *The economy is poised for 7% growth, but for that, we need political stability.*
>
> —**Rahul Bajaj,** managing director of Bajaj Auto, a leading manufacturer[18]

Prior to 1991, social and political fragmentation was generally suppressed by the unifying power of the Congress Party and its dynastic leaders.[19] But Rajiv's death and the corruption scandals that surrounded Prime Minister Rao sapped the Congress Party's legitimacy. The reform program increased tensions along India's traditional fault lines—religion and caste—and allowed opposition politicians to resort to increasingly divisive appeals, leading to increased political fragmentation. In December 1992, an army of militant Hindus marched on the Babri Masjid mosque, this time succeeding in tearing it down. Riots convulsed the country and left more than 3,000 dead. Three months later, a series of bombings in Bombay killed more than 260 people. Police suggested that the bombings were retaliation for the destruction of the mosque.

Religious tension was highest in India's north, where Muslims clashed with Hindi-speaking Hindus. Separatist movements continued to fester in the Punjab and Kashmir. The Hindu-nationalist BJP, which promoted a religious national identity and economic nationalism, had become a leading political force in the region. The BJP was wary of globalization, promising to prohibit FDI in "non-priority" sectors and to work toward an international trading system that was "more equitable, human, and free of exploitation."[20] Religious tensions were less visible in the south, where most people were Hindu but spoke a variety of regional dialects.[21]

The politics of caste opened up another fissure in Indian society. The Indian constitution guaranteed that 23% of government jobs would be reserved for members of lower castes, who made up 70% of the population.[22] However, the top castes—Brahmins, Ksratriyas, and Vaishyas, who make up only 22% of India's Hindu population—held 95% of all government jobs. The top castes have generally done well under reform, while the "backward" castes have lagged behind economically.[23]

Some states had their own job-reservation and social welfare programs aimed at lower castes. Local politicians appealed to caste interests, and the battle for power between upper and lower castes frequently resulted in violence. When caste-based parties won power in Bihar and Uttar Pradesh, caste-based policies were quickly implemented, resulting in violence. In Uttar Pradesh, caste conflict cleared the way for the Dalit (untouchable) chief minister, Mayawati, to fill government posts with members of her caste, while sacking thousands of employees from other castes. *The Economist* wrote, "There are fears of outright caste war in the country's most important state [Uttar Pradesh]. In neighboring Bihar, which is ruled by a member of the Yadev community, there are tensions."[24] Riots in Bombay and other cities of Maharashtra and Gujarat have left many dead.

The final split was between urban and rural. Most economic gains occurred in urban areas, while the overwhelming majority of Indians lived in small, rural villages where reform had little effect. Surveys suggested that rural voters' main concerns were inflation, food prices, corruption and "a sense that the government cares." This "caring" had traditionally been demonstrated with pork-barrel public spending and programs focused on the lower castes, both of which had been reduced since 1991.

Slow economic progress, combined with religious and cultural tension, provided fertile soil for political upheaval. Opinion polls suggest that the Hindu-nationalist BJP and the leftist parties who threatened to restrict foreign investment had become increasingly popular.

The Agenda in 1996

The 1996 elections demonstrated the regional splintering of Indian politics. A decade earlier, the Congress Party controlled the majority of state governments, but now controlled just five of the 25 states. The BJP emerged as the leading party, with 195 seats out of a total of 542. The Congress Party finished with only 150 seats, and the remaining seats were divided amongst the regional parties. The 13-member United Front partnered with regional parties and the Congress Party.[25]

This was the first time that these parties had joined, and the coalition appeared tenuous. Furthermore, the Congress Party had not been awarded any of the major Cabinet positions, despite the fact that it was the largest party in the coalition. Chidambaram himself had defected from the Congress Party during the Rao government to form his own regional party in Tamil Nadu. He was eager to continue the reform policies of the previous government but recognized that the coalition parties were unlikely to approve of his ambitious inclination toward reform. In order to lower the risk of splintering the coalition party, he needed to balance the pace and depth of reform. How, and whether, he could achieve these perhaps contradictory goals was an open question.

EXHIBIT 2.1   MAP OF INDIA

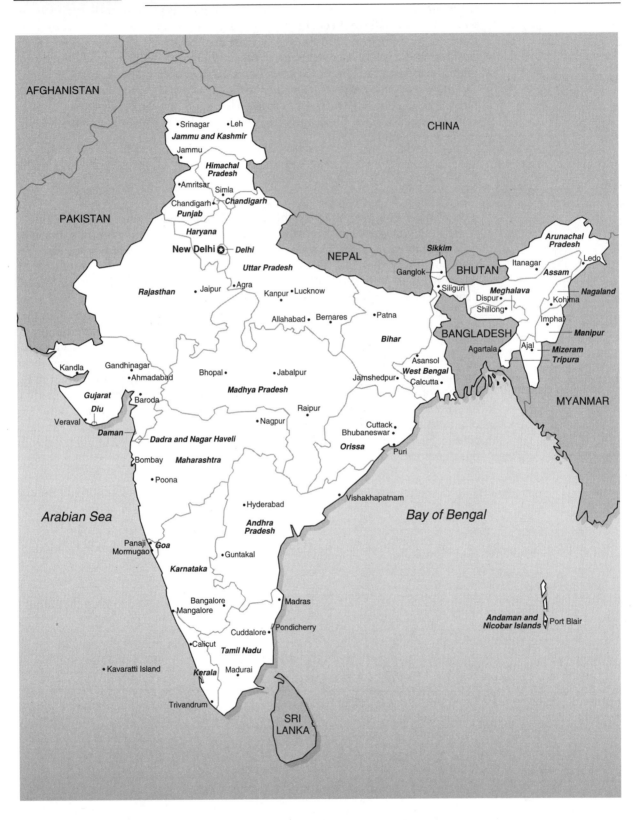

EXHIBIT 2.2A

NATIONAL INCOME ACCOUNTS 1970–1995
(BILLIONS OF CURRENT RUPEES, YEARS ENDING MARCH 31)

	1970	1974	1978	1980	1982	1984	1986	1988	1989	1990	1991	1992	1993	1994	1995
Private Consumption	323	533	725	966	1,225	1,601	1,955	2,623	2,944	3,304	4,112	4,670	5,502	6,413	7,227
Gross Domestic Investment	74	145	232	310	417	517	713	954	1,036	1,183	1,401	1,697	1,755	2,288	2,882
Govt Consumption	38	62	97	131	183	244	346	463	538	617	695	786	899	1,004	1,165
Exports	16	36	69	89	108	157	175	263	351	407	571	683	877	1,030	1,345
Imports	–19	–45	–81	–137	–157	–211	–255	–392	–475	–549	–610	–777	–935	–1,198	–1,633
GDP	**432**	**732**	**1,042**	**1,358**	**1,776**	**2,307**	**2,934**	**3,912**	**4,394**	**5,103**	**6,168**	**7,059**	**8,098**	**9,537**	**10,986**
Real GDP Growth (%)[a]	5.8	0.2	6.6	6.5	3.8	3.7	4.9	9.9	6.6	5.7	0.4	5.4	4.8	7.6	7.3
Private Cons./GDP	75%	73%	70%	71%	69%	69%	67%	67%	67%	65%	67%	66%	68%	67%	66%
Inflation	5.2%	28.6%	2.6%	11.5%	7.9%	8.4%	8.7%	9.4%	6.3%	8.9%	13.9%	11.8%	6.4%	10.2%	10.3%

[a]Over previous year.

SOURCE: 1970–1990, *World Tables 1992*; 1991–1995, India: Sustaining Rapid Economic Growth World Bank.

EXHIBIT 2.2B

GDP BY SECTOR OF PRODUCTION (PERCENTAGE CHANGE IN REAL OUTPUT)

	Average 1981/82–1990/91	1990/91	1991/92	1992/93	1993/94	1994/95	1995/96	Est.1996/97
GDP (factor cost)	5.7	5.4	0.9	4.3	4.3	6.2	7.1	6.2
Agriculture	3.5	3.8	–2.5	5.3	2.9	4.8	–0.1	3.7
Industry	7.2	6.6	–0.8	3.5	3.5	7.4	11.5	6.7
Services	6.3	4.4	5.4	4.9	5.9	6.1	8.8	7.4

SOURCE: *India, Economic Reform and Growth*, International Monetary Fund, 1995; *Country Report: India*, Economist Intelligence Unit (3rd Quarter, 1997), p. 10.

EXHIBIT 2.3 BALANCE OF PAYMENTS 1974–1995 (BILLIONS OF CURRENT US DOLLARS)

Year	1974	1978	1982	1986	1988	1989	1990	1991	1992	1993	1994	1995
Merchandise Exports	4.0	6.8	9.4	10.5	14.2	16.9	18.5	18.3	18.7	22.7	26.9	32.5
Merchandise Imports	-5.2	-9.0	-14.4	-17.7	-23.8	-25.1	-27.2	-21.1	-23.2	-25.1	-31.8	-41.4
Merchandise Trade Balance	**-1.2**	**-2.2**	**-5.0**	**-7.2**	**-9.6**	**-8.2**	**-8.7**	**-2.8**	**-4.5**	**-2.4**	**-4.9**	**-8.9**
Net Non-Factor Services	0.2	0.7	1.0	1.0	0.8	0.7	0.8	1.2	1.1	0.5	-0.4	0.1
Net Factor Payments	-0.2	0.0	-0.7	-2.0	-3.0	-3.3	-3.9	-3.8	-3.4	-3.3	-4.0	-4.5
Net Private Transfers	0.3	1.2	2.6	2.3	3.0	2.8	2.0	3.8	2.8	3.6	6.2	7.5
Net Official Transfers	0.1	0.5	0.4	0.4	0.4	0.5	0.5	0.5	0.4	0.4	0.5	0.4
Current Account Balance	**-0.8**	**0.2**	**-1.7**	**-5.5**	**-8.4**	**-7.5**	**-9.3**	**-1.1**	**-3.6**	**-1.2**	**-2.6**	**-5.4**
Foreign Direct Investment	0.0	0.0	0.1	0.2	0.3	0.4	0.3	0.2	0.3	0.6	1.3	1.9
Net Long-term Loans	0.9	0.6	2.0	2.9	4.4	4.2	2.9	2.2	0.9	0.8	-0.1	-1.2
Portfolio Investments	-0.7	0.9	-1.5	1.1	1.3	1.3	1.7	-0.9	1.4	3.8	3.3	2.2
Other Capital Flow, net	0.1	0.0	0.6	2.1	2.3	1.8	1.6	3.3	1.6	4.8	3.1	-0.4
Capital Balance	**0.3**	**1.5**	**1.2**	**6.3**	**8.3**	**7.7**	**6.5**	**4.8**	**4.2**	**10.0**	**7.6**	**2.5**
Overall Balance	**-0.5**	**1.7**	**-0.5**	**0.8**	**-0.1**	**-0.2**	**-2.8**	**3.7**	**0.6**	**8.8**	**5.0**	**-2.9**
Current Account Deficit as % of GDP	0.9%	0.2%	0.9%	2.4%	3.1%	2.9%	3.3%	0.3%	1.3%	0.5%	0.9%	1.6%
Exchange Rate (rupees/dollar)	8.1	8.2	9.5	12.6	13.9	16.2	17.5	22.7	25.9	30.5	31.4	32.4
Foreign Exchange Reserves as % of Imports	16%	82%	35%	45%	26%	20%	7%	18%	24%	45%	69%	49%

NOTE: Fiscal year runs from April through March.

SOURCE: 1974–1990—*World Tables*, 1992, World Bank; 1991–1995—India Economic Survey, Indian Ministry of Finance.

EXHIBIT 2.4A	GOVERNMENT RECEIPTS AND EXPENDITURES (BILLIONS OF CURRENT RUPEES)														
	1970	1974	1978	1980	1982	1984	1986	1988	1989	1990	1991	1992	1993	1994	1995
Total Revenues	33	76	132	165	229	301	425	563	683	730	902	1,014	1,022	1,269	1,456
Capital expenditures	na	11	17	21	31	50	74	86	100	108	119	130	155	193	200
Current expenditures	na	66	116	159	213	302	444	609	726	808	931	1,060	1,209	1,369	1,544
Total Expenditures	39	77	133	180	244	352	518	694	826	916	1,050	1,190	1,364	1,562	1,744
Primary Deficit	6	1	1	15	15	51	93	131	143	186	148	176	342	293	288
Lending less repayment	8	23	40	74	92	125	179	189	226	240	209	224	264	325	296
Overall Deficit	14	24	41	89	107	176	272	320	369	246	357	400	606	618	584
Overall Deficit as % of GDP	3.2%	3.3%	3.9%	6.6%	6.0%	7.6%	9.3%	8.1%	8.4%	4.8%	5.8%	5.7%	7.5%	6.5%	5.3%

SOURCE: International Monetary Fund, *International Financial Statistics.*
na: Data not available.

EXHIBIT 2.4B	CENTRAL GOVERNMENT REVENUES AND EXPENDITURES (PERCENTAGE OF GDP)				
	1990/91	1991/92	1992/93	1993/94	1994/95e
Total Expenditure	**19.1**	**17.8**	**17.0**	**17.8**	**17.7**
Current Expenditure	15.1	14.8	14.5	15.3	14.9
Interest	4.0	4.3	4.4	4.7	4.8
Major subsidies	1.3	1.4	1.2	1.3	1.2
Defense[a]	2.9	2.7	2.5	2.8	2.6
Grants to states	2.5	2.6	2.6	2.7	2.3
Wages	2.0	1.9	1.8	1.9	1.7
Other	2.4	1.9	1.9	1.9	2.3
Capital Expenditure	4.0	3.0	2.5	2.5	2.8
Consolidated Public Sector[b]					
Revenue and Grants	20.7	23.0	23.0	21.7	22.8
Expenditure and net lending	31.2	32.0	31.4	32.7	33.2
of which: interest payments	5.2	6.1	6.4	6.7	6.7

[a]Includes defense capital expenditure.
[b]The consolidated public sector comprises the operations of the central government, the state governments, and the central public enterprises.

SOURCE: *India, Economic Reform and Growth,* International Monetary Fund, 1995.

EXHIBIT 2.5A INDIA'S AND SELECTED COUNTRIES' INDICATORS FOR ECONOMIC DEVELOPMENT (1995 FIGURES UNLESS NOTED)

Country	Population (per km²)	Pop. Density (millions)	GDP (billion USD)	GNP Per Capita (USD)	GDP Growth Rate (1994)	External Debt (million USD)	Mean Tariff (1990–1993) %	Workers in Agriculture %	Population below $1 a Day %	Growth Food Prices (1990–1995) %	Inflation (%)	Paved Roads %
Brazil	159	19	702	3,640	4.1	159,131	11.1	23	28.7	1,235.4	84.4	9.2
China	1,200	129	693	620	10.5	118,090	36.3	74	29.4	na	16.9	89.7
France	58	106	1,538	24,990	2.1	na	6.7	5	na	1.0	1.8	na
India	929	313	289.5	340	5.8	93,766	56.3	64	52.5	11.1	14.8	50.1
Indonesia	193	107	198	980	8.2	107,831	19.4	57	14.5	9.2	9.4	45.5
Japan	125	333	5,134	39,640	1.3	na	6.3	7	na	1.1	-0.1	74.0
Malaysia	20	61	87.5	3,890	9.5	34,351	14.3	27	5.6	5.2	5.3	75.0
Mexico	92	48	286	3,320	-6.2	165,743	12.6	28	14.9	13.4	35	37.3
Morocco	27	60	32	1,110	-7.6	22,147	24.5	45	1.1	8.8	6.1	50.3
Pakistan	130	169	59	460	5.2	30,152	51.0	56	11.6	11.1	12.3	54.0
Poland	39	127	118	2,790	7.0	42,291	12.0	27	6.8	35.2	31.8	65.3
Singapore	3	4,896	85	26,730	8.8	na	0.5	0	na	2.0	1.7	97.3
South Africa	41	34	133.7	3,160	3.4	na	19.7	14	23.7	14.5	8.6	32.8
Thailand	58	114	165.3	2,740	8.6	56,789	23.1	64	0.1	5.4	5.7	97.4
United Kingdom	59	242	1,100	18,700	2.7	na	6.7	2	na	2.5	3.4	100.0
United States	263	29	7,030	26,980	2.0	na	5.9	3	na	3.5	2.8	59.9
Zaire	44	19	4.1	120	-3.9	13,137	na	68	na	na	370.3	na

SOURCE: *World Development Indicators*, The World Bank, 1997.
na: Data not available.

EXHIBIT 2.5B INDIA'S AND SELECTED COUNTRIES' INDICATORS FOR SOCIAL DEVELOPMENT (1995 UNLESS NOTED)

Country	Life Expectancy at Birth (male)	Infant Mortality Rate (per 1,000 births)	Births per Woman	Adult Illiteracy Rate (% males 15 and above)	Adult Illiteracy Rate (% women > 15)	Labor Force (millions)	People per Physician (1993)	Access to Sanitation (%)
Brazil	63	44	2.4	17	17	71	844	73
China	68	34	1.9	10	27	709	1,063	na
France	74	6	1.7	na	na	26	334	96
India	62	68	3.2	35	62	398	2,459	29
Indonesia	62	51	2.7	10	22	89	7,028	55
Japan	77	4	1.5	na	na	66	608	85
Malaysia	69	12	3.4	11	22	8	2,441	94
Mexico	69	33	3.0	8	13	36	615	70
Morocco	64	55	3.4	42	77	10	4,665	63
Pakistan	62	90	5.2	50	76	46	1,923	30
Poland	67	14	1.6	na	na	19	451	100
Singapore	74	4	1.7	4	14	1	714	100
South Africa	61	50	3.9	18	18	16	na	46
Thailand	67	35	1.8	4	8	34	4,416	87
United Kingdom	74	6	1.7	na	na	29	611	96
United States	74	8	2.1	na	na	133	549	82
Zaire	50	na	na	13	32	18	15,150	9

SOURCE: *World Development Indicators*, The World Bank, 1997.
na: Data not available.

EXHIBIT 2.6 EXTERNAL DEBT 1975–1995 (MILLIONS OF U.S. DOLLARS)

	1975	1978	1980	1982	1983	1984	1985	1986	1987	1988	1989	1990	1991	1992	1993	1994	1995
Total External Debt	13,708	16,466	20,582	27,438	32,004	33,826	40,971	48,278	55,727	58,443	73,393	81,994	83,952	90,131	91,781	102,611	94,414
Long-Term Debt (by debtor)	13,235	15,815	19,311	25,041	28,666	30,154	36,613	43,332	50,054	52,085	65,892	73,450	76,882	83,791	88,155	98,347	89,365
Central Bank	813	26	2,057	5,031	6,895	7,022	8,789	10,258	11,281	11,467	11,975	14,469	15,326	17,879	19,680	na	na
Central Government	9,809	12,769	14,005	15,556	16,668	17,019	20,367	23,931	27,799	28,383	40,327	44,760	45,443	49,573	50,789	na	na
Other General Govt.	46	36	27	18	15	18	21	19	74	63	68	71	175	345	388	na	na
Public Enterprises	1,728	1,920	2,138	2,575	3,005	3,875	4,891	6,307	7,322	8,349	9,434	9,800	9,882	9,942	10,432	na	na
Private Sector	838	1,064	1,084	1,862	2,084	2,221	2,545	2,817	3,578	3,824	4,087	4,350	6,056	6,053	6,866	na	na
Short-Term Debt	473	651	1,271	2,397	3,338	3,672	4,358	4,946	5,673	6,358	7,501	8,544	7,070	6,340	3,626	4,264	5,049
External Debt/GNP (%)			11.9		16.1	17.7	19.3	21.3	22.0	21.7	27.9	28.5	34.5	37.6	37.2	34.3	29.2
Ext. Debt/Exports (%)			136.0		207.9	209.5	265.2	294.8	288.2	276.2	310.0	320.8	311.0	336.5	300.8	264.1	198.8
Debt Service/Exports (%)			9.3		16.9	18.2	22.7	32.0	29.4	29.8	28.6	31.4	28.6	28.7	26.6	27.6	28.1

SOURCE: 1975–1993 Debt data: *World Tables*, The World Bank, 1995; 1994–1995 Debt data: Global Development Finance, Country Tables; 1998 Debt ratios: Global Development Finance, Country Tables, various issues.

na: Data not available.

EXHIBIT 2.7 **ECONOMIC AND SOCIAL DEVELOPMENT BY STATE**

	Per Capita Net Domestic Product (current rupees)			Annual Real GDP Growth (1990)		Per Capita GDP ($)	Index of GDP Per Capita (All India avg. = 100)	Annual Population Growth Rate	Density (pop. per sq. km)	Total Literacy Rate	Population (1995)
	1980/81	1989/90	1994/95	1980–90	1991–95	1994/95		1981–1991			
Andhra Pradesh	2,788	4,728	4,736	6.3	5.4	221	80	2.2	242	44.1	70,731,333
Arunachal Pradesh	3,173	5,397	5,780	8.2	8.0	270	98	3.1	10	41.6	943,504
Assam	2,594	4,281	3,965	6.6	3.8	185	67	2.2	286	52.9	24,234,039
Bihar	1,852	2,665	2,524	5.0	4.3	118	43	2.1	497	38.5	93,381,351
Delhi	8,141	11,043	11,282	6.7	7.8	526	191	1.5	6,352	75.5	10,681,392
Goa	6,353	8,797	9,740	3.8	8.2	454	165	1.9	316	75.5	1,254,750
Gujarat	3,919	5,917	6,992	5.4	9.8	326	119	2.4	211	61.3	44,042,352
Haryana	4,787	7,508	8,036	6.4	7.6	375	136	1.9	372	55.9	17,798,158
Himachal Pradesh	3,442	4,910	5,145	4.7	6.7	240	87	2.5	93	63.9	5,531,860
Jammu & Kashmir	3,588	3,625	3,041	1.4	0.4	142	52	na	na	na	8,043,478
Karnataka	3,070	4,605	5,342	5.3	9.1	249	91	1.9	235	56.0	47,538,796
Kerala	3,046	4,200	4,616	3.6	7.4	215	78	1.3	749	89.8	30,585,708
Madhya Pradesh	2,757	4,053	3,864	5.5	4.4	180	65	2.4	149	44.2	71,122,327
Maharashtra	4,919	7,367	8,667	5.6	10.0	404	147	2.3	257	64.9	84,676,632
Manipur	2,866	3,976	3,768	5.1	5.9	176	64	2.6	82	59.9	2,105,263
Meghalaya	2,749	4,530	4,056	7.4	3.6	189	69	2.8	79	49.1	1,965,450
Mizoram	2,604	4,474	5,354	8.8	14.8	250	91	3.3	33	82.3	864,198
Nagaland	2,925	5,498	4,627	11.2	1.8	216	79	4.5	73	61.7	1,342,857
Orissa	2,654	3,077	3,409	2.2	8.2	159	58	1.8	203	49.1	33,816,172
Punjab	5,401	8,341	9,378	5.6	8.6	438	159	1.9	403	58.5	21,702,847
Rajasthan	2,468	4,191	3,702	7.5	1.4	173	63	2.5	129	38.6	45,535,714
Sikkim	3,173	5,302	2,842	7.2	-1.9	133	48	2.5	57	56.9	604,651
Tamil Nadu	3,026	5,071	5,910	5.9	8.6	276	100	1.4	429	62.7	57,876,077
Tripura	2,640	3,370	3,041	4.6	5.5	142	52	3.0	263	60.4	3,260,870
Uttar Pradesh	2,582	3,590	3,524	4.8	4.9	164	60	2.3	473	41.6	148,234,853
West Bengal	3,581	4,710	4,546	4.0	4.4	212	77	2.2	767	57.7	72,386,215

SOURCE: *Economic Survey, 1996–97, Government of India.*
na: Data not available.

EXHIBIT 2.8	EMPLOYMENT IN THE PUBLIC SECTOR			
	1981	**1985**	**1990**	**1995**
Distribution of Government Employment				
Central government (%)	21	19	18	17
State governments (%)	37	36	37	38
Quasi-governments (%)	30	32	33	34
Local bodies (%)	13	13	12	11
By Industry (% of workers in public-sector firms)				
Agriculture, hunting	35	39	39	38
Mining and quarrying	87	90	91	91
Manufacturing	25	29	30	27
Electricity, gas, and water	95	96	95	96
Construction	94	91	95	96
Wholesale & retail trade	30	32	34	35
Transport, storage, and communications	98	98	98	98
Finance, insurance, and real estate	80	82	83	81
Community, social, and personal services	86	86	86	86

SOURCE: Economic Survey, 1996–1997, Government of India, Ministry of Finance, Economic Division, Table 3.1, p. S52.

EXHIBIT 2.9A	FINANCIAL MARKET STRUCTURE (PERCENTAGE OF TOTAL)							
	1987	**1988**	**1989**	**1990**	**1991**	**1992**	**1993**	**1994**
Households' savings in financial assets (in percent of total)								
Bank deposits	40.6	36.9	30.1	29.2	29.3	35.3	37.3	41.6
Nonbank financial assets	59.4	63.1	69.9	70.8	70.7	64.7	62.7	59.4
of which: shares and debentures	2.3	2.8	5.5	8.7	9.3	10.0	8.8	13.2
Commercial financing								
Domestic financing	99.4	99.2	97.4	96.3	97.9	99.9	84.9	81.5
Bank loans	66.3	68.0	61.9	53.0	34.4	46.7	37.0	32.6
Nonbank loans	15.0	14.3	19.1	25.6	35.7	27.4	11.4	9.3
Shares and debentures	18.1	16.9	16.4	17.7	27.8	25.8	36.4	39.6
Foreign Financing	0.5	0.7	2.5	3.6	2.2	0.2	15.1	18.5

SOURCE: *India, Economic Reform and Growth*, International Monetary Fund, 1995.

EXHIBIT 2.9B	SAVINGS IN INDIA (PERCENTAGE OF GDP)									
	1980	**1985**	**1986**	**1987**	**1988**	**1989**	**1990**	**1991**	**1992**	**1993**
Gross Savings	**21.2**	**19.8**	**18.7**	**20.9**	**21.5**	**22.3**	**23.7**	**23.1**	**20.0**	**20.2**
General government	2.1	0.4	–0.3	–1.0	–1.3	–1.9	–2.1	–1.4	–1.2	–2.7
Corporate and quasi-corporate enterprises	3.0	4.9	4.8	4.9	5.6	6.1	5.8	6.6	5.7	6.9
Household savings	16.1	14.6	14.2	17.0	17.3	18.1	20.0	17.8	15.5	15.9

SOURCE: India National Accounts Division of the Central Statistical Organization, 1994.

EXHIBIT 2.10A	EQUITY OWNERSHIP AND DEBT BY LENDER IN THE PRIVATE SECTOR

	Equity Distribution in the Private Sector				
	1950	**1955**	**1960**	**1965**	**1970**
Central government	7%	6%	12%	19%	25%
Local private	75	82	67	60	56
Foreign	18	12	21	21	19

	Distribution of the Flow of New Long-term Debt to the Private Sector				
	1950–55	**1956–60**	**1961–65**	**1966–70**	**1971–75**[a]
Central government	56%	72%	45%	45%	106%
Local private	39	20	49	54	–4
Foreign	5	8	6	1	–2

[a] Net repayment of capital and interest causes negative numbers.

SOURCE: Encarnation, *Dislodging Multinationals*, 1989, as reported in India (A), Harvard Business School Case #793-112.

EXHIBIT 2.10B	PUBLIC SECTOR SHARE OF TOTAL GROSS INVESTMENT (% BY SECTOR)

	1960	**1970**	**1980**	**1987**
Agriculture	29.7	28.7	39.5	35.6
Mining and manufacturing	36.5	26.2	47.1	43.4
Manufacturing	39.1	23.6	40.0	32.3
Power, transport, and communications	75.1	80.8	79.0	78.4
Electricity, gas, water	92.7	98.6	93.2	94.9
Railways	100.0	100.0	100.0	100.0
Other transport	27.4	43.4	39.6	23.5
Communications	100.0	100.0	100.0	100.0
Services	37.2	39.1	24.2	28.4
Total, all sectors	**42.4**	**42.1**	**49.4**	**46.5**

SOURCE: Center for Monitoring the Indian Economy, 1991, as reported in India (A), Harvard Business School Case #793-112.

EXHIBIT 2.11	PROFITABILITY OF CENTRAL GOVERNMENT PUBLIC ENTERPRISES (IN BILLIONS OF RUPEES, UNLESS OTHERWISE NOTED)

	1990/91	1991/92	1992/93	1993/94
Profits and losses of public enterprises				
Number of operating enterprises (nondepartmental)[a]	236	237	239	240
Percentage of public enterprises (ND) that are profitable	53%	57%	56%	51%
Total losses of departmental enterprises	18.9	18.3	na	na
As percentage of GDP	0.4	0.3	na	na
Total losses of state electricity boards (departmental)	41.7	48.9	47.0	na
As percentage of GDP	0.8	0.8	0.6	na
Return of sales in selected sectors				
Steel				
Public (ND)	–3.9	–5.8	–1.7	–1.1
Private	2.4	2.9	2.4	na
Fertilizer				
Public (ND)	–8.5	–7.5	–11.3	–8.0
Private	6.9	5.9	4.5	na
Chemicals and Pharmaceuticals				
Public (ND)	–2.9	–3.1	1.5	–0.6
Private	4.3	4.7	5.0	na
Heavy Engineering				
Public (ND)	–3.0	–2.7	–2.3	–7.9
Private	3.4	3.7	3.6	na
Textile				
Public (ND)	–16.7	–23.7	–39.2	–38.4
Private	3.9	2.3	2.2	na
Private firms average pretax return on invested capital	22.2%	21.7%	19.8%	19.8%
Nondepartmental public enterprises' pretax return on invested capital	10.9%	11.6%	11.4%	11.3%

[a]Nondepartmental (ND) enterprises are intended to be run for profit. Departmental enterprises (DP) that fall under government departments are not operated to maximize profits.
na: Data not available.

SOURCE: *India, Economic Reform and Growth*, International Monetary Fund, 1995.

EXHIBIT 2.12	INDIAN EXPORTS (MILLION $)

Exports fob	1993/94
Clothing and footwear	4,265
Diamonds	3,935
Textiles, fabrics, and manufactures	3,829
Agricultural products	3,227
Engineering goods (incl. software)[a]	3,020
Chemicals	2,155
Machinery and transport equipment	1,890
Leather and manufactures	467
Petroleum and products	423

[a] Includes electronics and computer software. The Indian Software Association estimates that software exports were approximately $325 million in 1993/94. These had grown to approximately $770 million by 1995/96.

SOURCE: Economist Intelligence Unit, 1997; Nascon: *The Software Industry in India*, 1997–98.

END NOTES

1   "Tiger or Tortoise?" *The Economist*, April 27, 1996, p. 21.

2   Quoted from "Survey of India," *The Economist*, May 4, 1991.

3   "Happy Anniversary?" *The Economist*, June 16, 1997, p. 17.

4   Ibid.

5   Vijay Joshi and I. M. D. Little, *India: Macroeconomics and Political Economy 1964–1991* (Washington, DC: World Bank, 1994), pp. 150–160.

6   "Tiger or Tortoise?" p. 21.

7   "India's Next 50 Years," *The Economist*, August 16, 1997, p. 11.

8   "Hello, World," *The Economist*, January 21, 1995, Survey, p. 3.

9   Ajai Chopra, et al., "India: Economic Reform and Growth," Washington, DC: International Monetary Fund Occasional Paper, December 1995.

10   "India's Next 50 Years," p. 11.

11   John F. Burns, "Second Thoughts on India," *The New York Times*, January 9, 1996, p. 48.

12   Ibid.

13   Ramesh Thakur, "India in the World: neither Rich, Powerful, nor Principled," *Foreign Affairs*, July/August 1997, p. 16; "Business Outlook: China," *Crossborder Monitor*, May 14, 1997.

14   Tony Tassell, "The Impatient Need Not Apply," *Accountancy*, May 1997.

15   Chopra, et al., "India: Economic Reform and Growth," p. 21

16   "Tiger or Tortoise?" p. 22

17   "Go West," *The Economist*, January 21, 1995, Survey, pp. 10–15.

18   Jonathan Karp and Sumit Sharma, "India's President Acts to Resolve Crisis; Uncertainty Jars Bombay Stock Market," *The Wall Street Journal*, March 31, 1997.

19   John F. Burns, "India's Prime Minister Wages Uphill Campaign," *The New York Times*, April 5, 1996.

20   BJP, "National Agenda for Governance," March 1998. Quoted from the India National News Network, http://indnet.org.

21   "India," *CIA World Factbook* (Washington, DC: Government Printing Office, 1996).

22   "India: The Hills Are Ablaze," *The Economist*, October 8, 1994.

23   Ibid.

24   "Casteing Stones," *The Economist*, July 19, 1997.

25   Peter Waldman and Miriam Jordan, "Indian Politicians Rush to Form Coalition," *The New York Times*, May 13, 1996, p. A16.

The Limits to Managed Growth

After growing at 10.1% annually for 17 years until 1971, Japan finally staggered with the Nixon Shocks. When the United States shifted to floating exchange rates and imposed a surcharge on Japanese imports, the Japanese miracle appeared to end. Late in 1973, the oil shock further staggered Japanese growth. Thereafter, Japan had to adjust to a slower growing world in which its own asymmetrical trade advantages were reduced.

But from 1971 until 1991, Japan still performed quite well, although without "miracle growth." It adjusted to high-cost oil and to a more and more valuable currency. Its targeted export sectors delivered huge trade surpluses in machinery, electronics, and automobiles. Even after *endaka* ("era of high yen") began in 1985, Japan struggled to remain competitive. And as it got richer, its people invested freely in domestic equities, in real estate, and eventually in Southeast Asia.

But when its central bank raised interest rates to curb inflation in 1989, the economy plunged into recession. Moreover, between 1991 and 1999, Japan never had a sustained recovery and remained mired in stagnation, which periodically slumped into recession.

Fiscal and monetary policy did not seem to work. That is, huge fiscal deficits and low interest rates barely prevented negative growth. Its banking system stopped working; its export sector experienced huge excess capacity. It appeared that the extraordinary institutions that had helped create the miracle now got in the way of structural adjustment required to deal with globalization. Business–government relations, labor relations, corporate governance, and even demographics all seemed a burden now and one that was difficult to change.

In 1997, Prime Minister Hashimoto proposed a thorough plan for institutional reform, to make Japan "free, fair, and global." But even before the Diet had considered his initiatives, Japan was again sinking into a recession—the deepest of the century. Should Hashimoto go forward with his broad plan for reform, or would a successor change direction? What did Japan need to do to adjust?

CASE STUDY

JAPAN: "FREE, FAIR, AND GLOBAL?"

The Japanese economy is currently facing its most difficult time ever. . . . If you look at what Hoover was saying at the start of the great depression and what Mr. Hashimoto is saying at the moment, they are very similar.

—**Norio Ohga,** Chairman and Chief Executive of
Sony Corporation (quoted in *Financial Times,* April 3, 1998)

By April 1998, Japan's prime minister, Ryutaro Hashimoto, faced two competing goals: a long-term plan of widespread institutional reform, and a short-term desire to stimulate the economy in an attempt to appease trading partners. To keep his job and restore the nation's economic glory, Hashimoto needed to choose the best method to bring the economy out of stagnation that had persisted for nearly six years.

In November 1996, Hashimoto announced a grand plan to restructure administration, deregulation, education, the financial system, fiscal policy, and social security. The cornerstone to this plan was financial market reform, dubbed the Big Bang. Modeled after British reforms in the 1980s, the Big Bang was to liberate the Japanese capital market by 2001. If all went according to plan, Japan's new capital market would be "Free"—completely following market principles; "Fair"—totally transparent and reliable; and "Global"—used by the entire world.

The collapse of its "bubble economy" in 1990 and 1991 had thoroughly deflated asset and land prices, and few companies had been able to restore profitability to anything like Western levels. Over the previous six years, Japan's economy remained in the doldrums, as government futilely attempted to restore growth both through monetary stimulus and through reducing fiscal deficits. As the fiscal year 1998 budget was being created, citizens clamored for renewed government stimulus, primarily through tax cuts. Japan also faced criticism internationally, especially from the United States, for its inability to rejuvenate its economy. In March 1998 the government announced its intention to provide a stimulus package of ¥16 trillion ($121 billion), primarily focusing on public works. Details of the package were due in late April.

In some circles, Hashimoto's viability as a leader remained in doubt. He had battled opposition and hesitation, even in his own Liberal Democratic Party. His original reform proposals had been substantially altered already and had yet to clear the Diet. A series of scandals, which had recently forced the resignations of Finance Minister Hiroshi Mitsuzuka and Bank of Japan Governor Yasuo Matsushita, persisted. And in the past half year, financial crises in Asia had undermined Japanese investments and markets, especially in Thailand, Malaysia, Indonesia, and South Korea.

Facing more recession in 1998, Japan moved forward with the financial reform, through its revisions of the Foreign Exchange Act. On April 1, investments abroad would be deregulated. Japanese citizens could, henceforth, buy equities on the New York Stock Exchange, U.S. Treasury bills, or shares in foreign mutual funds. With personal financial assets exceeding $10 trillion, and continuing low interest rates, no one really knew just what to expect.

Fruits of the Miracle

Although the Japanese economic miracle ended in 1971, the country reaped the benefits of its rapid growth over the next two decades. The economy continued to grow vigorously, despite severe supply-side shocks. Reinvestment and productivity made

Research Associate Stephen Lynagh prepared this case under the supervision of Professor Richard H. K. Vietor as the basis for class discussion rather than to illustrate either effective or ineffective handling of an administrative situation.

Japan's export business incredibly efficient. And on a macroeconomic level, the nation was able to achieve its goal of catching the United States—surpassing the United States in GDP per capita by 1989 (although purchasing power per capita was only 72% that in the United States). [See **Exhibit 3.1a.**]

Continued Economic Growth

Economic growth from 1971 to 1991 was consistently strong, at an average rate of 4.4% annually. In only four of those years did the rate drop below 3%, generally when some sort of shock was experienced. These shocks demonstrated both the exposure of Japan's system and its ability to make economic reforms. [Details of Japan's growth and spending are in **Exhibits 3.1–3.6.**]

Nixon Shocks   On August 15, 1971, U.S. President Richard Nixon ended the Bretton Woods system of fixed exchange rates, in effect since 1944. Under that agreement, the price of gold was fixed to the U.S. dollar, at $35 per ounce. All other currencies were pegged to the dollar; for Japan, the rate was ¥360/$1. When Nixon made his announcement, the dollar dropped and the yen rose to ¥308/$1. Nixon also imposed a 10% surcharge on imports, trying to push the Japanese into opening their markets.[1]

Within a year, President Nixon visited China. The Japanese were again caught totally unawares by this sudden realignment of world powers and were thoroughly embarrassed by their lack of foreknowledge. The entire affair reinforced Japanese sensitivity to their limited political connections in Washington and their overdependence on the United States.[2]

Oil Shocks   Late in 1973, the first oil shock hit the world, as OPEC countries enforced an oil embargo and quadrupled prices. Japan, which relied almost exclusively on imported oil, was forced to pay significantly more. Inflation skyrocketed in 1974, imports rose by 40%, and growth vanished. After a year, trade was back in balance and Japan took advantage of the gap created between the ¥/$ exchange rate and the country's purchasing power parity (PPP) based on export prices. The following years saw big trade surpluses as Japan continued to pursue energy conservation.

Again, at the end of the 1970s, the Iranian Revolution forced oil prices to double, engaging another round of inflation, a slump in the balance of trade, and conservation.[3] Japan was also reaching technological equality with the rest of the industrialized world, forcing a slowdown of its advantageous productivity growth.

Nonetheless, during the early 1980s, Japanese exports in a few industries began to swamp American production. The depreciation of the yen due to the second oil shock re-opened the gap between the ¥/$ exchange rate and export PPP, allowing extensive export growth. In cars and car parts, steel, consumer electronics, and machine tools, Japan was gaining U.S. market share annually. In response, the United States threatened Japan with "reciprocity" legislation that could close U.S. markets to asymmetrical trade. A series of U.S. trade complaints brought temporary and "voluntary" limitations to Japan's export onslaught, while the United States tried to adjust.

With the Reagan plan, U.S. real interest rates rose sharply in 1981 and the value of the dollar eventually climbed 63%. The yen weakened, which only reasserted Japan's export competitiveness. By 1985, the U.S. trade balance was negative $122 billion, while Japan's surplus rose to $56 billion. In September 1985, industrial countries decided that these currency trends had gone too far. G-5 finance ministers met at the Plaza Hotel in New York, and announced their agreement that the dollar had appreciated too much. Within weeks, the dollar began falling, reaching ¥128/$1 by 1988. This initiated the period of *endaka*—or "high yen." [See **Exhibit 3.7.**]

Endaka   Now the pressure was really on Japan, as the dollar prices of its exports rose sharply. If they were to prevent a balance of trade crisis, Japanese firms would have to cut costs, lower prices, and eventually reinvest in more modern plant and equipment. This they did with a vengeance. They benefited, of course, from the massive drop (yen terms) in the prices of their raw materials imports. Returns on equity, never much higher than 8%, now plunged to just 3% by 1991. As the Bank of Japan lowered interest rates to 2.5% by February 1987, real investment skyrocketed—from 27% to 32% of GDP by 1991—an unprecedented level for a developed country. Japan virtually rebuilt its industrial system.

As the trade surplus soared to more than $90 billion annually, the Japanese invested in their stock market, foreign equities, real estate, and foreign debt. Savings were immense, but there was no clear end to investment possibilities. Land prices in Tokyo and Osaka more than tripled, and the Nikkei stock market average rose from 11,000 to 39,000 points. Japanese banks and investment funds bought U.S. Treasury bills, and Japanese businesses bought nearly $140 billion of U.S. equities and real estate such as Columbia Pictures, Pebble Beach Golf, and New York's Rockefeller Center. Japan's manufacturers built plants in the United States, Europe, and Southeast Asia, to gain market access and avoid protectionism, to gain access to technology, or to lower their labor costs, grown high at home.

Adjustment to the Bursting Bubble and Globalization

Eventually, *endaka* caught up with Japan. Under the pressure of asset speculation and a threat of inflation in 1989, a new governor of the Bank of Japan moved to raise interest rates and cool off the economy. Rates rose further in 1990, and by 1991, Japan was in recession. The Nikkei fell back, bottoming at 14,309, and real estate values started to drop. Economic growth fell below 1% annually by 1993, and had barely recovered to 3% in 1996, when it fell once more. Partly due to its inept management, the Liberal Democratic Party (LDP), in control of the Diet since 1949, was ousted in 1993. Unemployment [see **Exhibit 3.7**], always low since the early 1960s, rose sharply, to a record 4.1% in April 1998.

After a long struggle to balance its budget (by 1992), the government attempted fiscal stimulus. For three years, through 1995, deficit spending rose dramatically. Although this drove government debt and debt service to record levels, it did little to stimulate growth. Then the government lowered interest rates, all the way down to 0.5% by 1995. Unfortunately, with asset prices still falling and bad debt plaguing the books of the nation's banks, even these low rates could not stimulate much borrowing.

Institutional Concerns

There was no simple explanation for Japan's continuing stagnation. But to the extent that many Japanese viewed Westernization as part of the solution, they tended to cite traditional institutions as part of the problem. Although labor and capital markets, the strong bureaucracy, corporate governance, and unique social arrangements had worked well in the past, they now seemed to fit less well with the imperatives of globalization.

Labor Markets

Job security was paramount for the Japanese: most people would choose a lower-paying, permanent-employment position in a prestigious company rather than work for a higher-paying startup company that did not guarantee job security. These positions generally were offered by medium- and larger-sized employers and accounted for about one-third of all positions; smaller employers did not strictly adhere to this policy.[4] For many years, this business practice was admired—companies garnered tremendous employee loyalty, and their substantial growth required increasing numbers of employees. Japan had a low unemployment rate relative to its industrial counterparts.

Japanese corporations promoted from within, following primarily a seniority system. Tax advantages even encouraged this policy; the longer employees worked for a company, the less tax was imposed on their retirement allowance.[5] Some people believed the seniority system was being slowly revised, and the Ministry of Labor reported a slight increase in wage disparity;[6] the gradual introduction of merit-based compensation could add to the disparity. But overall the seniority system was still intact, with few senior executives under the age of 55. Labor costs kept steadily rising.

Many Japanese were shocked in the late 1990s when major firms such as Yamaichi Securities declared bankruptcy, forcing their employees to find alternative positions. Despite that surprise, most Japanese companies maintained large payrolls through the slow growth period; few firms issued layoffs. Instead, companies instituted hiring freezes and offered some early retirement packages, reducing payrolls through attrition. These policies "worked well when the economy was constantly growing," said a president of a major research center. "But now companies cannot expect higher growth, so they must change the system."[7]

Capital Markets

Japanese banks dominated the country's financial markets, limiting equity market development. After the occupation, Japanese companies had a great need for funds, but individuals were risk-averse and had little money. Banks were tapped to take the funding risks for these companies, as individuals stored their assets in banks, which in turn loaned them to the companies. As a result, companies were financed predominantly through debt, not equity. Investors continued accumulating personal financial assets, which they then deposited in savings accounts. By 1997, personal financial assets had accumulated to ¥1,200 trillion, mostly in banks or postal savings.

Because banks played such a vital role in funding businesses, the relationship between businesses and their banks became increasingly mutually dependent. To protect themselves, the banks and businesses had formed interlocking relationships and taken equity positions in each other.[8] Moreover, restrictions on the security of a bank's portfolio were comparatively weak; Japanese banks could lend up to 20% of their capital to a single borrower, versus 10% in the United States, and there were no legal restrictions on the use of real estate as collateral, although banks could not hold real estate on their balance sheets.[9] [See **Exhibit 3.8.**]

Many Japanese institutions kept balance sheets based on book values rather than market values. In some situations this created hidden profits, as an asset's market value was much higher than its book value. However, in a large number of cases, this method of accounting held hidden losses; the dramatic decline in asset and land prices following the bubble forced financial institutions to hold on to depressed assets or sell them at a significant loss.

The collapse of the bubble also affected the massive bad debt problem. Many banks were leveraged beyond their means; as companies' collateral plummeted, they defaulted on their loans, turning worthless assets over to banks. In turn, the banks needed to face their own paper losses. Banks suffered additional losses in Southeast Asia due to financial crisis. But writing off bad debt was complicated, because land and buildings used as collateral for bad loans were sometimes owned by *yakuza*, the organized crime syndicates, which refused to write down their share.

April 1998 saw the introduction of "prompt corrective action" to protect a bank's capital adequacy ratio. Internationally active banks were required to meet the 8% minimum set by the Bank of International Settlements (BIS). Banks operating solely within Japan were forced to have at least a 4% ratio. Failure to meet these standards would require a management improvement plan or, in more severe cases, restructuring. Additionally, banks began to use marked-to-market accounting systems to increase their transparency. To meet these standards, many banks closed their international offices; in March 1998 the Ministry of Finance classification listed only 45 international banks and 102 domestic ones, compared with earlier respective figures of 80 and 67.

For a long time, the government would not allow banks to fail, either by injecting funds to prevent a bank from defaulting or encouraging a merger with a healthier bank. This policy changed dramatically when the government allowed Hokkaido Takushoku to collapse in November 1997. An even greater shock occurred when Yamaichi Securities collapsed a few weeks later, facing ¥260 billion in off-the-book debts. The bad loan problem was severe, as indicated in **Exhibit 3.9.**

Individuals had limited opportunities in the capital markets. The bulk of personal financial savings was held in commercial savings accounts (or in postal savings), which earned a nominal interest rate of 0.4% for deposits between one and two years. The postal accounts helped fund the Fiscal Investment and Loan Program, an off-budget fund financing public infrastructure. Individuals were also prohibited from foreign exchange transactions. As a result, few people held U.S. Treasury bills or foreign equity. Also uncommon were mutual fund holdings or derivative securities.

Bureaucratic Power

Japan was a representative democracy. There was a parliament (the Diet), which consisted of a 500-member House of Representatives and a 252-member House of Councillors. In the House of Representatives, elections occurred at least every four years. Members of the House of Councillors were elected to six-year terms. The Diet elected a prime minister, whose primary executive duty was to select a cabinet to oversee the bureaucracy. The legal system was headed by a U.S.-style Supreme Court, appointed by the cabinet, which sat atop a system of lesser courts.[10]

The Diet had traditionally been controlled by LDP factions—groups of powerful, senior politicians within the party. Kakuei Tanaka, who was prime minister for almost two years, was perhaps the best example. In 1974, Tanaka was forced to resign as prime minister due to financial improprieties. Thereafter, he built a faction of more than 100 Diet members and acted as "kingmaker" in Japanese politics for more than a decade. By so relying on Tanaka's leadership, the Japanese political system suffered in the years after his death. No one stepped forward to replace Tanaka, and Japanese politics stagnated. Problems merely festered until eventually the LDP splintered in 1992 and briefly fell from power.

Beyond the legislature lay the bureaucracy, which many people argued held the real power in Japanese politics. The bureaucracy consisted of 22 ministries or cabinet-level agencies. The head of each ministry, a member of the Diet, sat in the cabinet. All cabinet decisions had to be unanimous; effectively each minister had veto power over cabinet activity. Yet the true decision makers for each ministry were the vice-ministers, who began competing to head their ministry from the time they entered, usually just out of college. If the prime minister wanted to address policy, he needed the entire cabinet's permission, whose members in turn required the support of the vice-ministers in each of their ministries.[11] This desire for consensus was popular in Japan, as the people felt achieving *wa*, or harmony, was worth almost any cost.

Ministry of Finance

The Ministry of Finance (MOF) held power in all areas of the financial world. The ministry managed government fiscal policy and tariffs. In conjunction with the Bank of Japan, MOF was the linchpin for much financing of big business. Large city banks needed MOF consent for their lending policies.[12] And because the ministry controlled the tax code, maintaining tax advantages for its policies was simple, further securing MOF control.

MOF also held influence over monetary and securities policy. While the head of the Bank of Japan was officially appointed by the prime minister and cabinet, MOF officials were often involved in the selection process, and a MOF representative could sit in on BOJ policy meetings. Ministry officials managed restrictions throughout the capital markets, including limiting the scope of foreign exchange, derivative or individual stockholding transactions. In the United States, these responsibilities were spread throughout Congress, the Office of Management and Budget, the Treasury Department, the Federal Reserve Board, the Securities and Exchange Commission, and the Internal Revenue Service. MOF power was further augmented, like other Japanese ministries, through control over its own appointments and promotions.

The MOF responsibility for watching each bank's reserve capital led to scandals. Some ministry officials notified banks prior to inspections, allowing problem loans to be disguised. Also serious was the revelation that the MOF might have helped some banks and securities firms to hide losses to prevent them from failing. These scandals forced Finance Minister Hiroshi Mitsuzuka to resign in March 1998 and led to continued arrests in both the ministry and several major banks.

The ministry was slow to take responsibility for the continuing stagnation, despite its clearly ineffective policies. Numerous officials called for changes in fiscal policy and in the structure of the ministry, but its leaders were loathe to make that adjustment.

Ministry of International Trade and Industry

One of the crucial components of the Japanese economic miracle was the Ministry of International Trade and Industry (MITI). After the occupation, MITI used its control over trade and investment to "pick" and support a handful of industries to lead Japan's export-oriented growth. Its success continued into the 1970s, as MITI set its sights on the semiconductor and computer industries. [See **Exhibit 3.10.**]

But while MITI still had considerable influence in the business community, much of its original power had dissipated. So MITI had shifted its focus away from the heavy industries, more toward the service sector and telecommunications. Recently, a subcommittee of the Industry Structure Council had urged MITI to focus more structural measures to achieve economic reform—especially deregulation, promotion of competition, and acceleration of intellectual-capital formation.[13] Because MITI was "exposed to the outside world," commented Shijuro Ogata, approvingly, "it grew smarter and more aware as an organization."[14]

Bureaucracies like MITI often vied for power among themselves. One such conflict occurred between the Ministry of Posts and Telecommunications and MITI over telecommunications development. With the digital revolution, telecommunications became increasingly important, and MITI officials thought it should be the ministry's next focus. However, the Ministry of Posts and Telecommunications held more sway over the Diet members, so in 1998 the Diet conferred that industry's development on Posts and Telecommunications—a rare defeat for the once-powerful MITI.

Corporate Governance

Intertwined in the system of government and bureaucracy was Japan's business sector. Often government officials retired to a life of business when their government responsibilities ended around age 50. This process was called *amakudari*, or "descent from heaven," and bureaucrats could move from company to company as distinguished advisors, receiving large paychecks each step along the way. Playing a critical role in the business sector were the *keiretsu*, or business groups, which were giant conglomerations centered around a major bank. The *keiretsu* descended from the *zaibatsu*, industrial combines dominated by old industrial families, which were dissolved after World War II. Instead of being centered around a family, the *keiretsu* were centered around large city banks, which re-emerged in the late 1950s.

Initially, the main bank in each *keiretsu* played a crucial role in financing the businesses within the enterprise group. Businesses were allowed to borrow well beyond their capacity to repay, and often beyond their net worth (called "overborrowing"), giving the main bank significant control over the group's management process. The main bank then overborrowed from the Bank of Japan. Because the central bank held the ultimate responsibility for the system, it also had the ultimate control over lending decisions of dependent banks. By the 1980s, many of the larger companies had grown independent enough to generate funding on their own.

This debt-financing system permitted Japanese businesses to focus on long-term issues, as opposed to the shorter-term concerns of Western-style shareholders. Taking the long view allowed Japanese businesses to acquire market share, which could eventually be mined for profit. Tax incentives encouraged borrowing over equity funding; dividends on equity shares were paid from corporate profits after taxes, whereas interest on bank loans was tax deductible.[15]

Business groups with a strong main bank were known as "horizontal" *keiretsu*. Six large horizontal *keiretsu* dominated Japanese business: Mitsubishi, Mitsui, Sumitomo, Fuyo, DKB, and Sanwa. The Mitsubishi group, the largest of these with $392 billion in 1996 sales, entailed about 30 companies in businesses as diverse as heavy industries, electricity, aluminum, paper production, beer, and automobiles. [See **Exhibit 3.11.**] While the business group played a critical role in the past for creating partnerships between companies, leaders explained the relationship was decreasing in importance in the 1990s. Under equal conditions, members would choose to deal with other group members, but given a better deal with an outside company, the outsider would likely be selected.[16]

A smaller group of "vertical" *keiretsu* had also emerged. These groupings typically included a large manufacturer with its suppliers and distributors as subsidiaries. A prominent example of the vertical business group was the Toyota Motor Corporation. These groups were called vertical because they were managed in a rough pyramid structure, with the parent company maintaining a long-term relationship with the subsidiaries. This type of business structure was best suited for mass production of industrial products.

A third type of *keiretsu* was the "satellite" group, in which a core company formed subsidiaries to perform after-market functions or to engage in new ventures. Hitachi and NTT were this type of "satellite" group.

Cross-holding of shares was another distinctive feature of Japanese corporate governance. Much of the limited equity of Japanese firms was held by other members of the same group—especially the banks. The amount of cross-holding had generally risen, despite the Anti-Monopoly Act of 1977, reaching a high of 52% by the early 1990s.[17] Although it had tapered off slightly, to 45% by 1997, it continued to accommodate an environment of low equity earnings. [See **Exhibit 3.12.**] Corporations in other words, felt little pressure from shareholders, or "the market." Company priorities placed value on labor market issues and long-term market share. Thus while the Mitsubishi Corporation had 46 board members, all but two were insiders; the two outsiders were the chairman of Mitsubishi Heavy Industries and the president of Mitsubishi Electric.[18]

Finally, Japan's corporations increasingly faced scandals involving organized crime. Periodically reports would break about arrests in a *sokaiya* scandal, in which businesses would pay off criminals, known as *sokaiya*, with huge sums of money to prevent them from disclosing embarrassing information about the company, thereby disrupting its annual shareholders meeting. These scandals were widespread, affecting, among others, all four major securities houses: Daiwa Securities, Nikko Securities, Nomura Securities, and the now-bankrupt Yamaichi Securities.[19] Shijuro Ogata summed up the corporate climate by saying: "Corporate leaders became arrogant, thinking they had nothing to learn from outsiders because outsiders were coming to them to learn. The usefulness of the old-style corporate practice is over, and a revised approach might be necessary."[20]

Social Issues

A number of social issues had been developing during the past two decades. Demographics played a major role, with the rapidly aging population posing huge issues for government policy and personal savings. Women had a slightly larger part in government and business, although vast numbers of women maintained traditional roles in society. The quality of life was still a major concern, as prices were exceedingly high, salarymen worked long hours each week, and others lacked some basic facilities. Education levels were high, but creativity and innovation seemed to suffer.

Aging Problem   Like many industrial nations, Japan faced a serious aging problem. High life expectancy, partly due to the country's universal medical care, and low fertility made the Japanese problem especially potent. At the end of 1996, 15.1% of the Japanese population was elderly (aged 65 and older)—about 19 million people. Over the next 25 years, this percentage was expected to increase sharply, while the overall population stayed around 125 million. By 2049, the elderly population would comprise 32.3% of the population.[21] [See **Exhibit 3.14.**]

Medical Care   Since 1961, Japan's outstanding universal health insurance covered everyone. The Health Insurance Law, periodically revised, adjusted individual cost-sharing proportions and coverage issues to fit social needs. The Gold Plan for elderly medical care was last revised in 1994. This plan aimed to allow all elderly people to maintain their dignity and live independently as well as to provide care to everyone who needed it—the most serious concern for the elderly.[22]

Pensions   The Japanese pension structure too was reorganized to be more equitable and stable. The core of this system was the Basic National Pension, which covered the entire population and as of March 1996 provided an average monthly benefit of ¥45,000, although people did not receive benefits until age 65. In addition to this basic pension, private-sector retirees could collect from the Employees' Pension and public-sector retirees from the Mutual Aid Pension, both of which were paid in proportion to the beneficiaries' wages and salaries prior to retirement.

Japanese social security costs had expanded rapidly over the previous 25 years, rising from ¥4 trillion in 1971 to ¥60 trillion in 1994. As a percentage of national income, total social security expenditure was still only 16.2%, compared with 19.4% in the United States and 31.5% in Germany.[23] Yet, due to rapid aging, Japan was facing a sizable increase in social security costs. The Ministry of Health and Welfare estimated total social security expenditures to rise to between 29% and 35.5% of national income by 2025, depending on economic growth rates. Its most optimistic prediction was based on a nominal growth rate of 3.5% until 2000 and 3.0% thereafter: its least optimistic prediction still assumed nominal growth of 1.75% until 2000 and 1.5% thereafter.[24] [See **Exhibit 3.16.**]

The elderly saved relatively little, expecting previous savings and government pensions to support their retirement. Thus, the budget deficit was predicted to rise, as the government struggled to meet public pension obligations that were even less adequately funded than those in the United States. Stemming from this activity, it seemed likely that the personal savings rate would decline from its level of 12%–15% of income. [See **Exhibit 3.17.**] The trade surplus was expected to turn into a deficit eventually, as the declining pool of workers would limit the output that could be exported.

Role of Women   The place of women in Japan had advanced since the economic miracle but was still nowhere near Western standards and norms. In January 1970, women comprised 2.9% of the Diet; by the end of 1996, that number had risen to 7.6%, although women comprised only 4.6% of the more powerful House of Representatives. Hisako Takahashi became the first woman named Justice of the Supreme Court in 1994, but by April 1996, female judges throughout the country numbered 257, 8.9% of the total.

More than 27 million women sought work in 1996, over 40% of the total labor force. Women were especially prominent in education, representing over 61% of teaching staff at elementary schools, 11% of the teaching staff at universities, and 41% of the teachers at junior colleges. Over 97% of girls advanced to upper secondary school, and 46% continued to junior college or university—both figures higher than the ones for boys.[25]

Yet, despite the educational gains, few women held important positions in major corporations. Women had an easier time getting positions at smaller companies, many of which were apparel or retail focused. Several of these companies had relatively high profits, which activists argued encouraged opening companies to women.[26]

Standard of Living   Costs in Japan were extremely high. This was due in part to the fact that many items needed to be imported and that space was at a premium in an island nation of only 378,000 square kilometers (146,000 sq. miles, about the size of California with five times the population). However, part of this problem was also attributed to the lack of competition and extensive regulations on business activity in the economy.

Japanese workers historically worked long weeks, often more than five days per week, reaching over 2,200 hours per year in the 1980s. By 1996 that number had declined to about 1,900 hours per year,[27] but that figure did not include the after-work dinners and entertainment in which salarymen traditionally participated. Many nights each week, workers stayed away from home until late at night, only to get up early the next morning and begin the cycle again.

Finally, while the per capita GNP in dollars was substantially higher than in the United States or Germany, in terms of purchasing power parity it still lagged behind. Retail prices for food and clothes were almost twice as expensive in Tokyo than they were in either New York or London. Electricity cost 50% more in Japan than in the United States or France. And the 1994 average price of residential land in Tokyo was ¥560,000 per sq. meter, while the average house cost ¥132 million. By comparison, land costs in New York were only ¥10,000 per sq. meter and ¥33 million per house.[28]

Education   Japanese students scored well by international standards. In the Third International Mathematics and Science Study, Japanese eighth graders ranked third out of 41 countries in both mathematics and science. All Japan's eighth grade students had studied algebra, compared with only 25% in the United States, yet math instruction accounted for only 117 hours per year in Japan, instead of the 143 hours in the United States.[29] This success lay partly in the Japanese style of teaching. Students learned much through memorization and were periodically tested through competitive examination. By the time they finished university studies, they had an extensive command of facts, figures, languages (at least two), and history at their fingertips.

But the reasons favoring the Japanese educational dominance also contributed to some of the difficulties its leaders believed they faced. Students had little creativity, stifled by the rote learning. As a consequence, some Japanese criticized this loss in their business and government dealings. Critics argued that despite the strong educational statistics, Japan had only five citizens who received Nobel prizes in scientific fields; two of them worked predominantly in the United States.

The Hashimoto Era and Structural Reform

To regain governmental control, the LDP allied with the Social Democratic Party (SDPJ) in 1994, allowing Social Democrat Tomiichi Murayama to serve as prime minister. When support for the Murayama government collapsed in January 1996, Ryutaro Hashimoto, a prominent LDP politician and the minister of International Trade and Industry, ascended to the post of prime minister. Hashimoto was a political lone wolf but was hardly viewed as radical upon entering office. However, he surprised the country when he proposed radical reforms to the traditional Japanese system, ideas that even surpassed the Maekawa Report of 1986.[30]

Administrative Structure

"The ministries have a tremendous amount of power," complained a director at the Bank of Japan. "This centralized system must be decentralized to make changes for the future."[31] A year earlier, Hashimoto formed a 15-member Administrative Reform Council, with himself as the head. The council of political outsiders was charged with reorganizing the governing structure to be more efficient and responsive to the needs of the people. In the end the council issued a report with three recommendations:[32]

1. **Strengthen the Prime Minister and Cabinet.** The Prime Minister must no longer be required to seek approval from each ministry before addressing policy issues. The Cabinet should be allowed to act through majority agreement rather than unanimous approval.

2. **Reduce the number of ministries.** Reducing the number of ministries from 22 to 12, with a Cabinet Office, would reduce bureaucratic infighting and create a more streamlined government. Prefecture governments would get additional authority, and bureaucratic actions would become more transparent.

3. **Reduce the number of bureaucrats and civil servants.** The government would try to reduce costs and functions through privatization and conversion to British-style agencies. Once these revisions were completed, a further 10% reduction in personnel should occur.

The Basic Law outlining the intentions of the reform would be introduced in the Diet by June 1998, and specific proposals would be introduced in the following years. Administrative Reform Council member Ken Moroi defended this plan's importance: "We have now entered the era of megacompetition. Unless we do away with many of the regulations we currently have, the Japanese nation, industries, and companies won't survive."[33]

The plan's detractors thought that the proposal merely reorganized the current bureaucracy and did not cut enough government functions. There were also many doubts over the speed with which the administrative reforms would occur; ministries would not easily give up their power.

Economic Structure

By the time of Hashimoto's formal reform package, significant inroads had already occurred. Restrictions on large-scale retailers were reduced. Several foreign retailers had increased their presence—the most successful was Toys 'R' Us, with over 60 stores nationwide. Telephone deregulation dated to 1985, with the partial privatization of Nippon Telephone and Telegraph (NTT), although it remained a monopoly. In late 1997, the Ministry of Posts and Telecommunications announced its plans for the NTT breakup, which would occur by the end of 1999. In February 1998, the United States and Japan agreed on an open-air pact to increase flights between Tokyo and America.

These changes improved pricing on nonregulated goods [see table opposite] but overall they had not opened the Japanese economy—in 1995, foreign direct investment outflows surpassed inflows by a ratio of 15.5:1. [See **Exhibit 3.13.**] Explanations for this behavior included language difficulties, especially in grasping detailed information on business and the nuances of Japanese laws and regulations (and worse, the marked shortage of professional experts, such as lawyers and CPAs, to provide support for businesspeople); the limited supply of employees due to the employment appeal from Japanese companies; and the high taxes and fixed costs companies faced. A favorable environment for new business activities would be pursued through mass deregulation. MITI's focus had shifted from developing industries to developing the means to bolster economic growth.[34]

PREVAILING PRICES IN RETAIL TOY STORES

	1988	1993
Almost all toys sold at manufacturer's suggested retail price	70.10%	29.40%
Some items sold at less than suggested retail price	19.70%	57.10%
Almost all items sold at less than suggested retail price	10.30%	13.40%
Total	**100.00%**	**100.00%**

SOURCE: Japan Development Bank Research Report No. 72 by Akihiko Shinozaki & Kazumi Endo.

An Action Plan for Economic Structural Reform listed 15 growth fields to pursue: medical care and welfare; quality of life and culture; information and telecommunications; new manufacturing technology; distribution and logistics; environment; business support; ocean; biotechnology; improvement of the urban surroundings; aviation and space (civil demand); new energy and energy conservation; human resources; economic globalization; and housing.

MITI's deregulation plan spanned five main areas:[35]

1. **Logistics.** Controls on supply–demand adjustments would be abolished in areas of road cargo transport, rail, coastal shipping, and port transport.

2. **Energy.** Regulatory reforms aimed to increase competition in the electricity market by allowing for competition from independent power providers. Additionally, there would be a revision of electricity rates soon. Market principles would be further introduced in both the petroleum and natural gas markets.

3. **Information and telecommunications.** MITI proposed a fair and effective competitive environment through eliminating tariffs and diversifying services. Incentive regulations such as price caps and yardsticks would be introduced in FY1999. In subsequent years, the ministry would revise connection rules and long-term incremental cost calculations.

4. **Finance.** Through the Big Bang financial reform, the Japanese financial market would grow to a standard similar to that in New York and London.

5. **Distribution.** Continued efforts in deregulating distribution channels would provide more competition in the coming years.

MITI had simulated the effects of these deregulatory measures and found a potential benefit to real GDP of 6.0%. Specific benefits included an increase in plant and equipment investment of ¥39 trillion (2.6 GDP percentage points), a drop in consumer prices of 3.4%, and a consumer surplus increase of ¥365,000 per household.[36]

Education Structure

To improve the Japanese educational system, the proposed reforms aimed to introduce greater flexibility in the educational process, with the hopes of boosting creativity in students. The Program for Educational Reform had five main goals to achieve by 2003:[37]

1. **Reform of educational system and cultivation of rich humanity.** This goal proposed reducing the school week to five days, unifying the lower and upper secondary school system, encouraging autonomous learning instead of rote memorization, increasing computer training, and improving teacher quality and administration of schools.

2. **Prompt responses to changing social needs.** The educational system needed to be more flexible to the changing Japan. This flexibility included adjusting to the aging population, adapting to the information-oriented society, and keeping pace with cultural changes.

3. **School's active cooperation with communities.** To create a better learning environment, schools would strengthen their relationship with student families and communities.

4. **Promotion of internationalization by student exchange and other measures.** More exchange programs and improved foreign language education.

5. **Setting up of a forum with business community** for the expansion of the educational reform movement.

Financial Structure

Two themes dominated this program: the financial market reform and the disposal of the massive bad debts accumulated over the previous decade. The market reform revolved around the "Free, Fair, and Global" principles, to be strictly followed. Critical to this effort was the efficient disposal of banks' bad debt. On fruition, this reform would make Tokyo a financial center to rival New York and London.

Reformers developed four categories of changes to advance such a system:[38]

1. **To expand the choice of means for investors and borrowers.** The ban on derivative securities was lifted, increased use of asset-backed securities was proposed to increase liquidity, and banks became authorized to sell securities investment trusts and insurance.

2. **To improve the quality of intermediaries' services, and to promote competition.** An amended Anti-Monopoly Law would allow holding companies. Stock trading commissions were to be liberalized fully by the end of 1999. The April 1998 revision to the Foreign Exchange and Foreign Trade Control Law completely dismantled the foreign exchange banking system. Before this change, currency transactions were limited to authorized banks and a few securities firms; individuals and companies needed permission to bypass using an authorized foreign exchange bank.

3. **To develop a market with further utility.** Restrictions on trading stocks off-exchanges were to be eliminated, the short-term money market would be developed, and permission requirements for cross-border capital transactions were to be removed.

4. **To establish a reliable framework and rules for fair and transparent transactions.** Banks would be forced to report results through consolidated financial statements, to value financial instruments through a marked-to-market method, and to provide prompt corrective action to maintain their capital adequacy ratio. In addition, the system of inspection, surveillance, and punishment would be enhanced to provide further confidence in the system.

Beyond the structural reforms to liberate the market and remove the bad debt, the outcome of the administrative reform process would affect the financial system. To some degree the extent of change in the financial system would depend on the extent of change in the MOF.

The Bank of Japan was to have greater independence. "In the past, when the BOJ wanted to change the discount rate, it had a preliminary talk with MOF. Under the renewed regime with the revised Bank of Japan Law, it won't have to do that, as its policy board has the independent and ultimate power to make monetary policy judgment," according to Advisor to the Governor Eiji Hirano.[39] In March 1998, BOJ also began publishing the minutes of its board meetings. Despite this independence, for the BOJ to be successful in its goals of maintaining price and financial stability, it would have to work closely with the government, including the Ministry of Finance.

The regulatory functions of MOF would likely be transferred to a separate supervisory agency, so only the legislative functions would remain. However, MOF was to retain its banking bureau in light of the crisis in the banking sector, as the proposal stood to require this agency to consult with MOF before implementing measures such as employing public funds, thereby giving MOF control over bankruptcies.[40] Furthermore, others argued the Big Bang reforms were not enough to cause true change because the tax code was not overhauled, there was little to strengthen Japan's securities laws, and there was no move to protect shareholder rights. As a result of these factors, MOF still maintained tremendous control over the economy, and little changed for the future.[41]

Fiscal Structure

Although the Japanese economy had been the strongest fiscally in the Group of Seven from 1985 to 1992, by 1996 it had performed the worst. Its budget deficit had ballooned to 7% and showed few signs of improving.

Hashimoto's fiscal reform plan followed five major principles:[42]

1. To reduce the budget deficit to no more than 3% of GDP by FY2003, two years ahead of the original FY2005 deadline.

2. To devote the years 1998–2000 to fiscal reform.

3. To implement year-on-year reductions in general expenditures, with no area spared.

4. To reduce all current long-term spending programs, such as the spending goal of ¥630 trillion in public works over 10 years.

5. To maintain the ratio of taxes, social welfare premiums, and government deficit to national income, also known as the national burden, below 50%.

In June 1997, the Cabinet announced its policies to achieve these goals, including coordination with the social security reform plan, a three-year extension of the public works program in conjunction with reducing total spending to ¥470 trillion, a 10% reduction (¥920 billion) in defense spending, up to a 10% reduction in official development assistance expenditures, and settlement of the ¥28 trillion debt in the former Japan National Railways.[43]

The Japanese economy had not recovered by the end of 1997, and businessmen were deeply concerned over the lack of government fiscal stimulus. Without this stimulus, they feared Japan would never dig out of its slow growth period. At the same time, Hashimoto risked losing great face if he offered a stimulus package, expanding the budget deficit beyond the previous year's level.

Social Security Structure

The social security structural reform aimed to address Japan's changing demographics. Much of the reform was intertwined with the other proposals; the fiscal structural reform planned to limit the burden of government to 50% of national income. Also, continued economic growth would facilitate the social security system's stability.

The Ministry of Health and Welfare believed that its decision concerning this issue was of such importance that it created an education plan for the Japanese people, so individuals could register their opinions before any action was taken about the five proposals the ministry was considering:[44]

1. **Maintain the current benefit level.** To accomplish this, premiums would have to rise to 34.3% of income to overcome the additional costs with the elderly population.

2. **Keep the premium below 30%.** Under this proposal, the benefits would decline by 10%. To do so could involve raising the retirement age and increasing premiums slightly.

3. **Maintain the premium at 20% of income and tax employee bonuses.** Bonuses would be taxed at the same rate as monthly employee salary—currently bonuses were exempt from such taxation. This proposal would result in a total benefit reduction of 20%.

4. **Maintain the premium at the status quo.** By 2025, benefits would be reduced by 40%.

5. **Abolish the social insurance system for employees.** Citizens would still have the universal coverage portion of their social security, but the secondary part of social insurance would be completely privatized.

Ultimately, the ministry would design a pension reform based on these proposals, in addition to its plan to eliminate waste in medical care, current pension plans, and welfare policy. The complete reform of the pension system was scheduled to occur by 2000.

Other Measures

To reduce the budget deficit, the Japanese government raised the consumption tax from 3% to 5%, beginning in April 1997. This decision produced wild swings in consumption over the first two quarters of the year. Citizens rushed to make large purchases by March to avoid the additional 2% tax, and this increase in consumption caused GDP to grow at an annual rate of 5.6%. However, in the second quarter, residents dramatically curtailed their consumption, leading to an annualized drop in GDP of 11.6% for the three months ending June 1997.[45] Popular opinion about the consumption tax was that it would continue to inhibit consumption, increasing the difficulty of pulling out of the recession.

To support weak banks, the government announced a ¥30 trillion stabilization package in January 1998. Seventeen trillion yen would protect investor deposits in potentially unstable banks. The remaining ¥13 trillion was to recapitalize banks, although it would be possible for smaller banks to fail in the future. Most bankers felt if the estimates of problem loans were accurate, this package would be sufficient to stave off further problems, allowing financial reforms to continue.

At the end of April 1998, the government unveiled the details of its economic stimulus package, worth ¥16.65 trillion ($128 billion). The package included one-time ¥2 trillion tax cuts for 1998 and 1999, ¥7.7 trillion in public-works spending, ¥2.3 trillion to improve liquidity in the real estate market, ¥2 trillion in increased lending to small- and medium-sized companies and a much smaller sum in tax credits for investment and housing.[46]

Many leaders saw impending disaster if Japan failed to implement additional reforms after the Foreign Exchange Law. There would be little reason for personal financial assets to remain in Japan if postal savings rates remained significantly below those in Britain or the United States, and the hollowing-out of financial assets would continue.

Summary

Predictions for Japan's 1998 growth varied widely. The official estimate was for real growth of 1.9%, although the Industrial Bank of Japan predicted (0.5% growth, and most others foresaw flat growth at least for the near term.

Two schools of thought existed about Japan's future. On one side was Shijuro Ogata, who believed "some change is necessary, although I am not advocating an immediate switch to an Anglo-Saxon type system."[47] The ideas for a fundamental change were there but not yet implemented. On the other side was a senior Ministry of Finance official, who explained, "It is difficult to expect any quantum change in Japanese corporate climate. Such traditional values as long-term employment and coordinated human relationship have remained rooted deeply. In this context, an extension of the past is inevitable, and it is in fact impossible to abandon the whole of Japan's traditional way of corporate management."[48]

As the new fiscal year dawned with both the financial system reform and the economic stimulus, Hashimoto faced several questions in guiding Japan through this philosophical debate. Was his reform program feasible? Did it address the problems Japan was facing? Numerous officials described Hashimoto's political coalition as tenuous and wondered whether he would be strong enough to keep control over his reform proposals. How would the Asian financial crisis affect Japan in the coming year? Most important, Hashimoto was facing questions about stimulating the economy. The government stimulus package did not immediately win over the market; analysts awaited its results and hoped tax cuts would appear in the near future.

EXHIBIT 3.1A GDP AND COMPONENTS, 1971–1997

Year	Nominal GDP (trillions of yen)	Consumption (% of GDP)	Investment (% of GDP)	Government Expenditure (% of GDP)	Exports (% of GDP)	Imports (% of GDP)	Real GDP (1990 prices)	GDP Growth Rate	Real GDP per Capita ($U.S.)
1971	80.7	53.6%	35.8%	8.0%	11.7%	9.0%	190.7	4.3%	$5,145
1972	92.4	54.0%	35.5%	8.2%	10.6%	8.3%	206.2	8.1%	$6,346
1973	112.5	53.6%	38.1%	8.3%	10.0%	10.0%	222.1	7.7%	$7,519
1974	134.2	54.3%	37.3%	9.1%	13.6%	14.3%	220.9	-0.6%	$6,864
1975	148.3	57.1%	32.8%	10.0%	12.8%	12.8%	227.1	2.8%	$6,859
1976	166.6	57.5%	31.8%	9.9%	13.6%	12.8%	236.7	4.2%	$7,078
1977	185.6	57.7%	30.8%	9.8%	13.1%	11.5%	247.9	4.7%	$8,107
1978	204.4	57.7%	30.9%	9.7%	11.1%	9.4%	259.9	4.9%	$10,749
1979	221.5	58.7%	32.5%	9.7%	11.6%	12.5%	277.4	6.7%	$10,923
1980	240.2	58.8%	32.2%	9.8%	13.7%	14.6%	287.4	3.6%	$10,853
1981	258.0	58.1%	31.1%	9.9%	14.7%	13.9%	297.7	3.6%	$11,474
1982	270.6	59.4%	29.9%	9.9%	14.6%	13.8%	307.1	3.2%	$10,408
1983	281.8	60.2%	28.1%	9.9%	13.9%	12.2%	315.4	2.7%	$11,132
1984	300.5	59.4%	28.0%	9.8%	15.0%	12.3%	328.9	4.3%	$11,531
1985	320.4	58.9%	28.2%	9.6%	14.5%	11.1%	345.3	5.0%	$11,979
1986	335.5	58.6%	27.7%	9.7%	11.4%	7.4%	354.4	2.6%	$17,308
1987	349.8	58.9%	28.5%	9.4%	10.4%	7.2%	368.9	4.1%	$20,890
1988	374.0	58.2%	30.4%	9.1%	10.0%	7.8%	391.8	6.2%	$24,936
1989	400.0	58.2%	31.3%	9.1%	10.6%	9.2%	410.3	4.7%	$24,155
1990	430.0	58.0%	32.3%	9.0%	10.7%	10.0%	430.0	4.8%	$24,042
1991	458.3	57.1%	32.2%	9.0%	10.2%	8.5%	446.4	3.8%	$26,740
1992	471.1	57.8%	30.8%	9.2%	10.1%	7.8%	451.0	1.0%	$28,643
1993	475.4	58.6%	29.7%	9.4%	9.3%	7.0%	452.3	0.3%	$32,629
1994	479.3	59.7%	28.7%	9.5%	9.3%	7.2%	455.3	0.6%	$35,644
1995	482.9	60.2%	28.5%	9.8%	9.4%	7.9%	461.5	1.4%	$39,190
1996	500.4	59.8%	29.8%	9.8%	9.9%	9.4%	477.9	3.6%	$34,936
1997*	506.4	59.1%	30.7%	9.7%	9.9%	9.3%	482.2	0.9%	$30,841

SOURCE: Ministry of Finance, *The Budget in Brief, 1997*, Table 1.3. Bank of Japan, *Economic Statistics Monthly*, January 1998.
*Estimate.

EXHIBIT 3.1B	**SHARE OWNERSHIP:** **PERCENTAGE OF CORPORATION'S EQUITY** **HELD BY TYPE OF OWNER**

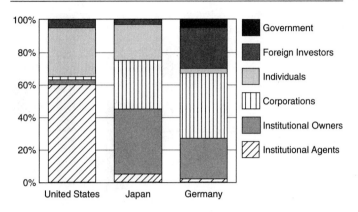

SOURCE: *The Economist*, January 25, 1992, p. 74.

Notes: *Institutional Owners* are institutions that hold equity for their own accounts (e.g., banks in Japanese *keiretsu*).
Institutional Agents hold equity as agents for other investors (e.g., pension funds).

EXHIBIT 3.2	**JAPAN: FISCAL INDICATORS (PERCENTAGE OF GDP)**

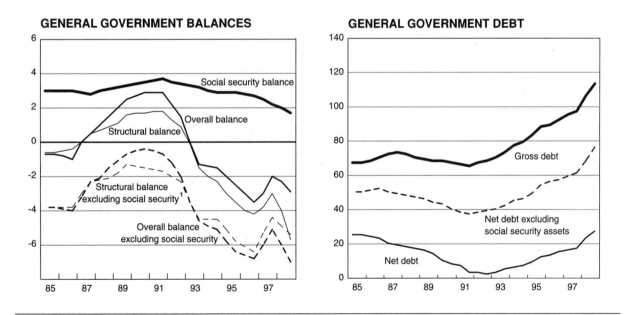

[1]Structural balances are calculated as percent of potential GDP.

SOURCE: *World Economic Outlook 1998: Financial Turbulence and the World Economy*, (Washington, DC: IMF), p. 116.

EXHIBIT 3.3   GENERAL EXPENDITURES BY MAJOR PROGRAM

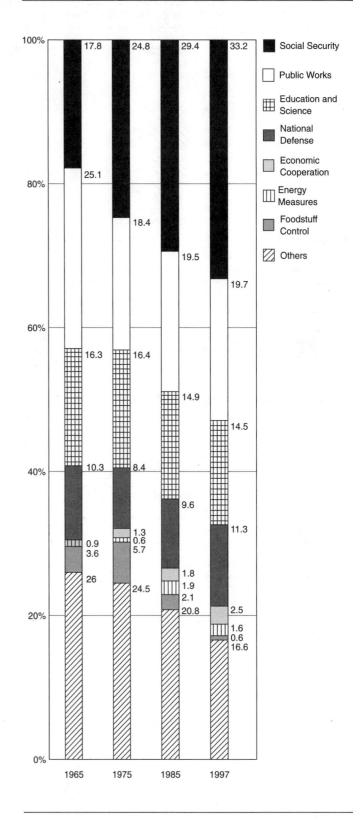

SOURCE: Ministry of Finance, *The Budget in Brief, 1997*, Chart II-2.
NOTE: The above figures are calculated on an initial budget basis.

EXHIBIT 3.4   BALANCE OF PAYMENTS (US$ BILLIONS)

	1977	1978	1979	1980	1981	1982	1983	1984	1985	1986	1987
Current Account	10.9	16.5	-8.7	-10.8	4.8	6.8	20.8	35.0	49.2	85.8	87.0
Exports	79.2	95.3	101.1	126.7	149.5	137.7	145.5	168.3	174.0	205.6	224.6
Imports	-62.0	-71.0	-99.4	-124.6	-129.6	-119.6	-114.0	-124.0	-118.0	-112.8	-128.2
Trade Balance	17.2	24.3	1.7	2.1	20.0	18.1	31.5	44.3	56.0	92.8	96.4
Net Services	-5.9	-8.0	-11.3	-12.1	-12.8	-11.4	-12.1	-11.9	-11.9	-14.2	-22.1
Net Income	0.1	0.9	2.0	0.8	-0.8	1.6	2.9	4.2	6.7	9.3	16.4
Net Transfers	-0.4	-0.7	-1.1	-1.5	-1.6	-1.4	-1.6	-1.5	-1.6	-2.1	-3.7
Financial Account	-5.0	-6.7	-6.8	18.9	-1.6	-16.2	-21.3	-36.6	-53.5	-73.5	-45.4
Direct investment	-1.6	-2.4	-2.7	-2.1	-4.7	-4.1	-3.2	-6.0	-5.8	-14.3	-18.4
Portfolio investment	0.8	0.8	-0.9	-6.3	-6.2	-2.7	-6.8	3.6	-0.3	8.7	26.0
Other capital (net)	-4.1	-5.1	-3.2	27.3	9.3	-9.4	-11.3	-34.2	-47.4	-67.9	-53.0
Errors & Omissions	0.5	0.1	2.4	-3.1	0.4	4.7	2.1	3.7	3.8	2.5	-3.7
Reserve assets	-6.5	-10.0	13.1	-5.0	-3.6	4.7	-1.6	-2.1	0.6	-14.8	-37.9

	1988	1989	1990	1991	1992	1993	1994	1995	1996	1997
Current Account	79.6	57.0	35.9	68.2	112.6	131.6	130.3	111.0	65.9	92.6
Exports	259.8	269.6	280.4	308.2	332.6	352.7	385.7	428.7	400.3	400.9
Imports	-164.8	-192.7	-216.8	-212.1	-207.8	-213.2	-241.5	-296.9	-316.7	-301.1
Trade Balance	95.0	76.9	63.6	96.1	124.8	139.4	144.2	131.8	83.6	99.8
Net Services	-31.9	-38.6	-44.7	-41.8	-44.0	-43.1	-48.1	-57.4	-62.2	-52.8
Net Income	20.6	23.0	22.5	26.0	35.6	40.4	40.2	44.3	53.5	54.3
Net Transfers	-4.1	-4.3	-5.5	-12.0	-3.8	-5.1	-6.1	-7.7	-9.0	-8.7
Financial Account	-66.2	-47.9	-21.5	-67.7	-100.3	-102.2	-85.1	-64.0	-28.1	-124.8
Direct investment	-34.7	-45.2	-46.3	-30.3	-14.6	-13.7	-17.2	-22.5	-23.2	-22.2
Portfolio investment	-9.8	-24.9	7.0	-50.2	-5.9	-35.1	-63.0	-50.5	-57.6	29.6
Other capital (net)	-21.7	22.2	17.8	12.9	-79.8	-53.4	-5.0	9.0	52.8	-132.1
Errors & Omissions	3.1	-21.8	-20.9	-7.7	-10.4	-0.5	-18.0	13.8	0.6	41.3
Reserve assets	-16.5	12.8	6.6	8.4	-0.6	-27.5	-25.3	-58.6	-35.1	-6.2

SOURCE: International Monetary Fund, *International Financial Statistics Yearbook* (1994), 1997, pp. 496–501; *Balance of Payments of 1997*, Ministry of Finance.

EXHIBIT 3.5		MONEY SUPPLY (TRILLIONS OF YEN)				
Year	M1	Time Deposits	M2	M2 Growth Rate	CPI	Inflation Rate
1971	27.7	39.7	67.4	0.2	36.8	6.4%
1972	34.5	49.5	84.0	0.2	38.5	4.6%
1973	40.3	57.9	98.2	0.2	43.0	11.7%
1974	45.0	64.5	109.5	0.1	53.0	23.3%
1975	50.0	75.4	125.3	0.1	59.2	11.7%
1976	56.2	86.1	142.2	0.1	64.8	9.5%
1977	60.8	97.2	158.0	0.1	70.1	8.2%
1978	68.9	109.8	178.7	0.1	73.0	4.1%
1979	71.0	122.7	193.7	0.1	75.7	3.7%
1980	69.6	137.4	207.0	0.1	81.6	7.8%
1981	76.5	152.7	229.2	0.1	85.6	4.9%
1982	80.9	165.7	246.6	0.1	88.0	2.8%
1983	80.8	182.8	263.6	0.1	89.7	1.9%
1984	86.4	195.4	281.8	0.1	91.7	2.2%
1985	89.0	217.8	306.8	0.1	93.5	2.0%
1986	98.2	237.1	335.3	0.1	94.1	0.6%
1987	103.0	269.7	372.7	0.1	94.2	0.1%
1988	111.8	297.5	409.4	0.1	94.9	0.7%
1989	114.5	343.1	457.6	0.1	97.0	2.2%
1990	119.6	375.4	495.0	0.1	100.0	3.1%
1991	131.0	375.5	506.5	0.0	103.3	3.3%
1992	136.1	370.7	506.8	0.0	105.1	1.7%
1993	145.6	372.6	518.2	0.0	106.4	1.2%
1994	151.7	382.4	534.1	0.0	107.1	0.7%
1995	171.5	377.4	549.0	0.0	107.0	−0.1%
1996	188.2	373.5	561.7	0.0	107.2	0.2%
1997	194.3	372.2	566.5	0.0	109.0	1.7%

SOURCE: International Monetary Fund, *International Financial Statistics Yearbook, 1997*, pp. 496–501. Bank of Japan, *Economic Statistics Monthly*, January 1998.

EXHIBIT 3.6 **NIKKEI STOCK PRICE INDEX AND BOND YIELD**

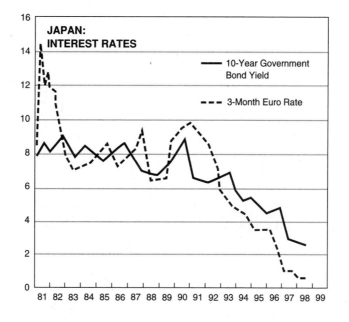

SOURCE: http://www.yardeni.com

EXHIBIT 3.7

CPI, OFFICIAL DISCOUNT RATE, EXCHANGE RATE, UNEMPLOYMENT RATE

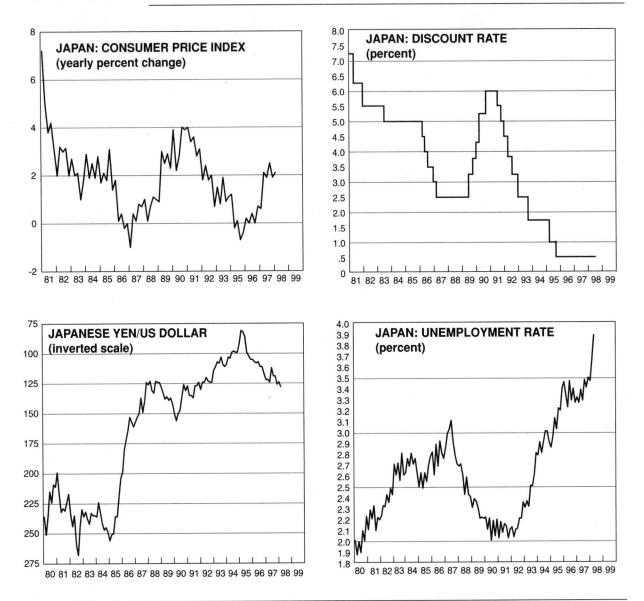

SOURCE: http://www.yardeni.com

EXHIBIT 3.8	ASSETS OF LARGEST JAPANESE BANKING INSTITUTION (IN MILLIONS OF DOLLARS)

Name	Total Assets	Name	Total Assets
Bank of Tokyo-Mitsubishi	648,161	Sumitomo Trust & Banking Co.	248,418
Dai-Ichi Kangyo Bank	434,115	Long-Term Credit Bank of Japan	231,761
Fuji Bank	432,992	Asahi Bank	230,080
Sanwa Bank	427,689	Daiwa Bank	212,967
Sumitomo Bank	426,103	Yasuda Trust & Banking	196,520
Sakura Bank	423,017	Toyo Trust & Banking	192,802
Norinchukin Bank	375,210	Zenshinren Bank	130,630
Industrial Bank of Japan	350,468	Shoko Chukin Bank	125,442
Mitsubishi Trust & Banking Corp.	284,528	Nippon Credit Bank	114,104
Tokai Bank	273,430	Chuo Trust & Banking	101,271
Mitsui Trust & Banking Co.	254,189	Bank of Yokohama	91,509

SOURCE: "The Largest Banks in the World by Country," *The American Banker*, July 29, 1997, p. 12.

EXHIBIT 3.9	LOAN CATEGORIZATIONS AND VALUES AS OF JANUARY 1998

Loan Category	Description	Total Value (¥ trillion)	Total Value ($ billion @ ¥130)
Category 1 (standard)	Credit Exposures that banks have not classified as Categories 2, 3, or 4.	¥548.2 trillion	$4,216.59
Category 2 (substandard)	Credit exposures on which banks have judged that adequate risk management on an exposure-by-exposurebasis will be needed.	¥65.3 trillion	$502.22
Category (doubtful)	Credit exposures on which banks have serious concerns in terms of their ultimate collection and thus are likely to incur losses but have difficulties with rational estimation of when or how much loss will actually occur.	¥8.7 trillion	$67.10
Category 4 (loss)	Credit exposures that banks have judged to be noncollectable or of no value.	¥2.7 trillion	$20.73

SOURCE: Industrial Bank of Japan

EXHIBIT 3.10	GROWTH IN IT INVESTMENT

	1980–1985		1985–1990		1990–1994	
	Real	Nominal	Real	Nominal	Real	Nominal
Japan	18.5%	16.8%	16.1%	9.4%	1.8%	–0.8%
United States	9.5%	12.0%	5.8%	3.8%	17.0%	9.5%

SOURCE: Shinozaki, Akihiko. "Analysis of the Primary Causes and Economic Effects of Information-Related Investment in the United States and Trends in Japan." The Japan Development Bank Research Report, August 1996, p. 35.
NOTE: The figures for Japan were deflated, using "Wholesale Price Index" prepared by the Bank of Japan for each product item. The base year is 1990.

EXHIBIT 3.11 DISTRIBUTION OF COMPANIES IN HORIZONTAL BUSINESS GROUPS

	Mitsubishi	Mitsui	Sumitomo	Fuyo	DKB	Sanwa
Financial Services	Mitsubishi Bank Mitsubishi Trust & Banking Meiji Mutual Life Tokio Marine & Fire	Mitsui Toiyo Kobe Bank Mitsui Trust & Banking Mitsui Mutual Life Taisho Marine & Fire	Sumitomo Bank Sumitomo Trust & Banking Sumitomo Life SumitomoMarine & Fire	Fuji Bank Yasuda Trust & Banking Yasuda Mutual Life Yasuda Fire & Marine	Dai-Itchi Kangyo Bank Asahi Mutual Life Taisei Fire & Marine Fukoku Mutual Life Nissan Fire & Marine Kankoku Securities Orient	Sanwa Bank Toyo Trust & Banking Nippon Life Orix
Computers, Electronics & Electrical Equipment	Mitsubishi Electric	Toshiba	NEC	Oki Electric Industry Yokogawa Electric Hitachi[1]	Fujitsu Fuji Electric Yaskawa Electric Mfg. Nippon Columbia Hitachi[1]	Iwatsu Electric Sharp Nitto Denko Kyocera Hitachi[1]
Cars	Mitsubishi Motors	Toyota Motor[1]		Nissan Motor	Isuzu Motors	Daihatsu Motor
Trading & Retailing	Mitsubishi	Mitsui Mitsukoshi	Sumitomo	Marubeni	C. Itoh Nissho Iwai[1] Kanematsu Kawasho Seibu Department Stores	Nissho Iwai[1] Nichimen Iwatani International Takoshimaya
Food & Beverages	Kirin Brewery	Nippon Flour Mills		Nisshin Flour Milling Sapporo Breweries Nichirei		Itoham Foods Suntory
Construction	Mitsubishi Construction	Mitsui Construction Sonki Engineering	Sumitomo Construction	Taisei	Shimizu	Toyo Construction Obayashi Sekisui House Zenitoko
Metals	Mitsubishi Steel Mfg. Mitsubishi Materials Mitsubishi Aluminum Mitsubishi Cable Industries	Japan Steel Works Mitsui Mining & Smelting	Sumitomo Metal Industries Sumitomo Metal Mining Sumitomo Electric Industries SumitomoLight Metal Industries	NKK	Kawasaki Steel Kobe Steel[1] Japan Metals & Chemicals Nippon Light Metal Furukawa Furukawa Electric	Kobe Steel[1] Nakayoma Steel Works Hitachi Metals Nisshin Steel Hitachi Cable
Real Estate	Mitsubishi Estate	Mitsui Real Estate Development	Sumitomo Realty & Development	Tokyo Taternono	Tokyo Dome	
Oil & Coal	Mitsubishi Oil			Tonen	Showa Shell Sekiyu	Cosmo Oil
Rubber & Glass	Asahi Glass		Nippon Sheet Glass		Yokohoma Rubber	Toyo Tire & Rubber

Chemicals	Mitsubishi Kasei Mitsubishi Petrochemical Mitsubishi Gas Chemical Mitsubishi Plastics Industries Mitsubishi Kasei Polytec	Mitsui Toatsu Chemicals Mitsui Petrochemical Industries	Sumitomo Chemical Sumitomo Bakelite	Showa Denko Nippon Oil & Fats Kureha Chemical Industry	Kyowa Hakko Kogyo Denki Kagaku Kogyo Nippon Zeon Asahi Denka Kogyo Sankyo Shiseido Lion	Ube Industries Tokuyoma Soda Hitachi Chemical Sekisui Chemical Kansai Paint Tonabe Seiyaku Fujisawa Pharmaceuticals
Fibers & Textiles	Mitsubishi Rayon	Toray Industries		Nisshinbo Industries Toha Rayon	Asahi Chemical Industry	Unitika Teijin
Pulp & Paper	Mitsubishi Paper Mills	Oji Paper		Sanyo-Kokusaku Pulp	Honshu Paper	
Mining & Forestry		Mitsui Mining Hokkaido Colliery & Steamship	Sumitomo Forestry Sumitomo Coal Mining			
Industrial Equipment	Mitsubishi Heavy Industries Mitsubishi Kakoki	Mitsui Engineering & Shipbuilding	Sumitomo Heavy Industries	Kubota Nippon Seiko	Niigata Engineering Iseki Ebara Kawasaki Heavy Industries Ishikawajimo-Harimo Heavy Industries	NTN Hitachi Zosen Shin Meiwa Industry
Cameras & Optics	Nikon			Canon	Asahi Optical	Hoya
Cement		Onoda Cement	Sumitomo Cement	Nihon Cement	Chichibu Cement	Osaka Cement
Shipping & Transportation	Nippon Yusen Mitsubishi Warehouses & Transportation	Mitsui OSK Lines Mitsui Warehouse	Sumitomo Warehouse	Showa Line Keihin Electric Express Railway Tobu Railway	Kawasaki Kisen Shibusowo Warehouse Nippon Express[1]	Navix Line Hankyu Nippon Express[1]

SOURCE: Dodwell Marketing Consultants, in *Fortune*, July 15, 1991, p. 81.
[1]Companies affiliated with more than one group.

EXHIBIT 3.12A   **CROSS-SHAREHOLDING ARRANGEMENTS**

PERCENTAGE OF JAPAN'S LISTED STOCKS HELD IN
CROSS-SHAREHOLDING ARRANGEMENTS

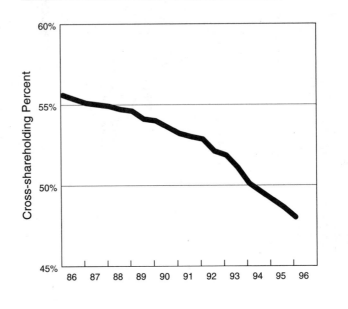

SOURCE: Daiwa Institute of Research, Baseline

EXHIBIT 3.12B   **RETURN ON EQUITY**

PERCENT RETURN ON EQUITY FOR JAPANESE COMPANIES
IN JANUARY FOR EACH YEAR

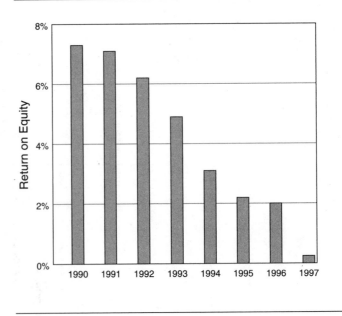

SOURCE: Datastream.

EXHIBIT 3.13   **FOREIGN DIRECT INVESTMENT**

CUMULATIVE DIRECT INVESTMENT INFLOWS
TO AND OUTFLOWS FROM JAPAN. 1980–1995

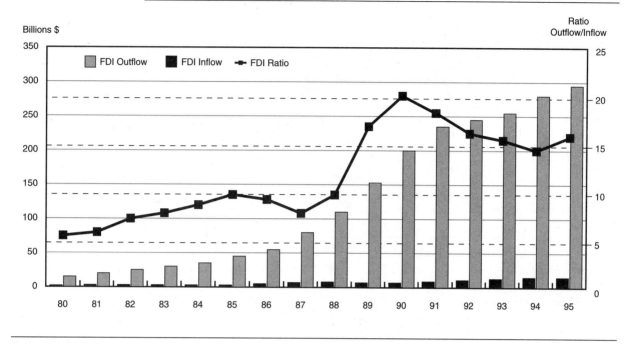

SOURCE: Akihiko Shinozaki and Kazumi Endo, "Analysis of Foreign Direct Investment and Foreign Affiliates in Japan," The Japan Development Bank, August 1997.

EXHIBIT 3.14   **SHIFTS OF POPULATION OF THE ELDERLY OF AGES OF 65 OR OLDER IN INDUSTRIALIZED COUNTRIES**

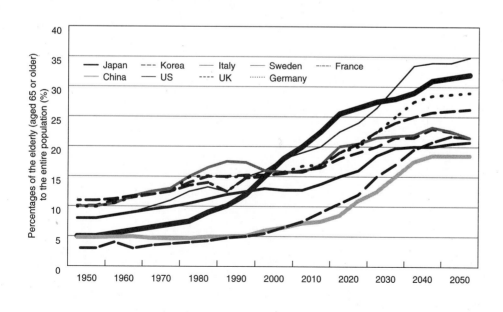

SOURCE: Japan International Corporation of Welfare Services, Textbook for the 7th Study Programme for the Asian Social Insurance Administrators, Tokyo, Japan, October 1997. p. 42.

| EXHIBIT 3.15 | MARKET YEN RATE AND PPPs(A) AGAINST U.S. DOLLAR |

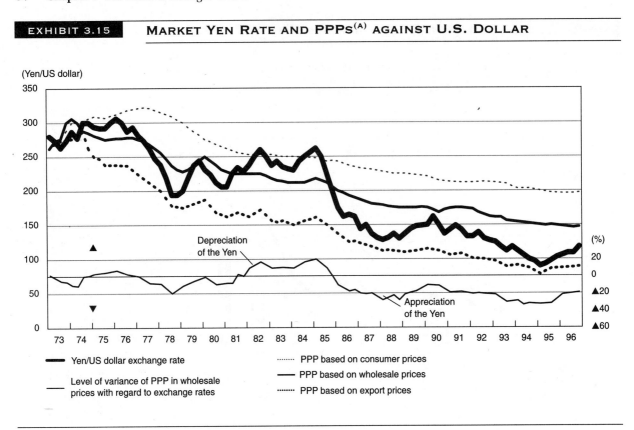

(Yen/US dollar)

Depreciation of the Yen

Appreciation of the Yen

——— Yen/US dollar exchange rate

······· PPP based on consumer prices

——— Level of variance of PPP in wholesale prices with regard to exchange rates

——— PPP based on wholesale prices

······· PPP based on export prices

(a) Purchasing Power Parities; reference: Purchasing Power Parity = 1973 yen/US dollar rate (Japan price index/US price index)
*MITI; IMF (IFS)

SOURCE: Keizai Koho Center, *Japan 1998: An International Comparison*, p. 59.

EXHIBIT 3.16	PROJECTIONS OF SOCIAL SECURITY COSTS (AS A PERCENTAGE OF NATIONAL INCOME)

FUTURE PROSPECTS FOR THE PUBLIC SUBSIDY FOR
THE SOCIAL SECURITY (AS OF SEPTEMBER, 1997,
BY THE MHW)

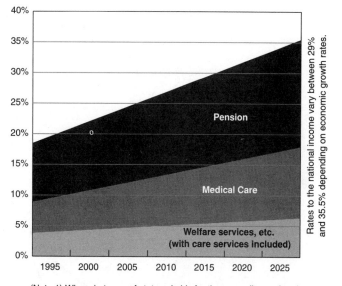

(Note 1) When, in terms of state subsidy for the expenditure other than
that of the social security system, its rate to the national income remains
unchanged compared to the present level (some 20%) and the present
such system is maintained, the future rate of taxation and social security
burden is expected to be 50%–56% depending on the growth rate of the
nominal national income (with the deficit of the general account excluded.)
In FY 1995, the deficit of the Government's general account was 8.8%
against the national income.

(Note 2) This estimatino was made on the assumption that the Long-Term
Care Insurance System is introduced.

SOURCE: Japan International Corporation of Welfare Services, Textbook for the 7th Study Programme for the Asian Social Insurance Administrators, Tokyo, Japan, October 1997, pp. 76–80.

EXHIBIT 3.17	HOUSEHOLD SAVINGS RATE

SAVINGS AS A PERCENTAGE OF DISPOSABLE INCOME

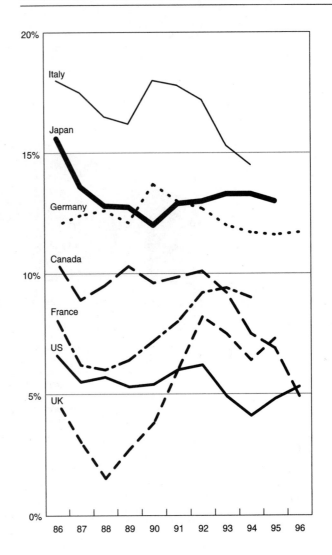

SOURCE: Bank of Japan, *Comparative Economic and Financial Statistics, Japan and Other Major Countries 1997*, p. 3.

1   W. G. Beasley, *The Rise of Modern Japan*, 2nd edition (New York: St. Martin's Press, 1995), pp. 263–264.

2   Takatoshi Ito, *The Japanese Economy* (Cambridge, Mass.: The MIT Press, 1992), p. 70.

3   Ibid., p. 71.

4   Karel Van Wolferen, *The Enigma of Japanese Power* (New York: Alfred A. Knopf Inc., 1989), p. 170.

5   Yasuhiko Hibata, Yomiuri Research Institute, *The Daily Yomiuri*, February 4, 1998, p. 5.

6   The Japan Institute of Labour, Ministry of Labour, "White Paper on Labour 1997," p. 91.

7   Personal interview with Mr. Yoshio Suzuki, President, Asahi Research Center, Co. Ltd.

8   Banks in Japan were allowed to own equity positions of up to 10% of the total outstanding shares in other businesses. The Anti-Monopoly Law Reform of 1977 reduced this number to 5%, effective in 1987.

9   Eisuke Sakakibara and Robert Alan Feldman, "The Japanese Financial System in Comparative Perspective," *Journal of Comparative Economics* 7 (1983), pp. 1–24.

10   The Economist Intelligence Unit, *EIU Country Report*, Japan, 3rd quarter 1997, p. 4.

11   Personal interview with Administrative Reform Council member Mr. Ken Moroi.

12   Van Wolferen, *The Enigma of Japanese Power*, pp. 121–124.

13   "Regarding the Report of The Subcommittee for Long-Range Issues of the Industrial Structure Council." News from MITI, October 1995. From the Internet website http://www.jef.or.jp/news/subcom1108.html.

14   Personal interview with Mr. Shijuro Ogata, former Deputy Governor of the Bank of Japan.

15   Chalmers Johnson, *MITI and the Japanese Miracle* (Stanford, Calif.: Stanford University Press, 1982), pp. 203–207.

16   Personal interview with Mitsubishi Corporation President Minoru Makihara.

17   Ito, *The Japanese Economy*, pp. 180–192.

18   Personal interview with Mitsubishi Corporation President Minoru Makihara.

19   Bill Spindle and Norihiko Shirouzu, "Mitsubishi Racketeering Probe Widens," *The Wall Street Journal*, October 27, 1997, p. A19.

20   Personal interview with Mr. Shijuro Ogata, former Deputy Governor of the Bank of Japan.

21   Statistics Bureau and Statistics Center, Management and Coordination Agency, Japan in Figures 1998, Section 2: Population, Tables 1 and 2. Internet address: http://www.stat.go.jp/1611m.htm.

22   Health and Welfare Bureau for the Elderly, Ministry of Health and Welfare, "New Gold Plan." December 1994, p. 32.

23   Ibid., p. 44.

24   Japan International Corporation of Welfare Services, Textbook for the 7th Study Programme for the Asian Social Insurance Administrators, Tokyo, Japan. October 1997, pp. 76–80.

25   "Women in Japan Today" website. URL: http://www.sorifu.go.jp/danjyo/index2.html.

26   Nihon Keizai Shinbun, February 9, 1998, p. 7.

27   The Japan Institute of Labour, Ministry of Labour, "White Paper on Labour, 1997," p. 19.

28   Japan Institute for Social and Economic Affairs, *Japan 1998: An International Comparison*, pp. 99–100.

29   *Facts on File World News Digest*, "Math, Science Education Study Released," December 5, 1996.

30   An advisory committee headed by former Bank of Japan Governor Haruo Maekawa proposed restructuring the Japanese economy to be less dependent on exports for growth. However, its report floundered in the bureaucracy, and its ideas were never implemented.

31   Personal interview with Mr. Koichi Koike, Director, Administration Department, Bank of Japan.

32   Final Report of the Administrative Reform Council (Provisional Translation), December 3, 1997.

33   Personal interview with Administrative Reform Council member Mr. Ken Moroi.

34   Personal interview with Mr. Akihiko Shinozaki, deputy director, Loan Division, Japan Development Bank.

35   "The Action Plan for Economic Structure Reform," Ministry of International Trade and Industry, May 1997.

36   "Estimated Economic Effects of Deregulation." Summary of Report of the Study Group on the Economic Effects of Deregulation. http://www.jef.or.jp/news/eco0609.html.

37   "Program for Educational Reform," Ministry of Education, Science, Sports and Culture, revised August 5, 1997.

38   "Financial System Reform," Ministry of Finance, June 13, 1997.

39   Personal interview with Mr. Eiji Hirano, advisor to the governor, Bank of Japan.

40   Naoki Okabe, "Fault Lines in the Financial Reform," *Japan Update*, July 1997, p. 7.

41   R. Taggart Murphy, "Don't Be Fooled by Japan's Big Bang," *Fortune*, December 29, 1997.

42   Hashimoto Yomiuri, "Hashimoto Wants Budget Deficit Reduced Earlier," *The Daily Yomiuri*, March 19, 1997, p. 1.

43 "On the Promotion of Fiscal Structural Reform," Cabinet decision, June 3, 1997.

44 Personal interview with Mr. Nobuyuki Takakura, senior policy coordinator, Policy Planning and Evaluation Division, Minister's Secretariat, Ministry of Health and Welfare.

45 The Economist Intelligence Unit, *EIU Country Report, Japan,* 4th quarter 1997, p. 22.

46 David P. Hamilton, "Japan Renews Blitz to Sell Its Stimulus Plan," *The Wall Street Journal,* April 27, 1998.

47 Personal interview with Mr. Shijuro Ogata, former deputy governor of the Bank of Japan.

48 Personal interview with Mr. Toshiharu Kitamura, executive vice president, Institute of Fiscal and Monetary Policy, Ministry of Finance.

Debt Crisis and Structural Adjustment

A s the first country to experience debt crisis and the first to undertake thorough-going structural reform, Mexico is our example for thinking about the 37 countries that experienced cross-border debt problems between 1982 and 1988.

After several decades of slow-growing import substitution, Mexico's economy nearly collapsed in the early 1970s. Having cut off foreign direct investment and then devaluing the peso, a new president opted for a development strategy leveraged on petroleum exports and foreign debt. Jose Lopez Portillo planned to build Mexico on oil, agriculture, and tourism. To do so, his government borrowed freely from American banks, which were flush with OPEC petrodollar deposits that they needed to loan out.

After several years of the "Mexican Miracle," the economy collapsed in 1982. Mexico simply lacked the dollars required to service its debt and maintain the fixed exchange rate. The first part of this case is structured around a discussion of what caused Mexico's debt crisis. Was it primarily an ineffective strategy? A weak social-political context? Or difficult circumstances in the world economy?

The case then develops Miguel de la Madrid's strategy for structural adjustment between 1982 and 1988. The International Monetary Fund required harsh medicine for Mexico, and de la Madrid had to implement it. Students need to discuss his eight-point strategy and evaluate its economic and political viability. This adjustment strategy came to constitute the "Washington consensus" used frequently by the IMF throughout Latin America and Africa.

The Salinas era (1988-1994) was the capstone to de la Madrid's turn-around approach. It is important to consider what Salinas added to adjustment and what he did not add. Free trade with the United States and Canada was a key piece of this adjustment, as was the fixed exchange rate policy. By December 1994, Mexico was back in a currency crisis, with which the new president Zedillo needed to cope.

In sum, this case provides the short history of debt crisis-from pre-1973 origins to second-round currency failure in the mid-1990s.

MEXICO IN DEBT

On December 1, 1994, Ernesto Zedillo Ponce de León took over as Mexico's president from his predecessor Carlos Salinas. Just three weeks later-on December 20-the Mexican stock market (known as the *Bolsa*) dropped 150 points. Foreign exchange reserves were already down from $25 billion at the start of the year to around $6 billion-less than one month of imports. The government had no choice but to float the peso. Financial markets reacted chaotically, sending the Mexican currency into a free-fall. The peso lost more than 35% of its value in just three weeks, falling from 3.4 pesos/dollar on December 20 to 5.7 pesos/dollar on January 9. Capital fled the country at an alarming rate. The economic strategies of Zedillo's predecessors Miguel de la Madrid Hurtado and Carlos Salinas de Gortari, whose reforms had won global admiration, were now in serious trouble.[1] Added to this was a peasant uprising in the southern state of Chiapas and damaging allegations of corruption in Zedillo's political party, the Partido Revolucionario Institucional (PRI). Barely a month into his job, the new president already had his work cut out for him.

Modern Mexico

Mexico is the 13th largest nation in the world, with a population in 1994 of approximately 93 million people.[2] The country's 1990 census showed that 71% of the population lived in cities and 29% in rural areas; 38% was under 14 years old.[3] Forty-eight percent of Mexico's land is suitable for livestock, 29% is forested, and 18% is arable. The country shares a 1,760-mile border with the United States.

Modern Mexico was built after the devastation of the 1910 revolution—a revolt against the 30-year dictatorship of Porfirio Díaz and U.S. "imperialism"—in which an estimated one million lives were lost. That bloody legacy shaped the national conscience and motivated policy makers and the population to search for nonviolent means of conflict resolution. The new Constitution in 1917 gave the state a leading role in national development and contained strong nationalist provisions. The state took on an arbitrating role between capital and labor and promised concessions regarding maximum working hours, minimum wages, and union rights. A six-year presidency was established that prohibited successive terms of office and granted primacy to the executive over the legislature and judiciary.

The current political system dates back to 1929, when the revolutionary elite founded the Partido Revolucionario Institucional or PRI. Over the years, noncompetitive elections were institutionalized within an officially multiparty, pluralistic framework.[4] The PRI had never lost an election, although the legitimacy of the results of the 1988 and 1994 presidential elections had been questioned.

After World War II, Mexico followed a deliberate policy of import substitution to reduce its dependence on raw material exports and imported manufactured goods. The fledgling manufacturing sector was protected from foreign competition by tariffs and quantitative restrictions on imports. In the 1950s, those restrictions covered about 10% of domestic production, rising to 60% in the 1970s and 100% in 1982–83. The government provided low-interest, long-term loans to industry through state investment banks. The public sector also invested directly in infrastructure and basic industries such as steel and petroleum.

Despite revolutionary constraints, foreign investors responded well to the import substitution policies and from 1950 to 1970 foreign direct investment (FDI) increased

Research Associate Eilene Zimmerman prepared this case under the supervision of Professor Richard H. K. Vietor as the basis for class discussion rather than to illustrate either effective or ineffective handling of an administrative situation. This case draws heavily on "Mexico: Escaping from the Debt Crisis?" by Professor Helen Shapiro, HBS case no. 390-174.

fivefold, with the United States swamping all other investors. From 1954 to 1970 Mexico followed a policy it termed *stabilized development (desarrollo estabilizador)*, which involved relatively tight fiscal policies and government restraint in using unsupported central bank credits to finance increased spending. As a result, average annual growth rates in per capita income of over 3% were accompanied by low inflation and a fixed exchange-rate regime.

By the mid-1960s, however, underlying problems in the system became apparent. Growth rates were slowing, agricultural production decreased, and exports of manufactured goods stagnated. The economy had become even more dependent on imported capital goods, and between 1965 and 1970 the current account deficit ballooned from US$367 million to US$946 million. With this economic stagnation came social unrest. In the summer of 1968, a series of peaceful student demonstrations were violently suppressed by the government, resulting in the army's massacre of hundreds on October 2. The PRI's use of outright repression precipitated further opposition. Grassroots movements began to organize outside the PRI umbrella, calling for increased democracy.

President Luis Echeverría (1970–1976) attempted to restore legitimacy and accommodate competing claims on the system through aggressive fiscal policies. In an attempt to increase the slackened growth rate and relieve infrastructural bottlenecks, the state increased investment and encouraged import substitution in intermediate and capital goods. But revenues failed to match the increasing fiscal demands on the state. Fiscal and current account deficits increased and inflation rose to an annual rate of 30%. In 1973, moreover, severe restrictions were placed on foreign investment. By August 1976 the situation had reached crisis proportions; for the first time since 1954, the president was forced to devalue the peso by more than 40%, from 12 to 19 pesos per dollar.

In 1977 the government of José López Portillo instituted an austerity program that improved the balance of payments by the following year. New oil discoveries led to increasingly optimistic estimates of the country's oil reserves, which in turn attracted foreign credit at low interest rates. López Portillo terminated a stabilization agreement previously reached with the International Monetary Fund and ushered in the era of the "Mexican Miracle." A development boom ensued, with rapid growth in state expenditures, especially for oil, agriculture, and tourism. Public sector outlays as a share of GNP went from 25% in 1970 to 42% in 1980. Nearly half of that investment was for oil exploration and production. López Portillo targeted oil exports at 1.3 million barrels a day (mmb/d), on top of 1.2 mmb/d for domestic use.

The "miracle," however, did not reach everyone. At the end of the 1970s, 35–40% of all households earned a total income below the prevailing minimum wage; approximately 20% of the population in 1979 was suffering from malnutrition; and 45% did not receive adequate health care. Approximately 50% of all homes lacked running water and sewage services, and 25% had no electricity. The lowest 20% of all households held 3% of national income while the top 20% held 41% of that income.[5] Imports were growing at a faster rate than exports as the fixed exchange rate became overvalued. The budget deficit grew to 17% of GDP in the last year of the López Portillo administration. Public external debt nearly doubled from US$40 billion to US$78billion in just two years. Anticipating a devaluation, investors began to move out of pesos. When oil prices began to soften in 1981, government income fell below projections. In February 1982, after vowing to "defend the peso like a dog," López Portillo was forced to devalue. By June, capital was leaving the country at a rate as high as US$400 million a day. On August 12, 1982, the so-called Mexdollar accounts—dollar-denominated deposits held in Mexican banks—were frozen.

When U.S. Secretary of the Treasury Donald Regan said to Mexican Finance Secretary Silva Herzog, "Mr. Secretary, you have a big problem," Silva Herzog replied, "No, Mr. Secretary, I'm sorry to tell you but *we* have a problem." On August

15, Mexico fired "the shot heard around the world" and announced it could no longer meet interest payments on its foreign debt. The country plunged into a period of financial crisis and economic stagnation unprecedented since the Great Depression.[6]

In September, López Portillo nationalized the banking system and inaugurated exchange controls. His surprise move, orchestrated by a small group of presidential intimates, sent shock waves through the private sector, shattering what little confidence remained. Although the move rallied popular support in the short-run, it aggravated capital flight and ruptured the implicit contract between the private sector and the government. In December, with foreign debt at US$91 billion, Mexico signed a stand-by agreement with the IMF, pledging to reduce the deficit, restrict growth in the money supply, devalue the peso, welcome foreign investment, privatize state-owned companies, restrain wages, and charge fees for public services.

Up until the economic crisis in 1982, the stability of Mexico's political system had been based on its capacity to maintain order and security and increase living standards, even in the face of rapid population growth and a highly unequal distribution of wealth. The government maintained a systemic equilibrium in the short to intermediate run but was unable to prevent long-term decay, both politically and economically. Rather than addressing the deeper, more fundamental problems that were undermining the system, reforms were designed to buy time through piecemeal adjustments. The result, by the 1980s, was a generalized crisis that increasingly encompassed the entire system.[7]

The 1982 Crisis and de la Madrid

The inauguration of de la Madrid in the immediate aftermath of the 1982 crisis signaled resurgence in the PRI's technocratic wing. De la Madrid was a 47-year-old graduate of Harvard's Kennedy School of Government who had spent most of his career in the Treasury and the central bank. He appointed an ideologically cohesive Cabinet, with Silva Herzog remaining as Secretary of the Treasury and Carlos Salinas, also from the Treasury, becoming Secretary of Planning and Budget. The new president's first task was to repair relations with the private sector, but he could not reverse the bank nationalizations. Although this disappointed the private sector, de la Madrid said he could "not reverse the decision for political reasons and because the nationalization was already introduced into the Constitution."[8]

The administration rapidly indemnified stockholders for the bank nationalizations, and within two years, all nonfinancial assets held by the banks were sold back to the private sector. But because of nationalization, throughout the 1980s Mexican banks were little more than an extension of government. Lending to the private sector was insubstantial—credit was directed to Mexican companies by the whim of politicians rather than allocated on market criteria.[9] Regulations were eased so that certain banking activity could be undertaken by mixed enterprises with significant private participation, and private brokerage houses were granted wide latitude to finance transactions in domestic capital markets.

Budget cutting was intense, particularly during the first two years of de la Madrid's presidency. Subsidies for basic commodities were cut, public-sector prices were increased for items such as electricity and gasoline, and the value-added tax was raised. In real terms, government spending on investment fell to 1960s levels. The real exchange rate and real wages were the principal instruments used to balance the external accounts and generate the surplus needed to service the debt. It was hoped that a sharply devalued peso would spark the growth and diversification of exports. The counterpart to deep devaluation was a sharp cut in the real wage, as import prices soared. Prior to 1982, nominal minimum wages were indexed to rates of past inflation; from 1983, minimum wages were set in accordance with expected inflation rates, which over this period were grossly underestimated. Tight fiscal and monetary policies were maintained until 1985, when the budget was loosened for the mid-term elections. In the meantime, Jesus Herzog worked with Paul Volcker to get much of Mexico's foreign debt rescheduled—stretched out over 14 years.

Then, in September 1985, a series of devastating earthquakes rocked Mexico City, causing thousands of deaths and physical damage of up to US$5 billion. On that same day, the IMF suspended payment on its previous Extended Fund Facility agreement, setting the stage for bitter negotiations throughout the following year. Shortly thereafter, oil prices took a nose-dive, falling as low as US$8.54 barrel in July 1986. This resulted in a US$10 billion loss in export revenues.

Private investment was not recuperating well enough to make up for the reduction in public investment. Despite export growth, the net effect of fiscal, monetary, and exchange reforms was deep recession. Employment growth had averaged 4% during the 1970s, not counting irregular or "off-the-books" employment in the informal sector. From 1982 to 1986 it fell to only 0.2%, while the labor force grew an estimated 3.6%. The World Bank estimated that by 1986, 20% of the workforce was employed in the informal sector or in the United States.

In October 1987 the Mexican stock market crashed, two weeks before the U.S. stock market collapsed. It had been the fastest-rising exchange in the world, becoming especially attractive after the 1986 peso devaluation. In the first nine months of 1987 alone, the market's value had gone up 330%. Much of this activity was speculative. The market lost 74% of its value less than 40 days after the crash, and this triggered a new wave of capital flight and further peso devaluation. Inflation was hitting an annual rate of 159%. A new policy direction was needed.

The Pacto

In December 1987 the administration introduced an unorthodox program of stabilization and reform. Macroeconomic stabilization was implemented through the introduction of the *Pacto*—an agreement between government and representatives of business, unions, and agriculture to cooperate and coordinate wage bargaining and price setting. Proponents of this approach argued that fiscal deficits were as much a result of inflation as they were a cause of it. Inflation had achieved a momentum all its own: expectations of inflation encouraged unions to demand higher wages to protect their members' standard of living, but this only succeeded in raising labor costs and prices, thereby validating the original expectations of inflation. Inflation required the government to pay ever-higher rates of interest on its debt, raising the deficit even further. Coordination in wage and price setting was required to break the inflationary spiral.[10]

The government worked with labor and the private sector to coordinate wage and price adjustments and impose a wage and price freeze. The peso was devalued by 22%. The maximum tariff on imports was reduced from 40% to 20%. Government expenditures were cut and revenues increased. Credit became extremely tight. Restrictions on foreign direct investment were eased, and in 1984 the government in many sectors abandoned its revolutionary principles, allowing 100% foreign-owned subsidiaries. In 1986–1987 IBM, and later Hewlett-Packard and Apple, were permitted to set up wholly owned subsidiaries.

An old exception to foreign investment restrictions was Mexico's special in-bond or *maquiladora* program, which dated back to the 1960s. Only permitted along the U.S. border, *maquiladoras* were essentially assembly operations. U.S. law said that goods assembled in Mexico and re-exported to the United States for final sale would be taxed only on the value added in Mexico. One hundred percent foreign ownership of *maquiladoras* was allowed, and at the end of 1986, 90% were U.S.-owned.

Mexico entered the GATT in August 1986, after having declined to do so in 1980. Over the next three years, the average tariff rates were dropped from 23% to 12.5%.

Many of the import licenses and quotas were to be freed up over an eight-year period. Surcharges of up to 50% of base tariff rates were allowed until December 1994. Entry into GATT by Mexico signified the country's ongoing commitment to liberalizing its trade policies.

Privatizing state-owned firms also became a priority of the de la Madrid administration, but it began slowly, with only 23 firms divested in 1983–1984. In February 1985, a new economic package was announced that targeted 765 firms to be privatized through 1988. The 116 firms sold through mid-1988 netted about US$422 million. In the last months of the de la Madrid administration, Aeromexico was added, for US$300 million.

De la Madrid's government hoped to improve the economy's competitiveness enough to maintain the current account deficit. This was done through increased private investment, including that from foreigners attracted by confidence in the stable exchange rate, anti-inflation policies, and productivity gains made possible by structural reforms.[11]

Political Reaction

Compared with many other indebted Latin American countries, Mexico imposed tough austerity measures and was one of the few to cut government spending and shrink its budget deficit. Silva Herzog said the reason this was possible in Mexico was its one-party system. "Even though you have opposition growing on the right and the left, the basic decisions . . . are still under the control of the majority party. . . . I think that is a good part of the answer," he said, "having a kind of monolithical political system."[12] President de la Madrid offered his explanation as well: "I believe that on the one hand, here in Mexico we—the government—had clearer ideas, a greater conviction in what we had to do. And on the other hand, the political organization of Mexico has institutions that are more developed, more mature, with a workers' movement that is more coherent, in solidarity with the government, and business organizations with which we could discuss and negotiate."

Nevertheless, the government's policies did elicit a strong response from some sectors of the population. The left organized and leftist parties began to make some electoral gains. Social forces that had previously been co-opted or excluded from the political system gave birth to new organizations, most of which focused on very specific demands. By the end of the 1980s, hundreds of independent nongovernmental organizations had been formed. Their ranks included political parties and business, labor, peasant, mass media, and human rights groups.[13] The political right was more organized and less fragmented, uniting within the National Action Party (PAN), which has historically been the PRI's main opposition party. PAN gathered strength in the 1980s and came close to winning governorships in some northern states. The party and its candidate, Manuel Clouthier, campaigned for even greater economic liberalization and for the democratization of the electoral process in order to gain a greater political voice within the PRI-dominated system.

The most serious electoral challenge to the PRI came from within its own ranks. Tension was growing between the traditional dominant *políticos* and the *técnicos* who had come to dominate national policy making under de la Madrid. Many old-guard politicos viewed reform measures such as privatizing state-owned enterprises and reducing subsidies as a betrayal of their party's revolutionary heritage. Those who favored traditional economic solutions got frozen out of power. In October 1987, some of these elements left the party to form an opposition movement under the leadership of Cuauhtémoc Cárdenas and Porfirio Muñoz Ledo.[14] Cárdenas criticized the administration for abandoning the PRI's commitment to social justice and national self-determination and argued that these views were not getting sufficient representation in the selection process of de la Madrid's successor. Cárdenas was essentially purged from the party but the split within the PRI allowed the fragmented opposition social movements to organize politically. Cardenás declared himself a candidate for president and the coalition of left-wing parties withdrew their candidate from the race in order to support him. A new coalition, the National Democratic Front (FDN), was formed.

The 1988 elections marked the most serious challenge to the hegemony of the ruling party since its consolidation in the 1930s. Historically, presidential elections had been a ritualistic ratification of candidates chosen behind closed doors by the PRI's political elite. For the first time the PRI's candidate, Carlos Salinas, faced organized opposition parties from the left and right. On election day, July 6, many traditional PRI voters abstained or joined the opposition. When the early returns showed Cardenás in the lead, the government's computers went dead, allegedly for "environmental reasons." After a week's delay in which Cardenás ballots were found "floating down rivers and smoldering in roadside bonfires," the official results were released: Salinas had won 50.7% of the vote, the narrowest margin of victory in the PRI's history. The opposition gained almost half the seats in the Chamber of Deputies and four seats in the Senate.[15]

Carlos Salinas

Amid this political and economic turmoil President Carlos Salinas de Gortari began his *sexenio* (six-year term). Salinas, like his predecessor, was a graduate of Harvard University with a Ph.D. in political economy. During the campaign, Salinas stressed that his would be a "modernizing" presidency. He promised both economic and political reform. But Salinas was acutely aware of the risks: undermining the PRI and jeopardizing political stability. He concluded the two reforms would proceed "at different rhythms," with economics taking priority, though the two were inextricably linked.[16] "The focal point of state reform," said Salinas, "is to reach decisions that benefit the people, to resolve the dilemma between property to be managed or justice to be dispersed, between a more proprietary state or a more just state."[17]

In the first months of his presidency, Salinas took a series of headline-grabbing actions to show he was serious about cleaning up government. The most striking was his arrest of Joaquín Hernández Galicia, or "La Quina," president of the Oil Workers Union, on charges of assassination, job peddling, and fraud. The union represented 210,000 PEMEX workers and had been a pillar of the PRI. It was financially the most powerful union group in Latin America. La Quina had long been accused of corrupt and wasteful management. He had initially opposed Salinas' candidacy and quietly backed Cardenas. On January 10, 1989, Salinas sent in the army, which demolished La Quina's front door with a bazooka and arrested him.

Turning to the private sector, Salinas locked up financier Eduardo Legorreta, who had contributed to his campaign, and four associates for securities fraud surrounding the stock market crash of 1987. In April, he jailed notorious drug trafficker, Miguel Felix Gallardo. And on November 1, having just delivered his first state of the nation address (*informe*), Salinas attended the inauguration of Ernesto Ruffo Appel as governor of Baja California Norte. Ruffo was a member of the right-wing opposition party PAN and was the first person allowed to win a state governorship from outside the ruling PRI. By being present at Ruffo's inauguration Salinas was emphasizing his stated commitment to opening up the political process.[18]

Economic Reforms

In his state of the nation address, Salinas repeated his government's commitment to modernization and reform. He stressed that key concerns were controlling inflation and boosting investment and production. And he said that agriculture was the sector of the economy that presented the country with its most serious challenge.

Salinas followed the strategy he had helped formulate during the de la Madrid government. He renewed the *Pacto*, maintained wage and price controls, and allowed the exchange rate to devalue by one peso a day. He expanded the privatization program by putting Telemex on the selling block.

In May 1989, the government announced a sweeping liberalization of foreign investment regulations. It revoked remaining restrictions on foreign investors to minority ownership positions and opened new areas to foreign investment. The new rules allowed 100% ownership in the tourism sector and the *maquiladoras*, hopefully to generate foreign exchange. *Maquiladora* legislation was aimed at expanding the industry and increasing the benefits to the domestic economy, primarily the generation of employment.[19]

Negotiating better terms on Mexico's foreign debt was a critical component of Salinas' strategy. Debt reduction was required to free the necessary resources to resume noninflationary growth. In April 1989, Mexico signed a $3.64 billion, three-year loan agreement with the IMF. This was to help build up reserves, which had declined as Salinas defended the peso in an effort to reduce inflation. Mexico then reached a landmark agreement with its foreign bank creditors in July 1989. The banks had been pressured by U.S. Treasury Secretary Nicholas Brady to reduce the volume of existing debt, instead of simply piling on additional debt to maintain interest payments. Although the final agreement, signed in February 1990, involved some debt forgiveness and injections of new lending, its main feature was the conversion of bank debt into so-called "Brady Bonds." These were 30-year zero-coupon bonds guaranteed by the U.S. Treasury on the collateral of Mexican oil revenues. They required no servicing in the years before maturity but only a single balloon payment in 30 years' time. This freed resources for development of the domestic economy in the intervening period.[20] It reduced the debt burden by as much as 20% and cut annual payments by US$3 billion over the next four years.

In January 1990, Salinas announced a program for reactivating the agricultural sector. Bean prices would be doubled, and the guarantee prices for maize, rice, and wheat were also raised. The government also announced it would liquidate Azúcar SA, the state sugar company, and Tabamex, the state tobacco company. The development of agri-business in seven selected areas was seen as a third aspect of the reform program. The government ended the country's land redistribution policy, a legacy of the revolution, giving farmers grouped together in *ejidos* (communal holdings) title to their land. This threatened to weaken PRI influence in rural areas (land or money given in exchange for votes), but Salinas saw that the dire poverty in which many of the approximately 20 million rural inhabitants lived was a far greater danger to long-term political stability.[21]

The Recovery

Although he was hailed by *Fortune* magazine as one of 1989's top 25 business leaders and his structural reforms termed *Salinastroika*, the president walked an economic and political tightrope at home. A *Los Angeles Times* poll taken a year after the election showed that although only a quarter of the population believed that Salinas had actually won, 79% gave him a positive presidential approval rating. Economic growth had reached 3% in 1989; inflation was down to about 20% (from 159% in 1987) aided by imports; and price controls were in place. Though GDP growth slowed some in 1991, per capital national income kept rising (to US$1,900, compared with US$1,710 in 1988).[22]

As U.S. interest rates fell during the early 1990s in response to recession, investors seeking high yields increasingly looked to the emerging markets. Mexico was in a prime position to receive a disproportionate share of these funds. Moreover, the investment community shared Mexican confidence in the prospects for economic reform. The mistakes of previous years were being aggressively reversed. New York fund managers scrambled to send money south to gain an early stake in Mexico's embryonic economic miracle. The country was caught in a virtuous cycle of reform, growing confidence, greater capital inflows, and accelerating expenditure growth. As capital flooded into the country, it stimulated domestic consumption and investment. Economic activity swelled tax revenues and further improved public finances. The apparent success of reform and stabilization made further liberalization and continued wage and price restraint under the *Pacto* more palatable to the parties concerned. Privatization of large state-owned firms, including the banks, took place during the 1990s; US$22 billion came in from the sale of 200 enterprises between 1988 and 1993.[23] Success in reducing inflation and raising the fiscal surplus only served to bolster foreign confidence and encourage even greater capital inflows.

Some argued that these gains were tenuous: the fiscal surplus was a product of creative accounting rather than actual improvements in financial control. Spending was moved off-balance sheet to nongovernmental organizations such as development banks. The reduction in inflation was an artifact of administrative *diktat* rather than improved monetary control. The parties to the *Pacto* were responsible for setting a large proportion of the prices that entered the statistical definition of inflation. But these facts were largely ignored in the clamor of the times.[24]

The peso's real exchange rate seemed to appreciate in the early 1990s. The peso/dollar rate had been confined within a fluctuation band since 1991. The lower boundary of the band declined a small amount each day, allowing for a gradual depreciation. But the magnitude of capital inflows kept the rate at the top of the band. There were incipient pressures for appreciation, rather than depreciation. From late 1992, the peso's exchange rate against the dollar demonstrated remarkable stability, evidence in the government's eyes of the success of reform and foreign confidence in Mexico's future. But some disagreed. Increasingly vocal critics argued the strength of the peso was evidence of macroeconomic mismanagement. A stable *nominal* exchange rate had resulted in an appreciating *real* exchange rate. The prices of Mexican goods, when converted to dollars at the market rate, were rising more rapidly than those of their American equivalents. The current account deficit was evidence of rapidly declining international competitiveness. Slumping exports were causing domestic economic stagnation.[25]

Nevertheless, Salinas' reforms were popular. Under his administration, social spending rose substantially, even as the overall budget deficit was reduced. Between 1988 and 1994, spending on education more than doubled; spending on health care and social security rose by 82% and on urban development by 51%. Thirteen and a half million more people were provided with potable water, 11.5 million with sewage services, and 4 million with electricity—all under President Salinas. By mid-term, Salinas was viewed as a strong leader with a vision of the future that appealed to millions of Mexicans. By entering into a partnership with the Bush administration to adopt free trade, he had acquired hemisphere-wide stature.

Under these conditions, the PRI made a dramatic recovery from the political trauma of 1988. The party—with a few exceptions—swept state and local elections in 1989 and 1990, culminating in their smashing victory in the August 1991 mid-term elections.[26]

NAFTA

In November 1993, the U.S. Congress ratified NAFTA and ushered in a new era in U.S.–Mexican relations, Mexican economic development and in Mexico's political evolution. Passage had not been easy and was attained only after a prolonged and fierce political struggle that included the negotiation of side agreements designed to make the pact more palatable to U.S. critics. In the months preceding the vote, Salinas had even distanced himself slightly from the agreement, seeking to deflate public expectations in the event the agreement was rejected.

The 1,400-page NAFTA document was essentially a treaty between Mexico, the United States, and Canada that converted all quotas between the countries to tariffs and removed all tariffs on trade over a ten-year period (except in special cases in which the schedule is 15 years). NAFTA began as an attempt by Salinas to cement his reforms and ensure Mexico's competitiveness in the world economy. The treaty was initialed by President George Bush, Canadian Prime Minister Brian Mulroney and Carlos Salinas in December 1992. Tariffs on approximately 50% of the 9,000 traded items covered by the treaty would disappear immediately, on another 15% within five years, and on all remaining goods over the next ten years. Mexico would also immediately eliminate any remaining licensing requirements and quotas, except for agriculture, autos, energy, and textiles. Sectors most sensitive to import competition were granted 15-year transition periods, and procedures were established to allow countries to reimpose tariffs in response to damaging import surges.

For textiles and apparel, duties would be phased out over a ten-year period, and NAFTA would take precedence over the existing Multifiber Agreement. To prevent other countries from using Mexico as an export platform to the United States or Canada, rules of origin required that all goods be produced from yarn made in North America; for cotton and man-made fiber yarns, the fiber itself had to originate in one of the three countries. The United States would immediately remove import quotas on goods that met the rule-of-origin standard from Mexico and gradually remove import quotas on Mexican goods that did not meet the rules of origin. For automobiles, the rule of origin was set at 62.5% for a zero tariff. After ten years, 62.5% of the value added had to be sourced in North America. In addition, Mexico's trade-balancing requirements would be phased out, and its domestic-content requirements would fall to 29% of value added in ten years. In agriculture, tariffs would be lowered over ten years, except for corn and soybeans in Mexico—15 years—and the same for orange juice and sugar in the United States. This would indeed be hard on Mexico's ten million *ejidos* (small revolutionary-era farms).

NAFTA stipulated that U.S. and Canadian firms could bid on as much as 50% of the service contracts offered by the government's oil and electricity monopoly. This would increase to 80% over eight years and to 100% in ten years. In the oil fields, firms would be allowed to compete only for "performance" contracts, which gave them a bonus for superior service, but not for "risk" contracts, which gave them a share of the oil itself (petroleum was exempted from NAFTA on constitutional grounds). The agreement also dealt with sanitary standards, dumping, government procurement, air service, telecommunications, financial services, social services, land transportation, and intellectual property.

President Clinton grudgingly endorsed free trade, but the work rules and environmental standards were weak and had to be renegotiated in 1993. Dispute settlement panels were strengthened, and penalties were included for environmental noncompliance. Congress approved the treaty in the fall, and Bill Clinton signed it into law in December.

With NAFTA now in place, the Mexico of the '90s—it was said—was about to enter the front ranks of trading nations, reforming and modernizing its industrial system and nationalist economic structure. The nation was now led by reform-minded technocrats who understood that Mexico must embrace global integration if it wished to prosper. In Mexico as well as in the United States, these progressive assumptions were articulated as the common understanding of the Mexican reality framed the context of NAFTA.[27]

The Fall

By the end of 1993, it appeared that Mexico seemed transformed. Its accession to the Organization for Economic Cooperation and Development (OECD) conferred on her membership in what had traditionally been regarded as the "rich countries' club."[28] The signing of the NAFTA agreement by Salinas was a high point in his *sexenio*. With Mexico's new standing in the world, the country soon became a main beneficiary of an unprecedented surge in private capital flow, a favorite son among "emerging markets." Between 1990 and 1994, Mexico became the world's second-largest recipient (after China) of foreign private investment.[29]

Beneath the surface, however, trouble was brewing. Since 1990, economic growth had steadily declined, from a growth rate of 4.4% in 1990 to 3.6% in 1991 to 2.6% in 1992. In 1993, it grew only 0.4% (manufacturing actually shrank 5%). By the end of 1993, the country was experiencing negative growth.[30] Job creation also slowed. Fewer than 500,000 new jobs were created in 1992, compared with 600,000 in 1991. At the same time, privatization, the introduction of new technologies, economic deceleration, and business failures eliminated many other jobs (labor sources put the figure as high at 400,000), leaving the net gain at the end of 1992 far short of the one million or so openings the economy needed to generate each year to absorb the new arrivals in the labor market.[31]

From 1992, bad loans in the banking system began to mount, although because Mexican accounting standards failed to meet international standards, the magnitude of the problem was not immediately apparent abroad. Perversely, the lack of regulation allowed the emergence of bad loans to encourage more destabilizing bank behavior, rather than conservatism. Close relationships between banks and industrial companies—often cemented by family ties that were opaque to the minimal official regulation—allowed banks to extend credit to affiliated companies or bank insiders, never expecting to be repaid. The absence of legal and regulatory infrastructure allowed such problems to multiply.[32]

At the macroeconomic level, the spending boom initiated by reform and facilitated by financial liberalization had caused a catastrophic collapse in private saving. Private savings went from 21.8% of GDP in 1983 to 15.7% in 1989 and dropped to 12.1% in 1994. Consumption and imports rose much more quickly than income because an overvalued currency made for inexpensive imports. Individuals denied foreign goods for so long were determined to obtain them while they had the chance. Foreign cars, appliances, and clothes demonstrated the rewards of Salinas' painful austerity programs. Even though public saving rose as the fiscal accounts moved into surplus, the precipitous decline of saving by the private sector implied a collapse in overall national saving. The implications of this for Mexico's development strategy were profound. If she could not generate the financial resources to fund investment and development herself, Mexico had to rely on financing from the rest of the world. Low national savings meant Mexican economic growth was dependent on continued inflows of foreign capital—the mechanism for transferring foreign savings into the Mexican economy.[33]

Mexico relied increasingly on its short-term capital (cash, stocks, and bonds) rather than foreign direct investment. The use of short-term capital was a testament to the sophistication of the Mexican economy, adjusting quickly to receive these inflows. Though short-term capital investment was a way to kickstart the economy, its downside was that the capital could be withdrawn as fast as it came in. Between 1991 and 1993, net foreign capital inflows into Mexico amounted to $78 billion, while foreign direct investment totaled only US$14 billion.[34]

Drug-related violence and corruption, meanwhile, muddied the waters of recovery. By 1993, roughly a dozen major drug lords and several minor ones were in control of drug cartels, and they were increasingly engaged in turf wars. During the first five months of the year over 80 people were killed in Culiacán, a city that had acquired the nickname, "Little Medellín"; and most killings were believed to be drug-related. In May, Cardinal Juan Jesús Posadas Ocampo and several other people were gunned down at point-blank range at the Guadalajara airport during a shoot-out between rival gangs. The government maintained the cardinal's murder was a case of mistaken identity, but critical questions remained unanswered. At the time, unidentified officials had ordered the delay of a Tijuana-bound Aeromexico passenger jet, allowing eight of the gunmen to board. Even after it became apparent to investigators on the ground that some of the killers had escaped by plane, Mexican officials made no effort to halt the jet or meet it in Tijuana. Upon arrival, the gunmen simply walked away.[35]

1994

Champagne corks should have been popping in Mexico City on New Year's Day 1994, the day NAFTA was to take effect, to mark a new era for Mexico. Instead, an hour into the new year the Zapatista National Liberation Army (EZLN) assaulted and captured four cities in the Los Altos region of Mexico's southernmost state, Chiapas. For 24 hours, rebels held the city of San Cristóbal de las Casas before retreating into the mountains. Disaffected and disenfranchised, the poor agrarian economy of the south stood to gain little from the introduction of free trade with the United States. The uprising caught Salinas by surprise and shocked the Mexican public. The violence ushered in a multifaceted political crises that brought into question prospects for Mexican democracy, economic development, and continued political stability.[36]

The rebellion had been developing for several years. In the two and a half decades prior to the uprising, a variety of groups had been active in promoting peasant organizational activities. The reasons for disaffection were many. Though Chiapas was a rich land containing fertile farmlands, pastures, and forests and was a major source of the nation's coffee, its wealth was maldistributed. According to available statistics, a little more than 100 people—just 0.16% of all coffee farmers—controlled 12% of the coffee lands. Some 6,000 families held over three million hectares of cattle land, the equivalent to almost half the territory of all the state's rural landholdings. A third of the households in Chiapas at the time were without electricity, 41.6% were without drinking water, and 58.8% lacked drainage.

The government responded to events in Chiapas with uncertainty. The Salinas administration tried to downplay the situation and deflect criticism by declaring the rebellion to be the work of external forces trying to destabilize Mexico. The government blamed Central American guerrillas, the drug cartels, and even the Catholic Church. The Mexican army was criticized for its slow response to the rebellion, but it was soon evident that political leaders had disregarded warning signs of trouble in the region. In March 1993, for example, the bodies of two junior military officers had been found hacked to pieces and buried in a shallow pit outside an Indian village in the Los Altos region. The heinous nature of this crime should have served as a warning that serious problems existed.

On January 12, Salinas declared a unilateral cease-fire in the region. By that time, the Mexican army's presence had swelled from approximately 2,000 soldiers to over 14,000, more than enough to cordon off the Zapatistas' stronghold in the Lacandona jungle. By mid-January, Congress passed an amnesty decree, clearing the way for peace negotiations.[37]

On March 23, Luis Donaldo Colosio, the PRI candidate for president—Salinas' hand-picked successor—was gunned down at a campaign rally in Tijuana. Colosio had vowed during the campaign to continue Salinas' reforms and continue the *Pactos*. His assassination was thought to be a conspiracy among those in the PRI who opposed reform. Suddenly, economic reform seemed in jeopardy. Foreign confidence was severely jolted, and the inflow of foreign capital dried up and began to reverse. To protect themselves from the financial consequences of possible devaluation, Mexicans again moved their savings offshore to safe dollar accounts in Miami and elsewhere.

Banco de Mexico was suddenly faced with reserve losses. The exchange rate, which had remained resolutely glued to the top of the fluctuation band for most of the preceding period, dropped to the bottom. Some argued that the currency depreciation brought on by Colosio's assassination was a blessing in disguise. Export growth picked up. At the same time, the Federal Reserve in Washington was raising U.S. interest rates. The Fed raised interest rates six times during 1994 after having left the rate at 3.0% since September 1992. On February 4, it raised the federal funds rate 25 basis points; on March 22, another 25 points; on April 18, the Fed raised it 25 points again; on May 17, 50 points; on August 16, another 50 points, and on November 15 the Fed announced an unexpectedly large 75 basis point increase.[38]

Authorities in Mexico decided to absorb the effect of the political shock on the capital account by raising interest rates and using reserves held at the central bank to maintain the value of the peso and prevent capital outflows. To maintain the gross level of reserves the government borrowed more dollars from abroad. In doing so they assumed the exchange rate risk on capital inflows that had previously been borne by foreign—particularly American—investors. The vehicle for this borrowing was the issuance of *tesobonos*—short-term Mexican government debt instruments indexed to the dollar. The government shifted its borrowing from *cetes*, domestic currency-denominated Mexican Treasury bills, and longer-term peso debt into *tesobonos* through the summer and fall of 1994 in order to replenish the central bank's stock of dollar reserves. As a result, the maturity of the public debt was shortening, while simultaneously its currency denomination became increasingly biased toward dollars. The government was making itself vulnerable to a liquidity crisis: If the *tesobono* debt could not be rolled over—as it had to be every three months given its short maturity—the central bank would simply not have enough dollars on hand to satisfy foreign creditors and finance the still-vast current account deficit.[39]

During 1994, Mexico pursued a strategy of retiring *cetes* and other longer-term debt instruments and replacing them with *tesobonos*. In fact, during 1994, the fraction of outstanding government debt funded thorough *tesobonos* increased from about 15% to over 71%. After Colosio's murder, the administration allowed the peso to fall from 3.1 to 3.4 new pesos/dollar (the new peso was one-thousandth of the old peso), the bottom of the allowable band. International reserves were used to buy up unwanted peso-denominated obligations, and peso-denominated debts were replaced with *tesobonos*. These events helped increase peso interest rates from about 10% to 18% during March and April, falling to 14% in August. In December 1993, the *tesobono* interest rate (three-month maturity) was 5. 09% per month; it fell briefly in January and February of 1994 and then steadily climbed. The first week of January 1995 the *tesobono* interest rate was 12.49%, making the interest rate differential between it and U.S. Treasury bills 6.94%.[40]

Ernesto Zedillo Ponce de León

On August 21, 1994, the Mexican people elected Ernesto Zedillo Ponce de León to be their next president. He won slightly over 50% of the vote in what was regarded as a reasonably honest election. But his election did not restore foreign confidence, and as a result, the renewed capital inflows anticipated by policy makers did not materialize. Instead of having a stabilizing influence, the election was overshadowed by another political assassination.

In late September, PRI Secretary General José Francisco Ruiz Massieu was assassinated. Massieu was to have been leader of the PRI caucus in the Chamber of Deputies, and as such he had been expected to play a crucial role in brokering the reforms planned by Zedillo. He was also the brother of Deputy Attorney General Mario Ruiz Massieu, who had presided over several high-profile drug raids, including the arrest of members of the Tijuana-based cartel accused of having killed Cardinal Posadas. Mario Ruiz had publicly vowed to jail the country's largest drug lords, and investigators speculated that his brother's killing was intended to send the attorney general a message to "back off." But shortly afterward, Mario Ruiz resigned his position, accusing his boss, the attorney general, of obstructing the investigation into his brother's murder.[41] After Zedillo took office, he appointed Antonio Lozano, a member of the PAN party, as the new attorney general, signaling his desire to see the investigation into Ruiz Massieu's death continue.

Mexico's problems were deepening. The trade deficit was worsening as the peso became more overvalued. During the spring and summer of 1994, Carlos Salinas was preoccupied with the presidential campaign, and with foreign exchange reserves falling, he refused to admit that foreign investors' demand for Mexican assets was declining. They issued more *tesobonos* and encouraged investors who feared devaluation to keep their capital in the country.[42]

Then, just three weeks into Zedillo's term, the peso took a nose-dive, falling from 3.4 pesos to the dollar to 5.7. The flow of foreign capital into Mexico dried up; the country had reached the bottom of its reserves. Zedillo's first move was to replace his finance minister, Jaime Serra Puche, with Guillermo Ortiz, a Stanford Ph.D. known as a straight-talking "tough guy."[43]

Zedillo freed the peso, and market reaction was severe. The peso fell 50%, far more than the 20% economists deemed necessary to restore equilibrium. Each investor in Mexico feared that other investors would pull their money out no matter what the cost and that the last investors to withdraw would lose the most as a result of hyperinflation, as the Mexican government frantically printed pesos to cover its peso-denominated debts. Capital controls might trap money in Mexico indefinitely, eroding its value. And a formal default would repeat Mexico's earlier commercial bank crisis of 1982.[44]

Arbitrage buying in the early '90s had also contributed to Mexico's woes. By borrowing, for example, in New York's money market, where interest rates at the time were comparatively low, an investor could buy Mexican stocks or short-term government notes and capture the spread between returns of 5 to 6% in America and 12 to 14% in Mexico. As more investors were inspired to do this, the price of Mexican stocks soared and the *Bolsa* index doubled, tripled, even quadrupled during a span of only three years. But after the 1994 crash, investors panicked and fled overnight en masse.[45]

The devaluation lowered the price of Mexican exports, a desirable effect, but it also made imports more expensive, provoking inflation and lowering the Mexican standard of living. Interest rates shot up. Mexican companies who had borrowed dollars now faced bankruptcy. And American companies in Mexico would receive fewer dollars for their peso sales.[46] By March, a quarter of a million more Mexicans had joined the ranks of the unemployed.[47]

With US$5 billion in reserves and US$23 billion in *tesobono* liabilities and no one willing to lend hard currency, Mexico faced two painful alternatives. The government could push interest rates sky-high in a bid to keep capital in the country, causing a Great Depression; or it could lose its ability to borrow and start rapidly printing money to meet its obligations, resulting in a spiral of hyperinflation and depreciation. To make things worse, the panic had spread—the so-called Tequila Effect—raising the possibility that developing countries throughout the world would be forced into contractionary policies leading to recessions.[48]

The question facing President Zedillo at the beginning of 1995 was this: Where would Mexico go from here? Zedillo had pledged to defend democratization by distancing the government from the PRI and curbing the powers of the presidency. The state's massive assistance to the party, he said, would be ended; and the PRI's candidate-selection process would be opened up by the introduction of primary elections. In his inaugural address, Zedillo had criticized the Salinas administration for tolerating graft, lax law enforcement, and neglect of the nation's poor. He promised to fight against poverty and reform the corruption-ridden judicial system.[49] But the new president now faced the country's fourth crisis in 20 years—not only an economic one, but a crisis that was equally political and social. Would Zedillo be able to provide the strong leadership necessary to restore confidence in Mexico and rebuild its economy? Or would the cycle of crisis–reform–recovery–crisis be repeated during his *sexenio* as well?

EXHIBIT 4.1 MEXICO'S REAL GNP 1976–1994 (BILLIONS OF 1987 MEXICAN NEW PESOS)

	1976	1980	1981	1982	1983	1984	1985	1986	1987	1988	1990	1992	1993[a]	1994
Gross National Product	131.17	171.54	185.25	177.98	172.48	179.83	186.67	177.19	183.75	187.12	204.0	218.21	218.67	226.3
Exports	13.74	20.92	23.35	28.43	32.39	34.13	32.62	34.34	37.69	39.88	42.28	44.91	46.47	60.9
Imports	22.43	42.04	49.49	30.76	20.36	23.99	26.62	23.32	25.88	35.37	51.39	72.48	71.61	79.4
Private consumption	96.13	126.76	137.33	128.42	119.47	124.73	129.90	126.29	127.27	132.24	154.03	174.49	174.44	na
General Government Consumption	10.45	13.64	15.04	15.34	15.76	16.80	16.95	17.2	17.0	16.91	17.29	18.37	18.92	na
Gross Domestic Investment	36.81	58.94	67.60	51.19	37.39	39.66	43.75	34.37	37.23	41.60	48.33	59.39	57.41	na
Average Annual GNP Growth Rate (%)	4.9	7.6	8.0	-3.9	-3.1	4.3	3.8	-5.1	3.7	1.8	4.4	3.4	.02	3.5

SOURCE: World Bank, *World Tables 1995*; The Economist, *EIU Country Report Mexico 4th Qtr. 1996*.
[a] World Bank estimates.
na: Data not available.

EXHIBIT 4.2	MEXICAN BUDGET DEFICIT 1980–1992 (PERCENTAGE OF GDP)	

	Total[a]	Primary[b]
1980	–7.9	–3.2
1981	–14.8	–8.3
1982	–17.6	–7.6
1983	–9.0	+5.8
1984	–8.7	+4.8
1985	–10.0	+4.5
1986	–16.0	+2.2
1987	–15.8	+4.9
1989	–5.3	+3.7
1991	–.2	+2.2
1992	+0.2	+5.6
1993	+0.3	na
1994	–0.7	na

SOURCES: "Mexico Escaping from Debt Crisis?" HBS case #390-174, Helen Shapiro; "Mexico (A): From Stabilized Development to Debt Crisis," HBS case #797-096, Huw Pill; International Monetary Fund, *International Financial Statistics*.
[a] Public-sector borrowing requirements.
[b] The difference between receipts and expenditures, excluding public debt.
na: Data not available.

EXHIBIT 4.3	US MERCHANDISE TRADE WITH MEXICO

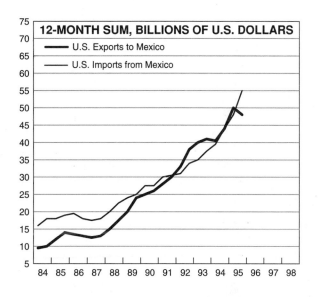

12-MONTH SUM, BILLIONS OF U.S. DOLLARS
— U.S. Exports to Mexico
— U.S. Imports from Mexico

SOURCE: Yardeni's Economic Network

EXHIBIT 4.4 MEXICO'S MONEY SUPPLY, INFLATION, REAL WAGES, EXCHANGE RATE, AND INTEREST RATES (BILLIONS OF NEW MEXICAN PESOS)

	1976	1980	1982	1984	1986	1987	1988	1990	1991	1992	1993	1994
M1 Money Supply		1.43	3.33	9.19	23.61	58.55	52.72	173.66	258.55	316.44	367.27	na
Yearly % Change		39.0	53.0	66.0	60.0	57.0	-10.0	81.0	49.0	22.0	16.0	—
Inflation	15.7	26.3	63.0	65.4	106.0	140.0	51.7	26.6	22.7	15.5	9.7	7.3
Real Wage Index[a] (1978 = 100)	100.0	96.0	100.0	72.0	69.0	68.0	69.2	79.1	82.7	85.3	na	na
Exchange Rate (old pesos/dollar)	19.95	22.95	22.95[b]	185.2	637.88	1,405.81	2,292.5	2,812.6	3,018.4	3,094.9	3,115.6	3,375.1[c]

SOURCES: World Bank, *World Tables 1995*; The Economist, *EIU Country Reports Mexico*; "Mexico: Escaping from the Debt Crisis?" HBS case #390-174, by Professor Helen Shapiro; and "Mexico 1995: The Crisis Returns," HBS case #795-126, by Professor George Cabot Lodge.

[a] After 1987, figures refer to real output per employee.

[b] In February, the peso devalued to 57.2; in August, it devalued further, to 115.

[c] In 1994, Mexico issued the neuvo peso = 1,000 old pesos. Thus, 3,375 old pesos = 3.375 new pesos.

na: Data not available.

| EXHIBIT 4.5 | INTEREST RATES, 1982–1993 |

	Mexican T-bills 90 Days	U.S. 90 Day T-Bills
1982	48.41	10.7
1984	49.47	9.6
1986	88.57	6.0
1988	69.15	6.7
1990	34.76	7.5
1991	19.28	5.4
1992	15.62	3.4
1993	14.93	3.0
1994	20.47	4.3

SOURCES: IPADE, *Sintesis Y Expectativas Economica De Mexico;* "Mexico: Escaping from the Debt Crisis?" HBS case #390-174, Helen Shapiro; "Mexico 1995: The Crisis Returns," HBS case #795-126, George C. Lodge; *Economic Report of the President,* 1997; and IMF, International Financial Statistics.

| EXHIBIT 4.6 | MEXICO'S FOREIGN INVESTMENT—1993 |

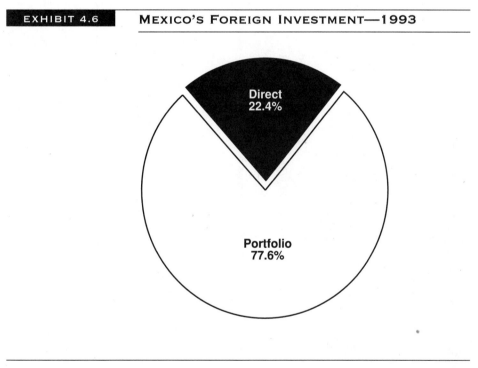

SOURCE: IMF data.

EXHIBIT 4.7A MEXICO'S CURRENT ACCOUNT, 1976–1994 (MILLIONS OF U.S. DOLLARS)

	1976	1979	1980	1981	1982	1983	1985	1987	1989	1991	1992	1993	1994 (est)
Merchandise Exports	4,980.0	11,517.0	15,512.0	23,307.0	24,055	25,953	26,757	27,600.0	35,171.0	42,688.0	46,196.0	51,886.0	60,882.0
Tourism	833	1,443	1,671	1,760	1,406	1,624	1,719	2,274	na	8,790	9,190	9,350	6,363.0
Merchandise Imports	6,564.0	12,149.0	18,897.0	27,184.0	17,011	11,848	18,359	18,812.0	28,082.0	49,967.0	62,129.0	65,366.5	79,345.0
Balance of Trade	-1,584.0	632.0	-3,385.0	-3,877.0	7,044	14,105	8,398.0	8,788.0	7,089.0	-7,279.0	-15,933.0	-13,480.5	-18,465.0
Interest on Debt[a]	na	3,737	5,437	7,573	11,059	10,163	6,450	4,927	7,915.8	6,405.2	5,971.3	5,534.1	9,107.0
Current Account[b]	-2,303.0	-2,763.0	-10,700.0	-16,507.0	-6,193	5,472	1,077.0	4,105.0	-5,930.0	-14,853.2	-24,803.6	-23,392.7	-29,663.0
Long-term net capital	5,299.0	5,198.0	10,535.0	19,183.0	16,661	7,828	861.0	2,756.0	3,723.0	20,509.0	20,586.0	30,416.4	20,254.0
Direct Investments	541.0	1,327.0	2,186.0	3,076.0	1,900	2,192	1,984.0	2,635.0	3,176.0	4,761.5	4,392.8	4,900.5	10,792.0
Loans	4,504.0	4,081.0	6,820.6	12,498.7	7,968.7	2,356	-22.3	3,778.9	-1,459.4	3,887.1	-347.5	3,055.7	3,000.0
Disbursements	6,489.4	12,139.6	11,580.7	17,002.9	12,500	7,187.7	5,049.9	7,174.0	3,973.6	8,141.1	11,896.9	15,783.8	11,500.0
Repayments	1,985.4	8,058.6	4,760.1	4,054.2	4,531.1	4,831	5,072.2	3,395.1	5,433.0	4,254.0	12,244.4	12,728.1	-8,500.0
Other Long-Term Capital	254	-210	1,528.4	3,608.3	6,792.3	3,279	-1,100.7	-3,657	2,006.4	11,860.4	16,540.7	22,460.2	4,100.0
Other net capital	-4,130.4	-1,923.0	-573.0	-1,540.0	-14,210	-12,260	-5,581.0	-2,967.0	1,825.0	2,051.2	7,112.6	-6,177.7	3,400.0
Errors & Omissions	na	703.0	-1,961.0	-8,373.0	-6,580	-1,022	-2,133.0	-2,709.0	2,775.0	-2,279.0	-1,266.0	-2,931.0	-1,200.0

SOURCE: World Bank, *World Tables 1995*; International Monetary Fund, *International Financial Statistic*; "Mexico: Escaping from the Debt Crisis?" HBS case #390-174, Helen Shapiro; IPADE.
[a]Combined public- and private-sector interest payments.
[b]After Official Transfers.
na: Data not available.

EXHIBIT 4.7B MEXICO'S SAVINGS RATE (PERCENT OF GDP)

	1987	1989	1990	1991	1992	1993 (est)
Gross National Savings	22.8	19.1	19.6	17.2	16.2	14
Gross Domestic Savings	25.3	21.2	20.7	19.3	17.7	15.9

NOTE:Gross National Savings (GNS) is a GNP-based measure and therefore includes factor payments to overseas residents. Because of Mexico's larger external debt, such factor payments were considerable. Hence the large discrepancy between GNS and the GNP-based measure, gross domestic saving.

| EXHIBIT 4.8 | MEXICAN EXTERNAL DEBT 1976–1993 (US$BN) |

	1976	1980	1982	1984	1985	1987	1989	1990	1991	1992	1993 (est)
Total external debt	23.97	57.38	86.08	94.82	96.87	109.47	93.84	106.3	115.36	113.42	118.03
Long-term debt	20.52	41.21	59.87	88.38	91.42	103.67	85.18	89.94	93.51	88.89	90.75
Short-term debt	3.45	16.16	26.21	6.44	5.45	5.8	8.66	16.08	21.86	24.53	27.28
Total Debt as % of GDP	31%	29%	50%	59%	63%	79%	46%	44%	40%	34%	34%

SOURCE: World Bank, *World Tables 1995*.

| EXHIBIT 4.9 | COMPOSITION OF TRADE, 1976–1994 |

	1976	1980	1982	1984	1986	1988	1990	1992	1994
Imports ($mns)	6,300	18,832	14,422	11,255	11,432	18,903	29,799	62,125	80,170
Intermediate Goods	498	2,012	1,099	1,696	783	1,396	17,930	42,830	56,542
Capital Goods	3,806	11,209	8,400	7,833	7,632	12,950	6,809	11,550	13,322
Consumer Goods	1,930	5,174	4,502	2,573	2,954	4,031	5,069	7,744	9,511
Exports ($mns) of which:	3,655	15,134	21,006	24,196	16,301	20,658	36,773	46,106	61,964
Agriculture	1,175	1,528	2,024	1,306	2,098	1,672	2,165	2,112	3,329
Chemical	227	390	442	756	830	1,397	3,126	4,329	2,773
Machinery[a]	203	242	229	711	1,082	1,837	13,831	20,983	24,307
Transportation	183	425	413	1,581	2,043	3,539	5,389	7,945	8,905
Oil	890	9,952	15,896	14,959	5,813	5,786	11,353	10,710	8,533
Textiles	156	201	150	119	310	510	1,217	1,962	941

SOURCE: "Mexico: Escaping from the Debt Crisis?" HBS case #390-174, Helen Shapiro; *The Economist*.
[a]Exports to major trading partners, Japan and United States.

| EXHIBIT 4.10 | MEXICO'S PETROLEUM PRODUCTION |

	1976	1979	1980	1981	1982	1984	1986	1987	1988	1990	1992	1994
Daily Oil Production (mns of barrels)	0.90	1.46	1.9	2.31	2.75	2.81	2.43	2.62	2.59	2.97	3.12	3.14
Amount for Export (mns of barrels per day)	0.20	0.78	0.82	1.06	1.34	1.47	1.30	1.35	1.31	1.28	1.43	1.36
Export price per barrel[a] (US$)	12.19	19.60	33.25	38.50	32.50	27.88	12.25	18.40	12.10	24.30	20.52	17.19

SOURCES: *BP Statistical Review of World Energy 1996; World Oil Trends 1997*, Arthur Anderson, Cambridge Energy Research Associates; "Mexico: Escaping from the Debt Crisis?" HBS case #390-174, Prof. Helen Shapiro.
[a] The average nominal price for West Texas Intermediate crude oil.

EXHIBIT 4.11	MEXICO'S EXTERNAL PUBLIC AND PRIVATE DEBT TO BANKS, 1976–1988

	External Debt ($ billions)	% Debt to U.S. Banks	% Maturity under One Year
Dec. 1976	17.9	59.78	40.78
Dec. 1977	20.3	55.17	40.89
Dec. 1978	23.3	45.49	31.33
Dec. 1979	30.9	36.89	34.63
Dec. 1980	42.5	36.94	44.24
Dec. 1981	56.9	37.79	48.68
Dec. 1982	77.1	38.23	52.27
Dec. 1983	93.8	36.99	50.50
Dec. 1984	96.4	35.98	29.22
Dec. 1985	97.0	32.51	32.46
Dec. 1986	101.7	30.44	23.09
Dec. 1987	102.3	28.83	25.24
Dec. 1988	100.4	25.44	26.78

SOURCE: "Mexico: Escaping from the Debt Crisis?" HBS case #390-174, Helen Shapiro.

EXHIBIT 4.12	COMPARATIVE SOCIAL AND ECONOMIC INDICATORS

	Mexico	Zambia	India	China	Singapore
Population (mid-1994)	88.5	9.2	914	1,191	2.9
Population growth rate					
(1980–1990)	2.0	3.5	2.1	1.5	1.7
(1990–1994)	2.0	3.0	1.8	1.2	2.0
Urban population	75	43	27	29	100
Life expectancy at birth	71	47	62	69	75
Public education (secondary enrollment)	57	16	48	54	58+
Adult literacy rate (1995)	90	78	52	81	91
GNP per capita in 1994 ($$)	4,180	350	320	530	22,500
GNP per capita (PPP, 1994)	7,040	860	1,280	2,510	21,900
Income distribution					
Lowest quintile	4.1	3.9	8.5	6.2	5.1
Second lowest quintile	7.8	8.0	12.1	10.5	9.9
Middle quintile	12.5	13.8	15.8	15.8	14.6
Second highest quintile	20.2	23.8	21.1	23.6	21.4
Highest quintile	55.3	50.4	42.6	43.9	48.9

SOURCE: World Bank, *World Development Report 1996*.

| EXHIBIT 4.13 | TARIFF LEVELS IN MEXICO, 1982–92 (PERCENT) |

Tariff Statistic	1982	1986	1992
Average tariff	27.0	22.6	13.1
Trade-weighted average	16.4	13.1	11.1
Tariff dispersion[a]	24.8	14.1	4.5

SOURCE: Taken from "Mexico (A) Reform and Crisis 1987–1994," HBS case #797-050, Professor Huw Pill.
[a] A measure of the uniformity of the tariff. A value of 1 would imply all imports face the same tariff. Greater tariff dispersion (when this statistic is higher) will be more disruptive because the domestic price system is subject to greater distortion.

| EXHIBIT 4.14 | CHRONOLOGY OF MAJOR EVENTS DURING 1994 |

1994

January 1	NAFTA takes effect. Chiapas rebels seize six towns.
February 4	U.S. Federal Reserve raises federal funds rate 25 basis points, having left the rate unchanged at 3% since September 1992.
March 22	U.S. Federal Reserve raises rates another 25 basis points.
March 23	Mexican presidential candidate Luis Donaldo Colosio is assassinated.
April 18	U.S. Federal Reserve raises rates another 25 basis points.
May 17	U.S. Federal Reserve raises rates by 50 basis points.
August 16	U.S. Federal Reserve raises rates another 50 basis points.
August 21	Victory for PRI candidate Ernesto Zedillo in the Mexican presidential elections.
September 28	Jose Francisco Ruiz Massieu, Secretary General of Mexico's ruling PRI party, is assassinated.
November 15	U.S. Federal Reserve raises rates by 75 basis points.
November 23	Mexican Deputy Attorney General resigns, alleging a cover-up of the murder of his brother, PRI Secretary General Massieu.
December 1	New Mexican government under Zedillo takes office.
December 19	Further violence in Chiapas.
December 20	Banco de Mexico announced 15% shift in the intervention limits for the *peso*, an effective devaluation of the Mexican currency.
December 22	Banco de Mexico withdraws from the foreign exchange market, allowing the *peso* to float against all other currencies.

SOURCE: Adapted from Exhibit 1 of "Mexico (A) Reform and Crisis 1987–1994," HBS case # 797-050, Prof. Huw Pill.

END NOTES

1 Trends in Developing Economies (Washington, DC: World Bank, 1996), p. 337; and George C. Lodge, "Mexico 1995: The Crisis Returns," HBS case #795-126, March 30, 1995.

2 International Monetary Fund, *International Financial Statistics*.

3 1990 Mexican Census data.

4 Donald E. Schulz, *Mexico in Crisis* (Strategic Studies Institute, U.S. Army War College, 1995).

5 World Bank, *World Bank Report*, 1987.

6 Schulz, *Mexico in Crisis*.

7 Ibid.

8 Interview with President de la Madrid conducted by Professor Helen Shapiro in January 1990.

9 Huw Pill, "Mexico (A): From Stabilized Development to Debt Crisis," HBS case #797-096, February 24, 1997.

10 Ibid.

11 World Bank, *Trends in Developing Economies*, p. 337.

12 Interview with Silva Herzog conducted and translated by Professor Helen Shapiro in January 1990.

13 Schulz, *Mexico in Crisis*.

14 Ibid.

15 Ibid.

16 Ibid.

17 Interview with Carlos Salinas conducted and translated by Professor Helen Shapiro in January 1990.

18 *EIU Country Report No. 1 1990, Mexico* (London: The Economist).

19 Ibid.

20 Pill, "Mexico (A): From Stabilized Development to Debt Crisis."

21 *EIU Country Report No. 1 1990 and No. 1 1992, Mexico* (London: The Economist).

22 Schulz, *Mexico in Crisis*.

23 Kenneth A. Froot, "The 1994–95 Mexican Peso Crisis," HBS case #296-056, October 2, 1996; and *EIU Country Report No. 1 1993, Mexico* (London: The Economist).

24 Huw Pill, "Mexico (C): Reform and Crisis 1987–1994," HBS case #797-050, draft, January 28, 1997.

25 Ibid.

26 Schulz, *Mexico in Crisis*.

27 William Greider, *One World Ready or Not: The Manic Logic of Global Capitalism* (New York: Simon & Schuster, 1997), pp. 259–260.

29 Pill, "Mexico (A): From Stabilized Development to Debt Crisis."

29 Moisés Naím, "Mexico's Larger Story," in *Foreign Policy* (Summer 1995).

30 Schulz, *Mexico in Crisis*

31 The Economist, *EIU Country Report No. 1 1993, Mexico*.

32 Pill, "Mexico (A): From Stabilized Development to Debt Crisis."

33 Ibid.

34 Douglas P. Handler, "The Mexican Economy in Perspective," published on the Internet by AC Nielsen Company, Inc., March 1995.

35 Schulz, *Mexico in Crisis*.

36 Donald E. Schulz and Stephen J. Wager, *The Awakening: The Zapatista Revolt and Its Implications for Civil–Military Relations and the Future of Mexico* (Strategic Studies Institute, December 1994); Pill, "Mexico (A): Reform and Crisis 1987–1994."

37 Schultz and Wager, *The Awakening*.

38 Froot, "The 1994–95 Mexican Peso Crisis."

39 Pill, "Mexico (A): From Stabilized Development to Debt Crisis."

40 Froot, "The 1994–95 Mexican Peso Crisis."

41 Schulz, *Mexico in Crisis*.

42 Bradford De Long, Christopher De Long, and Sherman Robinson, "The Case for Mexico's Rescue," *Foreign Affairs* (May/June 1996).

43 Lodge, "Mexico 1995: The Crisis Returns."

44 De Long, et al., "The Case for Mexico's Rescue."

45 Greider, *One World Ready or Not*, p. 261.

46 Lodge, "Mexico 1995: The Crisis Returns."

47 Naím, "Mexico's Larger Story."

48 De Long, et al. "The Case for Mexico's Rescue."

49 Schulz, *Mexico in Crisis*.

Transition from an Isolated Economy

The end of apartheid by peaceful revolution (between 1989 and 1994) is the turning point in this case. Out of a history of slavery, discrimination, and then brutal apartheid ("apartness"), South Africa finally emerged as a free and democratic state with a black-majority-ruled government. At issue is how this government can turn around the decades of damage while simultaneously making South Africa competitive in an open-world economy.

The case describes South African economic performance during the 1990s, as well as the difficult social problems (e.g., unemployment, crime, AIDS) it now faces. Students are expected to evaluate this situation and then consider the new strategy adopted by the African National Congress government in 1996. The GEAR (Growth, Employment, and Redistribution) strategy, with its ambitious goals, is a political compromise. Is it feasible? Will it work?

If not GEAR, then what? The case again provides opportunities to discuss other possible strategies for development—fiscal and monetary choices, industrial policies, trade policies, and others. But one must evaluate them in terms not only of political feasibility, but in the context of an already globalized world economy.

Last, the case allows consideration of the factors that affect foreign direct investment issues such as political stability, economic feasibility, growth, and profitability. Is the African Renaissance now on a firm footing? Is this the right time to invest in South Africa?

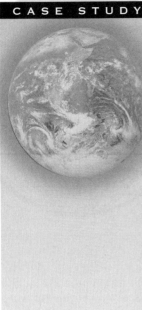

SOUTH AFRICA: GETTING IN GEAR

Don't ask the turkeys to vote for Christmas.
—**Christopher Stals,** Governor South African Reserve Bank

It was a cool midwinter evening in Johannesburg as Thabo Mbeki thumbed through the Reserve Bank's *Quarterly Bulletin* for June 1997.[1] The First Deputy President of the Government of National Unity, and likely successor to Nelson Mandela in 1999, wanted to see for himself the latest results of GEAR—the macroeconomic strategy for growth, employment, and redistribution that his government had adopted just one year earlier. Mbeki, with a masters degree in economics from Sussex University, searched the report for signs of good news. Although immensely pleased that South Africa seemed to be politically stable and recovering from Apartheid, he was looking for evidence of job creation, private investment, and disinflation. He wondered if Chris Stals was likely to lower interest rates soon to give the South African economy a needed boost.

GEAR was the political and economic culmination of a series of studies and plans proposed since 1990—the beginning of the end of Apartheid. First came the Change of Gears Scenario, proposed by an international team of analysts financed by Nedbank/Old Mutual.[2] Then there were Anglo–American's "High Road–Low Road" scenarios, the Platform for Investment in 1992, the African National Congress' (ANC) Reconstruction and Development Program in 1994, and Growth for All, from the business community in 1995.[3] GEAR, released in June 1996, was produced by a technical team supervised by Trevor Manuel, the new minister of finance.

The GEAR strategy was designed to deliver real GDP growth of 6% by the year 2000, with job creation of 400,000 per annum. This was more than double the present growth trajectory but was necessary to cut into structural unemployment, which had already surpassed 37%.[4] In the wake of Apartheid, the massive unemployment primarily of black South Africans underlay a wave of crime and violence that had reached epidemic proportions. Investment and savings, meanwhile, had dropped to record lows. Education, housing, and infrastructure desperately needed attention, while AIDS appeared to be spreading rapidly. With GEAR, the ANC acknowledged the limitations of government and recognized that the market would have to play a major role in rebuilding the economy. But first, to curb inflation, the government would have to curb fiscal deficits and credit growth. Although the Reserve Bank's effort appeared to be working, it left too few funds for needed programs and had pushed real short-term interest rates to 12%.

As he looked over the figures, Mbeki wondered if macroeconomic growth would be rapid enough to ease South Africa's severe social problems and sustain the extraordinary political stability that currently prevailed. Perhaps, he thought, more was needed than macroeconomic reform—possibly a more aggressive microeconomic strategy, to reposition South Africa in the increasingly competitive global economy.

Conquest by Europeans

In total area, South Africa is nearly as large as western Europe minus Spain and is home to about 44 million people.[5] It is divided into two main regions: a relatively arid inland plateau, fringed by coastal plains on three sides. An escarpment, dominated by the

---

Professor Richard H. K. Vietor prepared this case as the basis for class discussion rather than to illustrate either effective or ineffective handling of an administrative situation.

Drakensberg Mountains, separates the two. Climatically, it is divided into a winter-rainfall area in the southwest and one of summer rainfall in the east. [See map, **Exhibit 5.1**.] The zones were sufficiently different that relatively little interaction occurred between the pastoral people of the west (KhoiSan) and the iron-age cultivators (Bantu tribes) who occupied the east (Transvaal, Natal, Highveld) in the centuries prior to 1000 AD.[6] There are relatively few rivers or lakes in South Africa, but the coastline stretches 2,900 kilometers. South Africa shares borders with Namibia, Botswana, Zimbabwe, Swaziland, and Mozambique and completely surrounds Lesotho.

European settlers, representing the Dutch East India Company, established a fort and refueling station at Table Bay (Cape Town) in 1652. For the remainder of the century, immigrants gradually encroached on the grazing lands of Khoikhoi herders. Slave labor was imported from elsewhere in Africa, Malaya, and India. As colonial farmers penetrated northward, conflict between the Dutch and the Khoikhoi became endemic.[7] By the mid-18th century, colonial settlers had begun extending control over indigenous laborers, enforcing travel passes for the "bastard hottentots" and indenturing women and children. The Europeans' dialect, a simplified form of Dutch, evolved into the Afrikaans language. By 1795, the Xhosa tribes in the east came increasingly into conflict with colonists to the south and with competing African tribes.[8] In the early 1800s, a series of intertribal wars broke out, in which the Zulus, headed by Shaka, dominated for almost a decade.

Meanwhile, the British had captured Cape Town from the Dutch and had established a crown colony in 1806. Two years later, the slave trade was curtailed, and before long, antislavery sentiment in Great Britain put increasing pressure on South African slave owners. In 1828, Parliament outlawed slave ownership. Two days later, the governor of the Cape Colony then promulgated Ordinance 50—making "hottentots and other free people of colour" equal before the law with whites. The law, which was opposed by British settlers and Afrikaners, did not curtail discrimination, eliminate poverty, or usurp entrenched domination by whites.

Afrikaners who could not tolerate British domination picked up stakes and migrated northeast, to find new lands in territories they named Natal, the Orange Free State, and the Transvaal. The Great Trek, between 1836 and 1854, brought Afrikaners in conflict with the Zulus, where western rifles invariably prevailed. Over the next 30 years, European expansion into the northeast was marked by near-constant warfare with Zulu and other African tribes and the repeated reassertion of British colonial authority over new Afrikaner states.

As early as the 1860s, distinctions among four racial/ethnocultural groups were emerging in the Cape Colony. Census data in 1865 reported 180,000 Europeans (British and Afrikaners), 200,000 Hottentots and others collectively called "coloured," 100,000 Kaffirs—the black Africans who dominated eastern populations—and a few thousand Asians.[9]

In 1867, alluvial diamonds were found at the confluence of the Vaal and Harts rivers. Several years later, diamond-bearing formations were discovered, extending deep below the surface of what became Kimberly—the diamond city. As mining moved underground, masses of people were required to do manual labor. Skilled operatives, mostly white Europeans, commanded high wages, while manual labors, mostly black Africans, were paid far less. After a few chaotic years, the British high commissioner issued rules that *de facto* exclude black persons from owning mines. Gradually, a two-tiered, racially segregated workforce and migratory social system emerged. By 1887, a British immigrant named Cecil Rhodes had acquired control of the Kimberly mines, renamed De Beers Consolidated Mines.[10] About the same time, gold was discovered 30 miles from Pretoria—at what is today Johannesburg. Together, these discoveries, which inspired an immense immigration, changed the face of South Africa. Eventually, platinum, chrome, and other rare ores were discovered, making South Africa the world's leading producer of rare minerals [**Exhibit 5.2**].

The mining boom in the Transvaal led to a rapid expansion of British immigration and growing friction with the established Afrikaner population. The quasi-autonomous Transvaal Republic was managed by an elective Volksraad and a president named Paul Kruger. Kruger's efforts during the 1890s to expand Transvaal were thwarted by Cecil Rhodes, then governor of the Cape Colony. An attempted insurrection by British settlers led to a clampdown by Kruger, the importation of arms, and a tighter alliance with the Orange Free State. When negotiations failed, the Boer War ensued—lasting three years, from 1899 to 1902. The British engaged in a scorched earth policy, leaving thousands of Afrikaner women and children to die in concentration camps.

British victory and the Peace of Vereeniging led to the establishment of British colonial rule. South Africa would be, in the words of Lord High Commissioner Alfred Milner, "a self-governing white community, supported by well-treated and justly governed black labour from Cape Town to Zambesi."[11] Black Africans were disenfranchised, "pass laws" restricting travel were tightened, and labor conditions were enforced by the military. Colonial elections, held in 1907, resulted in Afrikaner victories for Louis Botha and Jan Smuts. Within two more years a constitution was drafted, and in 1909, the British Parliament passed the South Africa Act. On May 31, 1910, the Union of South Africa became a self-governing dominion of the British Empire.

Segregation and Apartheid

The era of formal segregation—1910 to 1948—was a period dominated by racist assumptions in Africa, much of Asia, and America. In South Africa, where whites dominated the capitalist economy, race and class coincided; blacks were poor, unskilled, and uneducated and were generally subordinated to whites. Even in industrial relations, race mattered. White mine workers earned 11 to 15 times as much as black mine workers. And as the material gap between whites and other ethnic groups narrowed, it widened between whites and blacks. In the 1990s, the top 10% of South Africa's population earned 67 times that of the bottom 20%.[12]

In the decades after 1948, the United Party, lead by Botha and Smuts, ruled an increasingly racist state. In 1911, the Mines and Works Act granted white workers a monopoly on skilled positions. In 1913, the Natives Land Act prohibited Africans from purchasing land outside the reserves. Subsequent legislation set aside 12% of South Africa's lands as native reserves—areas that would eventually become the "homelands." As urbanization accelerated, the government tried to limit the flow of Africans into cities with complex pass laws. Permits were required to leave the farm where one lived or the town where one worked. A 1922 law authorized urban governments to establish and enforce locations for black residence.

Black South Africans resisted but gradually adapted. They formed various political organizations; the most important turned out to be the African National Congress, established in 1912. The ANC, headed by lawyers, clergy, and journalists, elicited white support and used constitutional means to oppose racism. More radical organizations, such as the Industrial and Commercial Workers Union, were ruthlessly suppressed.[13] During World War II, a group of young ANC activists developed a platform against segregation—*Africans' Claims in South Africa*. Among these activists were young professionals from the best missionary schools and colleges, including Oliver Tambo, Walter Sisulu, and Nelson Mandela.

But World War II deepened Afrikaners' worries about race relations because of the massive influx of black Africans into the cities. Literary and political debate ensued over the need for complete separation of races. A 1946 government report was torn between the appeal of complete segregation and the labor needs of the industrial economy. The word *Apartheid* was coined by Afrikaner intellectuals to mean "apartness." When the National Party won the election of 1948, the prime minister appointed Hendrik Verwoerd to the Senate and then to Minister of Native Affairs. Over the next sixteen years, the last eight of which Verwoerd was prime minister, Apartheid was implemented in its most brutal form.

Four ideas, according to historian Leonard Thompson, were at the heart of Apartheid:

> First, the population of South Africa comprised four "racial groups"—White, Coloured, Indian, and African—each with its own inherent culture. Second, Whites, as the civilized race, were entitled to have absolute control over the state. Third, white interests should prevail over black interests; the state was not obliged to provide equal facilities for the subordinate races. Fourth, the white racial group formed a single nation with Afrikaans and the English-speaking components, while Africans belonged to several (eventually ten) [geographically] distinct nations or potential nations—a formula that made the white nation the largest in the country.[14]

These ideas were shortly written into law: the Prohibition of Mixed Marriages Act, the Immorality Act, and the Population Registration Act. Pass laws were strengthened, and Africans were removed from farms to homelands and from urban neighborhoods to satellite townships. Under the Group Areas Act (1950), government divided cities into zones where members of only one race could live. An estimated 3 million people were forcibly resettled from farms, "black spots," and strategic development areas to the new townships. These were fenced and guarded. Working papers were needed for residents to come and go. The government took charge and severely constrained the education of black Africans. "If the native in South Africa today, " testified Dr. Verwoerd in 1953, "is being taught to expect that he will live his adult life under a policy of equal rights, he is making a big mistake."[15] "Whites Only" notices appeared everywhere—taxis, buses, elevators, hearses, church halls, restaurants, cinemas, schools, and universities.

Repressive legislation kept coming: the Riotous Assemblies Act (1956), the Unlawful Organizations Act (1960), the Sabotage Act (1962), the Bantu Laws Amendment Act (1964), the General Law Amendment Act (1966), the Internal Security Act (1976), and so on. To enforce Apartheid, the bureaucracy was expanded, and a large Security Force operated with increasing impunity. By 1969, even white South Africans bluntly acknowledged the implications of Apartheid. As C. M. Botha, the Minister of Bantu Administration, put it in Parliamentary debate,

For whites and for each Bantu Nation separate development is the course. Bantu persons can be present in the white areas solely for their labour—not for a stake or a share in the Parliament, or for anything else. . . . The Bantu cannot strive towards the top on an equal footing with the whites in our politics, social matters, labour, economy and education in white South Africa. This is our territory, and here there are only limited opportunities of that nature for them. . . . In their homelands there are measureless and limitless opportunities for them. . . . That is the morality of our policy.[16]

Under the combined weight of poverty, repression, and forced resettlement, black community structure broke down. In Soweto, with a population over four million by today, eight to twenty people lived in typical four-room houses; many lived in two-room shacks, thrown together with cardboard, scrap lumber, and corrugated metal, that had sprung up after influx control laws collapsed in the mid-1980s. In Crossroads, outside of Cape Town, a single water tap was shared by 25,000 people. Uneducated children stole to survive and eventually acquired arms.

Opposition to Apartheid swelled. The laws of the early 1950s were actively protested by the African National Congress. Marches and meetings were repeatedly broken up by police, with thousands of volunteers arrested and jailed. In 1955, a huge meeting was organized in Kliptown, a village near Johannesburg. Three thousand delegates assembled as the Congress of the People, adopting the following charter:

> We the People of South Africa declare for our country and the world to
> know that South Africa belongs to all who live in it, black and white, and
> that no government can justly claim authority unless it is based on the will
> of all the people.[17]

As violence escalated, nonviolent protest became increasing difficult to sustain. In 1960, when 5,000 people demonstrated peacefully against pass laws in Sharpeville the police opened fire and killed 69, half of whom were women and children. This tragedy finally pushed the ANC leadership towards violence. Nelson Mandela organized Umkonto we Sizwe as a militant wing, with the following manifesto: "The time comes in the life of any nation when there remain only two choices—submit or fight. That time has come to South Africa."[18]

In 1963, the government arrested leaders of Umkonto we Sizwe. Among them, Nelson Mandela and Walter Sisulu received life sentences on Robben Island. A few years later, a twenty-two-year-old student named Steve Biko formed the South African Students Organization and began developing the ideology of Black Consciousness. In 1976, when black schoolchildren demonstrated in Soweto, a police crackdown eventually led to the killing of 575 people. Dozens of black South Africans died in detention of the Security Force. Steve Biko was among those arrested, beaten, and killed in August 1977.[19]

Later that year, the UN Security Council imposed an arms embargo on South Africa, and vice-president Walter Mondale told Prime Minister Vorster that America supported majority rule. During the next several years, South Africa's foreign relations deteriorated sharply, as more and more foreign powers denounced Apartheid. The government, meanwhile, imported oil and invested heavily in the economy to duplicate imported sources of capital goods. In 1985, Chase Manhattan Bank precipitated a financial crisis by refusing to roll over its loans to South Africa. In the wake of intensive citizen action, and over President Reagan's veto, the U.S. Congress passed the Comprehensive Anti-Apartheid Act, imposing a wide-ranging boycott on commerce with South Africa.

GDP growth had long since begun to slow, from a high of 6.5% in the mid-1960s to zero by 1986. Total factor productivity, which had slowed during the 1960s, became negative in the 1970s. It did not help that the real exchange rate actually rose in the 1970s when the price of gold rose to $800 per ounce. Income per capital peaked in 1981, long before sanctions were applied. Appreciation of the Rand made South African manufactured exports less competitive, causing a decline of investment, turning the current account negative, and undermining job creation.[20]

As the domestic situation deteriorated, the government began searching for reform. Some of the worst segregation laws were amended, and a series of dialogues commenced between ANC members in exile, church leaders, government officials, and business leaders. The economy, meanwhile, plunged into a deep recession, putting even greater pressure on the government. In 1989, when Prime Minister Botha resigned after a stroke, the National Party elected F. W. de Klerk in his place. De Klerk, nearly 20 years younger than Botha, realized that a negotiated settlement was the only feasible solution. On February 2, 1990, he lifted the bans on the ANC and the Pan African Congress, removed restrictions on thirty-three other organizations, suspended capital punishment, and freed political prisoners. Nine days later, after 27 years in prison, Nelson Mandela was released to a tumultuous public welcome.

Later that year, the basic Apartheid laws were repealed. Two more years of talks led to an interim constitution endorsed by de Klerk, Mandela, and 18 political parties. In April 1994, South African citizens went to the polls in a surprisingly free and peaceful election and gave the ANC 63 percent of the vote. Nelson Mandela was inaugurated president on May 10, 1994.

The New South Africa

The constitution, approved in December 1996, established a federal system of government: a two-house national parliament and nine provinces—each with a premier, regional legislature, and significant local authority. The parliament consisted of a 400-seat National Assembly, with direct elections and universal suffrage, and a 90-seat Senate appointed proportionally by elected parties. President (Nelson Mandela) and Deputy President (T. M. Mbeki) represented the dominant party—the African National Congress (with 252 seats) ; the National Party (with 82 seats) was also represented by a Deputy President (F. W. de Klerk), until he resigned in 1996. The Zulu-dominated Inkatha Freedom Party (with 43 seats) was lead by M. G. Buthelezi, who occupied the Ministry of Home Affairs. A cabinet of 27 ministers ran the executive branch. The president appointed a supreme court to head a three-tiered court system. Other distinctive features included a Bill of Rights, a council of traditional leaders, recognition of eleven official languages, and such specialized institutions as a public protector and a commission on human rights.

Gauteng was the smallest of the nine new states, but it had the largest, most urban population (in Johannesburg, Soweto, and Pretoria), the largest share of disposable income, and the highest population growth. The Western Cape, with the second largest city of Cape Town, also had a large share of disposable income, relatively low poverty, and a concentration of business. KwaZulu-Natal, where the city of Durban was located, was the third largest province by population and disposable income.

Because of the government's relatively high investment during the 1970s, South Africa's infrastructure, primarily serving the white population, was unusually well developed. Eskom, the state electric company, provided nearly 40,000 megawatts of power, at a mere 2.3 U.S. cents (compared with 7 cents, for example, in the United States) per kilowatt-hour. Twenty-one thousand kilometers of railroads, 58,000 km of highways, five million telephone connections, modern radio and television broadcasters, port facilities, and air transportation all made South Africa seem much like a European country. SASOL, the state petrochemical company, provided 45% of the nation's liquid fuel from coal, using unique liquefaction technology. A system of state-owned industrial and medical laboratories yielded a first-world health care system (for whites) and a weapons industry that was globally competitive.

South Africa's private business sector was modern but relatively labor intensive and high cost compared with global competitors. The mining industry accounted for about 9% of South Africa's GDP, nearly 50% of foreign exchange earnings, and provided 600,000 jobs. Half a dozen ores led world production, with a host of others providing export revenues and most domestic needs. Agriculture (and forestry) was another successful sector, producing about 5% of GDP. South Africa was one of only six countries that was regularly a net food exporter. In addition to grains, meats, and most vegetables it needed, South Africa also exported citrus fruits and fine wines. The timber industry provided 90% of South Africa's pulp and paper needs.

A third of South Africa's manufacturing sector was in metals refining and manufacturing. Ferroalloys and aluminum were exported, as were heavy fabrications. Electrical engineering and electronics were also successful sectors. Manufacturing contributed 24% of GDP and employed about 1.5 million. The finance sector—banks, insurance, brokerage firms, and building societies—were quite modern, although somewhat high cost. The Johannesburg Stock Exchange was the twelfth largest in the world, with market capitalization of $224 billion.[21]

Because of the years of inward-looking protectionism, South Africa's business structure was highly concentrated. Corporate acquisitions during Apartheid (by firms using their protected cash flows) resulted in a number of interlocking conglomerates, dominated by a few financial institutions. Old Mutual, Sanlam, SBIC, and ABSA each controlled more than R100 billion in assets; FNB, Anglo American,

Liberty Life, Nedcor, and Investec followed more than 50 billion. Eskom, the state electric utility, was tenth. Two dozen other financial companies, including three new black-owned conglomerates, and industrials, food companies, and mining houses followed—70 firms each with more than R4 billion in assets. There were also many large multinational firms—headed by Royal Dutch Shell, Daimler-Benz, Siemens, and Volkswagen—active in South Africa, although foreign investment still had not recovered from the trough of the Apartheid era [**Exhibit 5.3**].[22]

"Unbundling" and "black empowerment" were structural phenomena that had proceeded hand in hand since 1994. Unbundling referred to restructuring of business ownership by the selling off of diverse operating units owned by the large conglomerates. To ameliorate racial criticism, black empowerment encouraged the rise of black managers to senior executive positions, mostly in public-sector firms, and more specifically, the emergence of black-owned or black-controlled conglomerates. Through the use of pension funds from black unions and leveraged buyouts, a series of increasingly large mergers had resulted in 18 black-controlled firms listed on the Johannesburg Stock Exchange[23] [**Exhibit 5.4**]. Led by spin-offs from Anglo American of Johnic and JCI, more and more black-owned conglomerates had catapulted into the financial limelight. Metlife, New Africa Investment Ltd. (NAIL), and a dozen other firms controlled about R35 billion in assets.[24] A new black business leadership, headed by Cyril Ramaphosa, Dikgang Moseneke, and others was emerging. While they still had much to learn, their holding companies were at least performing satisfactorily.[25]

South Africa had a well-developed system of labor organizations. In 1996, there were some 200 unions, representing about 3.5 million workers. These were organized into several federations, the largest of which was the Congress of South African Trade Unions (COSATU, with 1.6 million members)—an ally of the ANC. Coming out of the 1994 election, organized labor negotiated with business and government in a trilateral forum—the National Economic Development and Labour Council (Nedlac). In the Labour Relations Act of 1995, the parliament promoted collective bargaining without compelling it. The Act created bargaining councils for wages, workplace forums for plant-level issues, and a Commission for Conciliation, Mediation, and Arbitration. In this format, large conglomerates of cartelized firms would settle on relatively generous terms, leaving small firms unable to make such concessions and thus be unable to compete.[26]

In 1997, problems were deepening between COSATU, the business community, and the ANC government. A Basic Conditions of Employment Act was pending, which would reduce weekly hours worked (from 46 to 45), increase overtime pay, and provide paid maternity leave of up to four months. Two other amendments were pending that would provide a payroll tax to ensure training and an affirmative action scheme. Although both laws obviously had good motives, they would entail complex regulation and greater cost—something that the business community did not need as it struggled to become competitive.[27] COSATU, moreover, had withdrawn its support of the GEAR and was beginning to agitate for more government spending to reduce unemployment.

Social Challenges

In the wake of the post-Apartheid boom, South Africa faced severe social challenges. Among the most pressing of these were crime, education, unemployment, infrastructural expansion (housing, electrification, and water), internal migration, immigration (and emigration), and AIDS. Racial issues bound most of these problems together.

Crime

Crime in South Africa had become endemic. As recently as the 1970s, South Africa had been a fairly low-crime society. But family and community life became increasingly fragmented as an immense number of black South Africans migrated from the countryside to the cities. Unemployment, poverty, and their new urban environment broke down the values that had governed personal and family relationships. This situation was exacerbated by years of civilian resistance to authoritarian government in the wake of the Soweto uprising. It became increasingly acceptable for armed teenage dropouts to attack the systems that had oppressed them. Violence and theft escalated as the government liberalized the Group Areas Act after 1986. Criminal syndicates eventually developed to organize the drug trade, auto theft, and truck hijacking.

The most serious problems were murder, rape, motor vehicle theft, and robbery. Rapes had doubled in the past six years, and murder was up 51 percent. In 1996, 26,000 people were murdered in South Africa. This was more than eight times the rate in the United States, which itself was the highest of the developed countries. More than 96,000 motor vehicles were stolen (three times the rate, per thousand vehicles, of the United States) and 13,000 hijacked (the driver was present); 3,700 trucks were hijacked.[28] Even political violence, while down from 1994, remained high—with 1,000 deaths and 1,600 injuries in a year.[29] A total of more than two million serious crimes was reported in 1996—about one for every 21 citizens.

Fear of crime had become palpable in some areas, such as Johannesburg, to the point at which people had changed the ways in which they behaved. Homes were surrounded by high walls, with barbed wire fencing and elaborate alarm systems. People thought twice about going out in the evening, about where they parked, and about what belongings they carried. Security services proliferated. Law enforcement, meanwhile, was underfunded, understaffed, and corrupt. The South African Police Service had fewer than half as many officers per capita than did the United States, and they tended to be poorly trained. Some 45,000 did not have drivers licenses; and as many as 30,000 were functionally illiterate. Even worse, the judicial system had broken down. Courts were underfunded; prisons were full. Of 1,000 crimes committed, 450 were reported to the police, 230 solved, 100 prosecuted, 77 convicted, 36 imprisoned, and one rehabilitated.[30]

Education

The start of the school year in 1996 marked history in South Africa. For the first time in 50 years, discrimination in public schools was ended. A single national education department was now responsible for compulsory education for children age seven to 15. The inequitable expenditures (e.g., R5,403 for whites, R2,184 for blacks per capita) would be rectified. But the task was sizable. An estimated 37% of the adult population was illiterate; approximately five million people over four years old had no education. To meet the needs of 12 million children, expenditures needed to be increased dramatically and redirected. Two thousand new schools, 65,000 new classrooms, and 50 million books would be needed. An average student-to-teacher ratio of 37:1 prevailed in primary schools. This ratio ranged as high as 60 or 70:1 in some areas.

Teacher training was also essential. About 40% of African teachers were unqualified or underqualified. Many of these teachers needed more basic education, as well as teacher training. State teaching colleges were fully enrolled but underfunded—despite the fact that 20% of the federal budget was being devoted to education.[31] Tertiary education in South Africa was much better but suffered from the same imbalances of racial discrimination that plagued primary schools. Some 350,000 students were enrolled at South Africa's 21 universities, but the pass rate for black students was far below that of whites. Other issues that had recently arisen included the conversion to more Afro-centric university life and the nonpayment of bills.[32]

Labor

South Africa's labor market was severely distorted. Years of segregation and Apartheid had rationed access to education, skills, jobs, housing, and health care according to skin color. To make matters worse, the state implemented various policies that directly undermined the opportunities for much of the population to earn income. As the South Africa Foundation noted, "Forced removals, Group Areas, the Land Act and assaults on the urban informal sector dispossessed millions of people of valuable assets and skills, and undermined the capacity of the economy to provide employment in rural areas. . . . The legacy of past labour and welfare inequalities is still powerful, and bedevils the efficient functioning of the labour market today."[33]

In the spring of 1997, the formal unemployment rate was 37.8%; the informal rate was estimated as high as 45%. The World Bank estimated that South African males aged 15–64 had one of the lowest labor force participation rates in the world.[34] The effects of this labor market on new entrants was devastating; only one in thirty new entrants could find a job in the formal economy. Thus, between 1980 and 1994, 97% of new workers—4.4 million—could find no work! Unemployment was worst among the unskilled [**Exhibit 5.5**]. The economy seemed to have no capacity to create jobs. Recent figures suggested that as companies consolidated and modernized, they had actually cut employment by 71,000 in 1996.

A related problem was the efficacy of the labor market. Unskilled unionized workers were paid 20% to 40% more than non-unionized workers—an exceedingly high gap by world standards. And the formal–informal gap was probably the highest anywhere. One study, for example, showed semiskilled unionized workers making R1,400 per month versus R650 in the informal sector.[35]

Long-term youth unemployment was awful. "About 2.3 million people in their teens and twenties, who have entered the labor market, have no gainful employment ... most have been unemployed for more than four years."[36] And if something did not change soon, another 200,000–300,000 would be unemployed in each of the next few years. A final problem aggravated by unemployment was income inequality. It was among the most severe in the world [**Exhibit 5.6**].

The high level of unemployment was a cumulative result of a macroeconomy that had not worked properly for many years. This was the problem that worried Chris Stals, Governor of the Reserve Bank, more than any other. He did not see any way for the economy to create the 400,000 jobs annually that were necessary to keep the unemployment rate from rising still further.[37] Most of South Africa's business and political leaders agreed. Land reform and government expenditures could provide some jobs, but if budget deficits were to be reduced, economic growth and a low-wage flexible labor market would have to do most of the work. The business community supported a two-tier labor market—one tier for organized workers maintaining their benefits and rules, and a second tier with minimal regulation to encourage "outsiders" to enter the labor-intensive formal sector.[38]

Infrastructure

The inequitable provision of infrastructure had caused additional problems. Too many homes still lacked electricity and plumbing—indeed, there were far too few homes. The latest statistics showed about 73% of urban households, and just 15% of rural households, had electricity. Among black South Africans, the numbers were worse. Eskom, the national electric company, had undertaken a program of making 1.5 million new connections in five years; this helped but was still not enough [**Exhibit 5.7**].[39]

Perhaps even more fundamental were water and sewage services. In 1994, 54% of African homes in urban areas had running water; only 8% in rural areas. Others had water on their site, or near their site, used tanks, wells, or public kiosks. The government had engaged in 12 huge water projects since 1994, but even when those were completed in 1998, many people would still not be served.[40] In urban areas, only 85% of the population (72% of Africans) had flush toilets. In rural areas, it was less than 12%. Chemical lavatories, latrines, and buckets were still widely used—even in cities.

Housing

Lack of adequate housing was another element of South Africa's infrastructural problem. With an estimated 8.3 million households in South Africa, the formal housing stock was about 3.4 million units. About 1.5 million urban households lived in "informal" housing units—service sites designated for water or electric service, where shacks had been constructed. There were also more than one million families living in squatters shacks and another 5% of households in hostels. In rural areas, another 17 million people lived in a mix of formal and informal structures. The backlog of housing needed was at least 1.5 million units, and this was increasing (due to immigration and population growth) by about 180,000 units annually.

> "Housing the nation," read the preamble of a 1995 White Paper on Housing, is one of the greatest challenges facing the Government of National Unity. The extent of challenge derives not only from the enormous size of the housing backlog and the desperation and impatience of the homeless, but stems also from the extremely complicated bureaucratic, administrative, financial and institutional framework inherited from the previous government.[41]

Although the 1994 Reconstruction and Development Programme targeted construction of one million homes in five years, the budget set aside R2.9 billion in the 1995/96 budget to support housing—an increase of 80% over the previous year. Households with incomes of R3,500 or less were eligible for state housing subsidies. Yet, by the end of 1995, just 6% of the 50,000 loans targeted had been granted; just 10,000 homes were built. Only about 35,000 were built in 1996, leaving a backlog of funds available of several billion Rand.

There were many housing-related problems. The cost of a cheap, four-room home, with sewage and electricity, was about R65,000 to R70,000. Several big banks had agreed to provide fixed-rate mortgages for up to 80% of the value of the house, at about 22% interest. A severe problem, however, was that many would-be borrowers did not understand either the concept of a mortgage or the difference between the bank and the government. Thus, by early 1996, the Mortgage Indemnity Fund (set up by the government) reported that banks had repossessed 70,000 properties due to nonperforming loans. In some of the townships, formal boycotts of mortgage payments had been organized by borrowers who did not have jobs.[42]

In the 1997/98 budget, R4 billion was allocated to housing—a 156% increase plus the roll-over of the unused R1.7 billion. The federal government had allocated Provincial Task Teams to implement and streamline construction and housing delivery. For 1997/98, 192,000 new homes were planned.[43]

Immigration and Emigration

Official immigration to South Africa in the most recent year was about 6,400 people: 43% from Europe, 25% from Asia, and 25% from Africa. Emigration, which amounted to more than 10,000, went mostly to Australia, Canada, and Europe. A rising concern in South Africa was that a growing number of professionals—doctors, managers, engineers—were leaving, amounting to something of a brain drain.

But informal, or illegal, immigration was far greater. The coordinator of border control for the South African Police offered an estimate (in 1995) of nearly five million, costing taxpayers as much as R5 billion, annually. Deputy President Mbeki still estimated the number of illegal immigrants in the country as two to three million.[44] The vast majority came from sub-Saharan Africa—Zimbabwe, Mozambique, Angola, and Botswana. Typically, males came to the townships around Johannesburg to find work, living with relatives or townsfolk already there. Eventually, their wives and children, and perhaps siblings and parents, would join them—severely aggravating the housing and services capacity of the township.

AIDS

These massive movements of people only aggravated South Africa's exposure to AIDS. Just a few years ago, South Africa was relatively free of AIDS. But in the past three years, surveys conducted on women attending antenatal clinics revealed an epidemic of HIV infection. By October 1995, an estimated 1.8 million people, 90% of whom were African, were infected. The demographics reflected the heterosexual character of the epidemic in Africa. The highest rate of infection was in females in their teens or early 20s. Figures showed a doubling rate of 15 months, which explained the estimate of 2.5 million HIV-positive cases by spring 1997. The official government estimate recently put the level of HIV infection at five to six million by 2005—17% to 24% of the sexually active population. Although the government was expanding educational programs as quickly as possible, lack of funds, extreme poverty, congestion in the townships, and cultural prejudices of African men all interfered with progress.[45]

Growth, Employment, and Redistribution (GEAR)

By 1996, South Africa had recovered from the stagnation that had prevailed since the early 1980s. GDP was growing at 3%, and inflation had declined to 8.5% [**Exhibit 5.8**]. Much as this pleased both business and political leadership, the government's fiscal deficit was still 5.6%—an amount that forced too much additional borrowing, a growing current account deficit, and a depreciating currency. This became all too obvious in February, when a run on the Rand drove its value down about 16%—or about 8% in real terms. Worse yet, growth was not enough to create new jobs. As mentioned, an estimated 71,000 jobs were actually lost for the year 1996. If nothing changed, the Ministry of Finance believed it faced the prospect of continuing slow growth with fiscal deficits causing higher inflation and interest rates and too little job creation.

It had become clear to almost everyone—including ANC leadership and the Government of National Unity—that the existing growth path would not reduce unemployment, provide revenues necessary for social services, or redistribute income. Something more was needed. So in June 1996, Financial Minister Trevor Manuel announced a new macroeconomic strategy—GEAR—that would hopefully accelerate nongold exports, private-sector investment, and infrastructural development. Doing so would push GDP growth to 6% and job creation to 400,000 by the year 2000. At the center of this program was deficit reduction—a real change of heart for the ANC government.[46]

The GEAR's medium-term strategy was as follows:

1. acceleration of fiscal reform, reducing the deficit to 3% of GDP by 2000, to help counter inflation; this included further revision of the tax structure and a more redistributive thrust of expenditures

2. gradual relaxation of exchange controls while maintaining monetary policies consistent with inflation reduction

3. trade and industrial policy reforms, including further reduction of tariffs, tax incentives to stimulate investment, small and medium business development, and a competitive policy with the development of industrial clusters

4. public-sector asset restructuring, including better governance and regulation of public corporations, the sale of nonstrategic assets, and public–private partnerships in transport and telecommunications

5. an expansionary public infrastructure investment program

6. structured flexibility within the collective bargaining system to support a competitive and more labor-intensive growth path; reduced minimum wage schedules for young trainees; increased incentives for more shifts, job sharing, and employment flexibility

7. a social agreement to facilitate wage and price moderation, accelerate investment and employment, and enhance public service delivery[47]

When the strategy was initially announced, it was immediately attacked by some members of the ANC and the trade union leaders. There was a sense that it was produced by "eight white men" and did not represent the interests of South African labor.[48] But as the government's commitment to GEAR appeared to deepen, business become increasingly enthusiastic. By March 1997, when Trevor Manual made his budget speech, there was general enthusiasm for the plan and for government's financial management.

Fiscal Policy

For the fiscal year ending in March 1997, the budget deficit stood at 5.6% of GDP. The budget proposed reducing it to 4% in 1998 [**Exhibit 5.9a and b**]. The primary balance (revenues minus expenditures, excluding debt service) was actually positive, 2.4% of GDP. Direct taxes remained high, but there were plans to shift more revenue dependence to the value-added tax. Budgetary reform was making progress, with reduced defense expenditures and some privatization revenues allowing somewhat greater expenditures on housing and infrastructure. One clear problem, however, was the government wage bill. Government's real wages were up 4.9% in 1996 [**Exhibit 5.10**].[49]

Monetary Policy

In March 1997, the Minister of Finance announced a series of exchange-rate liberalizations. Controls were to be lifted on capital outflows by individuals of up to R200,000. Corporations could hold foreign currency earnings offshore for 30 days and could transfer up to R30 million for approved foreign investments. Local institutional investors could invest up to 10% of total assets offshore.[50]

Overall, the monetary policy of the South African Reserve Bank was to control the growth of M3, so that inflation would fall toward 4% or 5%; an additional goal was to maintain a constant real exchange rate for the Rand. Chris Stals, the bank's governor, believed that he "didn't have much choice" regarding monetary policy, because global inflation rates were down to 2% to 3% in the economies with which South Africa competed. This had led to a very high, short-term interest rate—about 17.75% for short-term bonds and 20.25% for the prime rate. Stals understood that rates this high dampened investment, but they reflected the high inflationary expectations. As he put it, "You can't lower rates by creating more money."[51]

Real exchange rates were the other important reflection of monetary policy. The sharp fall in the value of the Rand in 1996 reflected a loss of confidence by investors. Although nonmineral exports were stimulated, imports recovered after about nine months, and the effects had begun to wear off after a year. Stals did not think real depreciation worked—at least for the South African economy. Thus, his target, to the extent that it mattered, was a constant real exchange rate. If inflation came down, exchange rates should stabilize [**Exhibit 5.11**].

Although sympathetic to the need to reduce unemployment, Stals seemed firm in his commitment to reduce inflation. The real problem, he thought, was structural inflexibility of labor markets. He had recently spoken out on this point and caused quite a political stir. But he believed real wages simply had to stop rising if South Africa were to effectively control inflation and if it were to expand nonmineral exports without further devaluation.[52]

Trade and Industrial Policy

Another important change in GEAR was a focus on supply-side policies to make South Africa's economy more competitive and productive. South Africa had already begun to lower tariffs (from an average of 15% to 9%) and proposed to go further in 1997. Export incentives, moreover, that did not comply with WTO rules were to be phased out.

The GEAR also offered several new policies. The National Infrastructure Investment Framework had identified R170 billion in needed capital spending. The 1997/98 budget provided R14.5 billion for capital and social infrastructure—mostly housing, water and sanitation, and municipal infrastructure. Two new programs included the Spatial Development Initiative (SDI) and small business development. The former designated ten development corridors where industries could be concentrated to achieve external economies—industrial areas, metro-service corridors, agri-tourism areas, etc. Most SDIs were designated along the coast of the Indian Ocean, but an additional ten had been identified for development inland.[53] For Small, Medium, and Micro Enterprises (SMME), a program of wholesale loans and loan guarantees was established to help broaden and deepen the structure of enterprise in South Africa.[54]

Most business executive and bureaucrats recognized the need for South African business to reduce costs and become more competitive. In some sectors, such as defense, metals, electronics, and petro-chemicals, there was potential for exporting more in competition with developed countries.[55] But that would not be enough. There needed to be some effort to grow labor-intensive businesses—for South Africa's own market and for markets throughout Africa and the Indian Ocean rim. These neighboring economies were now growing at 5% annually and created a market that South African business could potentially tap [**Exhibit 5.12a**].

Public Sector Asset Restructuring

Because the government was so heavily invested in the economy (i.e., 30% of GDP), there was a sense that public corporations needed a stronger, clearer set of principles to guide their behavior. The government was working on governance programs, including dividend and tax policies for government-owned corporations, a National Empowerment Fund to deepen employee ownership, treatment of pension and medical-aid fund deficits, and a more competitive and transparent bidding system.

The heart of this initiative, however, was privatization. But progress was slow, with opposition from labor unions intensifying. Six radio stations had been privatized, and restructuring committees were looking at sales of various airlines, airports, resorts, etc. Public–private Partnerships, a related initiative, had begun with the sale of 30% of Telkom to Southwestern Bell/Telekom Malaysia for $1.3 billion. According to Dikgang Moseneke, the chairman of Telkom, this not only provided an infusion of capital, but of management skills, of technology, and especially of training. More than 300 engineers were currently receiving specialized training and would eventually spend time in Malaysia or the United States. Mr. Moseneke planned to double Telkom's network in four years, at a cost of R53 billion. Doing so would indeed require an immense injection of capital and skilled labor.[56]

Flexible Wage and Labor Structure

In many ways, this was the element of GEAR on which the rest depended. The level of unemployment was intolerable and had to improve if political stability were to be maintained. GEAR envisioned creation of about 400,000 jobs annually by the year 2000 to reduce unemployment to 32%. Unlike previous plans, GEAR depended on the economic growth of 6% to accomplish at least 30% of this job creation; another

25% could be achieved by the infrastructural and public works expenditures of government; and 30% needed to come from institutional reforms in the labor market—skill development, wage moderation, and strategies to enhance flexibility through collective bargaining.[57]

These policies echoed the private sector's call for a dual wage strategy. In other words, as new jobs were created and younger workers were trained (either by government or by the private sector) and employed, they had to be willing to accept lower wages and benefits inferior to those guaranteed to unionized workers. Real wages could not rise significantly, not faster than productivity, if South Africa were to become more competitive. Unfortunately, organized labor could see the problem domestically but was less familiar with working conditions elsewhere—especially in India, China, and Indonesia, where wages were one-fifth as high. Thus, its willingness to tolerate low wages and harsh working conditions was increasingly doubtful.

A National Social Agreement

The final aspect of GEAR was its call for social cooperation. The government was committing to a tougher fiscal policy, with monetary restraint and constant fixed exchange rates. In return, it promised to deliver better income distribution and social policies; "orderly collective bargaining between organized labor and employers must remain the foundation of industrial relations."[58] Nedlac, the tripartite organization for discussions between business, government, and labor, was the primary vehicle for achieving this social pact. Yet the Nedlac mechanism was not working very well, and COSATU had recently opted out.

The Challenge

In just three years since its first democratic election, South Africa had remained incredibly peaceful and had grown, albeit slowly. But now the South African Chamber of Business concluded, "The challenge for the authorities lies in their political will to harness the economy's potential, and set the economy on the growth high road as set out in their GEAR strategy."[59] Although the economy had slowed during the last two quarters of 1996 and the first quarter of 1997, it appeared to be ready to expand again, with a more realistic budget, a somewhat depreciated currency, and stable inflation. The Department of Finance was projecting growth of 2.25%, with inflation of 8.5% and an increase in real wages of 2.5% [**Exhibit 5.13**].[60]

Even though growth was somewhat less than that which the GEAR had called for, most South African business executives were satisfied. It had, after all, been only a year since the GEAR was announced. Government was working hard to implement these various proposals, yet it would take some time to affect the real economy. Some people faulted the program for not reducing deficits fast enough.[61] Others believed that unemployment had to be addressed immediately, either by public works or reducing hours worked per employee.[62]

Delivery, as one economist put it, was the key; not strategy. The GEAR was fine, but its implementation through the political process over the next two years was crucial.[63] This, of course, would be the prime responsibility of Thabo Mbeki during the months running up to the election in April 1999. But as he dealt with one or another interest group, Mbeki had to wonder if the GEAR was adequate for dealing with South Africa's institutional weakness and if it was doable. As the ANC's candidate for the next presidency, and with Nelson Mandela's endorsement, Mbeki was almost certain to win. Yet, if the economy did not improve soon, organized labor would just be one of the interests abandoning ship.

EXHIBIT 5.1A   SOUTH AFRICA—PROVINCES

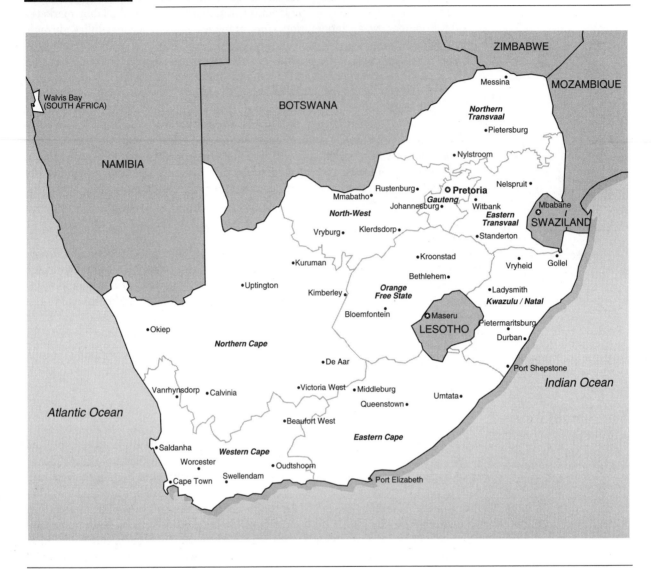

EXHIBIT 5.1B   SOUTH AFRICA—AGRICULTURAL REGIONS

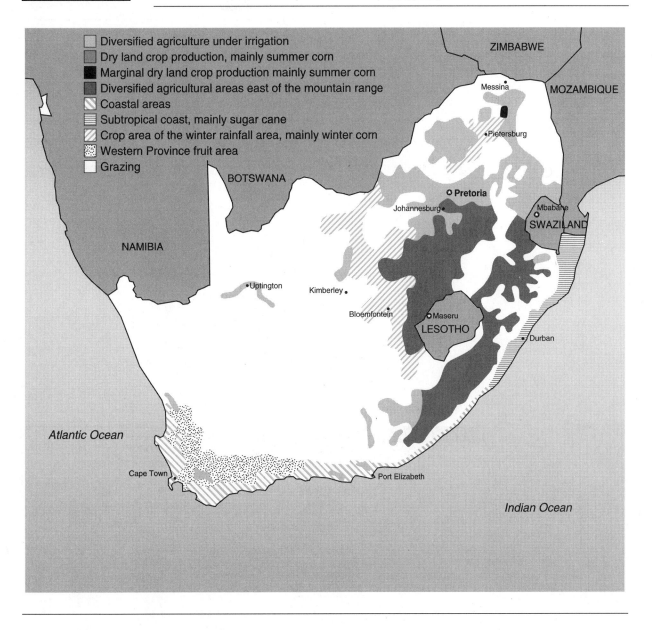

EXHIBIT 5.2

SOUTH AFRICA'S SHARE OF WORLD MINERAL PRODUCTION, 1994

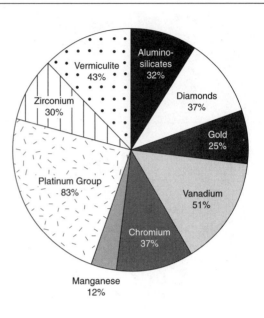

SOURCE: *South Africa at a Glance, 96–97* (Editors, Inc., 1997), pp. 102–103.

EXHIBIT 5.3A

ANNUAL FOREIGN DIRECT INVESTMENT IN SOUTH AFRICA, 1994–1997*

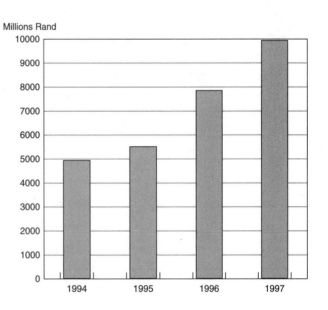

*May 1994 thru April 1997.

SOURCE: "FDI Essential for Economic Growth," *Financial Mail, Special Survey of Top Companies,* June 27, 1997, p. 314.

EXHIBIT 5.3B **FOREIGN DIRECT INVESTMENT IN SOUTH AFRICA, BY SOURCE**

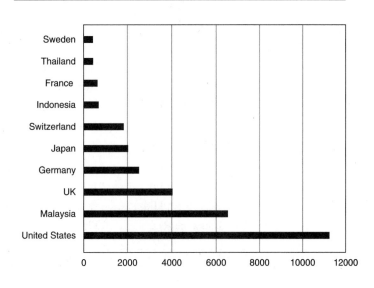

SOURCE: "FDI Essential for Economic Growth," *Financial Mail*, June 1997, p. 315.
Total FDI in millions of Rand, 5/94–4/97.

EXHIBIT 5.3C **FOREIGN DIRECT INVESTMENT IN SOUTH AFRICA, BY SECTOR**

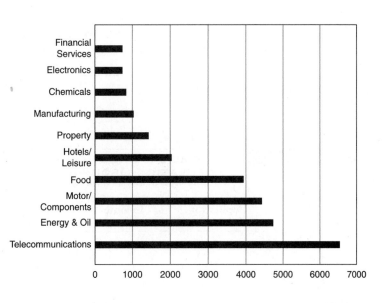

SOURCE: "FDI Essential for Economic Growth," *Financial Mail*, June 1997, p. 314.
Total FDI in millions of Rand, 5/94–4/97.

| EXHIBIT 5.4 | TOP BLACK-CONTROLLED FIRMS IN SOUTH AFRICA IN 1996 |

Ranked by Assets	Company	Sector	Total Assets (Rm)
1	Metlife	Insurance	10,910
2	Johnnic	Industrial Holdings	10,435
3	JCI	Mining	8,515
4	New Africa Inv.	Industrial Holdings	1,247
5	Saflife	Insurance	1,112
6	Aflife	Insurance	1,089
7	Cap Alliance	Insurance	1,059
8	Real Africa Inv.	Industrial Holdings	894
9	Real Africa Hld.	Industrial Holdings	890
10	Botswana Rst.	Copper	828

SOURCES: "Black Economic Empowerment," *Financial Mail*, Special Survey, June 1997, p. 174.

| EXHIBIT 5.5 | AVERAGE POPULATION, GROWTH RATE, AND UNEMPLOYMENT RATE, 1991, 1994 |

	Population in 1991 (000)	Population in 1994 (000)	Average Annual Growth Rate	Unemployment Rate
African	28,383	30,475	2.4%	41.1%
Asian	987	1,027	1.3%	17.1%
Coloured	3,280	3,424	1.4%	23.3%
White	5,061	5,165	0.07%	6.4%
Total/average	37,771	40,091	2.05%	32.6%

SOURCE: *South Africa Survey*, 1995/96, 12.262.

| EXHIBIT 5.6 | INCOME DISTRIBUTION BY POPULATION GROUP—1993 |

	Population Share	Income Share	Per Capita Income (R)	Disparity Ratio[a]
African	76.2%	29.3%	2,717	11.8
Asian	2.6%	4.8%	12,963	2.5
Coloured	8.3%	7.4%	6,278	5.1
White	12.9%	58.5%	32,076	1
Total/average	100%	100%	7,062	4.5

[a]White to other.

SOURCE: *South Africa Survey*, 1995/96, 12,280.

EXHIBIT 5.7	ELECTRICITY, WATER, TELEPHONE AVAILABILITY, 1994

	African	Coloured	Indian	White	Total
Electricity for lighting					
Urban	67%	90%	99%	99%	82%
Rural	16%	60%	74%	93%	21%
Telephone in dwelling					
Urban	25%	51%	73%	88%	51%
Rural	2%	7%	47%	83%	5%
Flush toilet					
Urban	72%	93%	98%	100%	85%
Rural	7%	45%	63%	99%	12%

SOURCE: *South African Survey*, 1995/96, 380,408.

EXHIBIT 5.8	NATIONAL INCOME ACCOUNTS

	1989	1990	1991	1992	1993	1994	1995	1996	1997 Q1*
Nominal GDP (R billion)	240.6	276.1	310.1	341.0	383.7	431.7	485.8	543.0	559.6
Real GDP (1990 prices)	276.9	276.1	273.2	267.3	270.7	278.1	287.5	296.5	293.9
Real GDP growth (%)	na	–0.3%	–1.0%	–2.2%	1.3%	2.7%	3.4%	3.1%	–1.0%
Real Values									
Private consumer expenditures	na	159.5	158.7	156.4	156.9	161.7	169.4	175.8	na
Gross domestic fixed investment	na	54.1	50.1	47.5	46.2	50.2	55.4	59.1	na
Govt. consumer expenditures	na	52.7	53.9	54.7	56.3	58.6	58.8	61.8	na
Exports of goods	na	70.7	70.7	72.5	76.0	76.7	83.9	90.4	na
Imports of goods	na	54.0	55.2	58.2	62.2	72.3	84.2	90.6	na
Change in inventories	na	–7.0	–4.9	–5.7	–2.4	3.1	4.3	–0.1	na
Gross domestic savings as a % of GDP	na	na	na	na	na	na	17.2	16.9	13.5
C/GDP %	na	57.8%	58.1%	58.5%	58.0%	58.1%	58.9%	59.3%	na
I/GDP %	na	19.6%	18.3%	17.8%	17.1%	18.0%	19.3%	19.9%	na
G/GDP %	na	19.1%	19.7%	20.5%	20.8%	21.1%	20.5%	20.8%	na
X/GDP %	na	25.6%	25.9%	27.1%	28.1%	27.6%	29.2%	30.5%	na
Im/GDP %	na	–22.1%	–22.0%	–23.9%	–23.9%	–24.9%	–27.8%	–30.6%	na
Nominal GDP per capita (US$)	na	na	2957.0	3079.0	2955.0	2955.0	3201.0	2977.0	na

*Q1 Annualized data.
na: Data not available.

SOURCE: *South Africa, A Country Report*, ABSA Bank Internal Data.

EXHIBIT 5.9A

SOUTH AFRICAN GOVERNMENT— REVENUES 1997/98 BUDGET

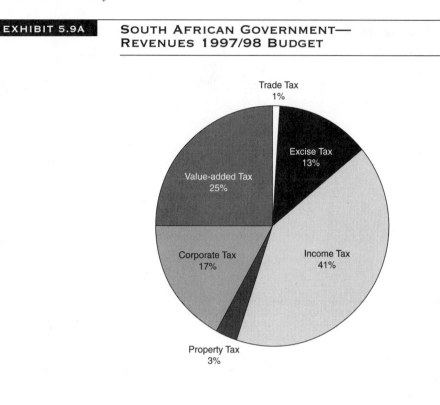

SOURCE: Department of Finance, *Budget Review*, 1997.

EXHIBIT 5.9B

SOUTH AFRICAN GOVERNMENT— EXPENDITURES 1997/98 BUDGET

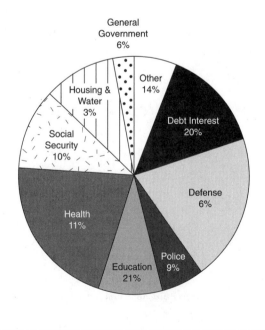

SOURCE: Department of Finance, *Budget Review*, 1997.

EXHIBIT 5.10A	**GNP PER CAPITA, REAL WAGES AND PRICES (PERCENT CHANGE FROM PREVIOUS YEAR)**

Year	GNP per capita*	Average Real Wages		CPI	PPI	GDP Deflator
		Private	**Public**			
1985	–3.2	–3.7	–4.3	16.3	16.9	16.2
1986	–1.7	–2.4	–2.7	18.6	19.6	16.3
1987	1.2	1.0	2.3	16.1	13.9	14.2
1988	1.7	2.7	–0.9	12.9	13.2	15.1
1989	–1.2	–0.6	3.7	14.7	15.2	17.2
1990	–3.8	0.0	0.7	14.4	12.0	15.1
1991	–2.7	0.7	2.1	15.3	11.4	13.5
1992	–4.5	1.5	1.4	13.9	8.3	12.4
1993	–0.5	0.1	–1.5	9.7	6.6	11.1
1994	2.0	1.4	6.0	9.0	8.2	9.5
1995	0.8	2.5	–1.9	8.7	9.6	8.9
1996	1.6	1.8	0.6	7.4	6.9	8.4

SOURCE: Republic of South Africa, Department of Finance, *Budget Review*, 1997, p. 2.10.

EXHIBIT 5.10B	**PRODUCTIVITY**

Index: 1960 = 100

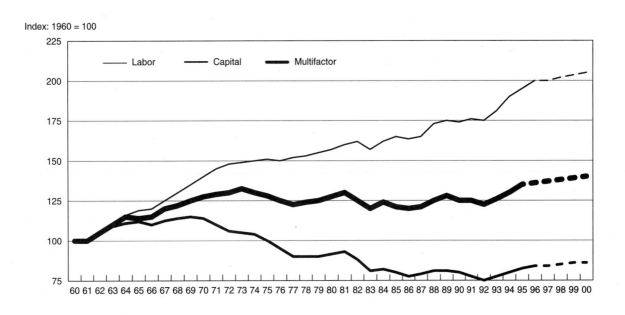

SOURCE: A. J. Jacobs, Chief Economist, ABSA Bank, *"Economy Presentation,"* July 1997.
— —: Projected

EXHIBIT 5.10C	AVAILABILITY OF NET SAVINGS

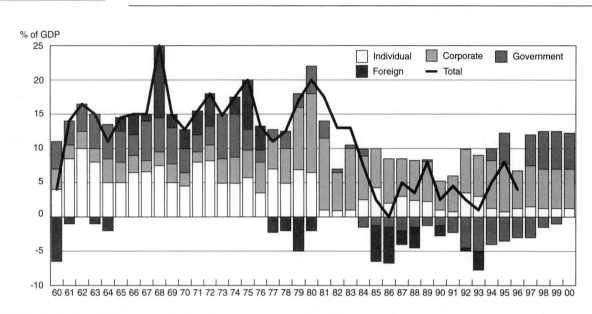

SOURCE: A. J. Jacobs, Chief Economist, ABSA Bank, "Economy Presentation," July 1997.

EXHIBIT 5.11	EXCHANGE RATE AND MONEY SUPPLY

Year	Nominal Exchange Rate		Real Exchange Rate		U.S. $ Exchange Rate		M3	Domestic Credit	Prim Rate
	1990 = 100	Pct. change	1990 = 100	Pct. change	Rand per $	Pct. change	Pct. change	Pct. change	Pct.
1985	151.8	–32.4	82.0	–22.6	2.228	–33.8	12.3	15.9	n/a
1986	127.8	–15.8	85.6	4.3	2.283	–2.4	9.3	8.3	n/a
1987	131.6	3.0	99.8	16.7	2.036	12.2	17.6	15.0	n/a
1988	114.7	–12.8	95.8	–4.1	2.273	–10.4	27.3	26.5	n/a
1989	103.3	–9.9	95.4	–0.4	2.622	–13.3	22.3	17.4	n/a
1990	100.0	–3.2	100.0	4.8	2.588	1.3	12.0	19.4	21.0
1991	94.0	–6.0	103.0	3.0	2.761	–6.3	12.3	12.3	20.2
1992	89.5	–4.8	104.8	1.8	2.852	–3.2	8.0	10.4	18.9
1993	81.2	–9.2	100.2	–4.4	3.267	–12.7	7.0	9.4	16.2
1994	73.7	–9.3	97.1	–3.0	3.550	–8.0	15.7	19.9	15.6
1995	69.5	–5.7	97.4	0.2	3.627	–2.1	15.2	13.2	17.9
1996	60.5	–13.0	89.4	–8.2	4.292	–15.6	13.6	16.1	19.7
1997 Q1*	59.6	–9.4	91.1	6.9	4.441	–14.6	12.9	17.1	20.25

*Rates of change for Q1 are annualized.

SOURCE: Republic of South Africa, Department of Finanace, *Budget Review* 1997, p. 2.11

EXHIBIT 5.12A SOUTH AFRICA BALANCE OF PAYMENTS, MILLIONS OF RAND

	1988	1989	1990	1991	1992	1993	1994	1995	1996	1997 1Q*
Merchandise exports (excluding gold)	32125	38384	42735	44709	49010	56512	64952	81289	98818	105610
Net gold exports	19701	19140	18177	19587	19391	22449	23671	22537	26294	26816
Service receipts	8884	11543	11346	12386	13310	14525	17970	20118	21978	26670
Merchandise imports	-39408	-44266	-43408	-47385	-51883	-59869	-76251	-97962	-116326	-122913
Service payments	-18011	-21539	-23711	-23312	-25153	-27997	-31709	-36259	-39060	-43681
Direct investment payments	-1750	-2105	-2227	-2195	-2466	-2127	-2204	-2392	na	na
Interest	-4615	-5588	-6118	-5594	-5228	-6046	-6531	-7555	na	na
Current account balance	3383	3467	5324	6187	4975	6049	-1207	-10157	-8479	-7940
Long term capital movements	na	-606	-102	-1730	-1511	-272	3503	15125	4885	na
Public authorities	na	-469	511	1051	3142	-2886	4102	6854	6913	na
Non-monetary private sector	na	-15	-650	-2657	-3964	2675	775	6448	-826	na
Basic balance	na	2861	5222	4457	3464	5777	2296	4968	-3594	na
Short-term capital movements not related to reserves	na	-2830	-1670	-424	-3197	-14969	825	4109	-1029	na
Total capital movements not related to reserves	na	-3436	-1772	-2154	-4708	-15241	4328	19234	3856	na
Change in net gold and other foreign reserves	na	31	3552	4033	267	-9192	3121	9077	-4623	na

*Annualized data.
na: Data not available.

SOURCE: South African Reserve Bank, *Quarterly Bulletin*, June 1997.

EXHIBIT 5.12B SOUTH AFRICA CURRENT ACCOUNT BALANCE IN MILLIONS OF U.S. DOLLARS

	1988	1989	1990	1991	1992	1993	1994	1995
Total Imports	-17,210	-16,810	-16,778	-17,156	-17,216	-18,287	-21,452	-27,001
Total Exports	22,432	22,399	23,560	23,289	24,009	21,438	24,947	28,611
Trade Balance	5,222	5,589	6,783	6,134	5,794	5,850	3,494	1,610
Net Services	-899	926	-680	-764	-1,222	-1,530	-1,494	-1,971
Net Income	-3,281	-3,286	-4,096	-3,183	-2,925	-2,577	-2,369	-2,476
Net Transfers	161	186	60	54	94	130	50	16
Current Account Balance	1,204	1,564	2,065	2,243	1,741	1,873	-319	-2,820

SOURCE: South African Reserve Bank, Annual Economic Report, 1998.

| **EXHIBIT 5.12C** | **TRADE AS A PERCENTAGE OF GROSS DOMESTIC PRODUCT** |

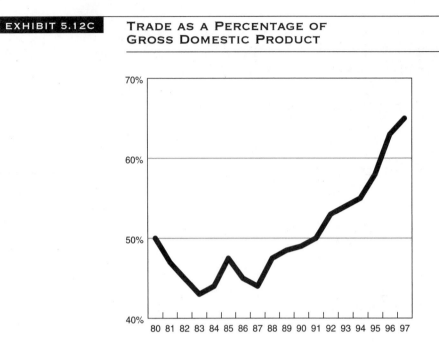

| **EXHIBIT 5.13** | **GEAR, INTEGRATED SCENARIO PROJECTION** |

Model characteristics	1996	1997	1998	1999	2000	Average
Fiscal deficit (% of GDP, fiscal year)	5.1	4	3.5	3	3	3.7
Real government consumption (% of GDP)	19.9	19.5	19	18.5	18.1	19
Average tariff (% of imports)	10	8	7	7	6	7.6
Average real wage growth, private sector	-0.5	1	1	1	1	0.8
Average real wage growth, government sector	4.4	0.7	0.4	0.8	0.4	1.3
Real effective exchange rate (% change)	-8.5	-0.3	0	0	0	-1.8
Real bank rate	7	5	4	3	3	4.4
Real government investment growth	3.4	2.7	5.4	7.5	16.7	7.1
Real parastatal investment growth	3	5	10	10	10	7.6
Real private sector investment growth	9.3	9.1	9.3	13.9	17	11.7
Real non-gold export growth	9.1	8	7	7.8	10.2	8.4
Additional foreign direct investment (US$m)	155	365	504	716	804	509

Results	1996	1997	1998	1999	2000	Average
GDP growth	3.5	2.9	3.8	4.9	6.1	4.2
Inflation (CPI)	8	9.7	8.1	7.7	7.6	8.2
Employment growth (non-agricultural formal)	1.3	3	2.7	3.5	4.3	2.9
New jobs per year ('000)	126	252	246	320	409	270
Current account deficit (% of GDP)	2.2	2	2.2	2.5	3.1	2.4
"Real export growth, manufacturing	10.3	12.2	8.3	10.5	12.8	10.8
Gross private savings (% of GDP)	20.5	21	21.2	21.5	21.9	21.2
Government dissavings (% of GDP)	3.1	2.3	1.7	0.7	0.6	1.9

SOURCE: *Growth, Employment and Redistribution: A Macroeconomic Strategy*, 14 June 1996, pp. 7–8

EXHIBIT 5.14 INTERNATIONAL COMPARATIVE EXHIBITS

Country	GNP per Capita in Dollars	Purchasing Power Parity of GNP per Capita, 1995 Int'l $	% Share of Income (lowest 20%)	% Share of Income (highest 10%)	% with Gini Index[a]	Access to Sanitation	Population Growth Rate	Electricity Production, kwh per Capita, 1994	Telephone Mainlines 1,000 Persons	Adult Literacy Percentage
South Africa	3,160	5,030	3.3	47.3	58.4	46	2.2	4,617	95	18
Argentina	8,030	8,310	na	na	na	89	1.3	1,885	160	4
Brazil	3,640	5,400	2.1	51.3	63.4	73	1.5	1,640	75	17
China	620	2,920	5.5	30.9	41.5	na	1.1	773	34	19
Ghana	390	1,990	7.9	27.3	33.9	29	2.8	360	4	na
India	340	1,400	8.5	28.4	33.8	29	1.8	416	13	48
Indonesia	980	3,800	8.7	25.6	31.7	55	1.6	277	17	16
Kenya	280	1,380	3.4	47.7	57.5	43	2.7	131	9	22
Mexico	3,320	6,400	4.1	39.2	50.3	70	1.9	1,608	96	10
Nigeria	260	1,220	4.0	31.3	45.0	63	2.9	140	4	43
Pakistan	460	2,230	8.4	25.2	31.2	30	2.9	450	16	62
Uganda	240	1,470	6.8	33.4	40.8	60	3.2	na	2	38
Zimbabwe	540	2,030	4.0	46.9	56.8	58	2.4	667	14	15

All data as of 1995, unless otherwise indicated. Income distribution data is from various surveys in the 1990s.
[a]The Gini index measures the difference between a perfectly equal distribution of income and the actual distribution. Index values range from zero (perfect equality in income distribution) to 100 (representing perfect inequality).
na: Data not available.

SOURCE: The World Bank, World Development Report 1997.

1 South African Reserve Bank, *Quarterly Bulletin* 204 (June 1997).

2 Bob Tucker and Bruce Scott, eds., *South Africa: Prospects for Successful Transition* (Cape Town: Juta & Co., Ltd., 1992).

3 South African Foundation, *Growth for All: An Economic Strategy for South Africa* (Johannesburg: February 1996).

4 Mike Brown, "The GEAR Economy," Societe Generale Frankel Pollak, May 1997, p. 24.

5 Although various sources list the population at 43–44 million, a new census reported in July 1997 a population of 38 million. Most observers think that this figure grossly understates population, especially in the black townships.

6 Merton Dagut, ed., *South Africa: The New Beginning* (London: Euromoney Publications, 1991), pp. 16, 40–41.

7 Nigel Worden, *The Making of Modern South Africa: Conquest, Segregation and Apartheid* (Oxford: Blackwell Publishers, 1994), 8–9.

8 Leonard Thompson, *A History of South Africa* (New Haven, Conn.: Yale University Press, 1995), chapter 2.

9 Ibid., pp. 50–66

10 William H. Worger, *South Africa's City of Diamonds: Mine Workers and Monopoly Capitalism in Kimberley, 1867–1895* (New Haven, Conn.: Yale University Press, 1987).

11 Alfred Milner, quoted in Thompson, *A History of South Africa*, p. 144.

12 South African Foundation, *Growth for All*, p. 2.

13 Thompson, *A History of South Africa*, p. 176.

14 Ibid., p. 190.

15 Quoted in Fatima Meer, *Higher than Hope*, (New York: Harper & Rowe, 1988), p. 67

16 *House of Assembly Debates*, 3 February 1969, quoted in *Racism and Apartheid in South Africa* (Paris: The Unesco Press, 1974), p. 75.

17 Quoted in Ibid., p. 90.

18 Quoted in Ibid., p. 96.

19 Donald Woods, *Biko: The Revised Edition* (New York: Henry Holt, 1987).

20 Peter Fallon and Loiz De Silva, *South Africa: Economic Performance and Policies*, discussion paper #7, World Bank, South African Department, Washington, DC, 1994, pp. 31–37, 43–51; Tucker and Scott, *South Africa: Prospects for Successful Transition*, pp. 50–53.

21 *SA 96–97: South Africa at a Glance*, pp. 103–110.

22 *Financial Mail*, "Top Companies—Special Survey," June 27, 1997, p. 330.

23 "Black Economic Empowerment," *Financial Mail*, pp. 173–178.

24 Marinus Daling, interview with the author, July 1997.

25 "Unbundling and Black Empowerment" and "Johnic Makes Determined Play for Small Black Investor," *Sunday Independent*, April 27, 1997; "Blacks Will Need to Be Proactive," *Business Daily*, January 18, 1997.

26 Duncan Innes, interview with the author, July 1997.

27 Ibid.

28 South African Foundation, *Growth for All*, pp. 32–33.

29 Criminal Information Management Center, *1996 Report on Crime* (http://196.33.208.55/miovs.html); South African Institute of Race Relations, *Fast Facts*, April 1997, p. 2.

30 South African Institute of Race Relations, "The Story of a Good Law, Its Bad Application, and the Ugly Results," Number 1, July 1997, pp. 22–23.

31 South African Institute of Race Relations, *South African Survey*, 1995/96, pp. 95–123.

32 *SA 96–97*, pp. 51–55.

33 South African Foundation, *Growth for All*, p. 84.

34 World Bank, *World Development Report 1995* (Oxford, UK: Oxford University Press, 1995).

35 Peter Moll, *Wage Developments in South Africa in the 1990's* (Geniva: ILO, 1995).

36 South African Foundation, *Growth for All*, pp. 88–90.

37 Chris Stals, interview with the author, July 1997.

38 South African Foundation, *Growth for All*, pp. 101–103

39 Eskom, *Statistical Yearbook, 1995; Annual Report 1996*.

40 South African Institute of Race Relations, *South Africa Survey*, 1995/96, pp. 403–410.

41 Department of Housing, *White Paper on Housing*, 1995, preamble, p. 1.

42 South African Institute of Race Relations, *South African Survey*, 1995/96, pp. 335–342.

43 Republic of South Africa, Department of Finance, *Budget Review 1997*, p. 8.9.

44 Department of Home Affairs, *Annual Report 1995*.

45 Department of Health, *Health Trends in South Africa 1994 (April 1995)*.

46 Department of Finance, *Growth, Employment and Redistribution: A Macroeconomic Strategy*, June 14, 1996, p. 2.

47 Ibid., p. 5.

48 Renee Grawitzky, "Cosatu "Will Not Help Implement Gear Strategy," *Business Times*, July 1, 1997.

49   Brown, "The 'GEAR' Economy," p. 6.

50   *GEAR*, pp. 10–11.

51   Chris Stals, interview.

52   Ibid.

53   Alan Hirsh, Ministry of Trade and Industry, interview with the author, July 1997.

54   *GEAR*, p. 13.

55   Alan Jacobs, Chief Economist, ABSA, interview with the author, July 1997.

56   Dikgang Moseneke, chairman Telekom, interview with the author, July 1997.

57   *GEAR*, pp. 16–17.

58   Ibid., p. 19.

59   South African Chamber of Commerce, "Prospects for the South African Economy in 1997," p. 4.

60   Department of Finance, *Budget Review 1997*, p. 6.2.

61   Ben van Rensburg, economist, South African Chamber of Commerce, interview with the author, July 1997.

62   Cheryl Carolus, executive director, ANC, interview with the author, July 1997.

63   Jac Laubscher, Chief Economist, Sanlam, interview with the author, July 1997.

Rapid Transition from a Centrally Planned Economy

This case compares the situation after the fall of communism in two countries, Poland and Czechoslovakia (prior to the Federation's division into the Czech Republic and Slovakia in January 1993). The case is set in the summer of 1990, six months after Poland's aggressive "shock therapy" reforms. Václav Klaus is charged with designing a reform program for Czechoslovakia. He would like to implement an aggressive program similar to Poland's, but there is no political consensus regarding reform.

The case is accompanied by a conceptual note, "Transition to a Market Economy: The Components of Reform," which makes a positive case for three broad categories of economic reform: macroeconomic stabilization, microeconomic liberalization, and institutional reform. Each type of reform is important, but they can only be implemented at different speeds. Microeconomic liberalization can be done quickly; simply deregulate prices and abolish licensing restrictions. Macroeconomic stabilization generally takes a few years. An institutional reform can take many years.

The case presents Poland's "shock therapy" reforms as one model for Klaus. Because the economic situation was grave in late 1989, Finance Minister Balcerowicz enjoyed broad political support for dramatic action.

The situation facing Klaus in Czechoslovakia is much different. There was no macroeconomic crisis and thus no sense of urgency. But this also meant that Klaus' constituents were less willing to bear the costs of rapid reform.

The case illustrates the interactions between different components of reform and the symbiosis between the economic situation and political support for policy changes.

SHOCK THERAPY IN EASTERN EUROPE: THE POLISH AND CZECHOSLOVAK ECONOMIC REFORMS

Following its resounding victory in Czechoslovakia's June 1990 federal elections, the Civic Forum/Public Against Violence (CF/PAV) coalition turned to the contentious issues of economic reform and development. The coalition's point man for this effort was Finance Minister Václav Klaus, who considered himself the Czech Milton Friedman. Klaus argued for quick action on reform, ideally a program similar to the shock therapy reforms that had been instituted in Poland six months before. Beyond this, however, he believed the market should guide development, not the government. Other powerful members of the coalition disagreed. They advocated a more gradual approach to reform and a more active role in guiding development.

Klaus had just a few months to build support for his reform program, which was scheduled to be introduced in January 1991. His task was complicated by several factors, both political and economic. First, the CF/PAV coalition was a weak alliance, not a traditional political party. In addition, growing ethnic tensions had expressed themselves in demands for Slovak independence, and many predicted the breakup of the federal state in the near future. Perhaps most important, Václav Havel, the newly elected and immensely popular president, did not support rapid action. He also insisted on a strong social safety net to mitigate the negative effects of the transition to a market economy.

The economics of reform and development were also complex. Most observers agreed that reform consisted of three elements (macroeconomic stabilization, microeconomic reform, and institutional reform) but differed sharply about how the pieces should fit together—specifically the timing and sequencing of various reforms. Poland offered a useful, but not wholly applicable, model for the Czech reformers. While both economies had been severely damaged by central planning, there were substantial differences. Inflation was much lower and the current account much healthier in Czechoslovakia than they had been in Poland on the eve of its reforms. On the other hand, there was reason to believe that structural distortions were larger in Czechoslovakia than in Poland. Beyond this immediate challenge, it was not clear what role Czechoslovakia would play in the new Europe. Would a laissez-faire approach serve the country well or leave it stranded between the high-productivity countries of the European Union and the extremely low-wage countries to the east?

Klaus knew that he had to find a balance between the elements of reform that was both economically logical and politically feasible. Because of different initial conditions and political constraints, the balance in Czechoslovakia was likely to be different from that in Poland, but Poland still provided a starting point.

Poland: Background and Economic Performance

Founded as an independent state in AD 966, Poland has a long and varied history. Trapped in the middle of the North European Plain, with no natural frontiers to protect it from potential invasion, the country had fought a 1,000-year battle for survival against two often more powerful neighbors, Germany and Russia. At times, Poland

Professor Robert Kennedy and Research Associate Amy Sandler, MBA '96, prepared this case as the basis for class discussion rather than to illustrate either effective or ineffective handling of an administrative situation.

has occupied a large portion of central Europe. In other periods, it did not exist.[a] After disappearing for much of the 19th century, Poland reemerged after the end of World War I, only to be carved up again with the signing of the Hitler–Stalin pact in 1939. As WW II ended, Soviet troops stood by while the Germans destroyed Warsaw. After the war, the Soviet Union forced Poland into its sphere of influence.[b] Although the Poles maintained official electoral freedom, by 1947 Stalinist terror and fraudulent elections brought the Communist Polish United Workers' Party (PZPR) to power, and the country effectively lost its sovereignty.[1] By the time the 1952 Constitution was adopted (modeled on the Soviet Union's 1936 Constitution), Communist rule in Poland was firmly entrenched.[2]

Several factors combined to curtail the Polish Communists' power. The country had always had a strong national identity, perhaps due to its long history of invasion and partition. Poland's national anthem reflects this. The refrain translates as "Poland will not be defeated as long as we are alive. What the foreign power has taken from us, we will recover with the sword." A second countervailing influence was the Catholic Church. The Church has been an integral part of both social and political life since Poland's establishment—marked by the baptism of Miesko I and the introduction of Roman Christianity. During Communist rule, the Church was a center of political activity and opposition, in addition to its traditional religious function.

Poland's agrarian and labor traditions also tempered the power of the Communists. Although the agricultural sector contributed only 11% to GDP in 1988, 40% of Poles still resided in rural areas and agriculture played an important role in Polish culture.[3] Poland was alone among Communist nations in rejecting attempts to collectivize agriculture. Finally, the labor movement had long played a pivotal role both in Polish society and in its economy. Since 1918, with the development of workers' councils, laborers had demanded greater self-management, economic decentralization, higher wages, and better working conditions. The power of the labor movement was a recurring theme throughout the Communist era and reflected the Poles' willingness to challenge the Communists when they felt pushed.

The Polish Communists were considered less repressive than many others in Eastern Europe, but repressiveness among Communist regimes is a relative term. When the government's power was threatened internally, or when repercussions from Moscow loomed, there was no shortage of violence, particularly as seen in the suppression of strikes.

The Communist Economic System

Following its 1947 takeover, the PZPR introduced a central planning system modeled on the Soviet system. Economic activity was organized much differently in this system than in Western market economies. Six distinctions illustrate the point. First, almost all economic activity was centrally organized and directed, most often in the form of five-year plans. Second, nearly all firms were state-owned, which meant that the central planning organization could simply order firms to meet certain goals. The plans set production targets, so managers' principal objective was to produce a certain quantity of output, not to maximize profits or use inputs efficiently. Third, profits from state-owned enterprises were the major source of government revenues, so the tax system was underdeveloped. Fourth, the government allocated all credit and investment funds. State-owned banks were the only source of credit, and industry—

---

[a] Poland controlled large areas of central Europe in the early 17th century and again between the first and second world wars. The Polish state did not exist from 1795 to 1807, from 1874 to 1918, and from 1939 to 1945.

[b] Stalin met with the U.S. president and Britain's prime minister Winston Churchill at the 1945 Yalta and Potsdam conferences to determine Eastern Europe's postwar destiny.

specific ministries allocated investment funds. Both bank credit and capital investment funds were allocated as much for political as economic reasons. Fifth, all foreign trade was handled by specialized foreign trade organizations. Finally, almost all prices were fixed and therefore contained no information about the balance between supply and demand.

This system led to an economic structure that differed sharply from developed market economies. Planners often focused on rapid industrialization, neglecting the agricultural and service sectors of the economy. They emphasized scale economies, import substitution, and the Soviet export market. The typical firm was much larger than its counterpart in the West, and concentration levels were often very high. Industrialization was achieved with high levels of business investment, which was financed with forced savings and severe restrictions on consumption.

The Polish system was typical, with two major exceptions. First, unlike many of its neighbors, Poland never successfully collectivized the agricultural sector. Second, as we see below, the PZPR experimented with limited decentralization in the early 1980s.

Because a large portion of Poland's industrial base had been destroyed during the second world war, re-industrialization was a top economic priority. The combination of central planning and the Communists' emphasis on heavy industry led to structural inefficiencies, misplaced incentives, and environmental degradation. Economics professor Leszek Balcerowicz, who would later serve as finance minister and architect of Poland's 1990 economic reforms, described the Polish economic system (like other centrally planned economies) as possessing five key features:

- domination of the state sector in the economy . . . ;

- heavily distorted prices due to price subsidies and controls . . . ;

- the absence of institutions needed in a market economy, such as a competitive banking system . . . a stock exchange, a system of government bonds to finance the deficit, genuine local government, etc.;

- a weak public administration . . . ; and

- a "socialist welfare state" that was extensive relative to the level of economic development but increasingly inefficient and financially insupportable. . . .[4]

In addition to these structural economic flaws, political tensions also arose under Communist rule. The post–World War II period in Poland was marked by three major reform efforts in 1956, 1970, and 1980. In each case, political tensions were exacerbated by economic problems. Each time, the government responded to political tensions with incremental economic solutions, but the reforms had little impact and the problems characteristic of centrally planned economies resurfaced. This eventually led to a new cycle of shortages, increased political tension, limited reform, and eventual crackdown. The cycle continued until the introduction of "shock therapy" in January 1990.

Political and Economic Interactions, 1947–1988

The Stalinist model of forced industrialization appeared to work for a few years. Polish national income grew (in real terms) by more than 76% from 1947 to 1950, while the investment share of national income increased by 35% in the same timeframe.[5] But this growth came at a cost. In the early 1950s, attempts to collectivize agriculture met with resistance and consumer well-being fell behind industrial growth. In June 1956, riots broke out in Poznan (killing 53 people) and spread throughout the nation.

This led to widespread strikes and armed clashes between workers and the security police. In response, popular leader Wladislaw Gomulka proposed the first major attempt at reform. He moved to decentralize economic decision making, decollectivize the small part of the agricultural sector still under public control, and increase worker participation. However, opposition to reform within the bureaucracy was strong. Minor reforms were eventually passed, but they had minimal long-term effect. National income increased at 3%,[6] and industrial output at 9.5%,[7] annually from 1955 to 1960.

Once the crisis of 1956 passed, the PZPR reasserted its control and the economy again slowed.[8] Throughout the 1960s, growth came primarily from capital accumulation, not increased efficiency, and the economy showed little growth in real wages or consumption. By 1968, the Party suffered from internal dissent. Gomulka's response was an anticonsumer policy of "economic rationalization"—primarily restrictions on wages and prices—implemented just a few days before Christmas 1970. This led to riots in Gdansk and to the death of about 300 civilians. Gomulka resigned in disgrace. Edward Gierek stepped in as the Party First Secretary in 1970 and introduced a second wave of reforms.[9] He proposed to improve living standards by increasing investment in *both* heavy industry and the consumer sector. He borrowed from Western banks to finance investment and granted real wage increases to ease social discontent.[10]

The foreign borrowing financed rapid growth in both investment and consumption. As before, the short-term results were impressive—between 1971 and 1975, real wages increased by 6.8% annually and real national income grew by 9.5%.[11] But the centrally engineered boom proved unsustainable, and by the mid-1970s, the economy was again in crisis. Growth in wages and output slowed, and rapidly increasing debt service costs led to a balance of payments crisis. Living standards declined as inflation rose and shortages returned. An attempt to rebalance the economy in 1976 by raising meat and agricultural prices met with strikes and protests. The strike leaders were arrested, setting the stage for the creation of the Solidarity movement four years later.[12] In the summer of 1980, the government sought to address a budget shortfall by increasing food prices. This led to demonstrations, riots, and threatened strikes. As in 1976, the price increases were rescinded, but this did not diminish public unrest. After a wave of strikes centered in the Lenin Shipyards in Gdansk in August 1980, the authorities agreed to the creation of an independent trade union, Solidarity. Ten days later, the PZPR, increasingly controlled by the Soviet Union and disturbed by Gierek's "reformist" ways, booted him out of office. General Wojciech Jaruzelski took over as Party First Secretary and was forced to face both an economic crisis and a fundamental political challenge to the Communist Party.

The first legal independent union in any Communist nation, Solidarity was a trade union in name only. At its peak, Solidarity claimed ten million members (of an adult population of 21 million)[13] and presented a unified political opposition to the Polish Communist authorities. Under the charismatic leadership of unemployed electrician Lech Walesa (the leader of the Gdansk strike committee), Solidarity quickly became a potent anti-Communist force. Confronted by intense domestic pressure and faced with potential invasion by the USSR, Jaruzelski imposed martial law on December 13, 1981.

Martial law brought with it the third attempt at economic reform, this time aimed at the decentralization of economic power and the gradual introduction of market forces into the economy. In theory, the reform was very similar to the 1956 reforms. The 1980–1981 reforms led to the restoration of the workers' councils, an increase in consumer goods prices, and increased production authority for individual enterprises, but these modest reforms still did not address the economy's structural problems. The reforms were characterized by the "three S's slogan": self-reliance for enterprises, self-financing of enterprises, and self-management for workers. As before, the reforms led to short-term growth—industrial output grew by 6.4% in 1983 and by 5.2% in 1984.

Although the decentralization of decision making was a relatively radical step, there had been no corresponding shift in incentives.[14] The fundamental flaws of the economy reemerged, leading to inflation and a wage explosion.[15] Real wages rose by 15% in 1988 and by another 9% in the first half of 1989. But increases in real wages led to queues, shortages, and black markets because the central plan was so unresponsive to consumer demands and did a poor job of allocating what was produced.[16] In 1988, the government responded with partial reforms. A new plan partially liberalized prices and increased workers' control over plants.[17] The public responded to price increases by raising wage demands. When the government relented, the result was further inflation, shortages, and increased foreign debt.[18]

Democracy Returns—Late 1989

Meanwhile, Mikhail Gorbachev's reform program of *glasnost* (political relaxation) and *perestroika* (economic restructuring) in the Soviet Union opened the door to political reform in Poland. Jaruzelski called for "Round Table" discussions with Solidarity leaders in the spring of 1989 in an effort to address the public's discontent. Led by Lech Walesa, Solidarity reached an agreement that legalized Solidarity and other independent associations and called for quasi-free elections for June 1989.[c]

In addition to political liberalization, the private sector was given equal rights to develop. But Solidarity's primary focus was on wage indexation and social benefits, and not on broad structural reforms. Neither side realized that they were negotiating the end of the Communist regime. The fall of the Berlin Wall was still several months away, and all Poland's neighbors were still governed by seemingly solid Communist governments (e.g., Honecker in East Germany and Ceausescu in Romania). Both sides were surprised when Solidarity won an overwhelming victory in the June 1989 elections, capturing 99 of 100 seats in the Senate and all of the 161 seats in the Sejm that it was permitted to contest.

After a failed attempt to form a government by Jaruzelski and his ally, General Czeslaw Kiszczak, Solidarity created a coalition with two other parties at the end of August. This government was led by non-Communist Tadeusz Mazowiecki, who appointed Balcerowicz as Deputy Prime Minister and Finance Minister. Charged with constructing an economic plan, the well-respected Balcerowicz and his team of energetic technocrats were concerned less with politics and than with restoring the economy. But they could not ignore a political landscape that offered only a limited timeframe for "shock therapy."

The Polish Reform Program

Balcerowicz's Challenge

The challenges confronting Balcerowicz and his team were enormous. The economy suffered from hyperinflation, widespread shortages, a collapsing currency, and huge fiscal and external deficits. While many of these problems could be attributed to the defects of a centrally planned economy, some aspects of the crisis were unique to Poland. These included the wage increases and price controls left behind by the Jaruzelski government and the high level of foreign debt. Balcerowicz believed that the most pressing crisis was macroeconomic. He was also constrained by the fact that

---

[c] After four decades with a unicameral legislature (the Sejm), the "April Amendments" created a bicameral structure. The amendments created a freely elected Senate (the upper house) and converted the Sejm into a powerful lower house. Solidarity was allowed to contest 35% of the 460 seats in Sejm and all the Senate seats in the June elections. See Bachman, pp. 187–189.

Solidarity had never offered a specific economic program. The movement had been formed to oppose the Communists and was primarily political. With that unifying force gone, the potential for political fragmentation was great. Solidarity's goal of wage indexation presented a tremendous political challenge to the planners. And while Poland's tradition of private farming reflected an entrepreneurial spirit, it also represented another strong and vocal interest group whose incomes might decline with reform.

Balcerowicz, a student of both Latin American debt crises and economic transformations, viewed the transition as having three elements: macroeconomic stabilization, microeconomic liberalization, and institutional reform.

Macroeconomic Stabilization Stabilization was to be achieved through tight macroeconomic policy. This included: tight monetary policy, particularly by maintaining positive real interest rates; fiscal balance, achieved primarily through budget cuts; and a tough tax-based wage restraint.[d] To address the foreign debt, Balcerowicz negotiated with the IMF to establish a $1 billion stabilization fund. He also initiated negotiations with the Paris and London Clubs (which represented public and private lenders, respectively) to help achieve radical debt reduction as part of the broader stabilization program.[19]

Microeconomic Liberalization Balcerowicz defined liberalization as "enlarging the scope of economic freedom by removing restrictions on setting up and developing private firms, eliminating price controls [and] bureaucratic and quantitative restrictions on foreign trade, introducing currency convertibility, etc."[20] He also strengthened property rights and removed many regulations, such as those on interest rates. The liberalization and deregulation components of Balcerowicz's plan included four elements, which were implemented immediately. These included

- further price liberalization (with the share of free prices in terms of volume of sales moving from 50% in late 1989 to more than 90% following reform)

- removal of [the] remaining restrictions on private economic activity

- trade liberalization through the removal of restrictions on imports and exports, the devaluation and unification of exchange rates, and the convertibility of the Polish zloty in current account operations

- financial liberalization, through positive real interest rates and the elimination of most household and industry subsidies[21]

Institutional Reform Balcerowicz believed that fundamental institutional restructuring was also essential. Because institutions—such as firms, the national government, and the capital allocation system—have such a large effect on economic behavior, any program that neglected institutions was bound to fail. Balcerowicz proposed to: privatize most state-owned enterprises; remove most regulatory barriers to foreign investment; introduce tough antimonopoly legislation; create an independent central bank; reform the financial sector; introduce tax reforms; streamline the budgetary process; reorganize local government; and reform the social safety net.[22]

In addition to these three elements, Balcerowicz had to consider the pace and sequencing of various reforms. His view was that late 1989/early 1990 was a period of "extraordinary politics"—radical times that called for radical policies. Not only was

---

[d] Known as the "popiwek," the excess wages tax was applied only to state-owned enterprises (SOE). The tax on "excessive wages" was 500% of the excess. The tax was designed primarily as a fiscal measure to hold down SOE spending (and thus state subsidies) over which the government had very little control. A secondary effect was to force workers out of the state sector and into private firms where wages quickly exceeded those in the SOEs.

the Polish economy at a critical juncture, the political landscape was also undergoing cataclysmic change. Balcerowicz argued that

> concentrating radical and drastic measures in the period shortly after a great change in a country's history enables one to tap a precious reserve of political capital. In contrast, delaying these measures by applying milder economic strategies involves a much lower probability of eventually getting them accepted or, conversely, a much higher risk of social protest. . . .[23]

He argued further that "if the macroeconomic situation is catastrophic . . . the 'cold turkey' approach to stabilization is the *safest* one."[24] The reforms were expected to reduce real incomes by 20% and create visible unemployment for the first time since the 1950s.[25] Balcerowicz felt that the window of opportunity for change was limited.

One area in which Balcerowicz chose to proceed less rapidly was in the financial markets. The draft securities law was modeled on the U.S. SEC, with strict regulation of financial intermediaries.[e] The law also imposed tough listing requirements on firms—including permission to list from the securities regulator, a high minimum capital requirement, quarterly financial disclosure, and strong protection of minority shareholders. Trading would be restricted to one financial exchange. The Warsaw Stock Exchange was scheduled to open in early 1991, and regulators anticipated that, when it did, fewer than ten firms would meet regulatory requirements. (In fact, seven firms listed when the exchange began trading in April 1991.)

With the exception of the financial sector, Balcerowicz generally chose to proceed rapidly, emphasizing stabilization and liberalization. Institutional reform was necessary but could not be allowed to slow other reforms. But this did not mean that the plan was entirely sequential. As Balcerowicz saw it, "Radical liberalization of prices had to be linked to the radical elimination of quantitative and other administrative restrictions in foreign trade. This was necessary in order to increase the competitive pressure upon the domestic enterprises."[26] Jeffrey Sachs, a Harvard economist advising Balcerowicz, described the transition process as

> a seamless web. Structural reforms cannot work without a working price system; a working price system cannot be put in place without ending excess demand and creating a convertible currency; and a credit squeeze and tight macroeconomic policy cannot be sustained unless prices are realistic, so that there is a rational basis for deciding which firms to close. At the same time, for real structural adjustment to take place, the macroeconomic shock must be accompanied by other measures, including selling off state assets, freeing up the private sector, establishing procedures for bankruptcy, preparing a social safety net, and undertaking tax reform. Clearly, the reform process must be comprehensive.[27]

Elsewhere, Sachs quotes Bolivia's Planning Minister, "If you are going to chop off a cat's tail, do it in one stroke, not bit by bit."[28] Balcerowicz's plan of shock therapy for Poland—known as the "Big Bang"—was launched on January 1, 1990. It did not take long for the cat to react. There was a sudden burst of inflation, with the price level jumping by about 80% in the first two weeks of January. Industrial output declined by more than 20% during 1990. As predicted, visible unemployment arrived for the first time in 40 years.[29] Real wages fell by about 30% between November 1989 and January 1990. To many, shock therapy meant soaring unemployment, decreased output, and plummeting living standards.

---

[e] Intermediaries included brokers, brokerage firms, investment banks, mutual funds, and financial advisors. Most positions involved licensing requirements and fairly strict testing standards.

But as inflation declined and shortages evaporated, the shock therapy began to bear fruit—for the first time since 1939, fresh fruit was available on the streets of Warsaw in the middle of winter.[30] Hundreds of thousands of new private businesses sprang up, as they could now register, obtain permits without bribing bureaucrats, and import goods to sell.[31] By May, the monthly inflation rate had fallen to 4.5%. Exports boomed and the fiscal balance moved from a deficit of 7.1% of GDP in 1989 to a surplus in 1990. The adherents of shock therapy celebrated.[32] Depending on one's perspective, the cat was either half-alive or half-dead.

Czechoslovakia: Background and Economic Performance

Situated on the territories of Bohemia, Moravia, and Slovakia, Czechoslovakia became a nation-state in 1918. These regions coexisted (with varying interdependence) for about 1,000 years, until the end of World War I. Following the collapse of the Austro-Hungarian Hapsburg Empire, the Czech and Slovak republics united into the federated state of Czechoslovakia. Although functioning well as a parliamentary democracy, and despite inheriting 70% of the industrial capacity of the former empire, the new federation was troubled by ethnic nationalism. In the east, Slovaks demanded greater autonomy from the more economically advanced Czechs. Additional minority demands—from the three million Sudeten Germans in the west and a smaller number of ethnic Poles and Hungarians—were silenced in 1939 with Hitler's annexation of Czechoslovakia.[33]

The Czechoslovak state and democratic politics were both restored after liberation in 1945. Initially, the post–second world war economy was mixed, with both a socialized sector and private industry.[34] But this changed after the Communist Party of Czechoslovakia (CPCS) won a 39% plurality in the 1946 elections. After the election, the political environment deteriorated. As the 1948 elections drew closer, the Communists gained control of the police force and formed a new government. Most non-Communist leaders fled the country, as did thousands of intellectuals and managers. The CPCS offered only a single list of candidates in the 1948 election and, as a result, gained control of the National Assembly,[35] dashing any hope of becoming a democratic socialist state. The Cold War brought with it the Stalinization of the economy and a centralization of the political system in the hands of the CPCS. The CPCS was one of the most repressive regimes in Eastern Europe, leaving little room for opposition or debate.[36]

Political and Economic Interactions 1947–1988

Unlike Poland, Czechoslovakia emerged from World War II with its industrial base largely intact. The country had a long tradition of fiscal and monetary conservatism as well as a refined business code, corporate law, and other legislative components of a market economy.[37] The Communists imposed a system of central planning, capital accumulation, state ownership of industrial enterprises, and collectivized agriculture. The mixed economy was quickly consolidated under centralized control. By 1960, 93% of net material product (NMP, the socialist version of GDP) was generated by state-owned enterprises (SOEs).[38] The Czechoslovak economic strategy was redirected from exporting light consumer goods toward an emphasis on heavy industry and the horizontal integration of key enterprises.

As in Poland, the strategy of suppressing consumption in favor of savings and investment led to strong initial economic performance. In the 1950s, annual labor productivity grew by 5.2% in industry and 6.5% in agriculture.[39] But this growth could not be sustained. Forced adherence to the central plan led to economic inefficiencies such as overinvestment in some sectors (leading to diminishing marginal returns to capital), underinvestment in others, and poor decisions at the firm level.[40]

The first efforts to address these inefficiencies came in 1958. The reforms were narrow in scope, allowing moderate decentralization of decision making. By 1962, the reforms were halted and the economy stagnated.[41] NMP growth slowed to only 1.8% between 1961 and 1965.[42]

This slowdown led to uncharacteristic student demonstrations and calls for political and economic liberalization. These demands, unusual for such a law-abiding nation, resulted in concessions and reforms by the party leadership. One reform—the reduction of censorship—eventually led to a revival of Prague's artistic, literary, and cultural heritage, culminating in what became known as the "Prague Spring" of 1968.

The Prague Spring brought with it calls for political democratization, a review of Communist rule, and the implementation of a radical economic reform package (the New Economic Model, or NEM). The NEM involved increasing workers' participation, liberalizing some prices, and separating economic policy from political decision making. As these changes began to be implemented, the economy started to improve and grew by about 7% a year between 1965 and 1970. Unfortunately, Alexander Dubcek, the reformist leader, was unable to convince a troubled USSR of his loyalty, and the Prague Spring was crushed by an invasion in August 1968. As the hard-liners returned to power, they reimposed the system of central planning that would remain in place until the late 1980s.[43]

Dubcek was replaced by Gustav Husak, whose program of "normalization" brought back central planning and a more repressive political environment. Economic stagnation soon returned.[44] Public dissatisfaction with the regime remained quiet, as memories of the suppression of the Prague Spring weighed heavily on the minds of reformers. In 1977, a group of ex-Communists, intellectuals (including the playwright Václav Havel), and religious representatives came together to issue "Charter 77," a defense of human rights. Throughout the 1970s and 1980s, however, reformers had little influence in economic and political decision making.

Some have called the 1980s in Czechoslovakia "a decade of economic stagnation." Annual growth averaged only 1.4%, discrepancies between the central plan's targets and actual growth increased, and net fixed investment fell from 20% of NMP to only 13%.[45] Still, inflation remained below 2%, and there were adequate supplies of basic consumer goods. But compared with the more industrialized nations with which it had been competing since before World War II, Czechoslovakia found itself falling behind. By 1989, GDP growth was only about one-third of the OECD average (1.3% vs. 3.5%).[46]

The Velvet Revolution: Democracy Returns

In the late 1980s, with the rise of Mikhail Gorbachev in the Soviet Union, economic and political reform swept the satellite states. In 1987, the Czechoslovak government recognized the changing political environment and approved the *Principles of Restructuring the Economic Mechanism.* The program called for partial, not systemic, transformation. The *Principles* included greater independence for state firms and a reform of wholesale prices.[47] But they did not make the decision makers responsible for the outcomes of their actions, nor did they address the economy's pervasive lack of competition.[48] Many perceived these reforms as an attempt by the Communist government to distract the public from the changes that were occurring elsewhere in Eastern Europe. It soon became impossible to ignore events in Poland. After a summer of demonstrations and activity in Czechoslovakia and throughout Central Europe, the Berlin Wall fell on November 9, 1989. A week later, Prague experienced its largest demonstration in 20 years, leading to clashes between police and students. Two days later, Václav Havel joined with other opposition groups to form Civic Forum, an unofficial coalition demanding major changes, including the resignation of Communist Party head Milos Jakes; the end of the Communist Party's leading role in society; freedom for the media; and democratization of the government. On November 24, 1989, Jakes resigned, and half a million people (out of a population of 15.6 million) lined the streets of Prague to hear Alexander Dubcek (the reformist leader from the Prague Spring) return to the political scene.

After a two-hour strike on November 27, the government agreed to negotiate with the opposition. Following a month filled with Communist resignations, reformers finally came to power. Dubcek became the chairman of the Federal Assembly on December 28. The next day, the Federal Assembly elected Havel to replace Husak as president. Though not great fans of Havel, the Communist deputies felt compelled to elect him (and preserve their future reelection) in the face of mass public support for the adored playwright. The transitional government was called a government of "national understanding" and announced free elections in June 1990, to be followed by economic reform.

The macroeconomic situation in Czechoslovakia was more stable than in Poland, but the structural weaknesses may have been worse. As with its northern neighbor, 40 years of central planning and overdependence on trade within the Soviet bloc (through the Council for Mutual Economic Assistance, or CMEA) had resulted in misaligned incentives, an outdated capital stock, a negligible private sector, and almost no unemployment. Growth in the 1980s had averaged less than 2%. Unlike many of its Soviet-bloc neighbors, however, this slow growth had been balanced by the monetary and fiscal responsibility. Because of tight credit and wage policies, annual inflation had averaged only 2%–3%, a figure considerably lower than that of other Central and Eastern European nations.[f] The Czechoslovak economy also benefited from a very modest hard currency debt—a total of $7.9 billion ($507 per capita) in 1989, compared with Poland's $39.1 billion ($1,032 per capita.)[g] Trade with the West was in balance, and Czechoslovakia boasted a 43.5 billion crown ($2.7 billion) trade surplus with other CMEA nations.[49]

The transitional government moved to secure macroeconomic stability and external balance. Fiscal and monetary policies were tightened, with targets of a fiscal surplus equal to 1% of GDP and zero money supply growth.[50] The koruna was devalued against both the ruble and convertible currencies. The government also initiated several institutional reforms, including the elimination of wage controls in the private sector, the separation of commercial banking from the central bank, and several reforms to the social welfare system.[51]

The first half of 1990 was devoted primarily to discussion and analysis. Several specific proposals were discussed, but none generated consensus. The greatest source of delay was the debate over the timing and sequencing of the proposed reforms. The fundamental issue was between those who favored a gradual, structured reform, and those who favored shock therapy similar to Poland's. An additional pressure on the federal government (renamed the Czech and Slovak Federated Republic) came from Slovak nationalists, who wanted to create their own economic policy as part of a desire for broader autonomy. Many in the government wished to wait until after the June 8–9 elections before launching a broad economic program.

June 1990: Klaus' Options and Constraints

The key proponent of Czechoslovakian shock therapy was Finance Minister Václav Klaus. Noted for his radical free market approach and a certainty that many characterized as arrogant, Klaus had spent the past six months debating his former patron, Dr. Valtr Komarek. Komarek had served as the first Deputy Prime Minister in charge

---

[f] Between 1970 and 1989, industrial wholesale prices rose by only 1.5% a year and consumer prices by about 1%. Because of excess demand (the result of suppressed prices), actual inflation was most likely 2%–3%.

[g] In addition to foreign hard currency debt, CMEA nations also had nonconvertible debt. In 1988, Poland's total debt stood at $42.1 billion, while Czechoslovakia ended 1989 with a total debt of $8.7 billion. For a more detailed external debt breakdown, see **Exhibit 6.8.**

of economic reform and was a strong voice for gradual restructuring and a "third way" that would retain the best aspects of socialism (like full employment). Klaus' personality and politics also clashed with the nation's most popular figure, President Václav Havel. Havel was not particularly well versed in economic issues and had been called a socialist by a government advisor.[52] His free-wheeling, socially oriented approach did not sit well with the economically trained Klaus, a virulent anti-Communist.

Klaus did not want to "repeat our mistakes of the 1960s, when we attempted to introduce a hybrid system between central planning and market economy—we are not interested in a 'third way.' As someone recently stated, the third way is the fastest way to the Third World." Klaus also did not "intend to wait for an all-embracing reform blueprint," as he believed that a "partial reform is much worse than a nonreform."[53] Economist Charles Wolf, Jr., summarized this perspective: "To attempt the transformation process on a piecemeal and gradual basis would be . . . like trying to shift a country's driving practices from the left side of the road to the right side in stages. The risk of serious accident is manifestly greater than if the change is accomplished all at once."[54]

But Klaus had already had to wait—for the June elections and to develop a reform coalition in the midst of political turf battles and ideological debates. Although Klaus preferred a Big Bang reform followed by a laissez-faire development policy, it was clear that these changes would not occur quickly. With the issue of pace deferred by political circumstance, Klaus turned to the sequencing of the reforms.

The Sequencing of Reforms

Sequencing raised many questions for Klaus. He confronted a basic tradeoff—should he focus on getting incentives right (which could be done rapidly) or on reforming institutions (which required more time)? Klaus later wrote, "It would be counterproductive to adjust and liberalize prices before economic agents have the incentives and sufficient freedom to respond. Yet at the same time, we realize that markets are unlikely to function effectively without an appropriate degree of price flexibility."[55]

Klaus came down on the side of rapid action and hoped to implement a program even more aggressive than Poland's. He proposed to free virtually all prices immediately, institute rapid privatization through an innovative voucher scheme,[h] and list nearly 1,500 newly privatized firms on one of several stock exchanges. His preference was to allow financial intermediaries to arise in response to market incentives, not regulators' dictates.

Because of the deep structural problems that plagued the economy, Klaus knew that the institutional piece of the transition process could not be ignored—even if it did not happen immediately. He acknowledged that a strong social safety net would have to be incorporated into any successful plan, especially if it were to gain the support of President Havel. As a free-market adherent, Klaus considered the social safety net a pragmatic necessity but not good economics. He recognized the dislocations that accompanied rapid liberalization, admitting that "the program will definitely have some negative consequences for industrial output and employment. There is no way around that. There will be dissatisfaction. There may be social unrest. But you have to try it, and then we'll see." The Czechoslovak reformers predicted that the nation's economic output would fall by 5%–10% in 1991 and that price inflation would rise from 10% to about 30%, perhaps even up to 60%.[56] Estimates for unemployment ranged from 7%–10% in 1991 to 8%–15% in 1992.[57]

---

[h] Klaus' plan was to institute a massive "voucher privatization" that would grant Czechoslovak citizens direct ownership in more than 1,500 state-owned firms. All adult citizens would receive coupon books, which could be used to bid on state-owned firms in a series of auctions. He believed that this was the quickest way to introduce private incentives for firms' managers and owners.

By contrast, Balcerowicz and his advisors had proposed a two-level privatization program, in which state-owned enterprises would be transferred to "National Investment Funds" that would be responsible for restructuring SOEs. Polish citizens would be granted shares in the NIFs, thus owning formerly SOEs only indirectly.

To mitigate the negative consequences of reform, the government made several changes to the social safety net. Unemployment insurance was extended to one year, with benefits set at 60% of salary.[58] Retail food subsidies were replaced with monthly allowances in mid-1990. Other reforms included parental allowances, indexing pensions for inflation, altering social security and family benefits, and legalizing collective bargaining. As a part of broader institutional reform, Klaus moved to recapitalize the banking system, which had been devastated by nonperforming loans made to SOEs, and established longer-term goals of reforming the tax system, the budgetary process, and labor regulations.

But these proposals did not appease those who favored a gradual approach. Deputy Prime Minister Komarek argued that "shock therapy could create as many problems as it solves." Komarek and others warned of the perils of rushing too quickly from socialism to capitalism: disrupted production, rising inflation, businesses forced into receivership, and large-scale unemployment. A senior official at Czechoslovakia's powerful Federation of Trade Unions voiced his concern that "the Minister of Finance prefers unemployment to inflation. That is politically unacceptable in a country where people have traditionally been guaranteed jobs." Gradualists like Minister of Labor and Social Affairs Petr Miller were also concerned that the pain stemming from radical reform could give the Communists ammunition against the government.[59]

Komarek compared Klaus' philosophy to that of Balcerowicz's and predicted "economic ruin," with "perhaps one million unemployed."[60] To help prevent inflation, Komarek and the gradualists argued that price controls should remain until the industrial monopolies were broken up and adapted to a more liberal competitive environment.[61] They believed that free market forces could safely be unleashed only after the SOEs had been restructured and Czechoslovakia's competitiveness had been restored.[62]

Monopolies presented a large political challenge for Klaus and an obstacle to market reform. Over two-thirds of state-owned enterprises had more than 1,000 employees, and in the mid-1980s, nearly 97% of Czechoslovakia's NMP was generated by SOEs. Only 0.7% came from nonfarm private enterprises.[63] The debate over reform led to public fears of bankruptcies, unemployment, and price gouging.

Professor Milan Zeleny, a Czech-American who headed the Christian Democratic Union's economic council, agreed with Dr. Komarek that breaking up the monopolies should come first. He also promoted employee ownership of companies, harkening back to an era of industrial democracy pioneered by Czech footwear maker Bata in the 1930s.[64] This contrasted with Klaus' ideas of privatizing state-owned firms through a unique voucher system aimed at citizen ownership.

A third view on sequencing came from Zdislav Sulc, a reformer from the 1960s, who argued that prices should be freed first but that currency convertibility should wait until the industrial sector had been restructured. Sulc felt that price liberalization was necessary for industrial restructuring to take place, although it would lead to moderate inflationary pressures (estimated at 12% in the year following reform). He warned that a simultaneous move to convertibility would lead to currency devaluation and additional inflation (perhaps as much as 30%), leaving firms unable to afford the Western technology needed for modernization. Without these investments and improvements, Czechoslovakian exports would be uncompetitive. To offset this, Sulc reasoned, the currency would need to be further devalued, which would lead to a vicious cycle of inflation, devaluation, chronic depression, and continuing inflation. Like Komarek and others, Sulc argued for government-led enterprise and sector restructuring before opening the economy to competition from abroad.[65]

The June 1990 elections—the first contested elections since 1946—were in some ways a referendum on which path Czechoslovakia would take: gradualism or shock therapy. For Klaus' plan to become reality required the support of the people, the government, and President Havel. Prior to the election, Klaus voiced concerns that the reform program could be jeopardized by the public's concerns over mass layoffs and price increases. "A really new government . . . would start new discussions, and that would be a tremendous waste," Klaus said. "This could just create a delay and we don't have time for delays."[66]

The coalition formed by the Czech Civic Forum and the Slovak Public Against Violence received 46.6% of the national vote and an overwhelming mandate. Klaus, a member of Civic Forum, emerged from the elections with the highest vote total of any government minister.[i] Václav Havel was elected President by the newly formed Parliament on July 5, 1990, on a vote of 224 to 50, opposed only by the Slovak nationalists. But in the midst of all this stability was uncertainty about the future direction of the government. Civic Forum was not a political party but an alliance, embracing a broad spectrum of ideological positions—from neo-Marxists to Thatcherites.[67] Without a strong opposition party, there was concern that the greatest resistance would come from within the government. The dispute between Havel and Klaus reflected this division. When introducing his newly appointed ministers, Havel avoided mentioning Klaus by name. Havel also tried to remove Klaus from his post as Finance Minister by offering him the governorship of the central bank. While this would have been an influential position, both Klaus and Havel saw the move as a demotion. Klaus managed to stave off this attempt during a series of heated negotiations, asserting his popularity with both the people of Czechoslovakia (he ranked second to Havel in the opinion polls) and with the international financial community.[68]

In Havel's address to the Federal Assembly on June 29, 1990, he stated that

> The transformation of our economy into a market economy does not mean that the general policy of our state should be subordinated solely to economic interests. If we wish to build a truly humane state and if, as such, we wish to open up to the world or, as they say these days, return to Europe, then all the state bodies must make their decisions with this fundamental aim in mind. Their task is to manage the economic consequences of this policy. Our oft-declared intention of implementing reform in such a way that it does not lead to great social shocks, great inflation, or even to the loss of basic social guarantees, must be understood by our economists as a task allotted to them—the objection "it can't be done" does not apply in this respect.[69]

Klaus knew that Havel's words were directed toward him and his band of free-market reformers. He also knew that there was a limited supply of public support for shock therapy. As Karel Dyba, a noted economist and later Minister of Economy in the Czech Republic, stated, "Nobody can tell what the tolerance limit of the population will be. People voted for a government that promised hardships, lower living standards, and some unemployment. It's one thing to be for a market economy, and another thing to experience the not-so-nice side of a market economy."[70]

A finely sequenced and well-planned transition was nice in theory, but Klaus was well aware of the many pitfalls along the path. He had to decide, Could he build support for shock therapy? Even if he could, was a Polish-style program appropriate for Czechoslovakia? Alternatively, was the finely sequenced approach too clever by half? If he recommended a more gradual approach to reform, which elements should he emphasize first? And even if the transition was successful, was an explicit longer-term strategy required? Was the country in danger of becoming stuck in the middle—less productive than the economies of the European Union but unable to compete with the low-wage countries to its east.

---

[i] Under proportional representation, only parties or groups with more than 5% of the vote in either the Czech or Slovak states were allowed representation. Civic Forum, the broad-based alliance that ushered in the Velvet Revolution, swept to victory in the Czech region, claiming 53.2% of the vote. Its Slovak counterpart, Public against Violence, emerged with 32.5% of the Slovak vote. The Communists and the Christian Democrats also passed the 5% hurdle, as did the Slovak National Party. See **Exhibit 6.12.**

CONCEPTUAL NOTE

TRANSITION TO A MARKET ECONOMY: THE COMPONENTS OF REFORM

"Time has finally run out for communism. But its concrete edifice has not yet crumbled. And we must take care not to be crushed beneath its rubble instead of gaining liberty."

—**Aleksandr Solzhenitsyn** (1991)[71]

The revolution that swept across Central Europe in 1989 was fueled by the desire for political and economic freedom—specifically democracy and capitalism. But while direction of movement was clear, the path from a one-party socialist state to democratic capitalism was not. This note focuses on the problems of economic reform. The transition from socialism to capitalism is complex, but we can simplify our discussion by grouping reforms into three broad categories—macroeconomic stabilization, microeconomic liberalization, and institutional reform. Both Leszek Balcerowicz and Václav Klaus, the architects of the Polish and Czechoslovak reform programs, used these categories to discuss their reform programs.

This note makes the positive case for each type of reform. It is organized into three sections, corresponding to the categories of reform. While most reform programs include reforms of each type, there is vigorous debate about the appropriate pace and sequencing of reforms.

Macroeconomic Stabilization

We first consider macroeconomic stabilization—specifically reforms designed to reduce inflation and stabilize the exchange rate. Rapid changes in the price level and exchange rate make long-term planning difficult and therefore increase the risk of any multiperiod economic commitment—such as borrowing, lending, or investing. Economic actors respond either by avoiding such long-term commitments, or by devoting resources to reduce this risk—resources that could be used elsewhere in a stable environment. Macroeconomic stability is restored by reducing domestic and external imbalances. Domestically, this includes fiscal and monetary tightening, as well as reducing subsidies to state-owned enterprises (SOEs). Externally, it involves policies that address the balance of payments and target the exchange rate.

Václav Klaus, the Czechoslovak Finance Minister during reform (and later the Czech Prime Minister), wrote that "reform must start with a heavy dose of restrictive macroeconomic policy. This prepares the ground for price and foreign trade liberalization and, by cutting subsidies, announces the dramatic change of the whole economic climate."[72]

Inflation is caused by excessive growth in the money supply and by supply–demand imbalances. Under communism, inflation was often hidden because prices were fixed and shortages were common. This resulted in forced savings, or 'monetary overhang,' which was an indirect measure of inflationary pressure.

Inflation is primarily a domestic phenomenon and is addressed with three domestic policy initiatives. First, fiscal tightening reduces aggregate demand, as well as the temptation to finance fiscal deficits by printing currency. Second, tighter monetary policy is used to reduce the growth of the money supply. Rapid money supply growth was a particular problem in economies where interest rates were controlled and rising inflation rates had caused real interest rates to become negative—which, in effect, paid debtors to borrow. This led to insatiable demand for credit and, eventually, to the political allocation of credit. Raising rates allows the reinstatement of price-based credit allocation. Third, hard budget constraints are imposed on state-owned enterprises (SOEs), and industrial subsidies are cut. These measures force SOEs to cover their own costs, relieve pressure on the fiscal deficit, and prevent SOEs from simply covering their losses with credit from other SOEs or banks.

Several formerly socialist countries also suffered from external imbalances, exacerbated by high debt and poor trade performance. This combination often led to a vicious cycle in which balance of payments problems led to currency devaluation. Devaluation led to inflation, which hurt export performance and made debt service (measured in foreign currency) more difficult. This led to further balance of payments pressures, perpetuating the downward spiral.

Reformers sought to break this cycle with a combination of policies. These included (1) tightening monetary policy; (2) renegotiating and rescheduling foreign debt to help reduce short-term hard currency requirements; and (3) fixing the exchange rate to reduce inflationary pressures (in many cases, following a large initial devaluation). These policies were often accompanied by restrictions on capital account transactions that allowed the government to maintain better control of monetary policy.

In theory, the internal and external reforms are complementary. Tighter monetary policy and a fixed exchange rate help reduce inflation. A fixed rate also reduces the risk of international investment, thereby increasing inflows of FDI, and eventually, domestic industries' competitive position. These reforms complemented trade liberalization, one of the microeconomic reforms, which is discussed below.

Microeconomic Liberalization

Microeconomic liberalization includes policies that decentralize economic decision making and increase the intensity of competition. These include eliminating price controls; reducing entry and exit restrictions on firms; and encouraging international trade by establishing currency convertibility and simplifying and lowering trade barriers. The authors of the World Bank's *World Development Report 1996: From Plan to Market* wrote that liberalization is important because

> [i]t decentralizes production and trading decisions to enterprises and households and directly addresses the two fundamental weaknesses of central planning: poor incentives and poor information. Liberalization exposes firms to customer demand, the profit motive, and competition, and it lets relative prices adjust in line with true scarcities . . . and when goods and services are traded freely, the price mechanism—Adam Smith's invisible hand—matches demand and supply.[73]

A second key microeconomic reform is the abolition of bureaucratic restrictions on the establishment and development of private firms. Without entry by new firms, SOEs might be tempted to raise prices rather than increase efficiency. In Poland, Balcerowicz suggested that "the spontaneous growth of the private sector should be as fast as possible, as it is the main engine of growth and flexibility in the transition to a market economy."[74] Many reformers were skeptical about how quickly SOEs could be privatized but believed that entry by new firms would provide the competitive pressure that would force SOEs to improve efficiency or to disgorge resources (workers or productive assets) that could be better used elsewhere.

A third key microeconomic reform involves policies designed to liberalize international trade. Most programs of reform include devaluation and unification of the exchange rate (after which the rate was often fixed); establishing currency convertibility; the elimination of most quotas; and the simplification and reduction of tariffs.

Increasing foreign trade broadens the effective market for a nation's inputs and outputs, introduces additional competition and allows a country to benefit from specialization and comparative advantage. Ideally, these factors will help to stabilize the balance of payments.

Several countries have allowed free convertibility for current account transactions while maintaining restrictions on capital account transactions. This partial convertibility is designed to achieve the benefits of trade without losing control of domestic monetary policy—an important tool for fighting inflation.

Jeffrey Sachs, a Harvard economist and advisor to more than a dozen reforming countries, describes the transition process as a "seamless web." In writing about Poland, he says:

> The basic goal was to move from a situation of extreme shortages and hyperinflation to one of supply-and-demand balance and stable prices. For this Poland needed tight macroeconomic policies with the decontrol of prices [*microeconomic reforms*]. To have a working price system, Poland needed competition. To have competition, it needed free international trade to counteract the monopolistic industrial structure. To have free trade, it needed not only low tariffs but the convertibility of currency. To have convertibility of currency at a stable exchange rate, it needed monetary discipline and a realistic exchange rate.[75]

Sachs discusses the tight links between macroeconomic stabilization and microeconomic liberalization, but without institutional reform, these changes will lack a solid foundation and will likely prove ephemeral.

Institutional Reform

Institutions can be thought of as "the rules of the game in a society or, more formally . . . the humanly devised constraints that shape human interaction."[76] Although sometimes difficult to observe directly, institutions have an important influence on all economic activity. Under socialism, the government's role in the economy was pervasive—it owned firms, was the sole source of financing, and had extremely powerful regulatory powers. As part of the transition to capitalism, all three roles must be transformed. Ownership must be shifted into private hands. The financial system must be restructured and depoliticized. And the regulatory apparatus must be redesigned. Under socialism, however, the nonstate institutions required to perform these functions (such as commercial and taxation codes, a system of private capital allocation, and institutions of corporate control) were severely underdeveloped.

Five types of institutional reform are thought essential for a successful transition. These include the reform of (1) the tax system and government administration; (2) property rights and the legal system; (3) the financial system; (4) industry ownership (privatization); and (5) the social safety net.

Reforms of the tax system and government administration are important elements of any reform program. For property rights to be secure, the taxation system must be transparent, predictable, and well enforced—conditions that rarely existed under communism. Legal reform that strengthens property rights also provides the basis for separating politics from economic activity. Additional key administrative reforms include establishing central bank independence and creating genuine local government.

A second reform involves the establishment and strengthening of property rights. In *Adam Smith Goes to Moscow*, Walter Adams and James Brock create a fictional advisor who explains,

[T]he simple fact is that no economic system can provide proper economic incentives unless individuals have the right to buy, own, and sell property as they see fit. Self-interest and voluntary exchanges won't be successful motivators unless there is private ownership of the means of production. . . . Only if people are owners, or have that prospect, do they care enough to preserve and maintain property, and to invest time, effort, and money in the hope of future reward. If they hire others to work for them, they have a strong incentive to monitor the workers' behavior; and since the workers know that their employer can reward or fire them, they, too, have a strong incentive to work efficiently. . . . It is the prospect of private profit that directs production into channels that best serve consumer demand at the least cost. It is private ownership that puts society's resources in the hands of those who best know how to use them.[77]

Legal reform is also required for property rights to have an effect. Categories of reform include contract law, regulatory law, labor law, company and foreign investment law (to facilitate entry of new firms), bankruptcy law (to establish exit procedures), and competition law (antimonopoly law). Because legal reform is complicated, it usually takes many years.

Third, restructuring the financial system is important because this system (e.g., banks, insurance companies, securities markets) is responsible for mobilizing and allocating investment capital and for pricing and allocating risk. Its task is to ensure that capital flows to its highest value use and is allocated for economic, not political, reasons. Many economists believe that this credit allocation role makes the financial sector "strategic." In order for a capitalist economy to prosper, the capital allocation system must function smoothly. Restructuring the banking sector has been considered a top priority in most reform programs.

Fourth, state-owned enterprises must be restructured and privatized. Restructuring includes reorganizing SOEs along economically rational lines and breaking up large monopolies. Privatization leads to a variety of benefits. First, it is easier to cut off industrial subsidies to private (as opposed to state-owned) firms. Second, private owners are more likely than SOEs to pursue economic rather than political goals, working to create and maximize economic value. Third, privatization decentralizes decision making, promising increased competition and innovation. Finally, privatization may yield revenues that the government can use to offset other costs of transition. In most countries, however, revenues from privatization have been minimal.

Finally, the transition from state-socialism to a market economy requires a complete reworking of the social safety net. In socialist economies, job security was absolute and most social benefits were provided through firms. These often included housing, vacations, retirement pay, and medical and disability benefits. The move toward a market economy puts pressure on firms to reduce these benefits, at precisely the time that unemployment becomes visible for the first time. To maintain political support, reform-minded governments are expected to soften the unpleasant effects of capitalism. At minimum, this requires reform of the pension, disability, and unemployment insurance systems and the establishment of welfare and job training programs.

The move from socialism to a market economy presents a complex challenge for many newly democratized nations. Some reforms can be accomplished quickly, while others take years of efforts. Some can be implemented in isolation, while others are dependent in complementary reforms. There has been vigorous debate about the proper pace and sequencing of reforms. While these theoretical debates are fascinating, the best lessons may be learned by simply observing the score of natural experiments currently taking place in Central and Eastern Europe.

EXHIBIT 6.1   AUGUST 1990: CENTRAL EUROPE AND THE BALKANS

SOURCE: Central Intelligence Agency, *Atlas of Eastern Europe* (Washington, DC: U.S. Government Printing Office, 1990), p. 5.

EXHIBIT 6.2   POLAND AND CZECHOSLOVAKIA: STARTING CONDITIONS IN 1989

Indicator	Poland	Czechoslovakia
Population (in millions, mid-1989)	37.9	15.6
GDP per capita (in 1989 US$)[a]	1,790	3,450
GDP growth (average annual rate, in % at constant prices):[b]		
1970s	5.5	4.6
1980s	−0.7	1.4
Structure of GDP (percentages):[c]		
Agriculture	11	6
Industry	41	60
Construction and services	48	34
Administered prices (% of total)	100[d]	100
State ownership (% of economy)	70	100
External debt/GDP (1990, %)	80	19
External debt-service ratio (1990)[e]	56	23
Exports to CMEA, 1990:[f]		
% of total exports	41	60
% of GDP	14	25

SOURCES: Michael Bruno, "Stabilization and Reform in Eastern Europe: A Preliminary Evaluation," in The *Transition in Eastern Europe: A National Bureau of Economic Research Project Report*, Blanchard, Froot, and Sachs, eds. (Chicago: University of Chicago Press, 1994), p. 23; Andres Solimano, "The Economies of Central Europe: An Historical and International Perspective," in *Reforming Central and Eastern European Economies: Initial Results and Challenges*, Corbo, Coricelli, and Bossak, eds. (Washington, DC: The World Bank, 1991), p. 19.
[a]Data are sensitive to the choice of exchange rates.   [b]Net material product (ICES, 1990).   [c]Data are for 1988. Czechoslovakia shares correspond to net material product.   [d]Excluding food prices.   [e]Debt service (principal and interest) as a percentage of export earnings.   [f]Estimates are very sensitive to distortions in intra-CMEA prices and exchange rates. Data for exports are based on estimated world market prices (considerably above the official traded prices); however, the GDP data are based on actual official prices.

EXHIBIT 6.3   PRODUCTIVITY (AVERAGE ANNUAL PERCENTAGE CHANGE)

	1971–1975	1976–1980	1981–1985	1986–1988
Total Factor Productivity				
Czechoslovakia	1.5	0.7	———0.1[a]———	
Poland	2.2	−0.6	———0.2[a]———	
Capital Productivity				
Czechoslovakia	0.5[b]	−1.9	−3.1	−2.1
Poland	0.9[b]	−5.5	−3.2	1.2
Labor Productivity				
Czechoslovakia	5.4	3.3	1.1	2.1[c]
Poland	8.1	0.9	−0.1	4.5[c]

SOURCES: Shen, pp. 60, 62; Mejstrik and Burger, "Privatization in Practice: Czechoslovakia's Experience from 1989 to Mid-1992," in *Privatization and Economic Reform in Central Europe: The Changing Business Climate* Rondinelli, ed. (Westport, Conn.: Quorum Books, 1994), p. 137.
[a]Data are for 1981–1988.   [b]Data are for 1970–1975.   [c]Data are for 1986–1989.

EXHIBIT 6.4	NATIONAL INCOME ACCOUNTS

POLAND, 1980–1988 (BILLIONS OF CONSTANT ZLOTYS)

	1980	1981	1982	1983	1984	1985[a] I	1985[a] II	1986	1987	1988
Gross domestic product	6,268	5,643	5,374	5,763	5,993	6,211	9,018	9,398	9,582	9,975
Government consumption	471	450	461	475	511	550	850	850	859	860
Private consumption	4,201	4,049	3,543	3,734	3,893	3,994	5,693	5,955	6,106	6,283
Investments[b]	1,714	1,333	1,287	1,357	1,443	1,532	2,341	2,446	2,449	2,658
Fixed investments	1,606	1,300	1,122	1,221	1,341	1,399	1,872	1,957	2,037	2,161
Changes in stocks	108	33	165	136	102	133	469	490	412	497
Exports	1,241	1,015	1,078	1,177	1,316	1,320	1,520	1,584	1,663	1,820
Imports	1,384	1,111	962	1,018	1,114	1,190	1,441	1,518	1,588	1,731
Growth Rates (%)										
Gross domestic product		–10	–5	6	6	4		4	2	4
Government consumption		–5	2	3	8	8		0	1	0
Private consumption		–4	–13	5	4	3		5	3	3
Investments		–22	–3	5	6	6		5	0	9
Fixed investments		–19	–14	9	10	4		5	4	6
Changes in stock		–70	400	–18	–25	30		5	–16	21
Exports		–18	6	9	12	0		4	5	9
Imports		–20	–13	6	9	7		5	5	9

CZECHOSLOVAKIA, 1980–1989 (BILLIONS OF CONSTANT KORUNY, IN JANUARY 1, 1984, PRICES)

	1980	1981	1982	1983	1984	1985	1986	1987	1988	1989
Gross domestic product	595.1	595.3	600.2	614.6	627.5	641.1	652.7	658.0	675.2	683.9
Total consumption	420.6	421.3	422.1	440.6	448.5	460.3	473.1	485.6	499.4	508.6
Gross investment	199.9	182.8	178.2	169.5	165.8	167.0	174.3	170.5	167.0	179.7
Fixed investment	164.9	167.2	160.0	152.2	153.8	152.6	156.1	146.7	156.7	170.8
Changes in stocks	35.0	15.6	18.2	17.3	12.0	14.4	18.2	23.8	10.3	8.9
Exports of goods and nonfactor services	181.0	184.7	195.0	204.6	227.5	236.3	236.0	241.0	251.3	254.8
Imports of goods and nonfactor services	206.5	193.5	195.1	200.0	214.3	222.5	230.7	239.1	242.5	259.2
Growth rates (%)										
Gross domestic product		0.0	0.8	2.4	2.1	2.2	1.8	0.8	2.6	1.3
Total consumption		0.2	0.2	4.4	1.8	2.6	2.8	2.6	2.8	1.8
Gross investment		–8.6	–2.5	–4.9	–2.2	0.7	4.4	–2.2	–2.1	7.6
Fixed investment		1.4	–4.3	–4.9	1.1	–0.8	2.3	–6.0	6.8	9.0
Changes in stocks		–55.4	16.7	–4.9	–30.6	20.0	26.4	30.8	–56.7	–13.6
Exports of goods and nonfactor services		2.0	5.6	4.9	11.2	3.9	–0.1	2.1	4.3	1.4
Imports of goods and nonfactor services		–6.3	0.8	2.5	7.2	3.8	3.7	3.6	1.4	6.9

SOURCES: World Bank Country Study, *Poland: Economic Management for a New Era* (Washington, DC: World Bank, 1990), p. 94; World Bank Country Study, *Czechoslovakia: Transition to a Market Economy*, p. 138.

[a]In 1985 the Polish statistical authorities changed the formula used to calculate constant Zlotys. The two columns of figures listed under 1985 represent the old and the new method of calculation. From 1980 to 1985 (I), 1982 Zlotys are used, and from 1985 (II) through 1988, 1984 Zlotys are used.

[b]Possible statistical discrepancy due to rounding.

EXHIBIT 6.5	PERCENTAGE DISTRIBUTION OF GDP/NMP BY INDUSTRIAL ORIGIN

POLAND (% GDP)

	1970	1975	1980	1985	1988
Production of Goods of which:	89.7	89.0	87.7	86.0	84.4
Agriculture	14.0	12.5	13.2	13.5	10.8
Industry	48.6	52.3	47.9	41.8	40.6
Construction	8.5	9.7	8.0	10.2	12.0
Transport and communications	7.2	7.0	7.5	6.1	4.9
Trade	8.1	4.6	8.4	11.5	13.9
Other	3.3	2.9	2.8	2.9	2.2
Other Services	10.3	11.0	12.3	14.0	15.6
Housing	1.2	1.0	1.3	2.5	na
Education	2.3	2.5	2.8	2.9	na
Culture and art	0.4	0.3	0.4	0.4	na
Health and social welfare	1.4	1.6	1.9	2.0	na
Other	5.0	5.6	5.9	6.2	na

CZECHOSLOVAKIA (% NMP)

	1970	1975	1980	1985	1988
Agriculture	10.1	8.3	7.2	6.7	6.4
Industry	61.0	64.7	63.6	59.8	59.6
Construction	11.2	12.4	10.5	10.9	10.7
Trade and catering	9.1	9.0	10.3	13.5	15.1
Other	8.6	5.6	8.4	9.1	8.2

SOURCES: *Poland: Economic Management for a New Era*, p. 92; *Czechoslovakia: Transition to a Market Economy*, p. 129.
na: Data not available.

EXHIBIT 6.6	STATE REVENUES AND EXPENDITURES

POLAND, 1980–1988 (BILLIONS OF CURRENT ZLOTYS)

	1980	1981	1982	1983	1984	1985	1986	1987	1988
Total Revenue	1,214.0	1,148.7	2,404.9	2,707.9	3,403.0	4,224.2	5,171.0	6,168.5	10,543.6
Total Expenditure of which:	(1,243.0)	(1,463.2)	(2,567.5)	(2,850.4)	(3,595.0)	(4,195.9)	(5,315.3)	(6,388.9)	(10,610.1)
Subsidies	719.9	848.8	1,146.2	1,140.1	1,486.6	1,671.8	2,108.1	2,687.9	4,393.5
To the population	300.0	363.3	572.6	576.2	748.6	806.7	1,183.1	1,690.8	2,966.5
To enterprises and economic units	419.9	485.5	573.6	563.9	738.0	865.1	925.0	997.1	1,427.0
Transfers to other units[a]	79.4	104.2	250.9	261.5	330.7	365.9	541.8	683.2	1,247.5
Other[b]	20.2	18.2	18.0	30.0	55.8	116.4	95.2	143.2	248.0
Accrual for interest in arrears[c]	na	na	(95.2)	(108.2)	(176.7)	(44.4)	217.4	(567.9)	(1,005.2)
Deficit/Surplus[d]	na	na	−257.7	−250.7	−368.7	−16.1	73.1	−788.4	−1,071.6
GDP in current values	2,511.2	2,752.6	5,546.4	6,924.0	8,575.9	10,367.2	12,953.0	16,939.9	29,628.7
Deficit/Surplus as % of GDP	na	na	−4.6	−3.6	−4.3	−0.2	0.6	−4.7	−3.6

CZECHOSLOVAKIA, 1980–1989 (BILLIONS OF CURRENT KORUNY)[e]

	1980	1981	1982	1983	1984	1985	1986	1987	1988	1989
Total Revenue	312.2	321.3	329.3	339.2	364.6	385.0	392.2	411.4	431.4	463.7
Total Expenditure of which:	314.6	323.3	332.6	342.3	367.6	388.5	397.9	415.2	449.5	473.3
Current expenditure, of which:										
Transfers to enterprises	53.8	68.4	65.3	69.8	82.6	84.6	90.9	93.6	99.5	102.2
Capital expenditure and net lending, of which:										
Transfers to enterprises	25.4	14.8	15.7	15.1	11.0	14.0	14.2	13.8	28.7	10.9
Deficit/Surplus	–2.4	–2.0	–3.3	–3.1	–3.0	–3.5	–5.7	–3.8	–18.1	–9.6
As a percentage of NMP	–0.5	–0.4	–0.7	–0.6	–0.6	–0.6	–1.0	–0.7	–3.0	–1.6

SOURCES: *Poland: Economic Management for a New Era*, pp. 93, 94, 101,103–104; *Czechoslovakia: Transition to a Market Economy*, p. 167.
[a]Consists mainly of transfers to extra budgetary funds and other organizations to finance expenditures for various cultural, educational, and social purposes.
[b]Includes interest payments on foreign credits extended by the government.
[c]Calculated by multiplying the annual change in interest arrears by the current market exchange rate [see **Exhibit 6.11**].
[d]Total revenue less total expenditure less accrual for interest in arrears.
[e]Only direct revenues and expenditures of the various parts of general government are included (i.e., data are presented net of intragovernmental transfers).
na: Data not available.

EXHIBIT 6.7 | **EXTERNAL DEBT**

POLAND, 1981–1988 (US$ BILLIONS)

	1981	1982	1983	1984	1985	1985	1987	1988
Convertible currency	$25.9	$26.5	$26.4	$26.9	$29.7	$33.5	$39.2	$39.1
Short-term	1.1	1.3	1.3	1.3	1.4	1.4	1.5	1.4
Medium- and long-term	24.3	23.6	22.4	21.5	23.9	28.8	32.6	30.6
Interest in arrears	0.5	1.6	2.7	4.1	4.4	3.3	5.1	7.1
Nonconvertible currency[a]	2.6	2.9	2.7	2.8	3.4	4.2	2.9	3.0
Short-term	1.0	0.5	0.2	0.6	na	0.1	na	na
Medium- and long-term	1.6	2.4	2.5	2.2	3.4	4.1	2.9	3.0
Total debt, including arrears	28.5	29.4	29.1	29.7	33.1	37.7	42.1	42.1

CZECHOSLOVAKIA, 1981–1989 (US$ MILLIONS)

	1981	1982	1983	1984	1985	1986	1987	1988	1989
Convertible currency	$6,316.2	$5,769.0	$5,159.5	$4,737.1	$4,607.8	$5,567.4	$6,657.0	$7,280.7	$7,915.1
Short-term debt	3,177.6	2,675.5	2,183.2	1,865.0	1,918.7	2,690.8	3,076.1	3,406.3	3,586.9
Medium- and long-term[b]	3,138.6	3,093.5	2,976.3	2,872.1	2,689.1	2,876.6	3,580.9	3,874.4	4,328.3
Nonconvertible currency	714.5	690.8	803.1	964.4	966.3	1,147.4	999.8	524.5	775.7
Short-term debt	567.7	549.5	689.4	878.0	887.2	1,079.2	928.9	454.3	706.3
Medium- and long-term	146.8	141.3	113.7	86.4	79.1	68.2	70.9	70.2	69.5
Total debt	7,030.7	6,459.8	5,962.6	5,701.5	5,574.1	6,714.7	7,656.8	7,805.2	8,690.8

SOURCES: *Poland: Economic Management for a New Era*, p. 101; *Czechoslovakia: Transition to a Market Economy*, p. 165.
[a]The external debt in nonconvertible currencies was converted from transferable rubles (TR) into US$ by using cross rates derived from the commercial rates of the zloty vis-à-vis the TR and US$; prior to 1982, the period average exchange rate was used, but since 1982 end-of-period rates have been used.
[b]Virtually all long-term commercial credits are guaranteed by the Czechoslovak Government.
na: Data not available.

EXHIBIT 6.8	BALANCE OF PAYMENTS

POLAND, 1980–1988 (US$ MILLIONS)

	1980	1981	1982	1983	1984	1985	1986	1987	1988
Current Account									
Exports (fob)	$14,170	$10,464	$10,457	$11,000	$11,800	$10,912	$11,558	$11,602	$13,211
Imports (fob)	15,806	12,564	10,654	10,582	10,962	10,436	10,914	10,803	12,064
Trade balance	–1,636	–2,100	–197	418	838	476	644	799	1,147
Total services Of which:	–2,320	–2,788	–2,653	–2,356	–2,967	–2,219	–2,538	–2,790	–2,883
Travel, net	16	–101	–65	–111	–123	–61	–45	–8	–16
Freight and insurance, net	64	288	332	271	89	85	88	–26	–23
Interest, net	–2,357	–3,060	–2,963	–2,592	–3,021	–2,383	–2,663	–2,915	–2,955
Other current items, net	–43	85	43	76	88	140	82	159	111
Transfers, net	656	655	323	380	467	768	946	1,413	1,434
Current account balance	–3,300	–4,233	–2,527	–1,558	–1,662	–975	–968	–578	–302
Capital Account									
Medium- and long-term capital	2,659	898	–2,371	–982	–107	84	–1,652	na	na
Revolving credits, net	0	0	196	338	240	–2	139	106	30
Short-term capital, and errors and omissions	239	–172	478	295	191	540	–421	na	na
Change in Reserves	402	–35	–369	–119	–340	236	173	–797	–561
Change in Arrears[a]		3,542	4,593	2,026	1,678	117	2,729	na	na

SOURCE: *Poland: Economic Management for a New Era*, p. 95.

[a]In 1981–1984, agreements for rescheduling the bulk of the annual principal obligations are treated as arrears until the effective operational date of the agreement, which for reschedulings with Western banks was in the year subsequent to the signing of the agreement.

na: Data not available.

CZECHOSLOVAKIA, 1980–1989 (CONVERTIBLE AND NONCONVERTIBLE CURRENCIES, IN MILLIONS OF US$)[a]

	1980	1981	1982	1983	1984	1985	1986	1987	1988	1989
Current Account										
Exports (fob)[b]	$5,237.3	$4,997.7	$4,887.6	$4,908.5	$4,862.6	$4,727.2	$5,255.7	$5,623.4	$6,124.6	$6,475.6
Imports (fob)[b]	5,226.0	4,679.3	4,314.6	4,064.0	3,934.5	4,013.9	5,055.8	5,667.4	6,211.3	6,236.9
Trade balance	11.3	318.4	573.0	844.5	928.1	713.3	199.9	−44.0	−86.7	238.7
Total services Of which:	−306.2	−309.0	−28.6	82.1	116.7	117.6	232.5	209.5	333.6	49.9
Shipment and other, net[c]	−57.9	95.4	75.8	113.3	125.6	145.6	138.2	157.5	144.2	106.6
Travel, net	0.6	−16.5	−0.1	−21.9	−39.8	−37.2	−33.2	−14.4	−15.6	−64.8
Interest, net	−500.2	−641.3	−448.5	−267.6	−234.9	−181.7	−137.8	−136.5	−180.3	−141.5
Other, net[c]	251.3	253.4	344.2	258.3	265.8	190.9	265.3	202.9	385.3	149.6
Unrequited transfers	−42.9	−34.8	−159.9	−35.2	−28.5	−39.7	−44.3	−43.0	−46.5	−36.1
Private	−2.3	−2.0	0.7	−1.0	−1.1	−2.6	−4.7	−1.1	−4.6	−5.7
Official	−40.6	−32.8	−160.6	−34.2	−27.4	−37.1	−39.6	−41.9	−41.9	−30.4
Current account balance	−337.8	−25.4	384.5	891.4	1,016.3	791.2	388.1	122.5	200.4	252.5
Capital Account										
Medium- and long-term capital, net	360.0	277.9	−9.6	−401.8	−627.6	−774.2	−390.6	349.0	58.4	221.3
Short-term capital, net	665.8	−802.5	−462.3	−267.8	34.4	15.3	547.4	96.9	215.3	150.3
Capital account balance	1,025.8	−524.6	−471.9	−669.6	−593.2	−758.9	156.8	445.9	273.7	371.6
Valuation changes	−330.5	−321.0	−98.3	−118.6	−274.6	−121.2	−253.7	−333.7	−212.3	−107.1
Errors and omissions	−0.7	−16.2	21.3	9.4	9.2	−5.5	−35.0	19.1	−52.8	46.2
Overall Balance	356.8	−887.2	−164.4	112.6	157.7	−94.4	256.2	253.8	209.0	563.2
Change in Reserves	−356.8	887.2	164.4	−112.6	−157.7	94.4	−256.2	−253.8	−209.0	−563.2

SOURCE: *Czechoslovakia: Transition to a Market Economy*, pp. 145, 147.

[a]This exhibit is intended to be used solely as a broad guide to Czechoslovakia's Balance of Payments statement. It does not include the Balance of Payments in transferable rubles. Also, please note that the translation to US$ may be misleading as part of the statement is comprised of *nonconvertible currency*.

[b]Excluding interest payments and receipts related to suppliers credits, which are part of the customs data.

[c]Excluding export-related expenditures and assembly costs and commissions related to transactions between nonresidents.

EXHIBIT 6.9	INFLATION AND REAL WAGES (AVERAGE ANNUAL PERCENTAGE CHANGE)

| | Average Wages | | | | |
| | Consumer Prices | | Poland | Real Wages | |
	Czech.	Poland	Poland	Czech.	Poland
1970–78	⊤ 1.1[a]	3.8	10.3	⊤ 1.6[c]	6.3
1979–81	⊥	13.1	16.3	⊥	2.8
1982	5.1	100.1	56.0	⊤	−28.7
1983	0.9	22.0	27.7	0.8[d]	19.0
1984	0.9	15.1	13.6		−1.3
1985	2.3	15.1	19.9	⊥	4.2
1986	0.5	17.7	21.1	1.6	2.9
1987	0.1	25.2	21.4	2.4	−3.1
1988	0.1	60.0	83.9	3.1	15.0
1989	1.4	257.1[b]	298.6	0.7	11.6

SOURCES: *Czechoslovakia: Transition to a Market Economy*, pp. 131, 181, 183; Lipton and Sachs, p. 105.
[a]Data are for 1970–1981.
[b]Changes are calculated from annual averages. With the acceleration of inflation in 1989, the rate of price increase was much higher on the basis of an end-of-year comparison. Consumer prices rose 636% between December 1988 and December 1989.
[c]Data are for 1970–1980.
[d]Data are for 1980–1985.

EXHIBIT 6.10	EXCHANGE RATES

| | Poland (end of period) (zloty per US$) | Czechoslovakia | | Discount of Black to Official Rate (percentage) |
| | | (koruny per US$) (period average) | | |
		Official Rate[a]	Black Market Rate[b]	
1980	46.1	5.38	26.18	387
1981	55.8	5.89	27.03	359
1982	86.5	6.10	28.25	363
1983	98.4	6.29	30.77	389
1984	126.2	6.64	33.22	400
1985	147.9	6.85	34.72	407
1986	197.6	6.00	29.76	396
1987	315.5	5.47	27.78	408
1988	502.6	5.32	33.44	529
1989	6,500.0	na	42.39	na

SOURCES: *Poland: Economic Management for a New Era*, p. iv; International Monetary Fund, 1996 *International Financial Statistics Yearbook* (Washington, DC: International Monetary Fund, 1996), pp. 630–631; *Czechoslovakia: Transition to a Market Economy*, p. 151.
[a]The official rate was discontinued on January 1, 1989.
[b]SOURCE: Schweizerischer Bankverein.
na: Data not available.

EXHIBIT 6.11	POLAND: 1989/1990

SELECTED INDICATORS, JANUARY 1989–MARCH 1990

Month and Year	Real Wage (index, January 1989 = 1.00)	Monthly Change in Real Wage (%)	Monthly rate of inflation (%)	Official Exchange Rate (zlotys per US$)
1989				
January	1.00	–40.1	11.0	506
February	1.18	18.2	7.9	526
March	1.46	24.0	8.1	566
April	1.29	–12.0	9.8	631
May	1.15	–10.9	7.2	746
June	1.24	8.1	6.1	849
July	1.19	–4.1	9.5	836
August	1.73	45.2	39.5	988
September	1.30	–24.5	34.4	1,340
October	1.06	–18.2	54.8	1,970
November	1.08	1.9	22.4	3,077
December	1.36	25.6	17.7	5,235
1990				
January	0.77	–43.2	78.6	9,500
February	0.66	–14.9	23.9[a]	9,500
March	0.69	4.3	4.7	9,500

ECONOMIC OPINION POLLS (PERCENTAGE)

Item	September 1989	November 1989	January 1990	February 1990	March 1990
Overall economic situation					
Very good	0.6	1.1	0.6	1.8	3.2
Good	0.4	2.7	1.6	3.7	10.6
Not good, not bad	4.8	9.6	9.8	15.9	25.4
Somewhat bad	17.2	34.1	29.1	34.0	30.2
Bad	32.8	30.2	32.0	27.6	18.3
Very bad	42.9	20.8	24.8	14.7	7.8
Undecided	1.3	1.4	2.0	2.4	4.5

PROJECTED AND ACTUAL MACROECONOMIC INDICATORS IN 1990

	Projected	Actual
Consumer price inflation (%)	267.6	352.2
Gross domestic product (% change)	–3.1	–11.6
Industrial output[b] (% change)	–5.0	–24.2
Unemployment rate (%)	2.0	6.1
Merchandise trade balance		
In dollars (billions)	–0.8	3.8
In transferable rubles (billions)	0.5	4.4
Consumption (% change)	–1.0	–11.7
Real wages (% change)	–20.0	–22.3

SOURCES: Sachs and Lipton, pp. 110, 117; Slay, p. 94.

[a]The official inflation data compare the average price level for each month with the average price level in the previous month. Estimates of inflation during February (i.e., comparing the price levels at the end of the month) show that inflation was about 5%. The difference derives from the fact that the price level was much higher at the end of January than on average in January because of the corrective inflation.

[b]Gross industrial sales.

EXHIBIT 6.12   CZECHOSLOVAKIA: 1990 ELECTION RESULTS

THE SHAPE OF FREEDOM
Seats in Czechoslovakia's parliament, June 1990
House of the People
Total Seats: 150*

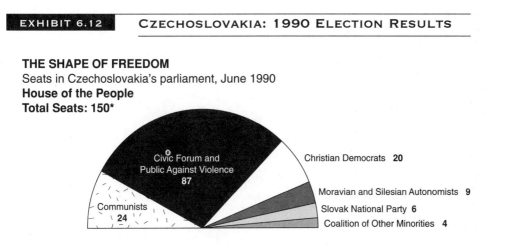

Civic Forum and Public Against Violence 87
Christian Democrats 20
Moravian and Silesian Autonomists 9
Slovak National Party 6
Coalition of Other Minorities 4
Communists 24

* 101 seats for the Czech Republic, 49 for Slovakia

HOUSE OF THE PEOPLE (% OF VOTES)[A]

	National Result	Czech Republic	Slovakia
Civic Forum and Public against Violence	46.6[b]	53.2 —	— 32.5
Communists	13.6	13.5	13.8
Christian Democrats	12.0	8.7	19.0
Moravian and Silesian autonomists	5.4	7.9	—
Slovak National Party	3.5	—	11.0
Coalition of other minorities	2.8	—	8.6
Other	16.1	16.7	15.1

SOURCE: *The Economist*, June 16, 1990, p. 54.

[a]Five percent of the vote in either republic is needed to win seats.

[b]National result for the Civic Forum and Public against Violence coalition.

EXHIBIT 6.13	GDP PER CAPITA AND WAGES: AN INTERNATIONAL COMPARISON (1990 US$)		

Country	GDP per Capita	Value Added per Worker	Average Wage, including Benefits
European Union			
Germany	15,687	76,368	38,440
France	14,873	57,376	36,111
Switzerland	18,873	85,691	—
Central and Eastern Europe			
Czechoslovakia	3,450	5,094	2,396
Poland	1,790	7,637	1,257
Bosnia and Herzogovina	2,786	10,796	4,488
Hungary	2,351	7,017	2,495
Romania	1,715	4,305	1,728
Russia	3,923	16,512	2,159
Slovenia	3,050	10,796	4,488
Kazakhstan	2310	—	—
Moldova	1330	—	—
Mongolia	201	—	—
Tajikistan	267	—	—
Other Countries			
India	354	3098	1502
Pakistan	423	7644	1689

SOURCE: *Statistical Abstract of the World*, 2nd ed., 1996.

END NOTES

1 Ben Slay, *The Polish Economy: Crisis, Reform, and Transformation* (Princeton, N.J.: Princeton University Press, 1994), pp. 23–25.

2 Ronald D. Bachman, "Government and Politics," in Glenn E. Curtis, ed., *Poland: A Country Study* (Washington, DC: Federal Research Division, Library of Congress, 1994), p. 184.

3 Until the 1989 reforms, private farmers controlled 75% of agricultural land. For further information, see Raphael Shen, *Economic Reform in Poland and Czechoslovakia: Lessons in Systemic Transformation* (Westport, Conn.: Praeger Publishers, 1993), p. 23. See also Andres Solimano, "The Economies of Central and Eastern Europe: An Historical and International Perspective," in Vittorio Corbo, Fabrizio Coricelli, and Jan Bossak, eds., *Reforming Central and Eastern European Economies: Initial Results and Challenges* (Washington, DC: World Bank, 1991), p. 19.

4 Leszek Balcerowicz, "Poland," in John Williamson, ed., *The Political Economy of Policy Reform* (Washington, DC: Institute for International Economics, 1994), p. 157.

5 Slay, *The Polish Economy*, p. 25.

6 Ibid., p. 31.

7 Shen, Economic Reform in Poland and Czechoslovakia, p. 46.

8 Slay, *The Polish Economy*, p. 30.

9 Ibid., pp. 34–35.

10 Shen, *Economic Reform in Poland and Czechoslovakia*, p. 69.

11 Slay, *The Polish Economy*, p. 41.

12 Ibid., p. 44.

13 Balcerowicz, "Poland,", p. 154.

14 Slay, *The Polish Economy*, p. 54.

15 Shen, *Economic Reform in Poland and Czechoslovakia*. p. 53.

16 Jeffrey Sachs, *Poland's Jump to the Market Economy* (Cambridge, Mass.: MIT Press, 1994), p 36.

17 Slay, *The Polish Economy*, pp. 66–68.

18 Sachs, *Poland's Jump to the Market Economy*, p. 36.

19 Balcerowicz, "Poland,", p. 160.

20 Leszek Balcerowicz, *Socialism, Capitalism, Transformation* (Budapest: Central European University Press, 1995), p. 239.

21 Balcerowicz, *Poland*, p. 161.

22 Ibid., pp. 161–162.

23 Balcerowicz, *Socialism, Capitalism, Transformation*, pp. 265–266.

24 Ibid., p. 261.

25 Slay, *The Polish Economy*, p. 94.

26 Balcerowicz, *Poland*, p. 163.

27 David Lipton and Jeffrey Sachs, "Creating a Market Economy in Eastern Europe: The Case of Poland," *Brookings Papers on Economic Activity*, 1990, no. 1, p. 99.

28 Ibid., p. 100.

29 Sachs, *Poland's Jump to the Market Economy*, p. 61.

30 Ibid., p. 59.

31 Ibid., p. 62.

32 Ibid., pp. 64–65.

33 *Czechoslovakia: EIU Country Profile 1989–1990* (London: Economist Intelligence Unit, 1990), p. 3.

34 Shen, *Economic Reform in Poland and Czechoslovakia*, p. 48.

35 *The New Encyclopedia Britannica*, Vol. 16 (Chicago: Encyclopedia Britannica, 1994), p. 915.

36 Shen, *Economic Reform in Poland and Czechoslovakia*, pp. 9–10.

37 Michal Mejstrik and James Burger, "Privatization in Practice: Czechoslovakia's Experience from 1989 to Mid-1992," in Dennis A. Rondinelli, ed., *Privatization and Economic Reform in Central Europe: The Changing Business Climate* (Westport, Conn.: Quorum Books, 1994), p. 135.

38 Ibid., p. 136.

39 Shen, *Economic Reform in Poland and Czechoslovakia*, p. 49.

40 Ibid., pp. 50–51.

41 Becky A. Gates, "The Economy," in Ihor Gawdiak, ed., *Czechoslovakia: A Country Study* (Washington, DC: Federal Research Division, Library of Congress, 1989), p. 140.

42 Shen, *Economic Reform in Poland and Czechoslovakia*, p. 72.

43 Karel Dyba and Jan Svejnar, "Stabilization and Transition in Czechoslovakia," in Olivier Jean Blanchard, Kenneth A. Froot, and Jeffrey D. Sachs, eds., *The Transition in Eastern Europe: A National Bureau of Economic Research Project Report*, vol. 1 (Chicago: The University of Chicago Press, 1994), pp. 94, 97.

44 Ibid., p. 97.

45 Ibid., pp. 23, 97.

46 World Bank Country Study, *Czechoslovakia: Transition to a Market Economy* (Washington, DC: World Bank, 1991), p. 19.

47 Shen, *Economic Reform in Poland and Czechoslovakia*, pp. 74–75.

48 *World Bank, 1994*, pp. 38–39.

49 David Fairlam, "Czechoslovakia: Instant Capitalism—The Rush for Reform Could Damage the Economy," *Institutional Investor,* May 30, 1990, pp. 125–129.

50 Dyba and Svejnar, "Stabilization and Transition in Czechoslovakia," p. 98.

51 *Czechoslovakia: Transition to a Market Economy,* pp. xix–xx.

52 Peter S. Green, "Czechoslovak Elections Could Jeopardize Economy," *United Press International,* June 1, 1990.

53 Václav Klaus, "Main Obstacles to Rapid Economic Transformation of Eastern Europe: The Czechoslovak View," in Herbert Giersch, ed., *Towards a Market Economy in Central and Eastern Europe* (Berlin: Springer-Verlag, 1991), p. 85.

54 Charles Wolf, Jr., "Getting to Market," *The National Interest* 23 (Spring 1991), p. 48.

55 Klaus, "Main Obstacles to Rapid Economic Transformation," p. 89.

56 Steven Greenhouse, "Czechs Begin Shift to a Free Market," *New York Times,* January 1, 1991, p. A3.

57 *Czechoslovakia: Transition to a Market Economy,* p. 82.

58 Naomi Caiden, "The Roads to Transformation: Budgeting Issues in the Czech and Slovak Federal Republic 1989–1992," *Public Budgeting and Finance* 13, 4 (Winter 1993), pp. 62–64.

59 Fairlam, "Czechoslovakia: Instant Capitalism," pp. 125–129.

60 John Lloyd, "Czech Voices Threaten to Slow Drive for Swift Economic Change," *Financial Times,* June 12, 1990, p. 2.

61 Fairlam, "Czechoslovakia: Instant Capitalism," pp. 125–129.

62 *Czechoslovakia: EIU Country Report No. 4 1990* (London: Economist Intelligence Unit, 1990), p. 13.

63 Mejstrik and Burger, "Privatization in Practice," p. 136.

64 Lloyd, "Czech Voices Threaten," p. 2.

65 *Czechoslovakia: EIU Country Report No. 4 1990,* p. 14.

66 Green, "Czechoslovak Elections Could Jeopardize Economy.".

67 "Now, Govern," *The Economist,* June 16, 1990, p. 54.

68 John Lloyd, "Prague Reformer Fends Off Havel Attempt to Sack Him; Václav Klaus Will Keep Finance Portfolio in New Czechoslovak Government," *Financial Times,* June 21, 1990, p. 2.

69 BBC Summary of World Broadcasts, "President Havel's Address to the Federal Assembly," *The British Broadcasting Corporation,* July 2, 1990, Part 2 Eastern Europe.

70 Greenhouse, "Czechs Begin Shift," p. A3.

71 Aleksandr Solzhenitsyn, *Rebuilding Russia: Reflections and Tentative Proposals* (New York: HarperCollins, 1991), p. 3.

72 Václav Klaus, "The Ten Commandments of Systemic Reform," Occasional Papers No. 43 (Washington, DC: Group of Thirty, 1993), p. 3.

73 The World Bank, *World Development Report 1996: From Plan To Market* (Oxford, UK: Oxford University Press, 1996), p. 23.

74 Leszek Balcerowicz, *Socialism, Capitalism, Transformation* (Budapest: Central European University Press, 1995), p. 180.

75 Sachs, *Poland's Jump to the Market Economy* (Cambridge, Mass.: The MIT Press, 1994), p. 54.

76 Douglass C. North, *Institutions, Institutional Change and Economic Performance* (Cambridge, UK: Cambridge University Press, 1990), pp. 3–4.

77 Walter Adams and James W. Brock, *Adam Smith Goes to Moscow: A Dialogue on Radical Reform* (Princeton, N.J.: Princeton University Press, 1993), pp. 72, 74. Adams and Brock are referring to concepts that can be found in Karen Pennar, "In Russia, a Journey Back to the Future," *Business Week,* July 27, 1992, p. 49; Milton Friedman, "Market Mechanisms and Central Economic Planning" [G. Warren Nutter Lecture in Political Economy, University of Virginia, 1981), p. 14; and Ludwig von Mises, *Socialism: An Economic and Sociological Analysis* (London: Jonathan Cape, 1936), pp. 119, 137–38, 311.

Regional Integration

This case examines the leading edge of globalization. Fifteen European countries are joined in an organization designed to create a single integrated market, and 11 of them have entered monetary union.

There are several issues to consider here. First, one ought to think about why the Europeans are doing this. What problems are they trying to solve? And is this the appropriate solution? Then one should think about this extranational form of government: How does it work? But the centerpiece of the case is the process of market integration since the passage of the Single Europe Act in 1985. At that time, the Europeans agreed to a program of reducing internal barriers to the movement of people, goods, and capital. Although its initiatives were originally planned for implementation in seven years, it has taken much longer and is still far from complete.

This case provides data for an evaluation of how far Europe has come and how far it still has to go in integrating product markets, capital markets, and labor markets. The exhibits provide important evidence that should be studied carefully.

The second part of the case explores monetary union—i.e., the adoption of a single currency and a single central bank, beginning in January 1999. Here, students must think carefully about what monetary integration means. What are its costs and benefits? And what does it mean for fiscal and social autonomy?

A supplemental case, European Monetary Union: Honeywell Europe, is designed to allow students to think about the effects of market and monetary integration on the competitiveness of firms. Honeywell Europe, a $2 billion subsidiary of the Honeywell Corporation in the United States, faces both challenges and opportunities as monetary union drives Europe further along its integrative path.

Finally, students are asked to think broadly about Europe's future trajectory. Is it likely to grow in an integrated fashion (i.e., all the parts converging to the same levels of GDP/capita), and is the whole likely to grow at the same rates as its largest competitor, the United States?

EUROPEAN MONETARY UNION

To achieve growth and further employment we need to improve the efficiency of the European economy by making our markets more flexible and improving manufacturing and service sector performance. To do this we must improve the regulatory framework in which our firms operate; develop a more entrepreneurial European economy, with more efficient capital markets and fewer barriers to easy entry/exit to markets; open protected markets to competition while securing affordable access to services of general interest and eliminate anti-competitive behavior by firms or by the public sector.[1]

—**The European Commission** (1998)

In the spring of 1999, Romano Prodi, newly designated chairman of the European Commission, prepared to help create an economically integrated Europe. Since the introduction of the euro on January 1, Europe had been operating with a single currency—at least for business-to-business transactions. Despite some technical problems with the changeover and an 8% depreciation of the euro against the dollar, this extraordinary step toward integration had gone fantastically well. Western Europe continued to experience healthy growth—in excess of 2% annually—and the Commission was expanding its plans to further integrate Europe's markets.

But before real integration could be achieved, many more reforms would be needed. While the Commission recently concluded that "thanks to the Single Market Programme, today's European product markets work much better than they did in the 1970s,"[2] they still exhibited wide price differentials, diverse regulations, and a lack of inter-European investment and competition. Capital markets had moved further, as members of the European Union had dropped regulations and encouraged competition across national borders. But even here, prices and margins remained high, and inter-European rationalization had only just begun. Finally, the markets for labor had barely begun to integrate. Here, high minimum wages, payroll taxes, unemployment benefits and diverse restrictions on flexibility had pushed Europe toward an employment crisis. Unemployment for the EU-11 had exceeded 11% for more than six years [**Exhibit 7.1**].

In little more than three years, at least 11 European countries planned to adopt the common currency for all their economic transactions. Transparency then should force more integration on these fragmented markets and on their macroeconomic policies, which varied as much as European cultures. The question on Prodi's mind was whether Europeans could really sustain the extraordinary pace of change. Tax systems, pensions, health care, work rules, agricultural subsidies, and fiscal budgets all needed significant adjustment and integration, while pressures mounted for the Commission to liberalize its own decision-making process and reform its generous budget. In the East, meanwhile, 13 more nations were seeking admittance to the Union—a pressure that was sure to make integration all the more challenging.

Research Associate Sabina M. Ciminero and Professor Richard H. K. Vietor prepared this case as the basis for class discussion rather than to illustrate either effective or ineffective handling of an administrative situation.

Copyright (c) 1998 by the President and Fellows of Harvard College. Harvard Business School case 799-131.

The Postwar Background of European Economic Integration

The destruction wrought by the Second World War gave rise to an outpouring of sentiment in favor of European unification. In 1946, Winston Churchill called for a "United States of Europe." Others talked of the need for some type of European federation. Yet all efforts to create political unity, such as the Council of Europe in 1949, failed because most governments would not surrender political sovereignty.

Economic integration proved more tractable. In 1951, France, West Germany, Belgium, Luxembourg, the Netherlands, and Italy established the European Coal and Steel Community (ECSC). The ECSC was essentially a customs union in coal and steel. It served to enhance efficiency and profitability in these two industries, and equally important, it fostered cooperation between former adversaries like France and Germany.

Treaty of Rome

In 1957, the six ECSC members signed the Treaty of Rome, which established the European Economic Community (EEC). The Treaty laid out a timetable by which its members would remove all internal tariffs and establish a common external tariff by 1970 (an objective that was reached two years ahead of schedule). It also provided for the creation of a common agricultural policy and the removal of some nontariff barriers to the free movement of people, services, and capital. Finally, the Treaty sought to "lay the foundations of an even closer union among the people of Europe and to preserve and strengthen peace and liberty."

Economic integration proceeded, albeit haltingly. In 1967, the European Economic Community, the European Coal and Steel Community, and the European Atomic Energy Community adopted a unified institutional structure. EEC membership also increased. Britain, Ireland, and Denmark joined in 1973, Greece in 1981, Spain and Portugal in 1986, and Austria, Finland, and Sweden in 1995, bringing the total number of member states to 15.[3]

Institutions of the European Community   Four principal institutions comprised the European Community (EC): the Commission, the Council of Ministers, the European Parliament, and the Court of Justice. Some of their responsibilities defined by the Treaty of Rome were amended by subsequent regulations. In particular, the Amsterdam Treaty of 1997 (effective May 1, 1999) increased the power of both the Council and the Parliament, relative to the Commission.

The Commission was the executive arm of the EC, directed by a president and 19 commissioners. The president was selected by member countries (for a five-year renewable term); the commissioners were appointed by national governments and the president-designate (two from each of the five large countries—France, Great Britain, Italy, Germany, and Spain—and one from each of the smaller EC countries). The Amsterdam Treaty mandated that the European Parliament approve the appointment of the entire commission and its president. Commission members were supposed to represent the interest of the EC as a whole. They were supported by a staff of approximately 14,000, who served in 24 directorates **(Appendix A)**.

The Commission performed three main functions: it initiated EC proposals, represented the EC in international trade negotiations, and managed the EC budget. It was also responsible for the management of some EC policies (agriculture, antitrust) and for overseeing national policies to ensure they were consistent with EC policy. It investigated violations of EC treaties, issued decisions when violations were found, and had the option of referring violations to the Court of Justice.

The Council of Ministers served as the EC's main decision-making body; it could not initiate legislation, but it had the power to approve, amend, or reject Commission proposals. It consisted of representatives from each government but was not a permanent group. Agricultural ministers sat on the Council when it dealt with agricultural policy, trade ministers sat on the Council when it dealt with trade matters, and so on. The Council presidency was responsible for setting the agenda, and it rotated among member states every six months. Decisions were mostly adopted by a qualified majority (62 votes out of a total of 87). Here too the Amsterdam Treaty had broadened the Council's range of qualified-majority voting to include many of the EC's new provisions, such as initiatives on jobs, public health, social exclusion, transparency, and customs cooperation but not taxation, which still needed unanimity.

The European Parliament comprised 626 members, directly elected by voters in each nation since 1979. It had offices in Brussels but gathered for meetings in Strasbourg. Parliament's role in the legislative process allowed it to help draft directives and regulations. In 1992, Parliament began to share joint decision-making powers with the Council on issues such as freedom of movement of workers, free circulation of products, freedom to set up business, and freedom to provide services. The Amsterdam Treaty extended Parliament's co-decision powers with the Council to include such areas as public health, transport policy, free movement of people, and social and economic policy. Together with the Council, Parliament had the power to adopt or reject the Commission's budget proposal. Parliament could also turn out the Commission through a vote of no confidence.

The Court of Justice interpreted EC treaties and directives and sought to apply Community law in a uniform way. Fifteen judges sat on the Court, one from each nation. The Amsterdam Treaty allowed the Court to rule on issues affecting peoples' freedom and security. Court decisions had precedence over national rulings, but in numerous cases companies and states disregarded the Court.[4]

EC regulations and directives began as Commission proposals. The process for approving proposals typically took from two to five years. Proposals were initiated by the Commission and then sent to Parliament for study and debate. Review by Parliament was followed by approval (or amendment) by the Council. A proposal was sent to the Parliament for a second reading. Once both Parliament and the Council accepted a proposal, it became a directive. Member states were then obligated to change ("transpose") their national laws to conform to it.

European Monetary System

Another step toward economic integration was taken with the formation of the European Monetary System (EMS) in 1979. Proposed by German Chancellor Helmut Schmidt and French President Valery Giscard d'Estaing in 1978, the EMS established a system of "fixed but adjustable" exchange rates, designed to insulate intra-European trade from the effects of floating exchange rates and to promote greater macroeconomic convergence.

Eight European states (Germany, France, Belgium, the Netherlands, Luxembourg, Denmark, Ireland, and Italy) joined the EMS on March 1, 1979. The basis of its Exchange Rate Mechanism (ERM) was the existing ("parity") exchange rates between member nations. While the parity rates were fixed, the system left room for some variability. Currencies could fluctuate within a band of ±2.25% from initial parity.[5] Central banks of member nations were required to use their foreign exchange reserves to maintain currencies within these bands. In addition, member nations could borrow from other ERM members whenever their currencies reached the lower end of the allowed band. Parity rates and exchange rates could be changed by unanimous agreement.

During the 1980s, the EMS seemed to work, haltingly, to reduce inflation differentials and foster convergence in economic cycles [**Exhibit 7.3**]. The relative success of the system eventually prompted Spain (1989) and the United Kingdom (1990) to join.

Single European Act

In 1985, the Commission released a White Paper that outlined a program to complete the internal market by December 31, 1992. It proposed 282 targets of growth, covering a variety of issues, products, services, and industries, each with its own timetable for implementation. The measures were designed to eliminate many of the costs and constraints facing European firms and thereby increase their efficiency and competitiveness. (**Appendix B** lists the major elements of the 1992 program.) This "adventure in deregulation," as *The Economist* put it, would create a stronger and more prosperous Europe.[6]

The Single European Act amended key parts of the original Treaty of Rome and aimed to remove three types of obstacles: (1) physical barriers, which included intra-EC border stoppages, customs controls, and associated paperwork; (2) technical barriers, which involved meeting divergent national product standards, technical regulations, conflicting business laws, and the opening of national protected public procurement markets; and (3) fiscal barriers, which mainly dealt with rates of VAT (value-added taxes) and excise duties.

Border Controls

A key component of the 1992 agenda was the elimination of border controls. These controls included tax collection (aggravated by differences in VAT and excise rates); agricultural checks (such as applications for adjustments to farm product prices); veterinary checks (which were necessitated by differing national health standards); and transportation controls. Such measures created delays and added considerably to costs. Smaller companies suffered the most. Customs cost per consignment were estimated to be up to 30%–45% higher for companies with fewer than 250 employees than they were for larger firms.[7]

Standardization

More than 100,000 different regulations and standards existed in the EC in the 1980s. These included regulations affecting health, safety, the environment, and technical standards within industries. EC countries set their own national standards for a wide range of industries, from automobiles to food processing, from electrical products to telecommunications. Firms were required to vary products and testing for each different national market; this increased marketing difficulties and added significantly to costs.

In the past, the Commission had sought to solve the problem of divergent standards and regulations by harmonizing national legislation throughout the EC (i.e., establishing similar laws in all member states). But given the entrenched interests in each country, this approach was scarcely feasible. The Court of Justice, in the Cassis de Dijon case, actually introduced a new approach, based on the principle of "mutual recognition": the practices, regulations, and other forms of control in one member state could be accepted in other countries, even if such regulations did not apply there. Thus, products lawfully produced or marketed in one EC nation, if legal at home, would have access to all other EC markets.

National Procurement

Public procurement amounted to some 12% of the EC's GDP. The 1992 program sought to end national protectionism for all public procurement contracts. In particular, the Commission aimed to open the four previously excluded sectors (energy, transport, telecommunications, and water supply) to competitive bidding. However, the Commission's proposal allowed national governments to give preference to products with at least 50% European content.

VAT Harmonization

The Commission intended to end the divergence in national indirect tax rates, which encompassed both VAT and excise taxes. Divergent VAT rates, from 1% to 38% (for different types of goods), distorted trade flows by encouraging consumers to buy goods in low VAT countries and ship them home without paying the higher VAT. One of the problems confronted by the Commission in considering changes in the VAT was that most EC countries had two, if not three, tiers of VAT rates. The *White Paper* proposed abolishing the highest tier of VAT rates (applied in only six countries). Two tiers would then remain: a reduced rate for basic necessity goods and a standard rate for all other products. The *White Paper*'s plan was to reduce the differences within each of these two tiers—to a band of 4% to 9% for the reduced rate and a band of 14% to 20% for the standard rate—over several years.

To reduce the need for border controls, the *White Paper* also proposed that the VAT should be applied in the country where a sale took place rather than collected at the border. Companies would report the value of their exports to their own governments, which would then seek reimbursement of the VAT from the government of the country where the good was sold.

Services

In the view of the Commission, "the establishment of a common market in services [was] one of the main preconditions for a return to economic prosperity."[8] Services encompassed a variety of activities, including finance, transportation, and telecommunications. It was one of the fastest-growing and most heavily regulated sectors in Europe.

In the three key areas of finance—banking, insurance, and securities—members states agreed that some regulation was justified on the grounds of consumer protection. The Single Market program placed a high priority on creating a common financial market. A central element in the 1992 program was the liberalization of capital movements—what one Commission official referred to as "the life-blood of cross-frontier trade in financial services."[9]

The second thrust of the 1992 banking program aimed to eliminate two other significant barriers found in most states: restrictions on the right of establishment (the right to set up branches or subsidiaries in another country) and on the freedom to provide services across frontiers (marketing and advertising of financial services). Finally, the Commission proposed that the principles of home country rule and mutual recognition should also govern banking supervision.

The Maastricht Treaty

Leaders of all 12 EC member nations gathered in the small Dutch town of Maastricht in December 1991 to discuss proposals for the creation of a European economic and monetary union (EMU). Together, they drafted the Maastricht Treaty. On the political side, the Maastricht agreement provided added powers for the European Parliament, increased regional funds for the poorer EC countries, and created a framework for a common foreign policy. More significantly, Maastricht established a clear timetable for achieving monetary union by January 1, 1997, or if that proved infeasible, by January 1, 1999. The Council of Ministers would decide (by qualified majority) whether a majority of countries had met five convergence requirements:

- **Price stability** Inflation must be within 1.5 percentage points of the average of the three EC countries with the lowest inflation rates.

Euro Timeline

Stage 1: July 1990–December 1993

- Coordination of economic policies

- Liberalization of capital markets

Stage 2: Phase A, January 1994–December 1998

- Adaptation of legal and administrative framework for conversion

- Establishment of the European Monetary Institution

- Early 1998: Decision on the starting date of Stage 3

- Decision as to the participating countries

- Establishment of the European Central Bank (ECB)

Stage 3: Phase B, January 1999

- Introduction of the euro for noncase transactions

- Irrevocable fixing of exchange rate to six significant figures for participating countries

- ECB adopts reasonability for centralized policy

Phase C, January 2002–July 2002

- Euro bank notes

- All remaining assets converted into euro

- Disappearance of national currencies

SOURCE: NatWest, *A Guide for Business*, December, 1997, section 1.1.

- **Interest rates** Long-term interest rates must be within 2 percentage points of the average of the three countries with the lowest rates.

- **Deficits** National budget deficits must not exceed 3% of GDP.

- **Debt** Public debt must not exceed 60% of GDP.

- **Currency stability** A currency must not have been devalued in the previous two years and should have remained within a normal fluctuation band (originally 2.25%) of its central parity rate in the exchange rate mechanism.

Once monetary union took effect, the exchange rates of member nations would be irrevocably fixed and a new European currency (euro) would be substituted over a three-year period. A European Central Bank in Frankfurt would set Europe's monetary policy. Independent of national authorities, its principal task would be the maintenance of price stability.

Maastricht represented one of the most significant milestones in European history. Soon after the December 1991 agreement, each member state had to approve the agreement by referendum. Denmark initially voted it down but subsequently approved it (with an opting-out clause). So did the rest of the EC nations. But the convergence criteria proved more difficult to achieve. After the German reunification in 1991, the Bundesbank raised interest rates under pressure from immense subsidies to rebuild East Germany. When the mark rose in value, EMU countries raised interest rates sharply to maintain the currency band. But they quickly gave up and devalued their currencies as Europe plunged into recession.

In little more than two years though, the European Monetary System was redesigned, with 15% fluctuation bands, new parity rates, and a new target of 1999 for monetary union. Member states began moving again to achieve the convergence criteria. Recovery helped these efforts, and by May 1998, low inflation, low interest rates, and reduced deficits had been substantially achieved by all but Greece. So the stage was set [**Exhibit 7.4**].

Market Integration

Over the past 13 years, the Commission has issued nearly 1,400 directives. **Exhibit 7.5** indicates that all but 13.2% of these had been implemented by national governments. Finland, with only 0.7% left to transpose, had done the most, while Portugal, with 5.5% of the directives left to implement, slightly lagged behind Ireland and Belgium. **Exhibit 7.6** shows where the problems lay. Telecommunications, until recently, remained dominated by state enterprises that were inefficient and monopolistic. For similar reasons, public procurement had remained a problem, although some progress had been made. And rules affecting social policies, not surprisingly, had difficulty getting implemented.

Diverse cultures appeared to remain the biggest barrier to market integration—by far. As one executive who ran an auto leasing company said, "Cultural barriers and language barriers were huge. Americans think integration will take one or two years, when really it is a process of hundreds of years." Thus, his organization did purchasing, maintenance, contracts, programs, accounting, and taxes locally; only finance was Europe-wide. A trade industry official agreed, but added that differences in tax systems and labor laws were nearly as problematic. A third executive suggested that culture overwhelmed much else. "Netherlands," he said, "is closer to the USA culturally than to France." This explained the slow progress in retail integration—in food, clothes, professional services, retail banking, and so on. Even branding had a long way to go.[10]

Product Markets

The Single Europe Act's first objective, to facilitate the free movement of people, goods, and services, had been substantially achieved. Border checks of passports and shipping invoices had been virtually eliminated. Most external tariffs had been liberalized, with the exception of some sensitive imports (automobiles, textiles, consumer electronics, and agricultural products). The voluntary import restriction negotiated with Japan in 1991 (holding Japanese market share in automobiles to a ceiling of 16.5%) was still in effect, although due to expire by the end of 1999.[11]

The standardization of diverse regulation had made significant progress, although it still had a ways to go [**Exhibit 7.7**]. The process of mutual recognition helped for consumer durables and capital goods but ran into problems with foodstuffs, pesticides, or drugs, where national regulatory authorities feared foreign risks. Here, the Commission developed another mechanism, the adoption of "essential requirements." Once those were agreed upon, European standards organizations were charged with harmonizing the standards. Some 17% of European trade was facilitated by this method.[12]

Despite the progress with regulatory harmonization, national governments had been balking at the newly agreed-upon rules and were creative at inventing new regulatory barriers. The number of "notifications," by which a member state notifies its intention to regulate a specific field, rose fairly steadily during the 1990s. Telecommunications, food products, transportation, and mechanical engineering engendered most of these notifications [**Exhibit 7.8a**].

All of this harmonization was intended to force rationalization of inefficient assets, increase competition, and drive down costs. If one considers cross-border, intra-EU mergers and intra-EU foreign direct investment, it appeared this process was indeed underway. After intensifying sharply in the late 1980s, intra-EU mergers peaked at about 4,000 annually between 1989 and 1991 and then receded somewhat during the remainder of the 1990s. Most of the mergers were intracountry tie-ups (Krupp/Thyssen), rather than EU-wide (Hoechst/Rhone-Poulenc), much less international. The Netherlands and the United Kingdom showed merger activity disproportionate to their relative size [**Exhibit 7.9a and b**]. However, by 1997 international mergers were picking up in both number and size. At the top of the list were the mergers of Daimler-Chrysler and of Deutsche Bank–Bankers Trust. It remained to be seen whether concentration would increase competition and lower prices and whether combination would increase the quality of management.[13]

To make sure that increasing integration and cross-border investment served the interests of economic efficiency, competition policy in Europe was intensifying. Stronger antitrust laws had recently been enacted—in Denmark and the Netherlands in 1997, and in Germany, Finland, and the United Kingdom in 1998. Across Europe, competition authorities had been strengthened, with at least nine countries enforcing the competition provisions (Articles 85–86) of the Treaty of Rome.[14]

Cross-border investment had also heated up. For the EU-15, intra-EU foreign direct investment had averaged 0.8% of GDP per year since 1992. Ireland, the Netherlands, and Belgium/Luxembourg had the most investment activity—generally three to four times this average. Among the large countries, only the United Kingdom exceeded the average. Most of the intra-EU FDI during the 1990s was in services; manufacturing's share dropped appreciably. In 1997, member states of the EU had invested 172 billion euros in other countries; of that, 42% was invested in other EU states. FDI inflows amounted to 99 billion euros—57.5 billion from other EU states. Net outflows increased by 8% from the previous year.[15]

Price Dispersion With deregulation and the intensification of competition, dispersion of prices across Europe should have narrowed. Indeed, this had happened in some areas. The OECD estimated that price variation decreased between 1985 and 1996, from a coefficient of 20% to about 16% [**Exhibit 7.10**]. A more careful examination by sector showed that in industries with relatively low productivity (e.g., pharmaceuticals, beverages, tobacco products, fabricated metals), price dispersion still exceeded 20% and ranged as high as 35%. However, where Europe's productivity was relatively higher (e.g., shipbuilding, rubber and plastic, mechanical engineering), price dispersion had shrunk to 11% or less [**Exhibit 7.11**].[16]

Among the most important products (from a consumer-purchasing perspective) were automobiles, the retail prices of which were carefully tracked. Price differentials had declined for most models since 1995. Then, a Ford Fiesta sold for 48% more in one EU country than another. By November 1998, the largest gap was down to 34.6% (a Ford Mondeo). However, price differentials on a dozen models still ranged from 16% to 32%. The United Kingdom showed the most expensive prices, while Portugal, Spain, and the Netherlands tended to have the cheapest. It appeared that manufacturers raised prices in cheap markets rather than lowering prices in less-competitive ones [**Exhibit 7.12**].[17]

Prices for consumer goods still varied significantly due to various factors—"structural (member states' differences in living standards and tastes, transport costs), regulatory (consumption and other taxes, nontariff barriers), and firm strategies (concentration, differentiated products, advertising, etc.)."[18] Thus, Lacoste shirts could vary from $63 to $80, Levi's 501 jeans from $66 to $88, and a Swatch watch by as much as 50%—from $30 to $45. Even the price of a Coca Cola (1.5-liter bottle) ranged 100%, from 0.77 euros in Spain to 1.57 euros in Germany. A Big Mac, which *The Economist* had long used as a currency standard, varied from 1.85 euros in Greece to 3.47 euros in Finland.[19]

Still, the Commission was hopeful that "by enhancing price transparency, in combination with competition policy . . . the euro's introduction should put pressure on firms seeking to segment markets."[20]

Value-Added Tax Another factor that artificially segmented markets was the dispersion of value-added tax rates. Dispersion of these rates by as much as 20% of price had long caused significant distortions in distribution channels, sourcing, and even manufacturing location. These imposed costs on enterprises, on consumers, and on governmental collection agencies.[21] The Single Europe Act's initial package resulted in a narrowing of tax bands, into "normal" rates on most goods but with broader rates for exceptions. These normal rates varied by 17% in 1992. Six years later, this spread had shrunk to 10%. Likewise, the gap for exceptional rates was reduced from 37% to 24%. But with the collection system still based on sales destination (and with a variety of special regimes), the Commission did not think market forces would force any further reduction in the remaining divergence.[22] The marginal tax rate on consumption still varied by almost 100%, from 12.3% in Spain to 21.2% in Denmark.[23] Thus, the Commission was preparing to propose an entirely new Europe-wide tax system with collection at the point of origin.

State Aid and Procurement The Commission remained particularly concerned about distortions to competition caused by government procurement and state aid. Because government purchases and subsidies were so important in Europe—averaging 12% of GDP—they significantly disrupted competition. Since the mid-1980s, privatization had made significant progress. In the United Kingdom, state enterprises had been thoroughly privatized. Progress was made in France and Italy, but little had changed elsewhere. During the 1990s, a 20% increase in total procurement had been accompanied by somewhat larger increases in bid notices and awards. Yet local preference and unwillingness to change suppliers persisted.[24]

State aid, although shrinking a bit since 1990, remained a problem. Nonagricultural aid represented 1.4% of the Community's GDP and was especially high in Italy (2.1%) and Germany (1.9%).[25] In 1997, aid to the manufacturing sector alone amounted to 38 billion euro annually. "Current levels are still too high," said Karl Van Miert, the commissioner for competition policy. "This level of spending continues to distort competition and trade and thus undermines the advantages offered by Economic and Monetary Union."[26]

Capital Markets

The Single Europe Act had clearly viewed capital markets, then diffusely regulated and fragmented, as an important barrier to integration and global competitiveness. Thus, one of the EC's principal thrusts had been to lower regulatory barriers in banking, securities, and insurance and foster a deeper, more modern finance system in Europe. The progress here, perhaps fostered by global competition and technological innovation, was less ambiguous.

Harmonization by the Commission had begun even before 1985, with the First Banking Coordination Directive (1977). But it was a series of directives after 1986 that really opened up European banking to competition and rationalization. Especially important was the Second Banking Directive in 1989, which established the principle of mutual recognition of a single banking license. Home country regulation would govern a bank's foreign branches for some product offerings and interest rates, while supervisory standards, capital requirements, and limitations to participation in the nonfinancial sector were harmonized. A few months later, a directive on solvency ratios sought to harmonize credit risk. In the early 1990s, these measures were followed by directives on capital adequacy, deposit guarantees, and liberalization of capital flows [**Exhibit 7.13**].[27]

The impact of this deregulation was dramatic. The value of EU bonds, equities, and bank loans exceeded those of the United States by 1995, and wholesale banking had grown more integrated. Prices and costs fell as a significant merger movement ensued. **Exhibit 7.14a** summarizes the changes in loan prices and mortgages. Not surprisingly, assorted evidence shows that commercial products benefited most in countries that had relatively less sophisticated financial systems. Fees and deposit prices showed similar trends, with Ireland and Denmark leading the way [**Exhibit 7.14b and c**]. Part of this was due to a significant increase in branching across borders, while the number of domestic branches shrank [**Exhibit 7.14d**].

The opening of competition across member states' retail markets had gone slowly, to date. There were few cross-border sales of life insurance, for example. Non–life insurance fared better, although cross-border sales merely ranged from 0.13% in Germany to 4.13% in Belgium. The price of credit cards in Belgium was more than twice that of the Netherlands. Mortgages in France cost 50% more than in the United Kingdom, more than 100% more than in Denmark, and another 100% more than in The Netherlands. At least through 1998, the need to "ensure a high-level of consumer protection" was "used as an excuse to hinder cross-border business." Yet as long as differences among member states persisted on bankruptcy provision, security, and pensions, developing Pan-European markets for retail financial products would remain difficult.[28]

The volume of mergers and acquisitions in the financial sector had clearly accelerated during the 1990s. **Exhibit 7.8b** shows more than 500 mergers annually, most of which involved domestic firms. Perhaps a third as many mergers involved firms crossing borders. "It is very difficult to merge across borders because of legal barriers," said one senior banker at Deutsche Bank.[29] The data also indicated more moves by EU banks outside of Europe, as well as some limited increase in entry. The average size of assets more than doubled in the 1990s, as firms attempted to consolidate and achieve economies of scale. Still, five-firm concentration ratios have remained in the range of 40% to 45% for most of Europe (except in Denmark and the Netherlands) and had actually fallen during the 1990s in France, Greece, and Luxembourg.[30]

Despite this substantial progress, significant obstacles to integration still remained. These included differences in implementation of financial market legislation, the absence of harmonization in areas such as pension funds, differences in national fiscal regimes, and technical barriers. Badly functioning financial markets especially affected small and medium-sized enterprises. These firms were obviously more dependent on banks, yet paid higher interest rates and were subject to credit rationing due to lack of collateral. Private equity and venture capital markets for smaller firms remained underdeveloped through most of Europe. One senior banker in Germany opined that it might take 50 years for European banking to achieve the degree of integration experienced in the United States.[31]

Labor Markets

Everyone seemed to agree that labor markets remained fragmented in Europe and required the most severe degrees of reform. Executives in Amsterdam said this, bankers in Germany said it, and regulators in Brussels nodded, sadly. Although migration of workers across member states had increased by 33%, the total numbers involved were pitifully small—311,000 in 1996, up from 233,000 earlier. Once again, culture and language remained a huge barrier to movement.[32]

The "low employment rates and high and persistent levels of structural unemployment suggest that . . . labour markets function relatively poorly in the EU." However, the problems differed immensely between regions, among member states, between declining industries and new high-tech sectors, and between categories of labor.[33] The employment rate in Austria, Denmark, Sweden, and the United Kingdom was about 70% or higher; but in Spain and Italy, employment was barely 50%. Unemployment had fallen sharply in Ireland and the Netherlands, while remaining high in Spain, Italy, France, and Germany. And regional differences were striking, especially in Italy, Spain, and Germany. These variations reflected, in part, differences in efforts at structural reform. But most people in Europe were not willing to work outside their own country.

The structure of employment varied significantly from the United States. In Europe, there was more farming, more industry, and less service than in the United States. For adult males, the unemployment rates were similar; but for youth, women, and older people, the rates in Europe far exceeded those of the United States.

The sources of these problems could be found in relative productivity differentials, in education and training, in geographic mobility, in minimum wage levels, in benefit levels, and in taxation. [These issues are treated carefully elsewhere, in HBS, *Unemployment in France*, HBS No. 9-795-065.] Recently, the Commission called more stridently for efforts at major reform of labor markets. The 1999 Employment Guidelines advised member states to implement tax reforms and curb expenditure growth, dependency, and social protection. "Flexibility criteria have been tightened, with stricter definitions of availability for work and tougher sanctions on those refusing to take up a job." The duration of benefits had been slightly reduced to curb disincentives to work, and several states had lowered high marginal effective tax rates [**Exhibit 7.15a and b**].[34]

Another area of reform related to work organization and working-time flexibility. A few member states were experimenting with work sharing, more part-time work, and more work-hour flexibility. Last year, for example, it became possible for social partners to agree on the annualization of work hours in Belgium, Spain, and France. In Austria, one could exchange overtime for time off. In the Netherlands, where barriers to part-time work were eliminated, 35% of total employment was now part-time [**Exhibit 7.16**]. Perhaps the biggest change in European labor markets was the reduction of the working week. If designed well, such reductions might redistribute work— but there were many difficult-to-meet conditions to achieve if unemployment was to be reduced.

Finally, the EC pointed to the importance of an "employment-friendly" regulatory environment. This pertained especially to employment protection. As the Commission urged, "Workers, management, the social partners [unions and employer associations] and policy makers alike [must] strike the right balance between *flexibility* and *security*." Where employment protection was strict—in Italy and Spain—unemployment was especially high. Where it was less strict—the United Kingdom and the Netherlands—unemployment had recently fallen. [35]

Monetary Union

In May 1998, the European Council selected 11 member states to participate in the EMU: Germany, France, Italy, Spain, Belgium, the Netherlands, Portugal, Austria, Ireland, Finland, and Luxembourg. While Greece wanted to be a part of the "Euro-zone," it had failed to meet the convergence criteria. On the other hand, Britain, Denmark, and Sweden were qualified to join EMU in its first wave but decided to opt-out for the time being.

EMU began on January 1, 1999. Yet as one senior economist noted, "EMU is not a revolution but an evolution."[36] While the EMU participants maintained control over their fiscal policy, the European Central Bank (ECB) was responsible for setting monetary policy for the entire Euro-zone. The ECB combined with the 15 national central banks (NCBs) to form the European System of Central Banks (ESCB), modeled after Germany's Bundesbank. While the national banks conducted banking activities for their respective countries, they were no longer directly involved in decision making for monetary policy, except through their membership on the Governing Board of the ECB. [37]

The primary objective of the ESCB was a "stability-oriented monetary policy strategy." Price stability was to be maintained over the medium term and was defined as "a year-on-year increase in the Harmonised Index of Consumer Prices (HICP) for the euro area of below 2%." According to one ECB economist, "We're given one tool and one objective and told to get on with it and that we shouldn't veer from it. We do the best we can do by maintaining price stability, and countries should know what we will do because that is our goal. We're serious about maintaining price stability. There

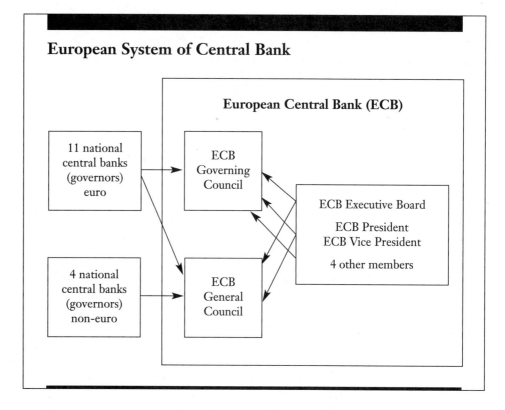

European System of Central Bank

European Central Bank (ECB)

11 national central banks (governors) euro

4 national central banks (governors) non-euro

ECB Governing Council

ECB General Council

ECB Executive Board

ECB President
ECB Vice President

4 other members

are a lot of very serious people here."[38] Driven by the central goal to maintain price stability, the ESCB had four key tasks: (1) define and implement the EC's monetary policy, (2) conduct foreign exchange operations, (3) hold and manage member states' official foreign reserves, and (4) ensure a smoothly operating payments system. Its monetary policy instruments included open market operations, "standing facilities" (e.g., overnight lending capacity), and minimum reserves.

Three decision-making bodies governed the ESCB: the Governing Council, the Executive Board, and the General Council. While the Governing Council made monetary decisions for the Euro-zone, the Executive Board implemented monetary policy. The General Council carried out such tasks as the collection of statistical data and the preparation of the ECB's annual reports. The Maastricht Treaty intended to free the ESCB from political pressures by mandating that "neither the ECB, nor a national central bank, nor any member of their decision-making bodies shall seek or take instructions from Community institutions of a Member State or from any other body."[39]

However, while the ECB represented one of the most independent central banks in the world, it seemed difficult for it not to be influenced by a country's political will. The economic cycles of the EMU participants varied widely, making it impossible to set a single interest rate that would be ideal for each member state. At one end of the spectrum was Germany, whose slow growth favored lower interest rates. At the opposite end, Ireland and Spain had rapid growth and tended to view Euro-zone interest rates differently. As economist Martin Feldstein put it, "The fall in demand in a country could not be offset, as it could be with an individual national currency, by an automatic decline in the exchange value of the currency . . . and the decline in its interest rates."[40] Interest rates had remained unchanged since the 11 EMU central banks simultaneously lowered their rates by at least 0.3% on December 4, 1998. Until his resignation on March 11, 1999, German Finance Minister Oskar LaFontaine had fought ardently for a cut in interest rates. Finally, after keeping interest rates constant for more than three months, the ECB on April 8 made a surprise cut in its benchmark interest rate from 3% to 2.5%. It was "an unexpectedly large fall," commented ECB President Willem Duisenberg, "but we want to add this is it. . . . We hope our goal to [get governments to] pursue a restructuring policy will be given a new incentive from the measures taken today. If they don't do that, monetary policy is no alternative." "We've done our bit," said another ECB economist, "[governments] can't wait for us to do it again. This is all."[41]

Making Firms Competitive

Although the Single Market Act had certainly begun to affect competition, it was the single currency regime that most businesses anticipated, some warily, some eagerly. Monetary integration entailed fairly clear-cut costs but offered significant, though less concrete, benefits. Harris Opinion Research, having surveyed large European companies, estimated transition costs of $30 million per firm, or around $50 billion (for companies with over 5,000 employees). *The Financial Times* had estimated total costs at $150 billion.[42]

Changes in accounting systems, pricelists and invoices, bank accounts, purchase orders, packaging, treasury operations (cash management, exposure management, cross-border cash pooling), and information technology systems loomed large on the cost side. Of course, these were one-time costs—any savings would be repeated annually. Lower interest rate differentials, more coherent finance strategy, less currency hedging, and especially lower exchange-rate charges were among the immediate and obvious savings.[43]

But the real threats were loss of competitive advantage based on domestic market dominance, lower prices, and more intense competition—throughout all of Europe. These threats, of course, could be counterbalanced by an effective adjustment strategy. Firms simply had to adapt to a regional market of more than 300 million people. They had to reorganize themselves, reduce unnecessary costs, better develop their distribution systems, and compete aggressively against a host of new competitors—from outside the EU, as well as internally.

Issues Facing the European Union

In the spring of 1999, the EU was faced with many other challenges. It was trying to enforce the Stability and Growth Pact, restructure its budget, and establish a plan for admitting new countries into the EU. The 1997 Stability and Growth Pact was designed to help maintain fiscal discipline in the Euro-zone [**Exhibit 7.19**]. The pact mandated that the deficits of EMU participants not exceed 3% of their GDP. In the case of noncompliant countries, sanctions in the form of a noninterest-bearing deposit with the Commission would be invoked within ten months. If a country's excessive deficit persisted, it could face fines up to 0.5% of GDP. Sanctions required the Council's qualified majority vote. A country would not face sanctions if it had taken immediate corrective actions. Also, exceptions would be made for countries suffering from severe recession (a GDP decline of 2% or more in a given year).[44]

Failure to enforce properly measures outlined in the Stability Pact could lead to loose fiscal policy, which could, in turn, interfere with the effectiveness of the ECB's monetary policy. Moreover, "The Stability Pact," claimed Feldstein, "tells governments that they cannot run fiscal deficits above three percent. . . . Since national monetary and fiscal policies would be precluded, the most likely outcome of the shift to a single monetary policy would be the growth of substantial transfers from the EU to countries that experience cyclical increases in unemployment."[45] Also, if EMU participants did not follow the pact's rules, they would be unlikely ever to achieve balanced budgets.

In terms of the EU's budget, there were plans to increase the efficiency of its revenues so as to allow for EU enlargement. In 1997, Agenda 2000 had set out to strengthen the Union in preparation for the addition of new EU members from Eastern and Central Europe. "We cannot think of pursuing agricultural reforms or the reform of structural policies without at the same time taking into account enlargement and the financial constraints," explained EU President Jacques Santer. "It is this mix of equations that the Commission has sought to solve in developing the communication, Agenda 2000."[46]

At its March 1999 meeting in Berlin, the European Council reached an overall agreement on Agenda 2000. While talks nearly collapsed, EU diplomats managed to arrive at a compromise that would eventually reduce farm expenditures and restrictive structural fund objectives [**Exhibit 7.20**]. For the 2000–2006 period, they agreed to keep the EU budget close to its current level of 85 billion euros. Over the next seven years, the final accord aimed to bring farm spending down to an annual average of 40.5 billion euros. The EU planned to cut cereal price guarantees by 15% and beef price guarantees by 20%. However, plans to reduce direct aid to farmers were dropped toward the end of discussions, and reforms in the dairy sector were delayed until 2005. A total of 213 billion euros was to be devoted to structural aid (programs to promote development of regions lagging behind). [47]

Finally, the Commission's mismanagement of the EU budget had placed the Union in a state of flux. After being accused of "chronic cronyism and corruption" by an independent panel of the European Parliament, the entire Commission resigned on March 15, 1999. The Parliament accused Commissioner Edith Cresson of basing her hiring decisions on favoritism; several other commissioners were also implicated in mismanagement. At the Berlin meeting less than two weeks later, EU diplomats chose former Italian Prime Minister Romano Prodi as the new Commission president. While Prodi's five-year term would not begin until the end of the year, it was hoped that his appointment would help bring order to the EC's crisis situation. In the meantime, the fired commissioners continued working in a "caretaker capacity." A new 626-member European Parliament would also be elected in early June.[48]

Meeting 21st Century Objectives

Europe had taken a huge and decisive step toward preparing itself to compete in a globalized world. Monetary integration would either force the completion of a single market, with all the benefits that entailed, or would derail European growth by faltering on cultural and political issues. European leaders had to think seriously about the process of moving forward.

The incredibly powerful ECB had chartered a course of monetary stability above all else. **Exhibit 7.21** reflects the growth trajectory that Europe had followed since the late 1970s. If it were to revitalize growth of GDP per capita, the EU needed to traverse effectively the host of problems still blocking integration. The successful creation of a single European market would depend on President Prodi's ability to fix the Commission's administration, its budgeting, and its external barriers while trying to continue the track of internal reform. Indeed, Prodi had a challenging job awaiting him.

EXHIBIT 7.1 EU COUNTRY PERFORMANCE

Country	Area (in square km)[a]	Population (in millions)	1998 GDP (in euros)	Average Real GDP Growth 1990 Prices, 1991–1998 (%)	Real GDP/Capita PPP Adjusted 1998 (US$)[b]	I/GDP 1998 (%)	Average Inflation Rate GDP Deflator 1991–1998 (%)	Average Unemployment Rate 1991–1998 (%)	Ratio of Top Decile Income to Bottom Decile[d]	Exports + Imports as a % of GDP[e] (1998)	Unit Labor Costs (National Currencies) 1998 (1991 = 100)	Current Account/ GDP Nominal 1998 (%)	Gross Savings/ GDP 1998 (%)
Belgium	30,260	10,222	222.8	1.7	23,137	18.2	2.3	9.0	4.8	141.9	112.3	5.1	22.9
Germany	349,270	82,150	1,906.2	1.6	22,210	19.5	2.4	8.5	3.1	53.4	109.9	0.2	21.6
Spain	499,440	39,418	493.8	2.0	16,129	21.1	4.0	21.5	6.0	58.4	122.3	0.1	21.5
France	550,100	59,145	1,283.4	1.7	21,502	17.1	1.6	11.8	4.5	50.7	108.4	2.9	20.2
Ireland	68,890	3,721	74.5	8.4	NA	19.3	2.3	12.6	5.9	149.5	98.0	3.6	23.9
Italy	294,060	57,754	1,044.9	1.2	20,817	16.8	4.0	11.2	5.4	51.6	113.7	3.1	20.9
Luxembourg	2,560	433.7	14.8	4.7	NA	22.7	2.2	2.7	4.8	172.2	NA	14.1	40.2
Netherlands	33,920	15,783	337.9	2.7	22,193	20.0	2.0	6.0	3.5	105.5	110.2	5.8	27.0
Austria	82,730	8,121	189.3	1.9	22,416	24.1	2.4	4.0	4.9	89.1	108.7	-1.9	24.3
Portugal	91,950	9,896	95.8	2.5	14,095	25.7	5.3	6.3	7.1	73.7	137.2	-2.1	20.0
Finland	337,030[c]	5,171	110.9	2.8	20,906	17.5	1.6	14.7	NA	72.7	92.2	5.8	24.0
EU-11	2,340,210	291,814	5,774.2	1.8	NA	19.1	2.7	11.2	NA	62.8	110.3[f]	1.9	21.7
Denmark	42,430	5,319	156.4	2.6	23,390	21.0	1.9	7.3	3.1	66.6	110.9	-0.9	21.2
Greece	128,900	10,623	107.1	1.7	NA	21.8	10.1	9.0	6.6	39.0	194.7	-2.4	19.1
Sweden	411,620	8,954	204.4	1.3	20,170	14.5	1.9	8.7	NA	82.9	110.3	1.5	16.4
United Kingdom	241,600	59,399	1,252.3	2.6	20,061	17.1	2.8	8.6	NA	54.5	115.6	0.2	18.0
EU-15	3,164,760	376,109	7,494.6	1.9	NA	18.5	2.8	10.5	5.5[f]	61.6	111.6[g]	1.5	20.9
United States	9,573,110	272,745	7,538.0	3.1	29,405	18.1	2.2	5.8	11.2[h]	24.7	115.5	-2.5	16.3
Japan	377,835	126,643	3,320.7	0.8	22,805	26.4	0.4	3.1	NA	20.9	104.1	3.3	29.8

SOURCES: Compiled from European Commission, *Statistical Annex of European Economy.* [a]World Bank, *World Data 1995.* [b]OECD, 1998. [c]CIA, *1996 World Fact Book.* [d]*Eurostat Press Release no. 6996,* September 14, 1998. [e]Includes intra-EU trade. [f]Does not include Finland, Sweden, and the United Kingdom. [g]Does not include Luxembourg. [h]US Census Bureau. NA:Data not available.

EXHIBIT 7.2   **EUROPEAN UNION**

EU Member States

EU-11
Austria
Belgium
Finland
France
Germany
Ireland
Italy
Luxembourg
Netherlands
Portugal
Spain

EU-15
Denmark
Greece
Sweden
United Kingdom

Countries That Want to Enter the EU
Bulgaria
Cyprus
Czech Republic
Estonia
Hungary
Latvia
Lithuania
Poland
Romania
Slovakia
Slovenia
Turkey

EXHIBIT 7.3	INFLATION RATES FOR EMS AND OTHER COUNTRIES

			Inflation Rates				Average Annual Inflation Differentials[a]	
	Non-EMS Europe[c]	United States	Germany	France	Italy	EMS 8	EMS[d]	Non-EMS 8[b]
1979	8.7	12.3	11.2	4.1	10.7	14.7	5.3	8.5
1980	12.0	14.7	13.6	5.4	13.3	21.3	7.4	6.9
1981	12.2	14.2	10.4	6.3	13.3	19.5	7.0	6.6
1982	10.8	12.3	6.2	5.3	12.0	16.5	5.7	7.7
1983	7.9	10.7	3.2	3.3	9.5	14.7	5.0	9.4
1984	6.5	10.7	4.3	2.4	7.7	10.8	3.5	9.8
1985	4.9	9.3	3.6	2.2	5.9	9.2	2.8	7.3
1986	2.5	7.7	1.9	−0.1	2.5	5.9	2.6	8.1
1987	2.3	6.7	3.7	0.2	3.3	4.7	2.5	5.3
1988	2.5	6.4	4.1	1.3	2.7	5.1	2.0	4.1
1989	3.7	7.5	4.8	2.8	3.5	6.3	2.0	4.4
1990	3.7	8.2	5.2	2.7	3.4	6.6	1.6	4.6
1991	3.6	NA	4.2	3.9	3.2	6.8	NA	NA

SOURCES: K. Froot and K. Rogoff, "The EMS, the EMU and the Transition to a Common Currency," *NBER Macroeconomics Annual 1991*; and IMF, *International Financial Statistics*.
[a]Computed by taking a simple average of the absolute value of all pairwise inflation differentials in each period.
[b]EMS 8 is comprised of Belgium, Denmark, France, Germany, Italy, The Netherlands, Ireland, and Luxembourg.
[c]Non-EMS Europe is comprised of Greece, Norway, Portugal, Spain, Sweden, Switzerland, and the United Kingdom.
[d]Non-EMS is comprised of non-EMS Europe and the United States.

EXHIBIT 7.4	CONVERGENCE

	Inflation (CPI) (%)			Long-term Interest Rate (%)			Government Deficit/GDP			Debt/GDP		
	1997	1998[a]	1999[a]	1997	1998[a]	1999[a]	1997	1998[a]	1999[a]	1997	1998[a]	1999[a]
Belgium	1.8	1.1	1.4	5.8	4.8	4.7	2.0	1.3	1.2	121.9	117.2	113.7
Germany	1.7	1.0	1.1	5.7	4.6	4.5	2.7	2.6	2.3	61.5	61.3	61.0
Spain	2.5	2.3	2.1	6.4	4.9	4.8	2.6	2.1	1.6	68.9	67.7	66.0
France	1.1	0.6	1.2	5.6	4.7	4.5	3.0	2.9	2.3	58.1	58.3	58.6
Ireland	0.9	2.7	3.3	6.3	4.8	4.6	−0.9	−2.1	−3.4	63.4	53.3	44.1
Italy	2.5	2.2	2.0	6.7	4.9	4.8	2.7	2.6	2.3	121.6	118.8	115.3
Luxembourg	1.1	1.4	1.7	5.6	4.8	4.5	−3.0	−2.2	−2.0	6.7	7.1	7.5
The Netherlands	2.0	2.2	2.3	5.6	4.6	4.5	0.9	1.4	1.4	71.4	68.6	66.6
Austria	2.0	1.1	1.3	5.7	4.7	4.5	1.9	2.2	2.1	64.3	64.0	63.6
Portugal	2.5	2.6	2.4	6.4	4.9	4.8	2.5	2.3	2.0	61.5	57.4	55.3
Finland	1.5	1.5	1.6	6.0	4.8	4.7	1.1	−0.7	−1.8	55.1	52.9	50.2
EU-11	1.9	1.4	1.5	6.0	4.7	4.6	2.5	2.3	2.0	75.1	73.8	72.5
Denmark	2.2	1.9	2.4	6.2	5.0	5.0	−0.5	−1.3	−2.7	64.1	58.8	54.3
Greece	5.5	4.8	2.9	9.3	8.5	6.7	4.0	2.4	2.1	109.5	108.7	107.0
Sweden	2.2	1.3	1.8	6.7	5.1	5.0	0.8	−0.9	−1.4	76.9	74.0	69.5
United Kingdom	2.6	2.0	2.2	7.0	5.6	5.2	2.1	0.01	−0.1	53.5	51.5	49.9
EU-15	2.1	1.6	1.7	6.2	4.9	4.7	2.3	1.8	1.4	72.0	70.3	69.0

SOURCE: European Commission, *Statistical Annex of European Economy*, November 1998.
[a]Forecast.

EXHIBIT 7.5 **PROGRESS IN IMPLEMENTATION OF SINGLE-MARKET DIRECTIVES, DECEMBER 2, 1998**

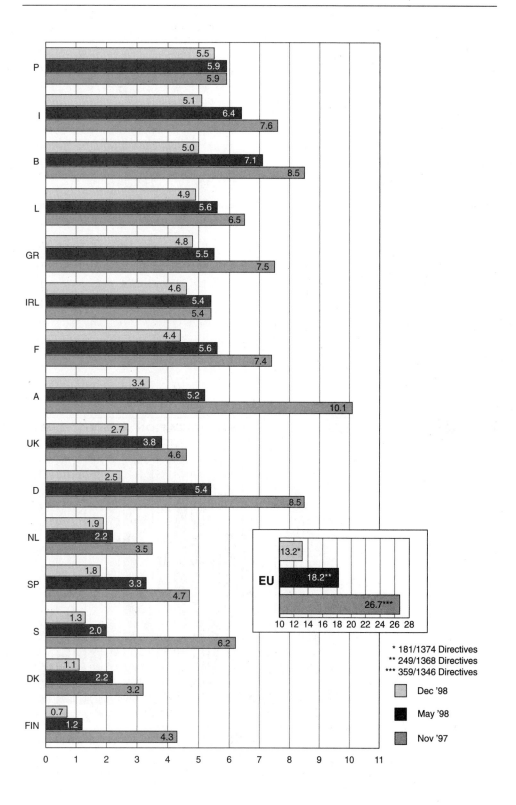

* 181/1374 Directives
** 249/1368 Directives
*** 359/1346 Directives

Dec '98
May '98
Nov '97

SOURCE: European Commission, 1998.

EXHIBIT 7.6	BREAKDOWN BY AREA AND MEMBER STATE OF NONTRANSPOSED DIRECTIVES, OCTOBER 15, 1998

	%	B	DK	GER	GR	SP	F	IRL	I	L	NL	A	P	FIN	S	UK
Telecommunications (15)	66.7	4	na	na	10	na	2	1	2	6	4	na	4	na	3	na
Public Procurement (10)	60	1	1	1	5	4	1	1	2	1	1	1	4	na	na	1
Transport (48)	52.1	12	7	4	5	7	9	17	12	9	8	9	11	3	3	9
Intellectual and Industrial Property (7)	42.9	na	na	na	2	na	na	3	1	1	1	na	1	na	na	na
Social Policy (38)	26.3	2	na	3	5	na	3	1	8	9	na	2	4	na	na	2
Chemical Products (74)	21.6	9	1	5	6	2	7	11	6	7	1	7	6	1	na	2
Veterinary Checks (193)	18.1	10	2	8	13	7	23	14	19	14	4	17	17	2	6	13
Environment (92)	17.4	11	3	4	7	5	6	6	6	4	4	3	5	2	3	6
Cosmetic Products (38)	15.8	1	na	na	2	na	3	4	1	3	1	3	2	na	1	na
Food Legislation (101)	14.8	3	1	4	4	3	4	10	7	3	na	6	11	1	na	2
Capital Goods (99)	12.1	8	2	2	2	1	3	4	7	4	na	2	2	1	1	1
Motor Vehicles (146)	8.2	na	1	1	1	1	3	1	na	7	1	1	1	1	1	11
Plant-Health Checks (172)	6.4	1	1	1	2	1	3	1	2	10	1	4	5	1	na	3
Total	na	64	20	33	64	32	67	76	74	80	26	55	74	12	18	50

SOURCE: European Commission.
(#) number of Directives concerned in each sector.
na: Data not available.

EXHIBIT 7.7	PROGRESS OF STANDARDIZATION ACTIVITIES BY THE EU

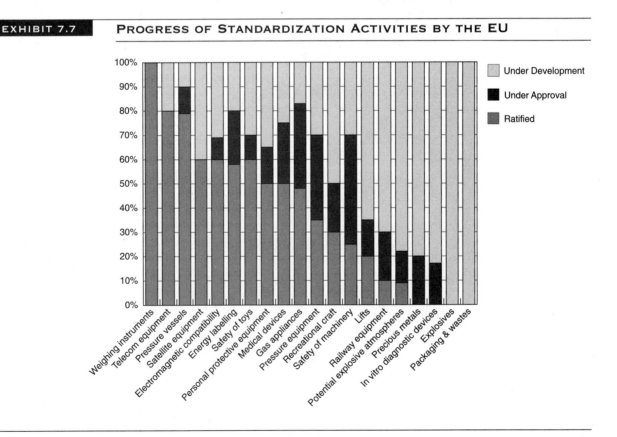

SOURCE: European Commission, "Economic Reform: Report on the Functioning of Community Product and Capital Markets," 1999.

EXHIBIT 7.8A

EVOLUTION OF NUMBERS OF NOTIFICATIONS AND DETAILED OPINIONS (1992–1998*)

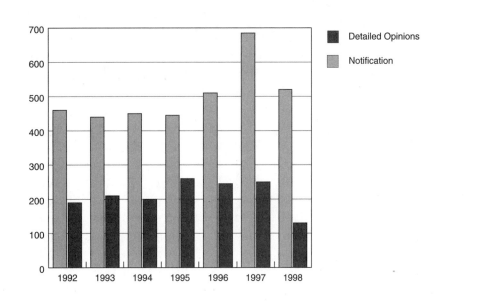

SOURCE: European Commission.

*These figures do not include 230 notifications from The Netherlands following from the case "CIA Securities" (1996) in the ECJ. Furthermore, the figures reflect the situations up to 11 November 1998.

EXHIBIT 7.8B

NUMBER OF MERGERS AND ACQUISITIONS INVOLVING EU FIRMS IN BANKING

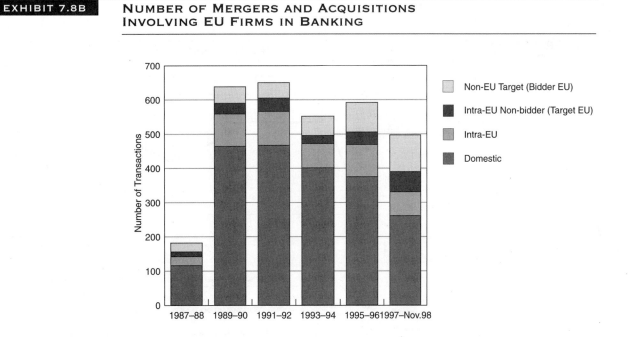

SOURCE: Compiled from *Acquisitions Monthly,* "European Community, Economic Reform: Report on the Functioning of Community Product and Capital Markets," 1998, p. A.12.

| EXHIBIT 7.9A | **CROSS-BORDER MERGERS AND ACQUISITIONS INVOLVING EU FIRMS** |

PERCENTAGE SHARES OF EACH MEMBER STATE, COMPARED WITH SHARES OF EU GDP, 1995–1998

Member State	Targeta (acquired company)	Bidderb (acquired)	GDP as % of EU Total (1996)
Belgium	4.4	3.3	3.1
Denmark	3.2	4.7	2.0
Germany	20.8	14.3	27.4
Greece	0.4	0.2	1.4
Spain	5.6	1.7	6.8
France	14.4	14.6	17.8
Ireland	1.3	3.3	0.8
Italy	7.5	3.2	14.1
Luxembourg	0.6	1.0	0.2
The Netherlands	7.2	12.4	4.6
Austria	2.2	1.6	2.7
Portugal	1.1	0.4	1.3
Finland	3.8	3.1	1.5
Sweden	4.9	8.1	2.9
United Kingdom	22.6	28.4	13.4
EU	100	100	100

SOURCE: European Commission, *Cardiff II*, p. 30.

ªTakeovers of EU firms, by another Member State or non-EU firms, classified by nationality of the acquired company.

ᵇTakeovers by EU firms, of firms in another Member State or outside the EU, classified by nationality of the acquired company.

| EXHIBIT 7.9B | **NUMBER OF COMPLETED MERGERS INVOLVING EU FIRMS (1986–1997)** |

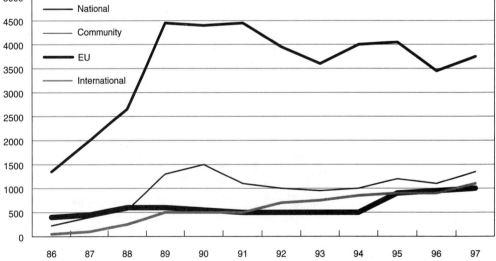

SOURCE: European Commission, "Cardiff I," fig A10.

National: mergers between firms based in the same Member State. Community: firms of different Member States. EU: non-EU firms acquired by EU firms.

EXHIBIT 7.10   DEVELOPMENTS OVER TIME IN EU PRICE DISPERSION (COEFFICIENT OF VARIATION)

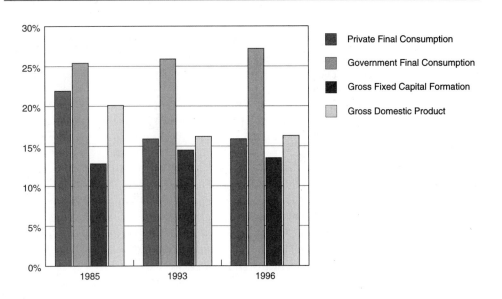

SOURCE: Compiled from Eurostat/OECD.
Unweighted, included excise and value-added taxes.

EXHIBIT 7.11   EU PRODUCTIVITY AND PRICE DISPERSION IN MANUFACTURING SECTORS (1996)

Sector	Relative productivity (Total manufacturing = 100)			Coefficient of price variation
	EU	U.S.	EU/U.S.	EU
Pharmaceuticals	165	277	0.60	32.1%
Food, beverage, tobacco	98	131	0.75	15.9%
Chemical industry	162	203	0.80	15.9%
Transport equipment	97	115	0.85	13.1%
Precision instruments	99	114	0.87	8.6%
Electrical engineering	102	118	0.87	10.9%
Motor vehicles	114	125	0.91	15.3%
Office machinery and computers	151	157	0.96	14.2%
Paper and printing	106	94	1.13	16.6%
Mechanical engineering	98	85	1.14	8.3%
Metal articles	83	69	1.21	16.2%
Rubber and plastic	91	73	1.25	11.4%

SOURCE: European Commission, *Eurostat*.
The "EU" column shows sectoral productivity levels in index relative to the EU's average manufacturing productivity level (= 100); the "U.S." column does the same for the United States. The "EU/U.S." column divides the EU's relative productivity levels by those of the United States—the result indicates in which sector the EU is relatively more productive than the United States. The final column provides a measure of price dispersion around the EU.

EXHIBIT 7.12	**PRICE DISPERSION FOR AUTOMOBILES IN THE EU MARKET, 1997–98 (% DIFFERENCE, HIGHEST AND LOWEST, INCLUDING LOCAL VAT)**

	1/11/98	1/5/98	1/11/97
Small Segments A and B			
Opel Corsa	16.2%	24.0%	43.5%
Ford Fiesta	28.8%	44.7%	26.9%
Renault Clio	27.7%	33.8%	30.4%
Peugeot 106	14.3%	21.1%	35.8%
VW Polo	32.0%	36.7%	54.3%
Medium Segment C			
VW Golf	31.0%	43.5%	40.1%
Opel Astra	19.5%	26.0%	25.3%
Ford Focus	27.8%	33.8%	45.4%[a]
Renault Mégane	19.8%	27.9%	31.7%
Peugeot 306	30.6%	46.2%	44.2%
Large Segments D, E, and F			
BMW 318 i	18.7%	12.0%	30.9%[b]
Audi A 4	19.1%	13.0%	12.5%
Ford Mondeo	34.6%	58.5%	34.7%
Opel Vectra	17.1%	18.2%	15.6%
VW Passat	24.0%	36.4%	33.5%

SOURCE: European Commission, "Car Prices in the European Union on 1 November 1998—Differences Decrease Sharply," February 1, 1999.
[a]Ford Escort/Orion, being replaced by Ford Focus.
[b]November 1, 1997: BMW 316i.

EXHIBIT 7.13	**THE TIMING OF FINANCIAL SERVICES DEREGULATION**

Measure	B	G	IRL	F	DK	GR	NL	I	L	P	SP	UK
73/183 Freedom of Establishment	1983	1974	1977	1975	1976	1986		1975	1975	1992	1987	1976
First Banking Directive	1993	1980	1989	1980	1978	1981	1978	1985	1981	1992	1987	1979
83/350 Consol. Surveillance	1985	1985	1985	1985	1984	1986	1986	1986	1986	1986	1985	1979
86/635 Consol. Accounts	1992	1990	1992	1991	1992	1994	1993	1992	1992	1992	1991	1994
89/117 Branches/ HQ Outside EU	1992	1990	1992	1991	1992	1994	1992	1992	1992	1992	1993	1993
89/299 92/16 Own Funds	1994	1990	1991	1990	1992	1992	1991	1993	1992	1993	1993	1992
Second Banking Directive	1994	1991	1992	1992	1992	1992	1992	1992	1993	1992	1994	1993
Solvency Ratio Directives	1994	1990	1991	1991	1992	1992	1991	1993	1993	1992	1993	1992
Money Laundering Directive	1995	1993	1995	1992	1993	1993	1994	1993	1993	1993	1993	1993
Large Exposures Directive	1994	1993	1994	1993	1995	1994	1993	1994	1993	1992	1993	1993
Deposit Insurance Directive	1994		1995	1995	1995	1995	1995			1995		1995
Interest Rate Deregulation	1990	1988	1993	1990	1981	1993	1981	1990	1990	1992	1992	1979
Liberalization of Capital Flows	1991	1982	1985	1990	1967	1994	1980	1983	1990	1992	1992	1979

SOURCE: EC, *Single Market Review: Credit Institutions and Banking* (Brussels, 1997), p. 12.

EXHIBIT 7.14A **PRICE CHANGES FOR DIFFERENT TYPES OF LOANS SINCE THE FULL IMPLEMENTATION OF THE SMP**

Product Area	IRL	UK	F	G	SP	P	B	NL	GR	DK	I	EU
Corporate customer loans (large firms)	–44	–22	–47	–32	–42	–19	–27	–22	–39	–36	–25	–29
Corporate customer loans (small firms)	–43	–22	–41	–26	–41	–18	–25	–23	–25	–21	–16	–24
Retail customer loans	–43	–25	–37	–8	–36	–4	–21	–24	–26	–25	–12	–21
Retail customer mortgages	–26	–29	–41	–19	–45	–30	–23	6	–39	–31	–18	–16

Price defined as margin between rate charged to customer and money market rate.
Changes in the margin due to business cycles effect excluded.
–50 is "large decrease," –25 is "small decrease," 0 is "no change," 25 is "small increase," and 50 is "large increase."

SOURCE: Postal survey.

EXHIBIT 7.14B **PRICE CHANGES FOR CORPORATE AND RETAIL CUSTOMER DEPOSITS SINCE THE FULL IMPLEMENTATION OF THE SMP**

Product Area	IRL	UK	F	G	SP	P	B	NL	GR	DK	I	EU
Corporate customer deposits (large firms)	–40	–21	–42	–31	–26	–29	–27	–22	–28	–18	–11	–25
Corporate customer deposits (small firms)	–37	–19	–35	–29	–29	–30	–27	–30	–30	–13	–8	–24
Retail customer deposits	–37	–11	–35	–30	–28	–25	–27	–32	–30	–31	–4	–23

Prices defined as margin between rate paid to customer and money market rate.
Changes in margin due to business cycle effects excluded.
–50 is "large decrease," –25 is "small decrease," 0 is "no change," 25 is "small increase," and 50 is "large increase."

SOURCE: Postal survey.

EXHIBIT 7.14C **THE EXTENT TO WHICH THE FEES CHARGED TO CUSTOMERS HAVE CHANGED SINCE THE FULL IMPLEMENTATION OF THE SMP**

Customer Type	IRL	UK	F	G	SP	P	B	NL	GR	DK	I	EU
Corporate customer (large firms)	–25	–14	–17	–22	–2	17	–3	–8	–5	15	4	–10
Corporate customer (small firms)	–23	–15	–5	–21	11	22	2	–8	–3	18	11	–6
Retail customers	–18	–3	12	–15	18	34	3	–6	0	25	18	0

–50 is "large decrease," –25 is "small decrease," 0 is "no change," 25 is "small increase," and 50 is "large increase."
"The last three years" was used as a proxy for the post-SMP period.

SOURCE: Postal survey.

EXHIBIT 7.14D **CHANGES IN THE NUMBER OF BRANCHES SINCE THE FULL IMPLEMENTATION OF THE SMP**

Market	IRL	UK	F	G	SP	P	B	NL	GR	DK	I	EU
Domestic market	4	–18	–7	–1	19	39	–4	–44	26	–39	46	–1
Market of other EU countries	25	19	–7	34	6	30	11	31	26	0	12	21

–50 is "large decrease," –25 is "small decrease," 0 is "no change," 25 is "small increase," and 50 is "large increase."

SOURCE: Postal survey; European Commission.

EXHIBIT 7.15A   MAIN FEATURES OF THE UNEMPLOYMENT IN THE EU 1997

	Unemployment Rate of Total Labor Force (1)	Share of Long-Term Unemployed among All Unemployed (≥ 12 Months) (2)	Unemployment Rate of Those with Low Educational Level (3)	Share of Unemployed with Low Educational Level among Total Unemployed (4)	Unemploy-ment Rate for Youth (15–24) (5)
Belgium	9.2	60.5	13.4	50.2	21.3
Denmark	5.5	27.2	14.6	37.3	8.1
Germany	10.0	50.1	13.3	26.5	10.7
Greece	9.6	55.7	6.3	37.3	31.0
Spain	20.8	51.8	20.6	62.6	39.2
France	12.4	39.6	14.0	45.1	29.0
Ireland	10.1	57.0	16.4	63.7	15.9
Italy	12.1	66.3	9.1	55.6	33.6
Luxembourg	2.6	34.6	3.8	71.5	7.3
The Netherlands	5.2	49.1	7.9	49.4	9.7
Austria	4.4	28.7	5.7	34.7	7.6
Portugal	6.8	55.6	6.2	76.6	14.1
Finland	13.1	29.8	21.6	38.2	35.4
Sweden	9.9	34.2	10.1	31.9	21.9
UK	7.0	38.6	12.2	55.0	13.6
Euro-Zone	11.6	50.9	na	47.0	23.5
EU-15	10.7	49.0	13.7	47.2	21.2
United States	4.9	8.7	10.0	na	11.3
Japan	3.4	21.8	na	na	6.6

SOURCE: EC, *Cardiff II*, Brussels, February 17, 1999, pp. 33, 36.

(1) Harmonized unemployment rates, *EUROSTAT.*
(2) *Labour Force Survey*, *EUROSTAT.* For United States and Japan, *OECD Employment Outlook 1998.*
(3) Educational level lower than upper secondary, persons aged 25 to 64 years old (1995), *OECD Employment Outlook 1998.*
(4) Educational level lower than upper secondary (lower secondary and less); persons aged 25–59 (1997 2Q), *LFS, EUROSTAT.*
(5) *Labour Force Survey*, *EUROSTAT.* For United States and Japan, *OECD Employment Outlook 1998.*
na: Data not available.

| EXHIBIT 7.15B | IMPLICIT TAX RATES ON LABOR AND CAPITAL (%)—1996 |

	Implicit Tax Rate on Employed Labor (1)	Taxes on Low-Skilled Workers (2)	Implicit Tax Rate on Consumption (3)	Total Tax Wedge (4)	Implicit Tax Rate on Other Factors (5)
Belgium	44.8	50.5	13.7	48.2	38.6
Denmark	47.1	41.3	21.2	54.2	35.8
Germany	43.3	46.5	13.7	45.6	36.1
Greece	44.9	34.9	16.6	34.5	9.7
Spain	38.3	34.4	12.3	37.4	24.0
France	44.9	44.3	14.6	51.1	47.6
Ireland	29.1	26.5	18.9	36.6	21.4
Italy	50.1	48.3	13.4	45.4	33.1
Luxembourg	30.2	29.1	17.9	44.8	49.8
The Netherlands	46.7	39.3	15.4	48.4	37.0
Portugal	42.0	30.6	15.9	34.2	18.0
UK	27.3	26.8	14.6	33.1	36.8
Austria	45.8	37.4	15.6	49.9	38.9
Finland	55.3	45.3	19.0	55.6	24.1
Sweden	57.6	48.6	16.1	56.3	47.4
Euro-Zone[a]	44.8	44.2	14.1	46.4	35.6
EU-15	42.6	41.8	14.4	44.8	35.6
United States	23.2	29.2	5.5	27.9	45.3
Japan	24.7	18.4	5.1	27.1	52.3

[a]Euro-Zone includes 11 countries: Belgium, Germany, Spain, France, Ireland, Italy, Luxembourg, The Netherlands, Portugal, Austria, and Finland.

(1) The ratio of taxes directly borne by the employed labor to the total compensation of employees. Employed labor taxes include social security contributions paid to the employers and the employees, the taxes on payroll and workforce, and personal income tax on employed labor.

(2) Tax benefit of singles with no children (wage level 67% of APW). Employees' and employers' SSC and personal income tax less transfer payments (% of gross labor costs: gross wage earnings plus employer's SSC).

(3) The ratio of consumption taxes to the after-tax value of consumption.

(4) The tax wedge includes all taxes borne by labor (social security contributions and personal taxes on labor income) plus the part of consumption taxes paid when spending labor income. The tax wedge is the difference between the producer wage and the consumer wage as a percentage of the former.

(5) Social security contributions and other taxes paid by the self-employed, plus taxes on capital income expressed as a percentage of the capital income (total operating surplus).

EXHIBIT 7.16	EMPLOYMENT RATE, EU

SOURCE: EC, "Commission Recommendation for the Broad Guidelines of the Economic Policies of the Member States and the Community," Brussels (CB-CO-99-152-EN-C), March 3, 1999, p. 15

EXHIBIT 7.17	NET REPLACEMENT RATE OF UNEMPLOYMENT BENEFITS IN 1995

| | Net Replacement Rates[a] | | | |
| | 2/3 of APW[b] | | APW[b] | |
Country	1st month	60th month	1st month	60th month
Belgium	79	86	61	58
Denmark	93	82	70	74
Germany	74	85	72	66
Greece[c]	N.A.	N.A.	57	N.A.
Spain	72	49	74	35
France	86	57	76	46
Ireland	60	60	49	49
Italy	41	7	42	5
Luxembourg	87	84	87	66
The Netherlands	87	92	79	71
Austria	65	62	63	61
Portugal	88	3	78	2
Finland	87	95	75	81
Sweden	80	109	78	82
UK	81	85	61	64

Note: The summary measure of net replacement rates and tax rates have been calculated as a simple average of the rates for three family types (single person, couple without children, and couple with two children). The net replacement for the 60th month of unemployment includes the possible topping-up of social assistance.

[a]This shows the percentage of a low wage worker's (2/3 of APW) wage recovered from unemployment benefits; and the same for an average wage worker (APW).

[b]APW = Average Production Wage.

[c]The Greek net replacement rate is from the study of the Central Planning Bureau for 1993.

N.A.: Data not available.

SOURCE: *OECD, Benefit Systems and Work Incentives, 1998,* and European Commission, *Cardiff II,* p. 37.

EXHIBIT 7.18	AVERAGE ANNUAL WORKED HOURS PER EMPLOYEE IN THE NETHERLANDS AND IN SELECTED OECD COUNTRIES

	1973	1979	1983	1990	1996*
The Netherlands	1,724	1,591	1,530	1,433	1,372
West Germany	1,804	1,699	1,686	1,562	1,508
France	1,771	1,667	1,558	1,539	1,529
SW[a]	1,557	1,451	1,453	1,480	1,554
UK[a]	1,929	1,821	1,719	1,773	1,732
United States	1,896	1,884	1,866	1,936	1,951

SOURCE: OECD, "Employment Outlook 1997, Paris: Organisation of Economic Cooperation and Development," July 1997, Table G.
[a]Total employment.

EXHIBIT 7.19	GENERAL GOVERNMENT NET LENDING/BORROWING (% OF GDP)

		STABILITY AND CONVERGENCE PROGRAM PROJECTIONS				
	Date[a]	1998	1999	2000	2001	2002
Stability Programs						
Belgium	12/98	−1.6	−1.3	−1.0	−0.7	−0.3
Germany	01/99	−2.5	−2.0	−2.0	−1.5	−1.0
Spain	12/98	−1.9	−1.6	−1.0	−0.4	0.1
France	01/99	−2.9	−2.3	−2.0	−1.6	−1.2[b]
Ireland	12/98	−2.6	−2.0	−1.5	−1.0	na
Italy	12/98	−2.6	−2.0	−1.5	−1.0	na
Luxembourg	02/99	2.1	1.1	1.2	1.3	1.7
The Netherlands[c]	10/98	−1.3	−1.3	na	na	−1.1
Austria	11/98	−2.2	−2.0	−1.7	−1.5	−1.4[d]
Portugal	12/98	na	−2.0	−1.5	−1.2	−0.8
Finland	09/98	−1.1	2.4	2.2	2.1	2.3
Convergence Programs						
Denmark	10/98	1.1	2.5	2.8	2.6	na[e]
Greece	6/98	−2.4	−2.1	−1.7	−0.8	na
Sweden	12/98	−1.5	0.3	1.6	2.5	na
United Kingdom[f]	12/98	0.8	−0.3	−0.3	−0.1	0.2[g]

[a]Date when program was adopted.
[b]Prudent scenario, favorable scenario projection: −1.7, −1.2, and −0.8% of GDP, respectively, in the years 2000 to 2002.
[c]No annual data provided for years 2000/01.
[d]Cautious scenario, middle and favorable scenario projections: −0.25 and 0.25% of SDP, respectively, in the year 2002.
[e]Projection for the year 2005: 3.5% of GDP.
[f]Data for the financial years beginning in each for the calendar years indicated.
[g]Projection in the financial year 2003/04: 0.1% of GDP.
na: Data not available.

SOURCE: EC, "Commission Recommendation for the Broad Guidelines of the Economic Policies of the Member States and the Community," Brussels (CB-CO-99-152-EN-C), March 3, 1999, p. 10.

| **EXHIBIT 7.20** | **AGENDA 2000 EUROPEAN UNION BUDGET** |

Euro million—1999 prices

Appropriations for committments	2000	2001	2002	2003	2004	2005	2006
1. Agriculture	40,920	42,800	43,900	47,770	42,760	41,930	41,660
CAP expenditure (excluding rural development)	36,620	38,480	39,570	39,430	38,410	37,570	37,290
Rural development and accompanying measures	4,300	4,320	4,330	4,340	4,350	4,360	4,370
2. Structural Operations	32,045	31,455	30,865	30,285	29,595	29,595	29,170
3. Internal Policies	5,900	5,950	6,000	6,050	6,100	6,150	6,200
4. External Action	4,550	4,560	4,570	4,580	4,590	4,600	4,610
5. Administration	4,560	4,600	4,700	4,800	4,900	5,000	5,100
6. Reserves	900	900	650	400	400	400	400
7. Preaccession Aid	3,120	3,120	3,120	3,120	3,120	3,120	3,120
Total Appropriations for Commitments	91,995	93,385	93,805	93,005	91,465	90,795	90,260
Total Appropriations for Payments	89,590	91,070	94,130	94,740	91,720	89,910	89,310
Appropriations for payments as % of GNP	1.13%	1.12%	1.13%	1.11%	1.05%	1.00%	0.97%
Available for Accession (appropriations for payments)	na	na	4,140	6,710	8,890	11,440	14,220
Ceiling on Appropriations for Payments	89,590	91,070	98,270	101,450	100,610	101,350	103,530

SOURCE: Berlin European Council, "Presidency Conclusions," March 24 and 25, 1999.
na: Data not available.

| **EXHIBIT 7.21** | **GDP PER CAPITA, 1970–1998 FOR THE UNITED STATES, JAPAN, AND THE EC (PPP ADJUSTED)*** |

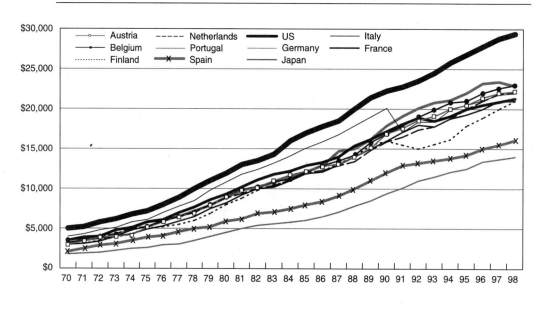

SOURCE: Bruce Scott, manuscript, 1999.
*Data for Germany represents unified East and West Germany beginning in 1991.

EXHIBIT 7.22	CONTRIBUTIONS TO EU BUDGET OF EU MEMBER STATES

	1995				1986	
	Net Contribution			GDP per Head as % of EC Average[a]		Net Contributions
	Total mecu	Per Head ecu	Per Head Rank		Total m ecu	per Head ecu
Germany	13,431	164.6	(1)	106.7	3,742	61.3
Britain	4,720	80.7	(6)	98.2	1,438	25.3
The Netherlands	2,005	129.7	(2)	100.4	–217	–14.9
France	1,727	29.6	(9)	107.2	561	10.1
Sweden	937	105.5	(5)	95.3	na	na
Austria	905	112.9	(3)	109.3	na	na
Italy	614	10.7	(10)	101.7	195	3.4
Belgium	311	30.6	(8)	110.4	284	28.7
Finland	165	32.3	(7)	92.5	na	na
Luxembourg	45	110.6	(4)	128.2	59	160.3
Denmark	–306	–58.6	(11)	112	–421	82.2
Ireland	–1,887	–526.8	(15)	85.3	–1,230	–374.4
Portugal	–2,381	–241.8	(13)	67.9	–319	–22.1
Greece	–3,489	–333	(14)	60	–1,273	–127.8
Spain	–7,218	–184	(12)	76.1	–95	–2.5

SOURCE: Court of Auditors Report; European Commission.
[a]Based on PPP.   na: Data not available.

EXHIBIT 7.23	COUNTRY DATA FOR PROSPECTIVE EU MEMBERS

Country	Population (millions)[a]	1995 GDP[a] (in bn US$)[b]	Real per Capita GDP, PPP Adj. ($)[c]	5 yr. Avg. Inflation Rate (%)[d]	% of 1995 X + M with EC Countries[e]	1994 Agri. as % of GDP[f]
Norway	4.4	146.1	15,518	2.67	75.5	2.92[g]
Switzerland	7.2	306.1	15,887	3.35	70.0	3.00[3]
Cyprus	0.7	na	9,203	4.7	47.5	4.97
Malta	0.4	na	6,627[h]	3.24	76.8	2.52
Turkey	61.4	169.3	3,807	76.14	48.7	15.46
Poland	38.6	115	3,826	129.6	269.5	6.29
Hungary	10.1	43.7	4,645	25.96	63.5	6.01
Czech Republic	10.3	47.3	4,095[i]	19.53	62.6	4.99[j]

[a] SOURCE: U.S. Bureau of the Census, International Data Base; CIA, 1996 World Factbook.
[b]SOURCE: Organization for Economic Cooperation and Development, National Accounts of the OECD Countries, 1996 Vol.1; Countries, submissions to the OECD and Secretariat estimates; CIA Directorate of Intelligence, *Handbook of International Economic Statistics*, 1996.
[c]Real GDP per capita in constant dollar using Chain index (1985 international prices); Penn World Tables.
[d]SOURCE: International Monetary Fund, *International Financial Statistics Yearbook*, February 1997.
[e]SOURCE: *International Monetary Fund, Direction of Trade Statistics Quarterly*, March 1997 and December 1996.
[f]SOURCE: United Nations Statistics Division.
[g]1991 data.
[h]1989 data.
[i]1990 data.
[j]1995 data.
na: Data not available.

The Directorates General

DGI External Relations: Commercial policy and relations with North America, the Far East, Australia, and New Zealand

DGIA External Relations: Europe and the New Independent States, Common Foreign and Security Policy and External Missions

DGIB External Relations: Southern Mediterranean, Near East, Latin America, South and Southeast Asia and North–South Cooperation

DGII Economic and Financial Affairs

DGIII Industry

DGIV Competition

DGV Employment, Industrial Relations, and Social Affairs

DGVI Agriculture

DGVII Transport

DGVIII Development

DGIX Personnel and Administration

DGX Audiovisual Media, Information, Communication, and Culture

DGXI Environmental, Civil Protection, and Nuclear Safety

DGXII Science, Research, and Development

DGXIII Telecommunications, Information Market, and Exploitation of Research

DGXIV Fisheries

DGXV International Markets and Financial Services

DGXVI Regional Policies and Cohesion

DGXVII Energy Policies

DGXIX Budgets

DGXXI Customs and Indirect Taxation

DGXXII Education, Training, and Youth

DGXXIII Enterprise Policy, Distributive Trades, Tourism, and Cooperatives

DGXXIV Consumer Policy and Consumer Health Protection

SOURCE: Frank McDonald and Steven Dearden, *European Economic Integration* (Great Britain: Henry Ling Ltd., 1999), p. 17.

Major Elements of the 1992 Program

In standards, testing, certification harmonization of standards for:

Toys

Automobiles, trucks and motorcycles and their emissions

Telecommunications

Construction products

Machine safety

Measuring instruments

Medical devices

Gas appliances

Cosmetics

Quick frozen foods

Flavorings

Food preservatives

Instant formula

Fruit juices

Food inspection

Definition of spirited beverages and aromatized wines

Tower cranes (noise)

Household appliances (noise)

Tire pressure gauges

Detergents

Fertilizers

Lawn mowers (noise)

Medicinal products and medical specialties

Radio interferences

New rules for harmonizing packing, labeling, and processing requirements

Ingredients and labels for food and beverages

Nutritional labeling

Classification, packaging, labeling of dangerous preparations

Harmonization of regulations for health

Harmonization of an extensive list of rules

Medical specialties

Pharmaceuticals

Veterinary medical products

High-technology medicines

Implantable electromedical devices

Single-use devices (disposable)

In-vitro diagnostics

Changes in government procurement regulations

Coordination of procedures on the award of public works and supply contracts

Extension of EC law to telecommunications, utilities, transport

Services

Harmonization of regulation of services

Banking

Mutual funds

Broadcasting

Tourism

Road passenger transport

Railways

Information services

Life and nonlife insurance

Securities

Maritime transport

Air transport

Electronic payment cards

Liberalization of capital movements

Long-term capital, stocks

Short-term capital

Consumer protection regulations

Misleading definition of products

Indication of prices

Harmonization of laws regulating company behavior

Mergers and acquisitions

Trademarks

Copyrights

Cross-border mergers

Accounting operations across borders

Bankruptcy

Protection of computer programs

Transaction taxes

Company law

Harmonization of taxation

Value-added taxes

Excise taxes on alcohol, tobacco, and other

Harmonization of veterinary and phytosanitary controls industry (including marketing)

Covering items such as:

Antibiotic residues

Animals and meat

Plant health

Fish and fish products

Live poultry, poultry meat, and hatching eggs

Pesticide residues in fruit and vegetables

Elimination and simplification of national transit documents and procedures for intra-EC trade

Introduction of the Single Administrative Document (SAD)

Abolition of customs presentation charges

Elimination of customs formalities and the introduction of common boarder posts

Harmonization of rules pertaining to the free movement of labor and professions within the EC

Mutual recognition of higher educational diplomas

Comparability of vocational training qualifications

Training of engineers and doctors

Activities in the field of pharmacy

Elimination of burdensome requirements related to residence permits

SOURCE: *Business America*, August 1, 1988, p. 2.

END NOTES

1   The European Commission, "Economic Reform: Report on the Functioning of Community Product and Capital Markets," 1998.

2   The European Commission, "Economic and Structural Reform in the EU (Cardiff II)," Brussels, February 17, 1999, p. 2.

3   Norway applied to join the EC, but in two national referenda (1973, 1994) its citizens voted against membership.

4   Michael Calingaert, *The 1992 Challenge from Europe: Development of the European Community's Internal Market* (Washington, DC: National Planning Association, 1988), p. 36; and Pascal Fontaine, *Europe in 10 Points* (Luxembourg: Office for Official Publications of the European Communities, 1998), pp. 9–13.

5   Because of its tenuous monetary position, Italy was given a wider band of ±6%.

6   "A Survey of Europe's Internal Market," *The Economist*, July 9, 1988, p. 8.

7   Paola Cecchini, et al., *The Benefits of a Single Market* (Aldershot, UK: Gower, 1988), pp. 8–10.

8   Commission of the European Communities, *Completing the Internal Market, White Paper from the Commission to the European Council*, Brussels, June 14, 1985.

9   European Community, *News*, No. 7/89, March 14, 1989.

10 Interviews by the authors in Amsterdam, April 7, 1999.

11 European Commission, "European Automobile Industry," Brussels, July 10, 1996; and Peter Holmes and Alasdair Smith, "Automobile Industry," in Pierre Buigues, et al., eds., *European Policies on Competition, Trade and Industry: Conflict and Complementarities* (Aldershot: Edward Elgar, 1995), pp. 132–147.

12 Mario Monti, *The Single Market and Tomorrow's Europe* (England: Clays Ltd., St Evives PLC, 1996), p. 31.

13 Duetshce Bank Research, *EMU Watch*, No. 67 (March 15, 1999), pp. 3–4.

14 EC, "Economic and Structural Reform," p. 10.

15 EC,"Economic Reform: Report on the Functioning of Community Product and Capital Markets" (Brussels, 1998), figure A.6; and Eurostat, News Release, "EU Member States Investment 46% More Abroad," August 3, 1998 (No. 59/98), p. 2.

16 Fabienne Ilzkovitz and Adriaan Dierx, "From the Single Market to the Single Currency: New Challenges for European Companies," IL/748/98-EN, Table A-1, pp. 17–18.

17 European Commission, "Car Prices in the European Union on 1 November, 1998—Differences Decrease Sharply," Brussels [IP/99/60], February 1, 1999, p. 2.

18 EC, "Economic and Structural Reform," p. 10.

19 Bureau Europeen des Unions des Consommateurs, "The Impact of the Euro on Price Transparency," 1998. It should be noted that the most recent issue of the "hamburger standard" in *The Economist*, April 3, 1999, reported a price variance of just 18%, as Greece and Finland were not included.

20 European Commission, "Economic and Structural Reform, p. 10.

21 European Commission, "A Common System of VAT-A Programme for the Single Market," XXI/1156/96-EN, July 1996, p. 3.

22 European Commission, "Economic Reform: Report on the Function of Community Produce and Capital Markets" [Cardiff I], 1998, p. 21.

23 European Commission, "Economic and Structural Reform," p. 36.

24 European Commission, "Economic Reform," p. 20 and figure B.12.

25 European Commission, "Economic and Structural Reform," p. 11.

26 Karle Van Miert, Brussels, March 30, 1999, quoted in Erik Berggren memorandum, April 2, 1999.

27 European Commission, *The Single Market Review: Impact on Services—Credit Institutions and Banking* (Brussels: European Community, 1997), vol. III, pp. 19–23.

28 EC, "Financial Services: Building a Framework for Action," (Brussels, COM (1998) 625), October 28, 1998, pp. 11–12; EC, "Implementing the Framework for Financial Markets: An Action Plan," May 11, 1998.

29 Interview with the authors at Deutsche Bank, Frankfurt, April 8, 1999.

30 European Commission, *The Single Market Review: Impact on Services*, p. 75.

31 Interview with the authors at Deutsche Bank, April 8, 1999.

32 European Commission, "Economic Reform: Report on the Function of Community Produce and Capital Markets" [Cardiff I], p. 6.

33 European Commission, "Economic Reform," p. 4.

34 Ibid., p. 21.

35 Ibid., p. 22.

36 Interview with the authors at Deutsche Bank, Frankfurt, April 8, 1999.

37 "The Euro: A Stable Currency for Europe," Deutsche Bank Research and http://www.ecb.int/.

38 Interviews with the authors at the ECB, Frankfurt, April 19, 1999.

39   "The European System of Central Banks," Federal Reserve Bank of Dallas, *Economic Review*, First Quarter 1999 and www.ecb.int/.

40   Martin Feldstein, "EMU and International Conflict," *Foreign Affairs*, November/December 1997, 76,6, p. 66.

41   Interview; "The European System of Central Banks," Federal Reserve Bank of Dallas, *Economic Review*, First Quarter 1999; Edmund L. Andrews, "European Banks, Acting in Unison, Cut Interest Rate," *The New York Times*, December 4, 1998; and "ECB Makes Surprise Half-Point Cut in Main Interest Rate," Financial Times, April 9, 1999.

42   "After the Euro . . . Now What?" *Chief Executive*, December 1998, p. 34.

43   William Hjerpe, in Peter Marsh, "When Transparency Leads to Added Value," *Financial Times*, January 26, 1999.

44   NatWest Markets, "Preparations for Economic and Monetary Union: A Guide for Business," December 1997.

45   M. Feldstein, "EMU and International Conflict," p. 66.

46   http://europa.eu.int/comm/agenda2000.

47   "Presidency Conclusions, Berlin European Council," 24 and 25 March 1999, and "EU Reaches Accord on Farm Aid, Budget Scandal Spurs Leaders to Protect Credibility," *The Globe and Mail*, March 27, 1999.

48   "Group Running European Union Quits en Masse," *The New York Times*, March 16, 1999, and "Former Italian Premier Chosen to Head European Commission," *The New York Times*, March 25, 1999.

EUROPEAN MONETARY UNION:
HONEYWELL EUROPE

William Hjerpe, the American president of Honeywell Europe, and Romano Prodi, newly designated chairman of the European Commission, shared at least one common interest in the spring of 1999: an economically integrated Europe. A stalwart enthusiast of integration, Hjerpe pondered how to move the U.S.-based leader in control technology forward. Looking at his organization's fragmented markets with their high-cost structure (relative to the U.S. parent), he saw monetary union as the push needed to integrate Honeywell's European market.

Over the past several years, Europe had made great strides toward becoming an integrated market. By July 2002, integration was expected to accelerate with the use of a common currency for all economic transactions among the EMU-11 countries. Given his company's leadership in technology and its strong and respected brand recognition, Hjerpe believed that real market integration was a huge opportunity for Honeywell to grow and prosper. Indeed, Honeywell Europe's savings from currency integration, including pan-European purchasing effects, was estimated as high as $30 million annually. While many Europeans wondered if they could keep up with competitive changes, Hjerpe was determined to move Honeywell to the forefront of integration.

Streamlining for Europe

When Bill Hjerpe came to Brussels from the United States to head up Honeywell Europe in 1997, he scarcely believed that Europe would really adopt a single currency. The European region of Honeywell Inc. generated about $2.1 billion in revenue with 13,000 employees—about a quarter of Honeywell's total. Honeywell Europe sold industrial controls (34%), commercial and residential control systems such as thermostats and building management systems (63%), and aerospace products (3%). Honeywell's reputation was for technological leadership and top quality, and it had great name recognition throughout Europe [**Exhibit 7.24**].

One problem, of course, was its cost structure. Honeywell Europe had a matrix organization; it was organized by both product market and country—with a full organizational structure in each European country. Thus, in Belgium, for example, there was a country manager, a finance manager, a human resources manager, etc.—and an organization of managers to run Honeywell's businesses in Belgium. Meanwhile, its manufacturing in Europe (with 17 sites) was fragmented and duplicative. And its product offerings, at least in commercial and residential, were resplendent with different models, systems, circuits, colors, sizes, labels, etc.; "the Honeywell product catalogue was an inch thick." The previous president of Honeywell Europe, Giannantonio Ferrari (now president of Honeywell Inc.), had already begun making Honeywell Europe more streamlined and cost-competitive.

By early 1998, Hjerpe realized that Europe was indeed going to integrate. At that point, he had two choices—to move fast and become an early adopter of an integrated strategy, or to delay adoption until 2002, holding down costs, avoiding uncertainty, and seeing what happened to the competition. Hjerpe quickly chose the former, adopting a strategy summarized as follows: "Exploit the opportunities in our vibrant marketplace, creating a future of competitive superiority by outperforming, with innovative and enhanced efficiency, for our customers and for Honeywell" [**Exhibit 7.25**].[a]

Hjerpe believed that in the face of price competition, Honeywell could press suppliers to lower their prices to Honeywell—by as much as $15 million annually. Since Honeywell believed that only 14% of its product offerings were exposed to downward

---

[a]Honeywell Europe, "Performance, Progress and Ambition," *1998 Review & 1999 Outlook*, February 4, 1999.

price pressure, Hjerpe thought he could actually increase margins if costs could be controlled. Thus, the centerpiece of strategy was to reorganize Honeywell Europe into business units and then to reduce personnel, manufacturing, and distribution costs by driving rationalization [see **Exhibits 7.25** and **7.26**]. This, plus continuing downward pressure on product differentiation (reducing "stinkers" by 10% annually) and closeness to the market, should yield most of Honeywell's improved margins. Sales initiatives and further acquisitions could help grow revenue by 10% annually.[b] Hjerpe intended to implement all this by the end of 2000.

Of course, he faced any number of difficulties—both inside Honeywell and without. Honeywell Europe's management was not initially enthusiastic about the kind of streamlining that would make it look like its American counterpart. It would entail bookkeeping changes, incentive changes, performance changes, and for sure, workforce reductions. Externally, Honeywell had to step lightly through member-state employment laws, established distributor patterns, and cultural preferences that differed sharply across boundaries. "We're wrestling with how to drive the economies of scale," said Mike Robinson, vice president of finance, "with banking issues, pension issues, tax issues and the labor issue all partly outside Honeywell's immediate control." Upstream concentration (pan-European factories) had to go together with the diversity of a local presence in sales and services. Customer intimacy still required a local presence, culture, and language.

Future

William Hjerpe thought Honeywell could meet its goals if Europe continued to grow for the next couple of years. He commented that "as we establish a strong vertically based SBU organizational structure, we will continue to build the benefits of a region-wide Honeywell philosophy . . . to reinforce economies of scale and globalization of strategy."[c]

Hjerpe was determined to make Honeywell Europe a more streamlined, more profitable competitor. But a lot depended on Prodi's course and the success or failure of the integrative process. For sure, Honeywell had its work cut out for it.

---

[b]Ibid.

[c]William Hjerpe, "Organization Change—Europe, Middle East & Africa," November 27, 1998.

EXHIBIT 7.24 | **HONEYWELL EUROPE, MIDDLE EAST, AND AFRICA (1998)**

Financials

Sales: $2.1 billion

Assets: $1.5 billion

Operating Profit: $210 million

Presence in 49 countries

31 through affiliates

5 through joint ventures

13 through national distributor and rep offices

With 17 manufacturing locations

And 13,000 people

8,500 in sales & services

4,500 in engineering & manufacturing

SOURCE: Honeywell Inc. 1998.

EXHIBIT 7.25 | **HONEYWELL EUROPE'S STRATEGY**

Our European Customers' Business Climate	**Honeywell**
Intensifying competition	Our goal is to achieve top tier performance
Global business consolidation	Our business is to increase our customers' productivity, lower their operating costs, enhance their profitability while improving their competitiveness
Pressure on prices	
Rising performance expectations	
Year 2000 system investment requirements exacerbated by euro adaptation costs	We provide Year 2000 services and compliant products
Labor mobility and cultural differences still a constraint	We are progressive "Early Adopters" of the Euro
	We enhance existing facilities and plan performance
EXTREME PRESSURE TO IMPROVE CUSTOMERS' COMPETITIVENESS	**WE IMPROVE OUR PERFORMANCE**

SOURCE: Honeywell Inc., 1998.

EXHIBIT 7.26   OLD ORGANIZATION STRUCTURE

Areas	SBU Operations	Support Functions
• Sales	• Marketing	• Infrastructure
• Service delivery	• R&D	• Shared services
• Customer support	• Manufacturing	• Logistics
• Strategic execution	• Distribution	• Supply management
• Tactical implementation	• Strategic planning	• Contract management
Affiliates	Center of Excellence	Area Centers

SOURCE: Honeywell Inc. 1998.

EXHIBIT 7.27   PAN-EUROPEAN SBU MANAGEMENT STRUCTURE

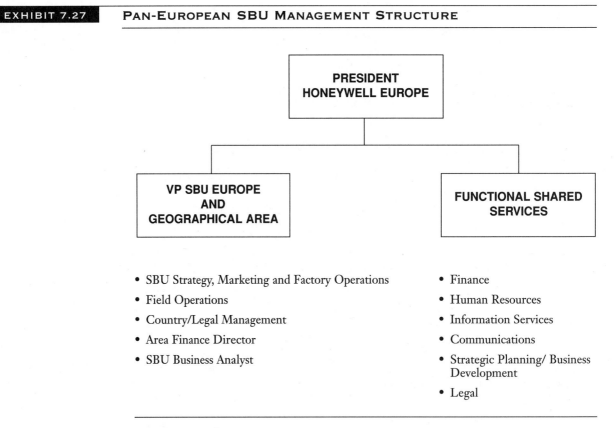

SOURCE: Honeywell Inc., 1998.

Recovery from Deficits and Debt

This last chapter is not really a case at all. It is an excerpt from the 1999 *Economic Report of the President*—the annual report, if you will, of the United States. The parts excerpted provide students with the opportunity to use raw data to evaluate (1) the costs and benefits of the Reagan Revolution in 1981, (2) the integration of the U.S. economy with the world economy, and (3) the issues facing President Clinton in 1999.

The case begins with description of the Clinton administration's strategy and the country's recent economic performance. But the numbers really dominate this case. Students should carefully analyze what has happened to the U.S. economy over the past 17 years. They need to look at the GDP and its components (inflation, unemployment, productivity and unit labor costs, the balance of payments and exchange rates) and at savings and the fiscal budget.

The second part of the discussion focuses on the linkage (in the United States) between fiscal deficits and trade deficits. That is, because of low savings, the United States is more closely linked to international trade and capital markets than most countries. These linkages, and what they imply for the United States, need to be carefully explored.

This case looks at the performance of the United States since President Clinton pushed through the Deficit Reduction Act in 1993. Again, students should consider carefully the causes of U.S. deficits and then solutions.

At last, President Clinton is proposing a strategy for using fiscal surpluses to address some of the United States' longer-term problems. Students should consider those proposals carefully (on both their economic and political merits), consider alternatives, and address additional problems not solved by the President's plan.

Finally, students should use this case to consider the future workings of a more integrated world economy. What parts of the world economy are likely to grow during the next decade? What will be the problems? How will these economies interact? What will it mean for foreign direct investment and the behavior of firms? And will globalization continue?

EXCERPTS FROM THE ECONOMIC REPORT OF THE PRESIDENT 1999

To the Congress of the United States:

I am pleased to report that the American economy today is healthy and strong. Our nation is enjoying the longest peacetime economic expansion in its history, with almost 18 million new jobs since 1993, wages rising at twice the rate of inflation, the highest home ownership ever, the smallest welfare rolls in 30 years, and unemployment and inflation at their lowest levels in three decades.

This expansion, unlike recent previous ones, is both wide and deep. All income groups, from the richest to the poorest, have seen their incomes rise since 1993. The typical family income is up more than $3,500, adjusted for inflation. African-American and Hispanic households, who were left behind during the last expansion, have also seen substantial increases in income.

Our nation's budget is balanced, for the first time in a generation, and we are entering the second year of an era of surpluses: our projections show that we will close out the 1999 fiscal year with a surplus of $79 billion, the largest in the history of the United States. We are on course for budget surpluses for many years to come.

These economic successes are not accidental. They are the result of an economic strategy that we have pursued since 1993. It is a strategy that rests on three pillars: fiscal discipline, investments in education and technology, and expanding exports to the growing world market. Continuing with this proven strategy is the best way to maintain our prosperity and meet the challenges of the 21st century.

The Administration's Economic Agenda

Our new economic strategy was rooted first and foremost in fiscal discipline. We made hard fiscal choices in 1993, sending signals to the market that we were serious about dealing with the budget deficits we had inherited. The market responded by lowering long-term interest rates. Lower interest rates in turn helped more people buy homes and borrow for college, helped more entrepreneurs to start businesses, and helped more existing businesses to invest in new technology and equipment. America's economic success has been fueled by the biggest boom in private-sector investment in decades—more than $1 trillion in capital was freed for private sector investment. In past expansions, government bought more and spent more to drive the economy. During this expansion, government spending as a share of the economy has fallen.

The second part of our strategy has been to invest in our people. A global economy driven by information and fast-paced technological change creates ever greater demand for skilled workers. That is why, even as we balanced the budget, we substantially increased our annual investment in education and training. We have opened the doors of college to all Americans, with tax credits and more affordable student loans, with more work-study grants and more Pell grants, with education IRAs and the new HOPE Scholarship tax credit that more than five million Americans will receive this year. Even as we closed the budget gap, we have expanded the earned income tax credit for almost 20 million low-income working families, giving them hope and helping lift them out of poverty. Even as we cut government spending, we have raised investments in a welfare-to-work jobs initiative and invested $24 billion in our children's health initiative.

Third, to build the American economy, we have focused on opening foreign markets and expanding exports to our trading partners around the world. Until recently, fully one-third of the strong economic growth America has enjoyed in the 1990s has come from exports. That trade has been aided by 270 trade agreements we have signed in the past six years.

Addressing Our Nation's Economic Challenges

We have created a strong, healthy, and truly global economy—an economy that is a leader for growth in the world. But common sense, experience, and the example of our competitors abroad show us that we cannot afford to be complacent. Now, at this moment of great plenty, is precisely the time to face the challenges of the next century.

We must maintain our fiscal discipline by saving Social Security for the 21st century—thereby laying the foundations for future economic growth.

By 2030, the number of elderly Americans will double. This is a seismic demographic shift with great consequences for our nation. We must keep Social Security a rock-solid guarantee. That is why I proposed in my State of the Union address that we invest the surplus to save Social Security. I proposed that we commit 62% of the budget surplus for the next 15 years to Social Security. I also proposed investing a small portion in the private sector. This will allow the trust fund to earn a higher return and keep Social Security sound until 2055.

But we must aim higher. We should put Social Security on a sound footing for the next 75 years. We should reduce poverty among elderly women, who are nearly twice as likely to be poor as other seniors. And we should eliminate the limits on what seniors on Social Security can earn. These changes will require difficult but fully achievable choices over and above the dedication of the surplus.

Once we have saved Social Security, we must fulfill our obligation to save and improve Medicare and invest in long-term health care. That is why I have called for broader, bipartisan reforms that keep Medicare secure until 2020 through additional savings and modernizing the program with market-oriented purchasing tools, while also providing a long-overdue prescription drug benefit.

By saving the money we will need to save Social Security and Medicare, over the next 15 years we will achieve the lowest ratio of publicly held debt to gross domestic product since 1917. This debt reduction will help keep future interest rates low or drive them even lower, fueling economic growth well into the 21st century.

To spur future growth, we must also encourage private retirement saving. In my State of the Union address I proposed that we use about 12% of the surplus to establish new Universal Savings Accounts—USA accounts. These will ensure that all Americans have the means to save. Americans could receive a flat tax credit to contribute to their USA accounts and additional tax credits to match a portion of their savings—with more help for lower income Americans. This is the right way to provide tax relief to the American people.

Education is also key to our nation's future prosperity. That is why I proposed in my State of the Union address a plan to create 21st-century schools through greater investment and more accountability. Under my plan, states and school districts that accept federal resources will be required to end social promotion, turn around or close failing schools, support high-quality teachers, and promote innovation, competition, and discipline. My plan also proposes increasing federal investments to help states and school districts take responsibility for failing schools, to recruit and train new teachers, to expand afterschool and summer school programs, and to build or fix 5,000 schools.

At this time of continued turmoil in the international economy, we must do more to help create stability and open markets around the world. We must press forward with open trade. It would be a terrible mistake, at this time of economic fragility in so many regions, for the United States to build new walls of protectionism that could set off a chain reaction around the world, imperiling the growth upon which we depend. At the same time, we must do more to make sure that working people are lifted up by trade. We must do more to ensure that spirited economic competition among nations never becomes a race to the bottom in the area of environmental protections or labor standards.

Strengthening the foundations of trade means strengthening the architecture of international finance. The United States must continue to lead in stabilizing the world financial system. When nations around the world descend into economic disruption, consigning populations to poverty, it hurts them and it hurts us. These nations are our trading partners; they buy our products and can ship low-cost products to American consumers.

The U.S. proposal for containing financial contagion has been taken up around the world: interest rates are being cut here and abroad, America is meeting its obligations to the International Monetary Fund, and a new facility has been created at the World Bank to strengthen the social safety net in Asia. And agreement has been reached to establish a new precautionary line of credit, so nations with strong economic policies can quickly get the help they need before financial problems mushroom from concerns to crises.

We must do more to renew our cities and distressed rural areas. My administration has pursued a new strategy, based on empowerment and investment, and we have seen its success. With the critical assistance of Empowerment Zones, unemployment rates in cities across the country have dropped dramatically. But we have more work to do to bring the spark of private enterprise to neighborhoods that have too long been without hope. That is why my budget includes an innovative "New Markets" initiative to spur $15 billion in new private-sector capital investment in businesses in underserved areas through a package of tax credits and guarantees.

Going Forward Together in the 21ˢᵗ Century

Now, on the verge of another American century, our economy is at the pinnacle of power and success, but challenges remain. Technology and trade and the spread of information have transformed our economy offering great opportunities but also posing great challenges. All Americans must be equipped with the skills to succeed and prosper in the new economy America must have the courage to move forward and renew its ideas and institutions to meet new challenges. There are no limits to the world we can create, together, in the century to come.

William J. Clinton

THE WHITE HOUSE
FEBRUARY 4, 1999

Reaching Surplus

Except during wars and economic downturns, the federal budget has stayed roughly balanced for most of the nation's history. Yet the large budget deficits that emerged in the early 1980s persisted throughout that decade of peace and economic expansion, and then worsened in the 1990–91 recession **[Exhibit 8.1]**. In 1992 outlays exceeded receipts by $290 billion, or 4.7% of GDP. When the President took office in January 1993, the deficit was projected to reach almost $400 billion in 1998 and over $600 billion in 2003, assuming no change in policy. By 1998, however, receipts exceeded outlays by $69 billion, or 0.8% of GDP. (All references to years in this section are fiscal years running from October through September, unless otherwise noted.)

In 1993 the President and the Congress enacted a deficit reduction package designed to cut more than $500 billion from the deficits expected to accumulate over the following five years. The program slowed the growth of entitlements and extend-

EXHIBIT 8.1   THE FEDERAL BUDGET BALANCE, 1946–98

AFTER A PERIOD OF PERSISTENT LARGE DEFICITS IN THE 1980S, THE FEDERAL
BUDGET SURPLUS IN 1998 WAS THE LARGEST AS A SHARE OF GDP SINCE 1957.

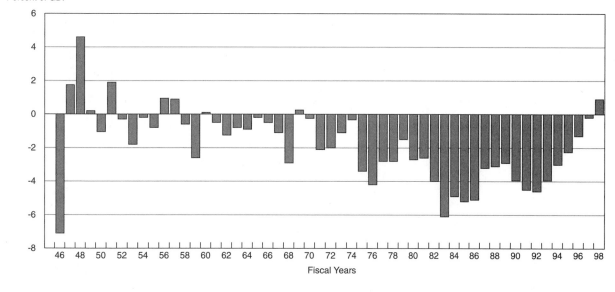

SOURCE: Office of Management and Budget.

ed the caps on discretionary spending put in place in 1990. It raised the tax rates of only the 1.2% of taxpayers with the highest incomes, while cutting taxes for 15 million working families. Four years later the President and the Congress finished the job of reaching budget surplus by passing the Balanced Budget Act of 1997, which incorporated additional deficit reduction measures.

Strong economic growth also played an important role in reducing the deficit. Faster-than-expected growth created more income and more tax revenue. In addition, it reduced unemployment insurance benefits and outlays for other means-tested entitlement programs, although the effect of better economic performance is considerably smaller on the spending side than on the revenue side.

The Demographic Challenge and Social Security

Social Security is an extremely successful social program. For 60 years it has provided Americans with income security in retirement and protection against loss of family income due to disability or death. Social Security retirement benefits are indexed for inflation and provide a lifetime annuity—a package that has been difficult if not impossible to obtain in the financial marketplace. In any case, fewer than half of all individuals aged 65 and older received any private pension benefits in 1994. Social Security benefits are the largest source of income for two-thirds of those in this age group and the only source for 18% of them. Social Security has achieved dramatic success in helping reduce the poverty rate among the elderly from 35% in 1959 to 10.5% in 1997.

The most commonly used yardstick to measure the financial soundness of the Social Security system is the 75-year actuarial balance—the difference between

EXHIBIT 8.2 — CONTRIBUTIONS TO ECONOMIC GROWTH IN
THREE LONG EXPANSIONS

MORE THAN A THIRD OF THE INCREASE IN REAL GDP IN
THE CURRENT EXPANSION CAME FROM FIXED INVESTMENT

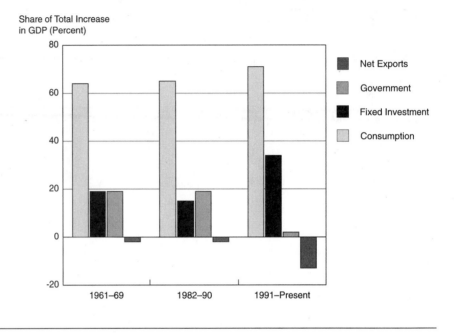

SOURCES: Department of Commerce (Bureau of Economic Analysis), National Bureau of Economic Research, and
Council of Economic Advisors.

expected income and costs over the next 75 years. The Social Security actuaries now
project that the current balance in the trust fund, together with projected revenues
over the next 75 years, will be insufficient to fund the benefits promised under current law. By 2013, payroll contributions, together with the part of income tax receipts
on Social Security benefits that is deposited in the trust fund, are expected to fall short
of benefits. By 2021, the shortfall is expected to exceed the trust fund's interest earnings, so that the fund will begin to decline. And by 2032, the trust fund is expected to
be depleted, although contributions would still be sufficient to pay about 75% of
current-law benefits thereafter. Of course, future taxes and benefits will depend on a
variety of economic and demographic factors that cannot be predicted perfectly, so the
actual problem may be smaller—or larger—than we now believe. Nevertheless, the
actuaries' intermediate projections imply that the imbalance in the old age, survivors,
and disability insurance program (OASDI, the main component of Social Security)
over the next 75 years amounts to around 2% of taxable payroll (which equals about
1% of GDP today).

The key factors contributing to the projected OASDI imbalance are improvements in life expectancy and a reduction in birth rates, which have put the United
States on a path of rapid decline in the number of employed workers for every retiree.

The Administration's Policy

In his 1998 State of the Union address, the President proposed to reserve the budget
surplus until agreement had been reached on a plan to secure the financial viability of

Social Security. To accomplish this task, the President suggested a process of public education and discussion, followed by the forging of a bipartisan agreement. The President later set forth five principles to guide the reform process:

- *Strengthen and protect Social Security for the 21ˢᵗ century.* This is an overriding goal, and it rules out proposals that fail to provide a comprehensive solution to the solvency problem. For example, a pan to divert existing payroll taxes into a new system of individual accounts, without other, offsetting changes, would fail the test to the extent that it would reduce Social Security's revenues and make the existing imbalance even larger.

- *Maintain universality and fairness.* The current program provides benefits on a progressive basis, and ensuring progressively is an important standard by which reform proposals should be judged.

- *Provide a benefit that people can count on.* Any proposed reform of Social Security must continue to offer people a secure base for retirement planning.

- *Preserve financial security for low-income and disabled beneficiaries.* The commitment to the disability and survivors' insurance aspects of the OASDI program must be maintained.

- *Maintain fiscal discipline.* Fiscal discipline is essential to ensure that the emerging budget surpluses are not drained before Social Security reform has been addressed, and that fiscal policy plays a helpful role in preparing for the retirement of the baby-boomers.

In his 1999 State of the Union address, the President put forward a comprehensive framework for Social Security reform that satisfies these principles. First, about three-fifths of the projected budget surpluses over the next 15 years would be transferred to the Social Security trust fund. Second, about one-fifth of the transferred surpluses would be invested in equities to achieve higher returns, just as private and state and local government pension funds do. The administration intends to work with the Congress to ensure that these investments are made by the most efficient private-sector investment managers, independently and without political interference. These two steps alone would extend the solvency of the Social Security system until 2055. Third, the President called for a bipartisan effort to make further reforms to Social Security that would extend its solvency to at least 2075.

The President repeated his commitment to "save Social Security first." He also stated that—if Social Security reform is secured—the remaining projected surpluses over the next 15 years should be dedicated to three purposes. First, about 15% of the projected surpluses would be transferred to the Medicare trust fund. The administration, the Congress, and the Medicare commission should work to use these funds as part of broader reforms. Even without such reforms, however, the transfers would extend the projected solvency of the Medicare trust fund to 2020. Second, about 12% of the projected surpluses would be used to create Universal Savings Accounts, which would help people save more for their retirement needs. The government would provide a flat tax credit for Americans to put into their accounts and additional tax credits to match a portion of each dollar that a person voluntarily puts into his or her account. These accounts would not be part of the Social Security system but would provide additional retirement resources. The remainder of the projected surpluses over the next 15 years would be reserved to improve military readiness and to meet pressing domestic priorities in such areas as education and research.

Within this framework, the national debt of the United States would decline dramatically. Debt held by the public would fall from about 45% of GDP today to less than 10% in 2014. That would be the smallest burden of government debt on the economy since the United States entered World War I in 1917.

EXHIBIT 8.3   **UNEMPLOYMENT RATE**

**IN 1998 THE AVERAGE UNEMPLOYMENT RATE FELL TO ITS LOWEST LEVEL
SINCE 1969**

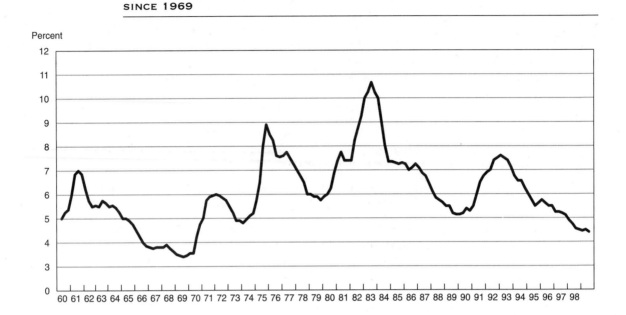

SOURCE: Department of Labor (Bureau of Labor Statistics).

EXHIBIT 8.4   **INFLATION RATE**

**INFLATION REMAINED LOW IN 1998, WITH THE CONSUMER PRICE INDEX
RECORDING ITS SECOND SMALLEST RISE SINCE 1964**

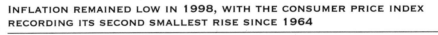

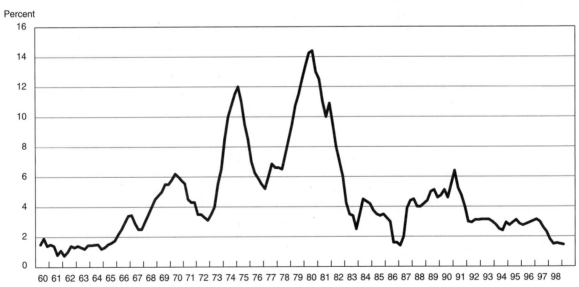

Note: Data are four-quarter percent changes in the CPI.

SOURCE: Department of Labor (Bureau of Labor Statistics).

| EXHIBIT 8.5 | NET WORTH AND THE PERSONAL CONSUMPTION RATE |

SURGING HOUSEHOLD WEALTH IN 1998 HELPED INCREASE CONSUMER
EXPENDITURES AND REDUCE THE PERSONAL SAVING RATE

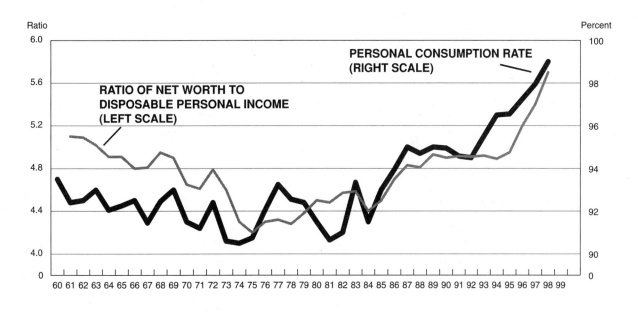

Note: Personal consumption rate is the ratio of personal outlays to disposable personal income. It equals one minus the personal saving rate. Household net worth for each year is constructed as the average of net worth at the beginning and the end of the year. Data for 1998 are approximate.

SOURCES: Department of Commerce (Bureau of Economic Analysis), Board of Governors of the Federal Reserve System, and Council of Economic Advisors.

Household Spending

Real personal consumption expenditures (PCE) surged during the first half of 1998, increasing at roughly a 6% annual rate. PCE growth downshifted during the third quarter to about a 4% pace (which still exceeded its growth rate for the four quarters of 1997) and remained strong in the fourth quarter, according to the partial data available.

Demand for homes was also very strong. Although real residential investment represents less than 5% of GDP, its growth during the first three-quarters of 1998 accounted for more than 10% of GDP growth. Single-family housing starts were the highest since 1978, and new and existing single-family home sales reached record levels. The percentage of Americans who own their own home reached an all time high of 66.8% in the third quarter (the latest period for which data are available). Growth in homeownership was especially fast for groups that have been underrepresented in the past, such as blacks and Hispanics.

This robust growth in household spending during 1998 occurred against a backdrop of extremely favorable fundamentals. First, real disposable income maintained its solid upward trend, rising about 3¼% at an annual rate over the first three quarters (based on the PCE chain-weighted price index). Second, household wealth soared to an extraordinary level—almost six times income—as a result of the dramatic runup in stock prices **[Exhibit 8.5]**. This expansion in household resources permitted spending to grow significantly faster than disposable income. Indeed, the personal saving rate—measured by the difference between disposable income and consumer outlays, as a percentage of disposable income—fell sharply again during 1998. After averaging roughly 4½% between 1992 and 1994, this rate dropped to about 3% in 1996, about

2% in 1997, and about ½% in the first three quarters of last year. (Last summer's revision of the measured saving rate is discussed later in this chapter.)

Household spending was also spurred by low interest rates and a ready availability of credit. In particular, housing affordability soared, as interest rates on 30-year fixed rate mortgages averaged more than half a percentage point below their 1997 values. Indeed, mortgage credit expanded more rapidly during the first three quarters of 1998 (the latest available data) than in any year since 1990. Over the same period, consumer credit grew at a somewhat faster rate than in 1997 but well below the torrid pace of 1994 and 1995. Total household debt appears to have increased faster than disposable income in 1998 for the sixth year in a row. Nevertheless, delinquency rates on consumer loans remained close to their 1997 values, and delinquency rates on mortgages stayed low. Personal bankruptcy filings reached a new record high in the third quarter of 1998, but the rate of increase over the preceding year was well below the pace recorded between 1995 and mid-1997.

Last year's *Economic Report of the President* included an extended discussion of the long-term upward trend in the bankruptcy rate. During 1998 the Congress considered various proposals to reform the bankruptcy law, and both the House and the Senate passed reform bills; however, the two houses were unable to agree on a compromise bill that incorporated the administration's key principles for bankruptcy reform. The administration supports reform of the bankruptcy law that would require both debtors and creditors to act more responsibly: Troubled debtors who can repay a portion of their debts should do so, but creditors should treat debtors fairly, in keeping with the creditors' superior expertise and bargaining power.

With respect to leverage, the degree of LTCM's leverage caused the risks in its portfolio to be transmitted more rapidly to other market participants. Creditors to hedge funds now appear to be reducing the amount of leverage they are willing to provide, which is another positive development. In addition, bank regulators can employ their existing regulatory tools to induce banks to make more prudent decisions. The working group is evaluating whether the government should do more to discourage excessive leverage, and if so, what specific steps might be appropriate.

Financial Market Influences on Spending

The financial market developments described in this section have had a significant impact on household and business spending. This impact has been felt through several channels, including wealth effects, effects on interest rates, and effects on the availability of credit to businesses.

Wealth and Consumption

An increase in a person's net worth raises the amount that he or she can consume, either today or in the future. Statistical evidence suggests that consumer spending has tended to rise or fall by roughly 2 to 4 cents per year for every dollar that stock market wealth rises or falls. This wealth effect usually occurs over several years, but much of the adjustment is seen within one year. The effect might be larger today than in the past because more Americans own stocks: The Survey of Consumer Finances shows that 41% of U.S. families owned stocks directly or indirectly in 1995, compared with 32% in 1989. However, there is little direct evidence on this point.

The dramatic increase in stock prices over the past few years has provided a significant impetus to consumer spending. Applying the historical relationship cited above to the change in total household wealth (which includes other assets and liabilities as well as stocks), one could conclude that rising wealth boosted consumption growth by nearly a percentage point during 1998, after a similar increase during 1997.

Robust spending has, in turn, led to a dramatic decline in households' saving out of income from current production, with the personal saving rate falling to a historical low of 0.2% in the third quarter of last year. (Net private saving, which combines personal saving and undistributed corporate profits, has also declined as a share of national income during the past few years but less sharply than has personal saving.)

The sharp decline in household saving in recent years became more apparent after the annual revision of the national income and product accounts in July 1998. Prior to the revision, capital gains distributions by mutual funds had been included in personal income (just as interest payments are), which bolstered measured personal saving.

Meeting the International Challenge

This administration has been committed from the start to outward looking trade and investment policies. And in his 1999 State of the Union address the President called for a new consensus in the Congress to grant him traditional trade-negotiating authority that permits trade agreements negotiated with other nations to be submitted to an up-or-down congressional vote without amendment. At the same time, he proposed the launch of an ambitious new round of global trade negotiations within the World Trade Organization. The general principle behind the administration's international economic policy is that open domestic markets and an open global trading system are a better way to raise wages and living standards over the longer term than are trade protection and isolationism. Recent strains on the fabric of the international economy have increased the allure of protectionism in some quarters. But the main lesson should be that it is essential to promote growth in the world economy, to help crisis-stricken economies recover, and to reform the international financial system in ways that make future crises less likely without abandoning the benefits that come with increased international trade and investment flows.

During the year and a half that has elapsed since the collapse of the Thai currency in July 1997, Asia's currency crisis has developed into a more widespread crisis affecting many countries around the globe. As the crisis has spread, it has affected global commodity markets, impaired economic development, and imposed extraordinary hardship in the crisis-afflicted countries, all the while posing risks to growth worldwide, including in the United States and other industrial countries. According to projections by the International Monetary Fund (IMF), global growth is now expected to reach a modest 2.2% in 1999, which represents a decline both from the 4.2% rate attained in 1997 and from its long-run historical average of 4%.

Beyond working to ensure growth in the industrial world, the administration has focused since the onset of the crisis on the need to contain the international contagion of financial disruption and to restore the confidence of market participants. The administration has supported the IMF in its goal of providing financial assistance to countries in crisis that are willing to implement the reforms needed to restore economic confidence and strengthen the underpinnings of their economies, including their corporate and financial sectors. The emphasis of IMF programs on financial-sector reform reflects the growing consensus, discussed in Chapter 6, that structural weaknesses, particularly in the process of financial intermediation, were a key element in initiating the crisis. It appears that many countries in East Asia have now made considerable progress toward establishing the foundation for recovery. In addition, an IMF stabilization package for Brazil, supplemented by bilateral financing, was arranged in November.

As the crisis spread, the administration recognized that its contagion threatened even countries that had taken great strides in implementing sound macroeconomic and structural policies and had worked to strengthen the fundamentals of their economies. The President therefore proposed, and the G-7 leaders agreed to establish, an enhanced IMF facility to provide contingent, short-term lines of credit that could be drawn upon by countries pursuing strong, IMF-approved policies, accompanied, as appropriate, by additional bilateral finance. As the scope of the crisis widened, the resources of the IMF became increasingly strained. A key step in expanding them was for the United States to meet its own financial obligations to the organization. The administration proposed, and In October the Congress approved, $18 billion in funding, opening the way for about $90 billion of usable resources to be provided by all IMF members to the liquidity-strapped institution.

Trends in Financial Integration

The phenomenal growth of international capital flows is one of the most important developments in the world economy since the breakdown of the Bretton Woods system of fixed exchange rates in the early 1970s. Their growth can be traced to the oil shock of 1973–74, which spurred financial intermediation on a global scale. Mounting surpluses in the oil-exporting countries could not be absorbed productively within those economies, and at the same time the corresponding deficits among oil importers had to be financed. The recycling of "petrodollars" from the surplus to the deficit countries, via the growing Euromarkets (offshore markets for deposits and loans denominated in key currencies, particularly the dollar), produced the first post–Bretton Woods surge of international capital flows. As a result, many developing countries gained access to international capital markets, where they were able to finance their growing external imbalances. Most of this intermediation occurred in the form of bank lending, as large banks in the industrial countries built up large exposures to developing countries' debt.

The buildup of these external liabilities eventually became excessive and, together with loose monetary and fiscal policies in the borrowing countries, sharp declines in their terms of trade, and high international interest rates, triggered the debt crisis of the 1980s. Starting in Mexico in 1982, that crisis rapidly engulfed a large number of developing countries in Latin America and elsewhere. The rest of the 1980s saw a period of retrenchment, with a significant slowdown in capital flows to emerging markets (especially in Latin America) as burdensome foreign debts were rescheduled, restructured, and finally reduced with the inception of the Brady Plan in 1989.

The resolution of the 1980s debt crisis led to new large-scale private capital inflows to emerging markets in the 1990s. Several factors encouraged this renewed surge of international financing. Many Latin American countries were adopting policies emphasizing economic liberalization, privatization, market opening, and macroeconomic stability. Countries in Central and Eastern Europe had embarked on their historic transition toward market economies. And rapid growth in a group of economies in East Asia had caught the attention of investors worldwide. Net long-term private flows to developing countries increased from $42 billion in 1990 to $256 billion in 1997.

The largest share of these flows took the form of foreign direct investment—investment by multinational corporations in overseas operations under their own control. These flows totaled $120 billion in 1997 **[Exhibit 8.6]**. However, bond and portfolio equity flows accounted for 34% of the total in that year, amounting to $54 billion and $33 billion, respectively. In contrast, commercial bank loans represented only 16% of net flows to developing countries, or $41 billion, in 1997, compared with about two-thirds in the 1970s. To the extent it went to bond rather than equity flows, this massive relative switch out of bank lending, which is characterized by a small number of substantial lenders, would eventually pose a problem not encountered in the 1980s, namely, how to coordinate the actions of a large number of creditors (an issue discussed further in Chapter 7).

The table reports gross inflows and outflows of both foreign direct investment and portfolio investment (two of the main components of capital flows) for both

EXHIBIT 8.6	NET CAPITAL FLOWS TO DEVELOPING COUNTRIES

FOREIGN DIRECT INVESTMENT IS THE LARGEST SOURCE OF NET CAPITAL FLOWS TO DEVELOPING COUNTRIES

SOURCE: World Bank.

TABLE 8.1	CAPITAL FLOWS TO INDUSTRIAL AND DEVELOPING COUNTRIES (BILLIONS OF DOLLARS)

	Industrial Countries		Developing Countries	
Flows	Direct Investment	Portfolio Investment	Direct Investment	Portfolio Investment
Gross Outflows				
1973–78	28.6	11.8	0.4	5.5
1979–82	46.9	35.0	1.1	17.8
1983–88	88.2	126.5	2.3	–5.1
1989–92	201.3	274.6	10.4	10.3
1993–96	259.6	436.4	19.2	19.2
Gross Inflows				
1973–78	17.9	24.4	5.0	1.3
1979–82	36.6	51.0	14.6	3.1
1983–88	69.3	139.1	15.5	4.0
1989–92	141.9	343.0	37.8	27.5
1993–96	173.0	549.9	106.4	95.9
Net Inflows				
1973–78	–10.7	12.6	4.6	–4.2
1979–82	–10.3	16.0	13.5	–14.7
1983–88	–18.9	12.6	13.2	9.1
1989–92	–59.4	68.4	27.4	17.2
1993–96	–86.6	113.5	87.2	76.7

SOURCE: International Monetary Fund.

Box 8.1   The Explosive Growth of Foreign Exchange Trading

The single statistic that perhaps best illustrates the dramatic expansion of international financial markets is the volume of trading in the world's foreign exchange markets. The Bank for International Settlements (BIS, an international institution in Basle, Switzerland, that acts as a kind of central bankers' bank) released in October 1998 a preliminary compilation of a triennial survey of 43 foreign exchange markets. It shows that, in current-dollar terms, the volume of foreign exchange trading in these markets grew 26 percent between April 1995 and April 1998, following a 45 percent increase between 1992 and 1995. That volume now stands at $1.5 trillion per day (after making corrections to avoid double counting). By way of comparison, the global volume of exports of goods and services for *all* of 1997 was $6.6 trillion, or about $25 billion per trading day. In other words, foreign exchange trading was about 60 times as great as trade in goods and services.

In the BIS preliminary survey, spot market purchases amounted to 40 percent of foreign exchange transactions in 1998, down from 44 percent in 1995. Forward instruments continued to grow in importance relative to spot sales. Over-the-counter derivatives, although still a smaller fraction of total transactions, have been the fastest-growing segment of the market.

A striking feature of the foreign exchange market is the small percentage of trades made on behalf of non-financial customers. In the most recent survey, transactions involving such customers represent only 20 percent of total turnover.

Trading also tends to be focused geographically in a few major centers. Arguably there is a natural equilibrium consisting of one major center in each of the world's three 8-hour time zones. New York is the major center in the Western Hemisphere, with U.S. volume now equal to $351 billion per day (18 percent of world turnover). Tokyo established itself in the 1980s as the major center in the third of the world that includes Asia. Its turnover, however, has fallen off recently, as markets in Singapore have gained. Average daily transactions totaled $149 billion (8 percent of the world total) in Japan and $139 billion in Singapore. London continues to handle the greatest volume of foreign exchange transactions, with its share of world turnover increasing to 32 percent, at an average daily volume of $637 billion.

To summarize, the volume of world trade in foreign exchange has continued to grow. Derivatives far exceed spot market transactions. Most trades take place between professional traders at banks and other financial institutions; only a fraction of foreign exchange sales and purchases directly involve those who import and export goods and services.

---

developing and industrial countries over several decades. Two points are noteworthy. First, although net flows have been large and growing, the magnitude of gross flows may be a better indicator of financial integration. As investors in one country diversify their portfolios by purchasing foreign assets, and as foreign investors increase their purchases of assets in the first country, gross flows may increase substantially without net flows changing nearly as much. And in fact, gross cross-border inflows and outflows have grown even faster than net flows. Second, the rise in cross-border capital flows has occurred in developing and industrial countries alike. Although the Mexican peso crisis of December 1994 led to a modest slowdown in capital flows to emerging markets in 1995, they surged again thereafter until the Asian crisis erupted in the summer of 1997.

Further evidence of the trend toward global financial integration is the sharp expansion of foreign exchange trading. This growth has been evident both in spot markets (where currency transactions are settled within two business days, or "on the spot") and in the use of derivative instruments (where trading is for future delivery of currencies, or in options to buy or sell currencies). Most purchases and sales of foreign exchange are related to financial transactions rather than merchandise trade, and indeed foreign exchange trading has grown much faster than international trade in goods over the past two decades (see box).

The Causes of Increased Capital Flows

Several factors have undoubtedly contributed to this phenomenal growth of international capital flows. First, countries have opened their financial markets, both domestically and internationally, as governments in industrial and developing economies alike have phased out restrictions on financial activity and progressively reduced or eliminated controls on cross-border capital transactions. In many instances, this financial liberalization has been accompanied by macroeconomic stabilization, privatization, trade liberalization, and deregulation. These structural reforms in capital-scarce developing countries have created significant investment opportunities, attracting a surge of foreign capital with the expectation of high rates of return. Growth in international trade has also increased the volume of trade-related financing and bolstered trade in derivative instruments, as buyers and sellers seek to hedge their exposures to currency and commercial risk.

At the same time, financial innovations in the United States and other industrial economies have rendered cross-border investments more accessible to institutional and individual investors. Revolutionary advances in information and communications technology, together with significantly lower transportation and transactions costs, have underpinned this rapid development. Mutual funds, hedge funds, and the growth of new financial instruments, including derivatives, have enabled investors to choose which risks they will and will not accept in their quest for higher returns. A radical increase in the available range of instruments and assets has afforded investors unprecedented opportunities to increase returns and decrease risks through global diversification. Although most wealth is still primarily invested in domestic assets, international portfolio diversification is now an option for both institutions and households.

The Financial Crisis of the 1990s

Although financial crises have a long history and have recurred throughout the century, the same two decades that have seen spreading financial liberalization and ever-growing global capital flows have also witnessed such crises, which imposed serious real costs on the economies affected. Since the resurgence of these flows after the 1980s debt crisis, three more financial crises of at least regional importance have struck. The first occurred in 1992–93, when several currencies in the Exchange Rate Mechanism (ERM) of the European Monetary System experienced speculative attacks. Italy and the United Kingdom were forced to abandon the ERM in the fall of 1992 and allow their currencies to depreciate; Sweden, whose currency was effectively pegged to the ERM currencies, was obliged to follow suit shortly thereafter. A series of devaluations of several other ERM currencies ensued, and the ERM exchange rate bands for France and the remaining members had to be widened in the summer of 1993, to cope with the speculative pressure on their currencies.

The collapse of the Mexican peso in December 1994 touched off the second crisis. Other Latin American currencies quickly came under attack through what became known as the tequila effect. The third crisis of the 1990s, the Asian currency and financial crisis that has now spread to Russia, Latin America, and beyond, was triggered by the devaluation of the Thai baht in July 1997. (The history and causes of that crisis are described in detail below.) Although each of these crises had distinct characteristics and causes, several common elements, which factor significantly into current debates surrounding the reform of the international financial architecture, can be identified.

Effects of the Emerging Markets Crisis on the United States

Macroeconomic Effects

The United States enjoyed strong economic growth before the onset of the Asian crisis and has continued to do so since. But the crisis has had an impact, both real and financial. One consequence has been a marked decline in net exports and a widening of the trade deficit. The growing trade deficit **[Exhibit 8.7]** is largely attributable to

EXHIBIT 8.7   REAL VALUE OF THE DOLLAR AND THE TRADE DEFICIT

THE TRADE DEFICIT IS A MACROECONOMIC PHENOMENON: INCREASES TYPICALLY
FOLLOW AN APPRECIATION OF THE DOLLAR

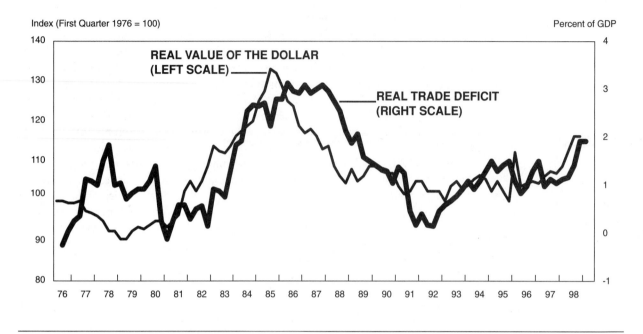

Index (First Quarter 1976 = 100)   Percent of GDP

REAL VALUE OF THE DOLLAR
(LEFT SCALE)

REAL TRADE DEFICIT
(RIGHT SCALE)

SOURCES: Department of Commerce (Bureau of Economic Analysis) and Federal Reserve Bank of Dallas.

three factors: faster income growth in the United States than in most other industrial countries, which raises imports; outright contraction in Japan and much of the rest of East Asia, which cuts U.S. exports; and an appreciation of the dollar in both nominal and real terms relative to both European and Asian currencies, and particularly the yen (from mid-1995 until September 1998). Since the summer of 1998, the dollar has depreciated against the yen, but the fall of the dollar against the other G-10 currencies is still modest on a trade-weighted basis **[Exhibit 8.8]**.

Two sectors adversely affected by the crisis were agriculture and manufacturing. Shrinking exports and low prices (attributable partly to the financial crisis, and partly to large global supplies of agricultural commodities following bumper harvests), on top of bad weather in some regions, led to a fall in farm incomes. In manufacturing, both export industries and industries that compete with imports sustained damage. The commercial aircraft industry, for example, suffered from the fall of exports to Asia. The steel industry and the textiles and apparel industry have come under import pressure as the dollar's appreciation reduced the price of imports from the crisis countries. As discussed in Chapter 2, U.S. financial markets also felt the impact, and financial institutions have suffered losses on their emerging market loans and investments.

The appreciation of the dollar since 1995 (illustrated in **Exhibit 8.8**) also had a number of beneficial effects at home. Import prices have fallen, especially for oil and other commodities, contributing to the drop in inflation and improving the U.S. terms of trade **[Exhibit 8.9]**. The terms of trade is a measure of the prices at which we sell our goods abroad, relative to the prices we pay for imports. An increase in the terms of trade translates into increased purchasing power of U.S. goods in world markets and higher real U.S. income. A strong dollar and subdued inflation have also supported lower interest rates, both short and long term, benefiting households, firms, and other borrowers.

| EXHIBIT 8.8 | DOLLAR EXCHANGE RATES |

THE DOLLAR HAS FLUCTUATED SHARPLY AGAINST THE CURRENCIES OF JAPAN
AND OTHER MAJOR TRADING PARTNERS BUT LESS SHARPLY AGAINST BROADER
INDEXES OF FOREIGN CURRENCIES

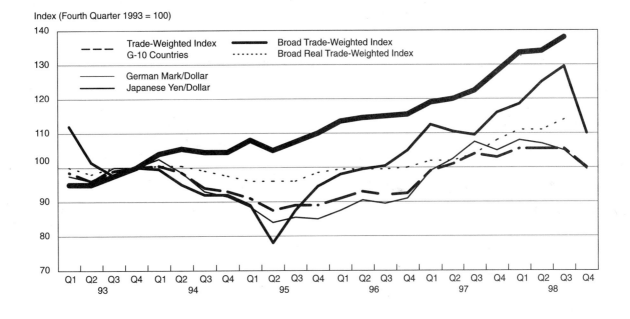

Index (Fourth Quarter 1993 = 100)

Note: The broad trade-weighted index is relative to 129 trading partners; the real measure is relative to 111 and is adjusted for domestic inflation. A rise in an index indicates an appreciation of the dollar.

SOURCES: Board of Governors of the Federal Reserve System and Federal Reserve Bank of Dallas.

The Current Account and the Saving–Investment Balance Unraveling misconceptions about the trade deficit requires an understanding of the trade balance and a closely related concept, the current account balance. A country's trade balance is equal to the difference between the value of its exports and the value of its imports—in other words, the value of goods and services sold by its residents to foreigners minus the value of the goods and services that its residents buy from foreigners. The current account balance simply adds other sources of foreign income to the trade balance to arrive at a complete accounting of the economy's current transactions (as distinct from its capital transactions, such as borrowing in the form of foreign loans). The most important of these other sources are interest and investment earnings received on foreign assets (and paid on foreign liabilities) and aid grants and transfers.

A country's current account balance also equals the difference between its gross national income (the sum of gross domestic production and net income received from abroad) and its spending (the sum of private and public consumption and investment spending). Because national saving is the difference between gross national income and total consumption, the current account is also equal to the difference between national saving and domestic investment. If a country's national income exceeds its spending, or, equivalently, if national saving exceeds domestic investment, the current account will be in surplus. If instead a country spends (that is, consumes and invests) more than its national income, investment will exceed saving, and the current account will be in deficit.

EXHIBIT 8.9   CURRENT ACCOUNT BALANCE

THE CURRENT ACCOUNT BALANCE HAS BEEN POSITIVE AND/OR INCREASING
DURING RECESSIONS AND HAS DECREASED DURING PERIODS OF ECONOMIC
EXPANSION

SOURCE: Department of Commerce (Bureau of Economic Analysis).

For the current account to be in deficit—that is, for investment to exceed saving—a country must be able to finance that deficit through capital inflows (borrowing) from the rest of the world. A country's current account deficit for a given period therefore equals the increase in its net foreign liabilities in that period (or the decline in its net foreign assets, if the country is a net creditor). Conversely, current account surpluses, which reflect an excess of saving over investment, increase a country's net foreign assets (or reduce its net foreign liabilities).

Business Cycles, Long-run Growth, and the Current Account The argument that current account deficits inevitably cause a net loss in jobs and output is at odds with the evidence. Rapid growth of production and employment is, in fact, commonly associated with large or growing trade and current account deficits, whereas slow output and employment growth is associated with large or growing surpluses. **Exhibit 8.9** shows, for example, that the U.S. current account improved during the recessions of 1973–75, 1980, and 1990–91 but declined during the cyclical upswings of 1970–72, 1983–90, and 1993 to the present. This reflects both a decline in demand for imports during recessions and the usual cyclical movements of saving and investment. During a recession, both saving and investment tend to fall. Saving falls as households try to maintain their consumption patterns in the face of a temporary fall in income; investment declines because capacity utilization declines and profits fall. However, because investment is highly sensitive to the need for extra capacity, it tends to drop more sharply than saving during recessions. The current account balance thus tends to rise. Consistent with this but viewed from a different angle, the trade balance typically improves during a recession, because imports tend to fall with overall consumption and investment demand. The converse occurs during periods of boom, when sharp increases in investment demand typically outweigh increases in saving,

EXHIBIT 8.10	ECONOMIC GROWTH AND TRADE BALANCES OF G-7 COUNTRIES, 1992–97

ACROSS THE MAJOR INDUSTRIAL COUNTRIES, POSITIVE TRADE BALANCES HAVE BEEN ASSOCIATED WITH WEAK ECONOMIC PERFORMANCE

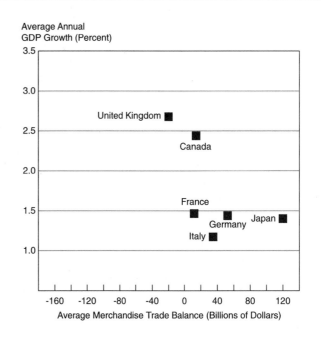

SOURCE: Organization for Economic Cooperation and Development.

producing a decline of the current account. Of course, factors other than income influence saving and investment, so that the tendency of a country's current account deficit to decline in recessions is not ironclad.

The relationship just described between the current account and economic performance typically holds not only on a short-term or cyclical basis, but also on a long-term or structural basis. Often, countries enjoying rapid economic growth possess structural current account deficits, whereas those with weaker economic growth have structural current account surpluses. This relationship likely derives from the fact that rapid growth and strong investment often go hand in hand. Whether the driving force is the discovery of new natural resources, technological progress, or the implementation of economic reform, periods of rapid economic growth are likely to be periods in which new investment is unusually profitable.

Investment must, however, be financed with saving, and if a country's national saving is not sufficient to finance all new profitable investment projects, the country will rely on foreign saving to finance the difference. It thus experiences a net capital inflow and a corresponding current account deficit. The current account deficit is then merely the result of thousands of individual firms issuing debt or equity or borrowing from banks to finance investment. As long as these individual decisions are sensible, the associated current account deficit should promote, not detract from, economic welfare. If the new investments are profitable, they will generate the extra earnings needed to repay the claims contracted to undertake them. Thus, when current account deficits reflect strong, profitable investment programs, they work to raise the rate of output and employment growth, not to destroy jobs and production.

| EXHIBIT 8.11 | EMPLOYMENT GROWTH AND TRADE BALANCES OF G-7 COUNTRIES, 1992–97 |

ACROSS THE MAJOR INDUSTRIAL COUNTRIES, POSITIVE TRADE BALANCES HAVE ALSO BEEN ASSOCIATED WITH WEAK EMPLOYMENT PERFORMANCE, AND VICE VERSA

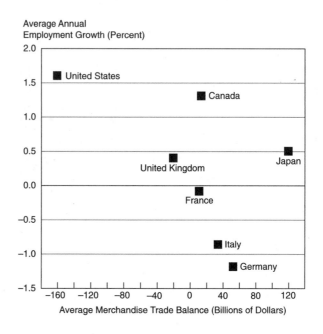

SOURCE: Organization for Economic Cooperation and Development.

Historically, countries at relatively early stages of rapid economic development, such as Argentina, Australia, and Canada in the early part of this century, have enjoyed an excess of investment over saving, running large structural current account deficits for long periods. The same general pattern has held in more recent times: faster growing developing countries have generally run larger current account deficits than the slower-growing mature economies.

The link between trade and current account deficits and growth is also confirmed by comparing the U.S. trade balance with those of its G-7 partners since the recovery from the 1990–91 recession. **Exhibits 8.10 and 8.11** show a clearly negative correlation between output growth and the trade balance, and between employment growth and the trade balance, respectively. The United States enjoyed the fastest output and employment growth—and the largest trade deficit—among the countries shown. Conversely, Japan had the largest trade surplus, but the second-slowest rate of growth. Trade surpluses are also the norm in Europe, where growth of output and employment has been disappointing. Similarly, unemployment in the United States has been low and falling since 1993, a period during which unemployment has remained high in Europe and has been growing rapidly in Japan.

Budget Deficits and the Current Account   Although current account deficits are not usually a cause for concern when they reflect strong investment opportunities, they may be worrisome if they instead reflect a decline in national saving. Because national saving includes the government's own saving or dissaving, one cause of a growing current account deficit can be rising government budget deficits. Such

| EXHIBIT 8.12 | SAVING, INVESTMENT, AND THE CURRENT ACCOUNT BALANCE |

THE CURRENT ACCOUNT DEFICIT GREW IN THE MID-1980S AS SAVING FELL FASTER THAN INVESTMENT. IN THE 1990S, HOWEVER, BOTH INVESTMENT AND SAVINGS ARE INCREASING

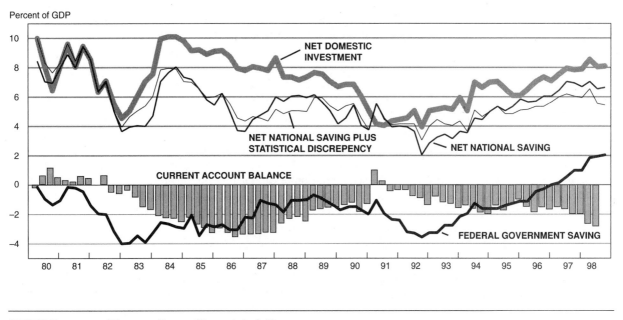

SOURCE: Department of Commerce (Bureau of Economic Analysis)

deficits may be harmful, resulting in an unsustainable buildup of foreign debt, if the government spending they permit is devoted to current consumption rather than productivity-enhancing public investment.

For example, in the late 1970s many developing countries ran large budget deficits, borrowing heavily in world capital markets to finance them and accumulating large foreign debts in the process. Much of this borrowing went to support excessive government spending in the face of insufficient tax revenue. By 1982 many of these governments were having difficulty servicing their foreign debts. A severe debt crisis erupted in that year, forcing many countries to negotiate a rescheduling of their foreign liabilities to avoid default.

The large U.S. current account deficits of the 1980s, also driven by large fiscal deficits, were a matter of concern for the same reason. These "twin deficits," as they were labeled, rates, a crowding out of productive investment (as evidenced by a fall in the national investment rate after its recovery from the 1982 recession), and a reduction in long-run growth opportunities. **Exhibit 8.12** presents the U.S. current account deficit, the national and public (federal government) saving rates, and the domestic investment rate. Conceptually, the current account is equal to net foreign investment, which is the difference between national saving and domestic investment; in practice, however, this equality may be obscured by measurement errors, which have been large in recent years both in the international transactions accounts and in the national income and product accounts. Thus, although over time there is a strong correlation between the current account balance and the saving–investment balance, in any given period the two measures may move in different directions. Exhibit 8.12 clearly shows the twin deficits of the 1980s: As fiscal deficits increased in an environment of tight monetary policy in the early 1980s, the dollar appreciated in real terms, and the current account moved into substantial deficit. The crowding out of productive investment, due to the high real interest rates associated with the fiscal deficit, is suggested by the fall in the investment rate between 1984 and 1990. The current account improved during the 1990–91 recession as the investment rate slumped sharply.

During the 1990s, the federal budget deficit first declined, then disappeared, and finally turned to a surplus in 1998. National saving increased as a consequence, despite a decline in the personal saving rate. Even so, the current account deficit has again increased. However, this increased deficit can be viewed as virtuous, because it has been driven by an even stronger increase in the pace of domestic investment. The U.S. gross investment rate rose from a low of 12.2% of GDP in the middle of 1991 to 16.0% in the third quarter of 1998.

The investment boom that the United States has enjoyed since 1993 has contributed to expanding employment and output and will provide payoffs for many years to come. It could not, however, have been financed by national saving alone: A current account deficit provided the additional capital inflow needed to finance the boom. In the absence of foreign lending, U.S. interest rates would have been higher, and investment would inevitably have been constrained by the supply of domestic saving. Therefore, the accumulation of capital and the growth of output and employment would all have been smaller had the United States not been able to run a current account deficit in the 1990s. Rather than choking off growth and employment, the large current account deficit, perhaps paradoxically, allowed faster long-run growth in the U.S. economy.

The Asian Crisis and the Current Account Deficit   The experience of the Asian crisis countries demonstrates that current account deficits can be dangerous not only when they finance unsustainable budget deficits but also when they finance investments of low profitability. As already noted, the crisis-afflicted East Asian economies all enjoyed high saving rates. Their large current account deficits were attributable to their even higher investment rates. Even so, the buildup of debt deriving from these current account imbalances became unsustainable, because, as discussed above, distortions in the operation of East Asian financial systems led to excessive investment in low-profitability projects. Investment-driven current account deficits enhance economic welfare only when expected investment returns exceed the cost of the borrowed funds. Throughout the East Asian region the rate of return to capital, although still positive, appears to have been falling in the 1990s, signaling a deterioration in the quality of the investment projects.

Moreover, foreign debt must be serviced and, at some point, fully repaid. Therefore, debtor countries must ultimately run trade surpluses, which may require adjustments in their real exchange rates. Borrowing in world capital markets is perhaps least problematic when the new investments it permits augment a country's capacity to produce goods for sale in foreign markets. In contrast, many Asian countries borrowed abroad to finance commercial and residential investments, producing goods, such as office buildings and houses, that are not usually traded internationally.

The U.S. International Investment Position   If current account deficits continue year after year, creditor countries eventually become net debtors: every year the stock of net foreign liabilities rises by an amount equal to the current account deficit (ignoring valuation effects). Not all these liabilities consist of debt: The capital inflows that finance current account deficits can take the form of equity investment, as in foreign direct investment. Thus an increase in a country's net foreign liabilities does not automatically translate into an increase in foreign debt, strictly speaking, but rather a decrease in the net international investment position.

Exhibit 8.13 shows the relationship between the U.S. current account and the change in the U.S. net international investment position (where direct investment is valued at current cost). In the 1970s, the United States was a net creditor country. However, the string of current account deficits in the 1980s led to a reduction of net

EXHIBIT 8.13	CURRENT ACCOUNT DEFICIT AND NET INTERNATIONAL INVESTMENT POSITION

AS THE UNITED STATES STARTED TO RUN LARGE CURRENT ACCOUNT DEFICITS IN THE EARLY 1980S, THE NET INTERNATIONAL INVESTMENT POSITION DECLINED

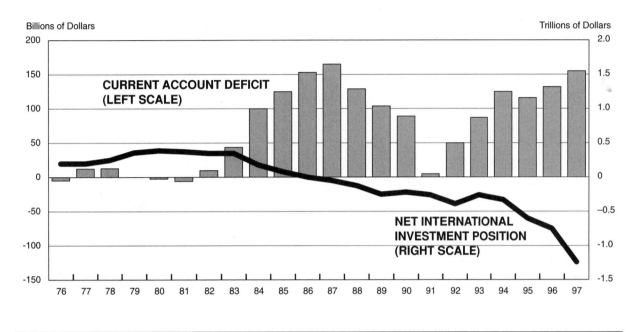

Note: Net international investment position at current cost.

SOURCE: Department of Commerce (Bureau of Economic Analysis).

foreign assets and eventually, in 1987, turned the United States into a country with growing net external liabilities.

Because the U.S. current account deficits of the 1980s were primarily driven by fiscal deficits and low national saving rates, the accumulation of net foreign liabilities was greeted with some concern. The large fiscal deficits were financed by government bonds, some of which foreign investors purchased directly. Since 1993, however, current account deficits have been driven by increases in investment, with foreign financing taking the form of both direct and portfolio investment. **Exhibit 8.14** shows trends in both inward and outward foreign direct investment.) At present, U.S. net foreign liabilities amount to a relatively modest 15% of GDP.

Policies toward the External Imbalance

Calls for protection from import competition typically increase when the U.S. trade deficit burgeons, as it has since the onset of the Asian crisis. Although the crisis has caused dislocations in some export and import-competing industries, overall employment growth remains strong in the U.S. economy. As we have argued, the growing U.S. trade imbalance primarily reflects strong investment and growth opportunities in the United States in comparison with our trade partners, rather than increased barriers to trade in foreign markets. Looked at another way, the countries affected by the crisis have been forced to reduce their own current account deficits by their sudden inability to finance those deficits through foreign borrowing. The increased U.S. trade deficit, at least through the first three quarters of 1998, primarily reflects falling exports to these economies—declines in their imports engendered by the sharp economic contractions those countries have suffered.

| EXHIBIT 8.14 | FOREIGN DIRECT INVESTMENT FLOWS |

THE 1980S SAW A SURGE IN FOREIGN DIRECT INVESTMENT INTO THE UNITED STATES. IN THE 1990S, HOWEVER, DIRECT INVESTMENT OUTFLOWS AGAIN SURPASSED INFLOWS.

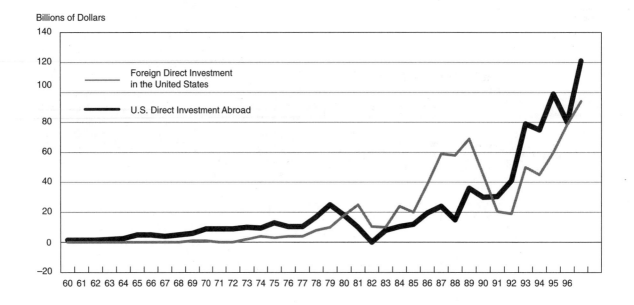

SOURCE: Department of Commerce (Bureau of Economic Analysis).

To restore world economic growth to its level before the crisis, the United States and other industrial countries must maintain open markets. Higher barriers to trade in the United States would not only hinder recovery in Asia and other crisis countries but provoke emulation and retaliation by our trading partners, which would hamper our own growth prospects. It is worth remembering that it was a dramatic switch to protectionist policies in the United States and other industrial countries that deepened the Great Depression. As the crisis economies recover, their demand for U.S. goods and services will increase as well, once again fueling our own export growth.

Recognizing the need to maintain open markets worldwide, the President has called for a new consensus on trade, to continue to expand America's opportunities in the global economy while ensuring that all our citizens enjoy the benefits of trade, through greater prosperity, respect for workers' rights, and protection of the environment. The President asked the Congress to join him in this new consensus by restoring his traditional trade-negotiating authority (so-called fast-track authority), to allow him to pursue an ambitious trade agenda. At the top of this agenda is a far-reaching new round of global trade negotiations within the World Trade Organization aimed at shaping the world trading system for the 21st century.

Conclusion

During a period of great turmoil in the global economy, the first imperative of the administration has been to work with the international community to sustain worldwide growth. That is a prerequisite for the recovery of the countries now afflicted by crisis. No country, not even the United States, is an island in the world economy. The growth prospects of all the world's industrial nations will suffer unless all do their part. The United States and its G-7 partners have clearly recognized this imperative.

The United States remains committed to opening markets to international trade, recognizing that an open trade environment will be the best policy for domestic growth, support the recovery of the crisis-afflicted countries, and ensure the continued growth of the world economy. At the start of his administration in 1993, the President declared, "The truth of our age is this—and must be this: Open and competitive commerce will enrich us as a nation. . . . And I say to you in face of all the pressure to do the reverse, we must compete, not retreat." Now, as then, the administration remains strongly committed to outward-looking, internationalist policies.

National Income or Expenditure

| TABLE B-1 | GROSS DOMESTIC PRODUCT, 1959–98 |

[BILLIONS OF DOLLARS, EXCEPT AS NOTED; QUARTERLY DATA AT SEASONALLY ADJUSTED ANNUAL RATES]

Year or Quarter	Gross Domestic Product	Personal Consumption Expenditures				Gross Private Domestic Investment						Change in Business Inventories
		Total	Durable Goods	Non-durable Goods	Services	Total	Fixed Investment					
							Total	Nonresidential			Residential	
								Total	Structures	Producers' Durable Equipment		
1959	507.2	318.1	42.7	148.5	127.0	78.8	74.6	46.5	18.1	28.3	28.1	4.2
1960	526.6	332.2	43.3	152.9	136.0	78.8	75.5	49.2	19.6	29.7	26.3	3.2
1961	544.8	342.6	41.8	156.6	144.3	77.9	75.0	48.6	19.7	28.9	26.4	2.9
1962	585.2	363.4	46.9	162.8	153.7	87.9	81.8	52.8	20.8	32.1	29.0	6.1
1963	617.4	383.0	51.6	168.2	163.2	93.4	87.7	55.6	21.2	34.4	32.1	5.7
1964	663.0	411.4	56.7	178.7	176.1	101.7	96.7	62.4	23.7	38.7	34.3	5.0
1965	719.1	444.3	63.3	191.6	189.4	118.0	108.3	74.1	28.3	45.8	34.2	9.7
1966	787.8	481.9	68.3	208.8	204.8	130.4	116.7	84.4	31.3	53.0	32.3	13.8
1967	833.6	509.5	70.4	217.1	222.0	128.0	117.6	85.2	31.5	53.7	32.4	10.5
1968	910.6	559.8	80.8	235.7	243.4	139.9	130.8	92.1	33.6	58.5	38.7	9.1
1969	982.2	604.7	85.9	253.2	265.5	155.0	145.5	102.9	37.7	65.2	42.6	9.5
1970	1,035.6	648.1	85.0	272.0	291.1	150.2	148.1	106.7	40.3	66.4	41.4	2.2
1971	1,125.4	702.5	96.9	285.5	320.1	176.0	167.5	111.7	42.7	69.1	55.8	8.5
1972	1,237.3	770.7	110.4	308.0	352.3	205.6	195.7	126.1	47.2	78.9	69.7	9.9
1973	1,382.6	851.6	123.5	343.1	384.9	242.9	225.4	150.0	55.0	95.1	75.3	17.5
1974	1,496.9	931.2	122.3	384.5	424.4	245.6	231.5	165.6	61.2	104.3	66.0	14.1
1975	1,630.6	1,029.1	133.5	420.6	475.0	225.4	231.7	169.0	61.4	107.6	62.7	–6.3
1976	1,819.0	1,148.8	158.9	458.2	531.8	286.6	269.6	187.2	65.9	121.2	82.5	16.9
1977	2,026.9	1,277.1	181.1	496.9	599.0	356.6	333.5	223.2	74.6	148.7	110.3	23.1
1978	2,291.4	1,428.8	201.4	549.9	677.4	430.8	403.6	272.0	91.4	180.6	131.6	27.2
1979	2,557.5	1,593.5	213.9	624.0	755.6	480.9	464.0	323.0	114.9	208.1	141.0	16.9
1980	2,784.2	1,760.4	213.5	695.5	851.4	465.9	473.5	350.3	133.9	216.4	123.2	–7.6
1981	3,115.9	1,941.3	230.5	758.2	952.6	556.2	528.1	405.4	164.6	240.9	122.6	28.2
1982	3,242.1	2,076.8	239.3	786.8	1,050.7	501.1	515.6	409.9	175.0	234.9	105.7	–14.5
1993	3,514.5	2,283.4	279.8	830.3	1,173.3	547.1	552.0	399.4	152.7	246.7	152.5	–4.9
1984	3,902.4	2,492.3	325.1	883.6	1,283.6	715.6	648.1	468.3	176.0	292.3	179.8	67.5
1985	4,180.7	2,704.8	361.1	927.6	1,416.1	715.1	688.9	502.0	193.3	308.7	186.9	26.2
1986	4,422.2	2,892.7	398.7	957.2	1,536.8	722.5	712.9	494.8	175.8	319.0	218.1	9.6
1987	4,692.3	3,094.5	416.7	1,014.0	1,663.8	747.2	722.9	495.4	172.1	323.3	227.6	24.2
1988	5,049.6	3,349.7	451.0	1,081.1	1,817.6	773.9	763.1	530.6	181.3	349.3	232.5	10.9
1989	5,438.7	3,594.8	472.8	1,163.8	1,958.1	829.2	797.5	566.2	192.3	373.9	231.3	31.7

TABLE B-1	CONTINUED

Year or Quarter	Net Exports of Goods and Services			Government Consumption Expenditures						Sales of Domestic Product	Gross Domestic Purchases[1]	Addendum: Gross National Product[2]	Percent Change from Preceding Period	
					Federal			Final State and Local					Gross Domestic Product	Domestic Purchases[1]
	Net Exports	Exports	Imports	Total	Total	National Defense	Non-defense							
1959	−1.7	20.6	22.3	112.0	67.2	55.7	11.5	44.8	503.0	508.9	510.1	8.5	9.0
1960	2.4	25.3	22.8	113.2	65.6	54.9	10.8	47.6	523.3	524.1	529.8	3.8	3.0
1961	3.4	26.0	22.7	120.9	69.1	57.7	11.4	51.8	582.8	541.5	548.4	3.5	3.3
1962	2.4	27.4	25.0	131.4	76.5	62.3	14.2	55.0	579.1	582.8	589.4	7.4	7.6
1963	3.3	29.4	26.1	137.7	78.1	62.2	15.9	59.6	611.7	614.1	621.9	5.5	5.4
1964	5.5	33.6	28.1	144.4	79.4	61.3	18.1	65.0	658.0	657.6	668.0	7.4	7.1
1965	3.9	35.4	31.5	153.0	81.8	62.0	19.7	71.2	709.4	715.3	724.5	8.5	8.8
1966	1.9	38.9	37.1	173.6	94.1	73.4	20.7	79.5	774.0	785.9	793.0	9.5	9.9
1967	1.4	41.4	39.9	194.6	106.6	85.5	21.0	88.1	823.1	832.2	839.1	5.8	5.9
1968	−1.3	45.3	46.6	212.1	113.8	92.0	21.8	98.3	901.4	911.8	916.7	9.2	9.6
1969	−1.2	49.3	50.5	223.8	115.8	92.4	23.4	108.0	972.7	983.4	988.4	7.9	7.8
1970	1.2	57.0	55.8	236.1	115.9	90.6	25.3	120.2	1,033.4	1,034.4	1,042.0	5.4	5.2
1971	−3.0	59.3	62.3	249.9	117.1	88.7	28.3	132.8	1,116.9	1,128.4	1,133.1	8.7	9.1
1972	−8.0	66.2	74.2	268.9	125.1	93.2	31.9	143.8	1,227.4	1,245.3	1,246.0	9.9	10.4
1973	.6	91.8	91.2	287.6	128.2	94.7	33.5	159.4	1,365.2	1,382.0	1,395.4	11.7	11.0
1974	−3.1	124.3	127.5	323.2	139.9	101.9	38.0	183.3	1,482.8	1,500.0	1,512.6	8.3	8.5
1975	13.6	136.3	122.7	362.6	154.5	110.9	43.6	208.1	1,636.9	1,617.1	1,643.9	8.9	7.9
1976	−2.3	148.9	151.1	385.9	162.7	116.1	46.6	223.1	1,802.0	1,821.2	1,836.1	11.5	12.6
1977	−23.7	158.8	182.4	416.9	178.4	125.8	52.6	238.5	2,003.8	2,050.5	2,047.5	11.4	12.6
1978	−26.1	186.1	212.3	457.9	194.4	135.6	58.9	263.4	2,264.2	2,317.5	2,313.5	13.0	13.0
1979	−24.0	228.7	252.7	507.1	215.0	151.2	63.8	292.0	2,540.6	2,581.5	2,590.4	11.6	11.4
1980	−14.9	278.9	293.8	572.8	248.4	174.2	74.2	324.4	2,791.9	2,799.1	2819.5	8.9	8.4
1981	−15.0	302.8	317.8	633.4	284.1	202.0	82.2	349.2	3,087.8	3,130.9	3,150.6	11.9	11.9
1982	−20.5	282.6	303.2	684.8	313.2	230.9	82.3	371.6	3,256.6	3,262.6	3,273.2	4.1	4.2
1983	−51.7	277.0	328.6	735.7	344.5	255.0	89.4	391.2	3,519.4	3,566.2	3,546.5	8.4	9.3
1984	−102.0	303.1	405.1	796.6	372.6	282.7	89.9	424.0	3,835.0	4,004.5	3,933.5	11.0	12.3
1985	−114.2	303.0	417.2	875.0	410.1	312.4	97.7	464.9	4,154.5	4,294.9	4,201.0	7.1	7.3
1986	−131.5	320.7	452.2	938.5	435.2	332.4	102.9	503.3	4,412.6	4,553.7	4,435.1	5.8	6.0
1987	−142.1	365.7	507.9	992.8	455.7	350.4	105.3	537.2	4,668.1	4,834.5	4,701.3	6.1	6.2
1988	−106.1	447.2	553.2	1,032.0	457.3	354.0	103.3	574.7	5,038. 7	5,155.6	5,062.6	7.6	6.6
1989	−80.4	509.3	589.7	1,095.1	477.2	360.6	116.7	617.9	5,407.0	5,519.1	5,452.8	7.7	7.0

Continued

TABLE B-1   CONTINUED

Year or Quarter	Gross Domestic Product	Personal Consumption Expenditures				Gross Private Domestic Investment						Change in Business Inventories
							Fixed Investment					
								Nonresidential				
		Total	Durable Goods	Non-durable Goods	Services	Total	Total	Total	Struc-tures	Producers' Durable Equip-ment	Resi-dential	
1990	5,743.8	3,839.3	476.5	1,245.3	2,117.5	799.7	791.6	575.9	200.8	375.1	215.7	8.0
1991	5,916.7	3,975.1	455.2	1,277.6	2,242.3	736.2	738.5	547.3	181.7	365.6	191.2	−2.3
1992	6,244.4	4,219.8	488.5	1,321.8	2,409.4	790.4	783.4	557.9	169.2	388.7	225.6	7.0
1993	6,558.1	4,459.2	530.2	1,370.7	2,558.4	876.2	855.7	604.1	176.4	427.7	251.6	20.5
1994	6,947.0	4,717.0	579.5	1,428.4	2,709.1	1,007.9	946.6	660.6	184.5	476.1	286.0	61.2
1995	7,269.6	4,953.9	611.0	1,473.6	2,869.2	1,043.2	1,012.5	727.7	201.3	526.4	284.8	30.7
1996	7,661.6	5,215.7	643.3	1,539.2	3,033.2	1,131.9	1,099.8	787.9	216.9	571.0	311.8	32.1
1997	8,110.9	5,493.7	673.0	1,600.6	3,220.1	1,256.0	1,188.6	860.7	240.2	620.5	327.9	67.4
1993:I	6,444.5	4,365.4	506.4	1,354.4	2,504.6	854.3	823.5	580.5	171.7	408.9	243.0	30.7
II	6,509.1	4,428.1	524.2	1,366.3	2,537.6	357.4	842.9	598.8	175.2	423.6	244.1	14.5
III	6,574.6	4,488.6	537.2	1,373.9	2,577.4	872.8	858.8	606.4	177.8	428.6	252.4	14.0
IV	6,704.2	4,554.9	553.1	1,388.0	2,613.8	920.3	897.5	630.6	180.7	449.9	266.8	22.9
1994: I	6,794.3	4,616.6	563.2	1,404.4	2,649.0	963.4	911.0	634.6	175.4	459.3	276.4	52.4
II	6,911.4	4,680.5	572.4	1,416.0	2,692.2	1,017.9	941.7	652.9	185.2	467.7	288.7	76.3
III	6,986.5	4,750.6	583.3	1,439.5	2,727.8	1,007.1	956.9	667.4	186.8	480.6	289.5	50.2
IV	7,095.7	4,820.2	599.3	1,453.7	2,767.2	1,043.1	977.0	687.5	190.7	496.8	289.5	66.2
1995: I	7,170.8	4,862.5	598.4	1,459.6	2,804.5	1,058.9	1,000.0	713.6	197.9	515.6	286.4	59.0
II	7,210.9	4,931.5	606.0	1,470.7	2,854.7	1,029.6	1,004.3	728.1	201.8	526.3	276.2	25.3
III	7,304.8	4,986.4	616.9	1,476.8	2,892.7	1,030.6	1,013.5	729.5	203.0	526.5	284.0	17.1
IV	7,391.9	5,035.3	622.8	1,487.5	2,925.0	1,053.6	1,032.1	739.5	202.2	537.2	292.6	21.5
1996: I	7,495.3	5,108.2	632.3	1,506.8	2,969.0	1,075.3	1,059.1	759.0	206.5	552.6	300.1	16.3
II	7,629.2	5,199.0	647.3	1,537.9	3,013.7	1,118.3	1,089.7	774.8	211.3	563.5	315.0	28.5
III	7,703.4	5,242.5	642.5	1,543.6	3,056.3	1,167.9	1,118.1	801.1	218.0	583.1	317.0	49.8
IV	7,818.4	5,313.2	651.1	1,568.3	3,093.9	1,166.0	1,132.2	816.8	232.1	584.8	315.3	33.8
1997: I	7,955.0	5,402.4	668.9	1,589.7	3,143.9	1,206.4	1,146.7	827.1	236.2	591.0	319.5	59.7
II	8,063.4	5,438.8	659.9	1,588.2	3,190.7	1,259.9	1,176.4	850.5	234.3	616.2	325.9	83.5
III	8,170.8	5,540.3	681.2	1,611.3	3,247.9	1,265.7	1,211.1	982.3	243.8	638.5	328.8	54.6
IV	8,254.5	5,593.2	682.2	1,613.2	3,297.8	1,292.0	1,220.1	882.8	246.4	636.4	337.4	71.9
1998: I	8,384.2	5,676.5	705.1	1,633.1	3,338.2	1,366.6	1,271.1	921.3	245.0	676.3	349.8	95.5
II	8,440.6	5,773.7	720.1	1,655.2	3,398.4	1,345.0	1,305.8	941.9	245.4	696.6	363.8	39.2
III	8,573.9	5,846.7	718.9	1,670.0	3,457.7	1,364.4	1,307.5	931.6	246.2	685.4	375.8	57.0

TABLE B-1 CONTINUED

Year or Quarter	Net Exports of Goods and Services			Government Consumption Expenditures					Final Sales of Domestic Product	Gross Domestic Purchases[1]	Addendum: Gross National Product[2]	Percent Change from Preceding Period	
	Net Exports	Exports	Imports	Total	Federal			State and Local				Gross Domestic Product	Domestic Purchases[1]
					Total	National Defense	Non-defense						
1990	−71.3	557.3	628.6	1,176.1	503.6	373.1	130.4	672.6	5,735.8	5,815.1	5,764.9	5.6	5.4
1991	−20.5	601.8	622.3	1,225.9	522.6	383.5	139.1	703.4	5,919.0	5,937.2	5,932.4	3.0	2.1
1992	−29.5	639.4	669.0	1,263.8	528.0	375.8	152.2	735.8	6,237.4	6,274.0	6,255.5	5.5	5.7
1993	−60.7	658.6	719.3	1,283.4	518.3	360.7	157.7	765.0	6,537.6	6,618.8	6,576.8	5.0	5.5
1994	−90.9	721.2	812.1	1,313.0	510.2	349.2	161.0	802.8	6,885.7	7,037.9	6,955.2	5.9	6.3
1995	−83.9	819.4	903.3	1,356.4	509.1	344.4	164.7	847.3	7,238.9	7,353.5	7,287.1	4.6	4.5
1996	−91.2	873.8	965.0	1,405.2	518.4	351.0	167.4	886.8	7,629.5	7,752.8	7,674.0	5.4	5.4
1997	−93.4	965.4	1,058.8	1,454.6	520.2	346.0	174.3	934.4	8,043.5	8,204.3	8,102.9	5.9	5.8
1993: I	−46.6	647.1	693.7	1,271.5	521.3	363.6	157.7	750.1	6,413.8	6,491.1	6,468.1	3.9	4.1
II	−57.5	661.2	718.7	1,281.2	517.8	361.7	156.1	763.4	6,494.7	6,566.7	6,525.3	4.1	4.7
III	−72.1	646.8	718.9	1,285.3	515.7	358.0	157.7	769.6	6,560.6	6,646.7	6,596.9	4.1	5.0
IV	−66.6	679.4	746.0	1,295.5	518.5	359.4	159.1	777.0	6,681.3	6,770.8	6,717.1	8.1	7.7
1994: I	−76.6	678.5	755.1	1,291.0	506.9	344.9	162.0	784.1	6,741.9	6,870.9	6,811.2	5.5	6.0
II	−87.9	710.1	797.9	1,300.8	505.3	348.5	156.8	795.5	6,835.1	6,999.2	6,920.3	7.1	7.7
III	−103.4	732.6	936.0	1332.3	520.4	359.7	160.7	811.9	6,936.3	7,090.0	6,992.3	4.4	5.3
IV	−95.6	763.7	859.2	1,328.0	508.3	343.6	164.7	819.6	7,029.6	7,191.3	7,096.8	6.4	5.8
1995: I	−94.7	787.8	882.5	1,344.1	512.3	346.1	166.2	831.8	7,111.8	7,265.5	7,189.3	4.3	4.2
II	−108.0	803.4	911.4	1,357.8	511.7	348.1	163.6	846.2	7,185.6	7,318.9	7,233.3	2.3	3.0
III	−74.5	835.1	909.6	1,362.3	511.2	345.5	165.7	851.1	7,287.7	7,379.3	7,313.2	5.3	3.3
IV	−58.4	851.5	909.9	1,361.4	501.2	337.9	163.3	860.2	7,370.4	7,450.3	7,412.6	4.9	3.9
1996: I	−75.7	856.6	932.3	1,387.5	517.1	350.3	166.8	870.4	7,479.1	7,571.0	7,515.0	5.7	6.6
II	−94.0	863.0	957.0	1,406.0	523.1	355.6	167.4	882.9	7,600.6	7,723.2	7,643.3	7.3	8.3
III	−115.5	861.4	976.9	1,408.6	519.0	351.3	167.7	889.6	7,653.6	7,818.9	7,708.6	3.9	5.1
IV	−79.6	914.2	993.8	1,418.8	514.6	346.7	167.9	904.2	7,784.6	7,898.0	7,829.0	6.1	4.1
1997: I	−93.3	930.2	1,023.5	1,439.4	517.0	341.1	175.9	922.4	7,895.2	8,048.2	7,952.4	7.2	7.8
II	−86.8	961.1	1,047.9	1,451.5	522.9	349.1	173.8	928.6	7,979.9	8,150.2	8,062.3	5.6	5.2
III	−94.7	981.7	1,076.4	1,459.5	521.0	347.1	173.9	938.5	8,116.2	8,265.5	8,162.0	5.4	5.8
IV	−98.8	988.6	1,087.4	1,468.1	520.1	346.5	173.6	947.9	8,182.6	8,353.3	8,234.9	4.2	4.3
1998: I	−123.7	973.3	1,097.1	1,464.9	511.6	331.6	180.0	953.3	8,288.7	8,508.0	8,369.4	6.4	7.6
II	−159.3	949.6	1,108.9	1,481.2	520.7	339.8	180.9	960.4	8,401.3	8,599.9	8,421.8	2.7	4.4
III	−165.5	936.2	1,101.7	1,492.3	519.4	343.7	175.7	972.9	8,480.9	8,703.4	8,510.9	4.7	4.9

[1]Gross domestic product (GDP) less exports of goods and services plus imports of goods and services.
[2]GDP plus net receipts of factor income from rest of the world.

SOURCE: Department of Commerce, Bureau of Economic Analysis.

| TABLE B-2 | REAL GROSS DOMESTIC PRODUCT, 1959–98 |

[BILLIONS OF CHAINED (1992) DOLLARS, EXCEPT AS NOTED; QUARTERLY DATA AT SEASONALLY ADJUSTED ANNUAL RATES]

Year or Quarter	Gross Domestic Product	Personal Consumption Expenditures				Gross Private Domestic Investment						Change in Business Inventories
							Fixed Investment					
								Nonresidential				
		Total	Durable Goods	Non-durable Goods	Services	Total	Total	Total	Structures	Producers' Durable Equipment	Residential	
1959	2,210.2	1,394.6	—	—	—	271.7	—	—	—	—	—	—
1960	2,262.9	1432.6	—	—	—	270.5	—	—	—	—	—	—
1961	2,314.3	1,461.5	—	—	—	267.6	—	—	—	—	—	—
1962	2,454.8	1,533.8	—	—	—	302.1	—	—	—	—	—	—
1963	2559.4	1,596.6	—	—	—	321.6	—	—	—	—	—	—
1964	2,708.4	1,692.3	—	—	—	348.3	—	—	—	—	—	—
1965	2,881.1	1,799.1	—	—	—	397.2	—	—	—	—	—	—
1966	3,069.2	1,902.0	—	—	—	430.6	—	—	—	—	—	—
1967	3,147.1	1,958.6	—	—	—	411.8	—	—	—	—	—	—
1968	3,293.9	2,070.2	—	—	—	433.3	—	—	—	—	—	—
1969	3,393.6	2,147.5	—	—	—	458.3	—	—	—	—	—	—
1970	3,397.6	2,197.8	—	—	—	426.1	—	—	—	—	—	—
1971	3,510.0	2,279.5	—	—	—	474.9	—	—	—	—	—	—
1972	3,702.3	2,415.9	—	—	—	531.8	—	—	—	—	—	—
1973	3,916.3	2,532.6	—	—	—	595.5	—	—	—	—	—	—
1974	3,891.2	2,514.7	—	—	—	546.5	—	—	—	—	—	—
1975	3,873.9	2,570.0	—	—	—	446.6	—	—	—	—	—	—
1976	4,082.9	2,714.3	—	—	—	537.4	—	—	—	—	—	—
1977	4,273.6	2,829.8	—	—	—	622.1	—	—	—	—	—	—
1979	4,503.0	2,951.6	—	—	—	693.4	—	—	—	—	—	—
1979	4,630.6	3,020.2	—	—	—	709.7	—	—	—	—	—	—
1980	4,615.0	3,009.7	—	—	—	628.3	—	—	—	—	—	—
1981	4,720.7	3,046.4	—	—	—	686.0	—	—	—	—	—	—
1982	4,620.3	3,081.5	285.5	1,080.6	1,728.2	587.2	610.4	464.3	207.2	260.3	140.1	–15.6
1983	4,803.7	3,240.6	327.4	1,112.4	1,809.0	642.1	654.2	456.4	185.7	272.4	197.6	–5.7
1984	5,140.1	3,407.6	374.9	1,151.8	1,883.0	833.4	762.4	535.4	212.2	324.6	226.4	75.3
1985	5,323.5	3,566.5	411.4	1,178.3	1,977.3	823.8	799.3	568.4	227.8	342.4	229.5	30.2
1986	5,487.7	3,708.7	448.4	1,215.9	2,041.4	811.8	805.0	548.5	203.3	345.9	257.0	11.1
1987	5,649.5	3,822.3	454.9	1,239.3	2,126.9	821.5	799.4	542.4	195.9	346.9	257.6	26.4
1988	5,865.2	3,972.7	483.5	1,274.4	2,212.4	828.2	818.3	566.0	196.8	369.2	252.5	11.7
1989	6,062.0	4,064.6	496.2	1,303.5	2,262.3	863.5	832.0	588.8	201.2	387.6	243.2	33.3

TABLE B-2 CONTINUED

Year or Quarter	Net Exports of Goods and Services			Government Consumption Expenditures						Sales of Domestic Product	Gross Domestic Purchases[1]	Adden-dum: Gross National Product[2]	Percent Change from Preceding Period	
	Net Exports	Exports	Imports	Total	Federal			Final State and Local					Gross Domestic Product	Domestic Pur-chases[1]
					Total	National Defense	Non-defense							
1959	—	71.9	106.6	618.5	—	—	—	—	2,206.9	2,268.0	2,222.0	7.4	7.8
1960	—	86.8	108.1	617.2	—	—	—	—	2,264.2	2,304.1	2,276.0	2.4	1.6
1961	—	88.3	107.3	647.2	—	—	—	—	2,318.0	2,354.3	2,329.1	2.3	2.2
1962	—	93.0	119.5	686.0	—	—	—	—	2,445.4	2,503.0	2,471.5	6.1	6.3
1963	—	100.0	122.7	701.9	—	—	—	—	2,552.4	2,604.2	2,577.3	4.3	4.0
1964	—	113. 3	129.2	715.9	—	—	—	—	2,705.1	2,745.9	2,727.8	5.8	5.4
1965	—	115.6	143.0	737.6	—	—	—	—	2,860.4	2,932.1	2,901.4	6.4	6.8
1966	—	123.4	164.2	804.6	—	—	—	—	3,033.5	3,134.0	3,087.8	6.5	6.9
1967	—	126.1	176.2	865.6	—	—	—	—	3,125.1	3,221.1	3,166.4	2.5	2.8
1968	—	135.3	202.5	892.4	—	—	—	—	3,278.0	3,382.7	3,314.5	4.7	5.0
1969	—	142.7	214.0	887.5	—	—	—	—	3,377.2	3,485.6	3,413.3	3.0	3.0
1970	—	158.1	223.1	866.8	—	—	—	—	3,406.5	3,478.5	3,417.1	.1	−.2
1971	—	159.2	235.0	851.0	—	—	—	—	3,499.8	3,602.4	3,532.1	3.3	3.6
1972	—	172.0	261.0	854.1	—	—	—	—	3689.5	3,806.2	3,726.3	5.5	5.7
1973	—	209.6	272.6	848.4	—	—	—	—	3,883.9	3,989.3	3,950.1	5.8	4.8
1974	—	229.8	265.3	862.9	—	—	—	—	3,873.4	3,928.6	3,930.2	−.6	−1.5
1975	—	228.2	235.4	876.3	—	—	—	—	3,906.4	3,875.9	3,903.3	−.4	−1.3
1976	—	241.6	281.5	876.8	—	—	—	—	4,061.7	4,124.6	4,118.8	5.4	6.4
1977	—	247.4	311.6	884.7	—	—	—	—	4,240.8	4,345.7	4,314.5	4.7	5.4
1978	—	273.1	338.6	910.6	—	—	—	—	4,464.4	4,574.9	4,543.7	5.4	5.3
1979	—	299.0	344.3	924.9	—	—	—	—	4,614.4	4,674.6	4,687.4	2.8	2.2
1980	—	331.4	321.3	941.4	—	—	—	—	4,641.9	4,581.5	4,670.8	−.3	−2.0
1981	—	335.3	329.7	947.7	—	—	—	—	4,691.6	4,693.1	4,769.9	2.3	2.4
1982	−14.1	311.4	325.5	960.1	429.4	316.5	113.3	531.4	4,651.2	4,619.3	4,662.0	−2.1	−1.6
1983	−63.3	303.3	366.6	987.3	452.7	334.6	118.5	534.9	4,821.2	4,864.3	4,844.8	4.0	5.3
1984	−127.3	328.4	455.7	1,018.4	463.7	348.1	115.9	555.0	5,061.6	5,276.2	5,178.0	7.0	8.5
1985	−147.9	337.3	485.2	1,080.1	495.6	374.1	121.8	584.7	5,296.9	5,482.8	5,346.7	3.6	3.9
1986	−163.9	362.2	526.1	1,135.0	518.4	393.4	125.2	616.9	5,480.9	5,663.9	5,501.2	3.1	3.3
1987	−156.2	402.0	558.2	1,165.9	534.4	409.2	125.3	631.8	5,626.0	5,816.7	5,658.2	2.9	2.7
1988	−114.4	465.8	580.2	1,180.9	524.6	405.5	119.1	656.6	5,855.1	5,986.1	5878.5	3.8	2.9
1989	−82.7	520.2	603.0	1,213.9	531.5	401.6	130.1	682.6	6,028.7	6,147.8	6,075.7	3.4	2.7

Continued

TABLE B-2   CONTINUED

Year or Quarter	Gross Domestic Product	Personal Consumption Expenditures				Gross Private Domestic Investment						Change in Business Inventories
							Fixed Investment					
								Nonresidential				
		Total	Durable Goods	Non-durable Goods	Services	Total	Total	Total	Struc-tures	Producers' Durable Equip-ment	Resi-dential	
1990	6,136.3	4,132.2	493.3	1,316.1	2,321.3	815.0	805.8	585.2	203.3	381.9	220.6	10.4
1991	6,079.4	4,105.8	462.0	1,302.9	2,341.0	738.1	741.3	547.7	181.6	366.2	193.4	−3.0
1992	6,244.4	4,219.8	488.5	1,321.8	2,409.4	790.4	783.4	557.9	169.2	388.7	225.6	7.0
1993	6,389.6	4,343.6	523.8	1,351.0	2,468.9	863.6	842.8	600.2	170.8	429.6	242.6	22.1
1994	6,610.7	4,486.0	561.2	1,389.9	2,535.5	975.7	915.5	648.4	172.5	476.8	267.0	60.6
1995	6,761.7	4,605.6	589.1	1,417.6	2,599.6	996.1	966.0	710.6	180.7	531.7	256.8	27.7
1996	6,994.8	4,752.4	626.1	1,450.9	2,676.7	1,084.1	1,050.6	776.6	189.7	589.8	275.9	30.0
1997	7,269.8	4,913.5	668.6	1,486.3	2,761.5	1,206.4	1,138.0	859.4	203.2	660.9	282.8	63.2
1993: I	6,327.9	4,286.8	504.0	1,337.5	2,445.3	845.5	814.8	577.9	168.0	409.8	237.0	32.3
II	6,359.9	4,322.8	519.3	1,347.8	2,455.9	846.1	831.1	595.1	170.3	424.9	236.1	16.6
III	6,393.5	4,366.6	529.9	1,356.8	2,480.0	858.6	844.5	602.3	171.7	430.7	242.2	15.3
IV	6,476.9	4,398.0	542.1	1,361.8	2,494.4	904.0	880.8	625.6	173.1	452.9	255.1	24.2
1994: I	6,524.5	4,439.4	550.7	1,378.4	2,510.9	939.9	887.8	626.2	166.3	460.6	261.3	53.1
II	6,600.3	4,472.2	555.8	1,385.5	2,531.4	987.8	913.2	641.2	174.5	467.3	271.5	75.9
III	6,629.5	4,498.2	561.7	1,393.2	2,543.8	972.2	922.7	653.2	174.0	480.0	269.4	49.7
IV	6,688.6	4,534.1	576.6	1,402.5	2555.9	1,003.0	938.5	672.9	175.0	499.1	265.9	63.6
1995: I	6,717.5	4,555.3	575.2	1,410.4	2,570.4	1,013.5	957.1	698.4	179.5	520.4	259.9	54.3
II	6,724.2	4,593.6	583.5	1,415.9	2,594.8	982.0	957.8	710.2	181.7	529.9	249.5	21.7
III	6,779.5	4,623.4	595.3	1,418.5	2,610.3	983.4	965.8	711.7	181.5	531.8	255.6	14.7
IV	6,825.8	4,650.0	602.4	1,425.6	2,622.9	1,005.4	983.1	722.3	179.8	544.8	262.1	20.1
1996: I	6,882.0	4,692.1	611.0	1,433.5	2,648.5	1,029.3	1,011.4	744.8	182.6	565.0	268.0	14.4
II	6,983.9	4,746.6	629.5	1,450.4	2,668.4	1,072.8	1,043.5	764.4	185.9	581.6	280.2	26.1
III	7,020.0	4,768.3	626.5	1,454.7	2,688.1	1,118.1	1,067.1	790.1	189.9	604.0	279.0	47.5
IV	7,093.1	4,802.6	637.5	1,465.1	2,701.7	1,116.1	1,080.4	807.0	200.6	608.8	276.3	32.1
1997: I	7,166.7	4,853.4	656.3	1,477.9	2,722.1	1,156.6	1,096.0	820.9	202.5	621.0	278.4	56.3
II	7,236.5	4,872.7	653.8	1,477.1	2,743.6	1,211.3	1,127.0	848.2	199.3	653.8	282.5	79.0
III	7,311.2	4,947.0	679.6	1,495.7	2,775.4	1,215.8	1,159.3	882.2	205.2	682.6	282.3	51.0
IV	7,364.6	4,981.0	684.8	1,494.3	2,804.8	1,241.9	1,169.5	886.2	205.7	686.4	287.9	66.5
1998: I	7,464.7	5,055.1	710.3	1,521.2	2,829.3	1,321.8	1,224.9	931.9	203.1	738.8	298.5	91.4
II	7,498.6	5,130.2	729.4	1,540.9	2,866.8	1,306.5	1,264.1	960.4	201.9	771.3	309.1	38.2
III	7,566.5	5,181.1	733.7	1,549.1	2,904.8	1,331.6	1,270.9	958.7	202.0	769.3	316.5	55.7

TABLE B-2   CONTINUED

Year or Quarter	Net Exports of Goods and Services			Government Consumption Expenditures					Sales of Domestic Product	Gross Domestic Purchases[1]	Addendum: Gross National Product[2]	Percent Change from Preceding Period	
					Federal			Final State and Local				Gross Domestic Product	Domestic Purchases[1]
	Net Exports	Exports	Imports	Total	Total	National Defense	Non-defense						
1990	−61.9	564.4	626.3	1,250.4	541.9	401.5	140.5	708.6	6,126.7	6,199.8	6,157.0	1.2	.8
1991	−22.3	599.9	622.2	1,258.0	539.4	397.5	142.0	718.7	6,082.6	6,101.6	6,094.9	−.9	−1.6
1992	−29.5	639.4	669.0	1,263.8	528.0	375.8	152.2	735.9	6,237.4	6,274.0	6,255.5	2.7	2.8
1993	−70.2	658.2	728.4	1,252.1	505.7	354.4	151.2	746.4	6,368.9	6,459.0	6,408.0	2.3	2.9
1994	−104.6	712.4	817.0	1,252.3	486.6	336.9	149.5	765.7	6,551.2	6,712.7	6,619.1	3.5	3.9
1995	−96.5	792.6	889.0	1,254.5	470.6	323.5	146.9	783.9	6,731.7	6,855.0	6,779.5	2.3	2.1
1996	−111.2	860.0	971.2	1,268.2	465.6	319.1	146.2	802.7	6,961.6	7,101.1	7,008.4	3.4	3.6
1997	−136.1	970.0	1,106.1	1,285.0	458.0	308.9	148.6	827.1	7,203.7	7,396.5	7,266.2	3.9	4.2
1993: I	−54.7	647.2	701.9	1,250.1	512.1	359.2	152.9	738.0	6,297.3	6,382.3	6,351.3	.1	1.0
II	−62.6	660.1	722.7	1,253.1	507.8	356.7	151.1	745.3	6,344.9	6,422.0	6,375.9	2.0	2.5
III	−83.1	646.3	729.4	1,250.5	501.6	351.1	150.3	749.1	6,379.3	6,475.6	6,415.3	2.1	3.4
IV	−80.5	679.1	759.7	1,254.7	501.3	350.8	150.4	753.4	6,453.8	6,556.2	6,489.7	5.3	5.1
1994: I	−97.6	676.0	773.6	1,241.9	487.2	335.1	151.9	754.7	6,473.0	6,620.2	6,540.5	3.0	4.0
II	−103.9	704.1	808.0	1,243.3	481.2	335.9	145.1	762.2	6,526.7	6,701.8	6,609.3	4.7	5.0
III	−111.1	722.1	833.2	1,268.1	496.4	347.0	149.4	771.7	6,580.4	6,737.5	6,635.6	1.8	2.1
IV	−105.9	747.3	853.2	1,255.8	481.7	329.6	151.7	774.1	6,624.8	6,791.3	6,691.2	3.6	3.2
1995: I	−109.5	763.9	873.4	1,256.2	478.6	328.3	150.0	777.6	6,661.8	6,823.3	6,735.9	1.7	1.9
II	−114.7	774.0	888.7	1,259.9	476.2	328.4	147.6	783.7	6,700.0	6,834.6	6,746.3	.4	.7
III	−86.8	806.3	893.1	1,257.6	473.1	323.9	148.8	784.5	6,761.7	6,863.5	6,788.9	3.3	1.7
IV	−74.8	826.1	900.9	1,244.5	454.6	313.3	141.1	790.0	6,803.3	6,898.4	6,846.8	2.8	2.0
1996: I	−95.5	833.6	929.1	1,254.5	463.5	318.7	144.5	791.0	6,863.6	6,974.0	6,902.1	3.3	4.5
II	−113.5	845.5	958.9	1,276.2	472.6	325.0	147.3	803.6	6,954.7	7,092.8	6,999.0	6.1	7.0
III	−140.1	849.9	990.0	1,271.1	467.0	319.8	146.8	804.2	6,970.3	7,152.6	7,027.1	2.1	3.4
IV	−95.9	911.1	1,007.0	1,271.2	459.5	313.0	146.1	811.8	7,057.9	7,185.2	7,105.3	4.2	1.8
1997: I	−121.5	929.4	1,050.9	1,277.7	456.3	305.0	150.7	821.5	7,108.1	7,281.3	7,167.8	4.2	5.5
II	−131.6	963.6	1,095.2	1,284.4	460.4	311.7	148.2	824.2	7,155.5	7,359.4	7,239.3	4.0	4.4
III	−142.4	988.1	1,130.5	1,288.9	458.9	310.2	148.2	830.1	7,256.3	7,443.1	7,307.0	4.2	4.6
IV	−149.0	998.8	1,147.8	1,289.2	456.5	308.7	147.3	832.9	7,294.8	7,502.1	7,350.7	3.0	3.2
1998: I	−198.5	991.9	1,190.4	1,283.0	446.1	293.3	151.9	837.1	7,372.5	7,644.9	7,455.2	5.5	7.8
II	−245.2	972.1	1,217.3	1,294.8	454.1	300.3	152.9	840.9	7,456.4	7,718.6	7,485.9	1.8	3.9
III	−259.0	965.3	1,224.3	1,299.6	452.5	303.5	148.4	847.3	7,507.6	7,798.8	7,546.7	3.7	4.2

[1] Gross domestic product (GDP) less exports of goods and services plus imports of goods and services.
[2] GDP plus net receipts of factor income from rest of the world.

SOURCE: Department of Commerce, Bureau of Economic Analysis.

TABLE B-32 — GROSS SAVING AND INVESTMENT, 1959–98

[BILLIONS OF DOLLARS, EXCEPT AS NOTED; QUARTERLY DATA AT SEASONALLY ADJUSTED ANNUAL RATES]

	Gross Saving													Capital Grants Received by the United States (Net)[3]
		Gross Private Saving					Gross Government Saving							
				Gross Business Saving				Federal			State and Local			
Year or Quarter	Total	Total	Personal Saving	Total[1]	Undistributed Corporate Profits[2]	Corporate and Non-corporate Consumption of Fixed Capital	Total	Total	Consumption of Fixed Capital	Current Surplus or Deficit (–)	Total	Consumption of Fixed Capital	Current Surplus or Deficit (–)	
1959	108.5	82.3	25.2	57.1	16.5	40.5	26.2	12.8	10.2	2.6	13.5	3.9	9.6	—
1960	113.4	81.6	24.2	57.4	15.3	42.1	31.8	17.8	10.5	7.4	14.0	4.0	9.9	—
1961	116.3	98.0	29.2	58.8	15.7	43.1	28.3	13.6	10.7	2.9	14.7	4.3	10.4	—
1962	126.8	96.5	30.4	66.1	21.5	44.6	30.3	14.0	11.2	2.8	16.3	4.6	11.7	—
1963	134.9	99.3	29.5	70.2	24.0	46.2	35.1	17.2	11.8	5.4	17.9	4.9	13.0	—
1964	145.3	112.3	36.4	75.9	27.3	48.7	32.9	13.0	12.1	.9	19.9	5.2	14.7	—
1965	160.4	123.8	38.7	85.1	33.1	52.0	36.6	15.9	12.5	3.4	20.8	5.7	15.1	—
1966	171.1	131.9	40.1	91.9	35.2	56.7	39.2	15.6	13.0	2.6	23.5	6.3	17.3	—
1967	173.8	144.1	49.9	94.2	32.7	61.5	29.7	5.6	13.9	–8.3	24.1	6.8	17.3	—
1968	185.1	145.4	47.8	97.6	30.2	67.3	39.7	12.0	14.9	–2.8	27.6	7.6	20.0	—
1969	202.1	148.2	47.9	100.3	26.0	74.2	53.9	24.3	15.6	8.7	29.6	8.5	21.1	—
1970	197.3	163.8	62.0	101.8	20.7	81.2	32.6	2.2	16.2	–14.1	30.4	9.6	20.8	0.9
1971	214.3	189.7	69.9	119.8	30.5	88.9	23.9	–8.5	16.9	–25.3	32.4	10.7	21.7	.7
1972	243.9	201.7	65.2	136.5	39.0	97.8	41.5	–2.4	18.2	–20.5	43.9	11.7	32.2	.7
1973	296.4	241.3	91.5	149.7	42.7	107.1	55.1	8.7	19.9	–11.1	46.4	13.0	33.4	0
1974	301.2	251.7	100.2	151.5	27.0	124.5	51.5	5.1	22.0	–16.9	46.5	16.0	30.5	2.0[6]
1975	297.3	301.2	107.8	193.5	47.2	146.3	–3.9	–49.9	24.0	–73.9	46.0	18.4	27.6	0
1976	340.0	316.5	100.4	216.1	54.8	161.3	23.5	–31.9	25.4	–57.2	55.3	19.4	35.9	0
1977	394.7	348.6	97.2	251.4	70.5	181.0	46.1	–19.3	27.0	–46.3	65.4	20.7	44.7	0
1978	476.9	404.5	118.2	286.3	79.5	206.8	72.4	–2.8	28.9	–31.7	75.1	22.5	52.6	0
1979	540.6	448.8	136.2	312.5	72.6	239.9	90.7	13.0	31.5	–18.4	77.7	25.4	52.3	1.1
1980	547.2	489.2	169.1	320.1	44.1	276.0	56.8	–26.8	34.1	–61.0	83.6	29.2	54.4	1.2
1981	650.8	581.7	207.2	374.4	56.4	318.1	68.1	–20.6	37.1	–57.8	88.7	33.3	55.4	1.1
1982	604.3	609.6	210.9	398.7	52.5	346.2	–5.3	–92.8	41.9	–134.7	87.5	36.2	51.3	0
1983	589.0	618.4	169.7	448.7	83.6	365.2	–29.4	–131.8	42.6	–174.4	102.4	37.5	64.9	0
1984	750.7	736.7	241.5	495.2	116.8	378.4	14.0	–111.9	44.1	–156.0	125.9	39.0	86.9	0
1985	745.6	730.5	207.4	523.1	123.6	399.4	15.2	–116.9	46.1	–162.9	132.0	41.0	91.0	0
1986	719.8	708.9	188.6	520.3	95.9	424.4	10.8	–127.9	49.6	–177.5	138.8	43.9	94.9	0
1987	779.6	726.0	168.9	557.1	110.0	447.1	53.6	–77.2	51.7	–128.9	130.8	47.1	83.8	0
1988	876.0	807.2	195.2	612.0	134.0	478.0	68.9	–67.0	54.3	–121.3	135.8	49.9	85.9	0
1989	906.3	814.3	194.8	619.5	104.3	515.1	92.0	–56.4	57.0	–113.4	148.4	53.3	95.1	0

Year or Quarter	Gross Investment				Statistical Discrepancy	Addenda	
	Total	Gross Private Domestic Investment	Gross Government Investment[4]	Net Foreign Investment[5]		Gross Saving as a Percent of Gross National Product	Personal Saving as a Percent of Disposable Income
1959	106.9	78.8	29.3	−1.2	−1.6	21.3	7.2
1960	110.2	78.8	28.2	3.2	−3.2	21.4	6.6
1961	113.5	77.9	31.3	4.3	−2.8	21.2	7.7
1962	125.0	87.9	33.2	3.9	−1.8	21.5	7.6
1963	131.9	93.4	33.5	5.0	−3.0	21.7	7.0
1964	143.8	101.7	34.5	7.5	−1.5	21.7	7.9
1965	159.6	118.0	35.4	6.2	−.8	22.1	7.8
1966	174.4	130.4	40.1	3.9	3.3	21.6	7.5
1967	175.1	128.0	43.5	3.5	1.3	20.7	8.7
1968	186.0	139.9	44.3	1.7	.9	20.2	7.7
1969	200.7	155.0	43.9	1.8	−1.5	20.5	7.2
1970	199.1	150.2	44.0	4.9	1.9	18.9	8.5
1971	220.4	176.0	43.1	1.3	6.1	18.9	8.8
1972	248.1	205.6	45.4	−2.9	4.3	19.6	7.6
1973	299.9	242.9	48.3	8.7	3.4	21.2	9.5
1974	306.7	245.6	56.0	5.1	5.5	19.9	9.5
1975	309.5	225.4	62.7	21.4	12.1	18.1	9.3
1976	359.9	286.6	64.4	8.9	19.9	18.5	7.9
1977	413.0	356.6	65.4	−9.0	18.2	19.3	6.9
1978	494.9	430.9	74.6	−10.4	18.1	20.6	7.5
1979	568.7	480.9	85.3	2.6	28.2	20.9	7.7
1980	574.8	465.9	96.4	12.5	27.6	19.4	8.5
1981	665.7	556.2	102.1	7.4	14.9	20.7	9.4
1982	601.8	501.1	106.9	−6.1	−2.5	18.5	9.0
1983	626.2	547.1	116.5	−37.3	37.1	16.6	6.7
1984	755.7	715.6	131.7	−91.5	5.0	19.1	8.6
1985	748.0	715.1	149.9	−116.9	2.4	17.7	6.9
1986	743.1	722.5	163.5	−142.9	23.3	16.2	5.9
1987	764.2	747.2	173.5	−156.4	−15.4	16.6	5.0
1988	828.7	773.9	172.9	−118.1	−47.3	17.3	5.4
1989	919.5	829.2	182.7	−92.4	13.2	16.6	5.0

Continued

TABLE B-32   CONTINUED

Year or Quarter	Gross Saving Total	Gross Private Saving Total	Personal Saving	Gross Business Saving Total[1]	Undistributed Corporate Profits[2]	Corporate and Non-corporate Consumption of Fixed Capital	Gross Government Saving Total	Federal Total	Federal Consumption of Fixed Capital	Federal Current Surplus or Deficit (−)	State and Local Total	State and Local Consumption of Fixed Capital	State and Local Current Surplus or Deficit (−)	Capital Grants Received by the United States (Net)[3]
1990	903.1	860.3	213.3	647.0	112.7	534.3	42.7	−94.0	60.7	−154.7	136.7	56.6	80.1	0
1991	934.0	930.6	243.5	687.1	130.8	556.4	3.3	−132.2	63.9	−196.0	135.5	59.6	75.8	0
1992	904.3	970.7	264.1	706.6	137.1	585.4	−66.5	−215.0	65.9	−280.9	148.6	62.3	86.3	0
1993	949.5	979.3	210.3	769.0	170.1	594.5	−29.1	−182.7	67.9	−250.7	152.9	65.5	87.4	0
1994	1,079.2	1,030.2	176.8	853.4	201.4	638.6	49.0	−117.2	69.5	−186.7	166.2	69.4	96.8	0
1995	1,187.4	1,106.2	179.8	926.4	256.1	657.0	81.2	−103.7	70.7	−174.4	184.8	73.2	111.7	0
1996	1,274.5	1,114.5	158.5	956.0	262.4	684.3	160.0	−39.6	70.6	−110.3	199.6	77.1	122.6	0
1997	1,406.3	1,141.6	121.0	1,020.6	296.7	720.1	264.7	49.5	70.6	−21.1	215.2	81.1	134.1	0
1993: I	932.0	1,001.1	181.2	819.9	159.2	590.5	−69.1	−211.2	67.0	−278.2	142.1	64.3	77.8	0
II	942.1	977.3	231.0	746.3	158.3	588.0	45.2	−181.7	67.5	−249.2	146.5	65.2	81.3	0
III	943.8	973.3	200.5	772.8	171.8	601.1	−29.4	−182.2	68.4	−250.6	152.7	65.8	86.9	0
IV	980.1	965.6	228.7	736.9	191.0	598.1	14.5	−155.8	68.8	−224.6	170.4	66.6	103.7	0
1994: I	1,062.4	1,048.6	132.3	916.3	178.7	685.2	13.8	−139.9	69.1	−209.0	153.7	69.0	84.7	0
II	1,065.5	995.7	179.3	816.4	201.2	614.9	69.7	−93.6	69.6	−163.2	163.3	68.5	94.8	0
III	1,071.0	1,021.2	188.1	833.1	209.5	623.3	49.7	−118.3	69.3	−187.6	168.0	69.6	98.4	0
IV	1,118.0	1,055.3	207.5	847.8	216.2	631.2	62.7	−117.0	69.8	−186.8	179.7	70.4	109.3	0
1995: I	1,161.5	1,098.7	214.9	883.8	229.3	641.1	62.8	−119.4	70.3	−189.6	182.1	71.7	110.4	0
II	1,153.8	1,075.8	164.0	911.8	247.3	651.1	78.0	−107.2	70.7	−177.9	185.2	72.6	112.6	0
III	1,190.4	1,110.0	162.4	947.6	275.0	659.2	80.4	−106.2	70.7	−176.9	186.6	73.6	113.0	0
IV	1,224.0	1,140.5	178.0	962.5	272.7	676.4	103.5	−82.0	71.0	−153.0	185.4	74.7	110.7	0
1996: I	1,233.0	1,119.4	173.5	945.9	264.4	672.2	113.6	−79.4	70.7	−150.1	193.0	75.7	117.3	0
II	1,255.3	1,091.6	140.5	951.1	262.6	679.2	163.7	−41.9	70.7	−112.6	205.6	76.5	129.1	0
III	1298.8	1,128.6	172.2	956.4	258.7	688.5	170.2	−29.6	70.5	−100.1	199.8	77.5	122.3	0
IV	1,311.0	1,118.4	147.6	970.8	264.2	697.3	192.5	−7.6	70.7	−78.3	200.2	78.5	121.7	0
1997: I	1,353.9	1,126.3	135.4	990.9	281.4	705.8	227.5	19.6	70.8	−51.2	207.9	79.5	128.4	0
II	1,416.3	1,169.5	151.9	1,017.6	299.0	715.0	246.9	36.1	70.9	−34.8	210.7	80.6	130.1	0
III	1,427.0	1,139.0	98.5	1,040.5	311.5	725.2	288.0	70.0	70.3	−.3	218.0	81.4	136.6	0
IV	1,428.0	1,131.6	98.2	1,033.4	295.0	734.7	296.4	72.3	70.2	2.2	224.1	82.7	141.4	0
1998: I	1,482.5	1,130.1	73.0	1,057.1	312.0	741.1	352.4	128.7	69.9	58.8	223.7	83.5	140.2	0
II	1,448.5	1,079.0	25.6	1,053.4	300.9	748.5	369.4	143.9	69.5	74.4	225.6	84.3	141.3	0
III	1,474.5	1,078.7	12.6	1,066.1	304.8	757.3	395.7	161.6	69.6	92.0	234.2	85.4	148.7	0

[1] Includes private wage accruals less disbursements not shown separately.
[2] With inventory valuation and capital consumption adjustments.
[3] Consists mainly of allocations of special drawing rights (SDRs).

TABLE B-32   CONTINUED

Year or Quarter	Gross Investment				Statistical Discrepancy	Addenda	
	Total	Gross Private Domestic Investment	Gross Government Investment[4]	Net Foreign Investment[5]		Gross Saving as a Percent of Gross National Product	Personal Saving as a Percent of Disposable Income
1990	920.5	799.7	199.4	−78.6	17.4	15.7	5.1
1991	944.0	736.2	200.5	7.3	10.1	15.7	5.6
1992	949.1	790.4	209.1	−50.5	44.8	14.5	5.7
1993	1,002.1	876.2	204.5	−78.6	52.6	14.4	4.4
1994	1,093.8	1,007.9	205.9	−120.0	14.6	15.5	3.5
1995	1,160.9	1,043.2	218.3	−100.6	−26.5	16.3	3.4
1996	1,242.3	1,131.9	229.7	−119.2	−32.2	16.6	2.9
1997	1,350.5	1,256.0	235.4	−140.9	−55.8	17.4	2.1
1993: I	1,003.0	854.3	202.9	−54.2	771.0	14.4	3.9
II	989.0	857.4	206.5	−74.9	46.9	14.4	4.8
III	991.3	872.8	203.4	−84.9	47.5	14.3	4.2
IV	1,025.1	920.3	205.2	−100.4	45.0	14.6	4.7
1994: I	1,068.7	963.4	197.0	−91.6	1.3	15.6	2.7
II	1,107.8	1,017.9	202.4	−112.5	42.4	−15.4	3.6
III	1,086.2	1,007.1	213.2	−134.2	15.2	15.3	3.7
IV	1,112.6	1,043.1	211.2	−141.8	−5.4	15.8	4.0
1995: I	1,164.6	1,058.9	216.3	−110.7	3.1	16.2	4.1
II	1,131.1	1,029.6	219.6	−118.0	−22.7	16.0	3.1
III	1,147.3	1,030.6	216.8	400.1	43.0	16.3	3.1
IV	1,200.8	1,053.6	220.7	−73.5	43.2	16.8	3.3
1996: I	1,206.7	1,075.3	229.2	−97.8	−26.3	16.4	3.2
II	1,234.7	1,118.3	231.3	−114.9	−20.6	16.4	2.6
III	1,249.5	1,167.9	227.9	−146.2	−49.3	16.8	3.1
IV	1,278.3	1,166.0	230.3	−118.0	−32.6	16.7	2.6
1997: I	1,310.8	1,206.4	235.3	−130.9	−43.1	17.0	2.4
II	1,368.6	1,2593	232.6	−123.9	−47.7	17.6	2.6
III	1,361.9	1,265.7	237.3	−141.0	−45.1	17.5	1.7
IV	1,360.7	1,292.0	236.5	−167.8	−47.3	17.3	1.7
1998: I	1,428.4	1,366.6	237.4	−175.6	−54.1	17.7	1.2
II	1,362.7	1,345.0	232.5	−214.8	−85.7	17.2	.4
III	1,372.5	1,364.4	239.7	−231.6	−102.0	17.3	.2

[4]For details on government investment, see Table B-20.

[5]Net exports of goods and services plus net receipts of factor income from rest of the world less net transfers plus net capital grants received by the United States/ See also Table B-24.

[6]Consists of a U.S. payment to India under the Agricultural Trade Development and Assistance Act, This payment is included in capital grants received by the United States, net.

SOURCE: Department of Commerce, Bureau of Economic Analysis.

TABLE B-35	CIVILIAN POPULATION AND LABOR FORCE, 1929–98

[MONTHLY DATA SEASONALLY ADJUSTED, EXCEPT AS NOTED]

Year or Month	Civilian Non-institutional Population[1]	Civilian Labor Force					Not in Labor Force	Civilian Labor Force Parti-cipation Rate[2]	Civilian Employment/ Population Ratio[3]	Unemploy-ment Rate Civilian Workers[4]
		Total	Employment			Unem-ployment				
			Total	Agri-cultural	Nonagri-cultural					
		Thousands of Persons 14 Years of Age and Over						Percent		
1929	—	49,180	47,630	10,450	37,180	1,550	—	—	—	3.2
1933	—	51,590	38,760	10,090	28,670	12,830	—	—	—	24.9
1939	—	55,230	45,750	9,610	36,140	9,480	—	—	—	17.2
1940	99,840	55,640	47,520	9,540	37,980	8,120	44,200	55.7	47.6	14.6
1941	99,900	55,910	50,350	9,100	41,250	5,560	43,990	56.0	50.4	9.9
1942	98,640	56,410	53,750	9,250	44,500	2,660	42,230	57.2	54.5	4.7
1943	94,640	55,540	54,470	9,080	45,390	1,070	39,100	58.7	57.6	1.9
1944	93,220	54,630	53,960	8,950	45,010	670	38,590	58.6	57.9	1.2
1945	94,090	53,860	52,820	8,580	44,240	1,040	40,230	57.2	56.1	1.9
1946	103,070	57,520	55,250	8,320	46,930	2,270	45,550	55.8	53.6	3.9
1947	106,018	60,168	57,812	8,256	49,557	2,356	45,850	56.8	54.5	3.9
		Thousands of Persons 16 Years of Age and Over								
1947	101,827	59,350	57,038	7,890	49,148	2,311	42,477	58.3	56.0	3.9
1948	103,068	60,621	58,343	7,629	50,714	2,276	42,447	58.8	56.6	3.8
1949	103,994	61,286	57,651	7,658	49,993	3,637	42,708	58.9	55.4	5.9
1950	104,995	62,208	58,918	7,160	51,758	3,288	42,787	59..2	56.1	5.3
1951	104,621	62,017	59,961	6,726	53,235	2,055	42,604	59.2	57.3	3.3
1952	105,231	62,138	60,250	6,500	53,749	1,883	43,093	59.0	57.3	3.0
1953[5]	107,056	63,015	61,179	6,260	54,919	1,834	44,041	58.9	57.1	2.9
1954	108,321	63,643	60,109	6,205	53,904	3,532	44,678	58.8	55.5	5.5
1955	109,683	65,023	62,170	6,450	55,722	2,852	44,660	59.3	56.7	4.4
1956	110,954	66,552	63,799	6,283	57,514	2,750	44,402	60.0	57.5	4.1
1957	112,265	66,929	64,071	5,947	58,123	2,859	45,336	59.6	57.1	4.3
1958	113,727	67,639	63,036	5,586	57,450	4,602	46,088	59.5	55.4	6.8
1959	115,329	68,369	64,630	5,565	59,065	3,740	46,960	59.3	56.0	5.5
1960[5]	117,245	69,628	65,778	5,458	60,318	3,852	47,617	59.4	56.1	5.5
1961	118,771	70,459	65,746	5,200	60,546	4,714	48,312	59.3	55.4	6.7
1962[5]	120,153	70,614	66,702	4,944	61,759	3,911	49,539	58.8	55.5	5.5
1963	122,416	71,833	67,762	4,687	63,076	4,070	50,583	58.7	55.4	5.7
1964	124,485	73,091	69,305	4,523	64,782	3,786	51,394	58.7	55.7	5.2
1965	126,513	74,455	71,088	4,361	66,726	3,366	52,058	58.9	56.2	4.5
1966	128,058	75,770	72,895	3,979	68,915	2,875	52,288	59.2	56.9	3.8
1967	129,874	77,347	74,372	3,844	70,527	2,975	52,527	59.6	57.3	3.8
1968	132,028	78,737	75,920	3,817	72,103	2,817	53,291	59.6	57.5	3.6
1969	134,335	80,734	77,920	3,606	74,296	2,832	53,602	60.1	58.0	3.5

TABLE B-35   CONTINUED

Year or Month	Civilian Non-institutional Population[1]	Civilian Labor Force					Not in Labor Force	Civilian Labor Force Participation Rate[2]	Civilian Employment/ Population Ratio[3]	Unemployment Rate Civilian Workers[4]
		Total	Employment			Unem-ployment				
			Total	Agri-cultural	Nonagri-cultural					
		Thousands of Persons 16 Years of Age and Over						Percent		
1970	137,085	82,771	78,678	3,463	75,215	4,093	54,315	60.4	57.4	4.9
1971	140,216	84,382	79,367	3,394	75,972	5,016	55,834	60.2	56.6	5.9
1972[5]	144,126	87,034	82,153	3,484	78,669	4,882	57,091	60.4	57.0	5.6
1973[5]	147,096	89,429	85,064	3,470	81,594	4,365	57,667	60.8	57.8	4.9
1974	150,120	91,949	86,794	3,515	83,279	5,156	58,171	61.3	57.8	5.6
1975	153,153	93,775	85,846	3,408	82,438	7,929	59,377	61.2	56.1	8.5
1976	156,150	96,158	88,752	3,331	85,421	7,406	59,991	61.6	56.8	7.7
1977	159,033	99,009	92,017	3,283	88,734	6,991	60,025	62.3	57.9	7.1
1978[5]	161,910	102,251	96,048	3,387	92,661	6,202	92,661	63.2	59.3	6.1
1979	164,863	104,962	98,824	3,347	95,477	6,137	59,900	63.7	59.9	5.8
1980	167,745	106,940	99,303	3,364	95,938	7,637	60,806	63.8	59.2	7.1
1981	170,130	108,670	100,397	3,368	97,030	8,273	61,460	63.9	59.0	7.6
1982	172,271	110,204	99,526	3,401	96,125	10,678	62,067	64.0	57.8	9.7
1983	174,215	111,550	100,834	3,383	97,450	10,717	62,665	64.0	57.9	9.6
1984	176,383	113,544	105,005	3,321	101,685	8,539	62,839	64.4	59.5	7.5
1985	178,206	115,461	107,150	3,179	103,971	8,312	62,744	64.8	60.1	7.2
1986[5]	180,587	117,834	109,597	3,163	106,434	8,237	62,752	65.3	60.7	7.0
1987	182,753	119,865	112,440	3,208	109,232	7,425	62,888	65.6	61.5	6.2
1988	194,613	121,669	114,968	3,169	111,,800	6,701	62,944	65.9	62.3	5.5
1989	186,393	123,869	117,342	3,199	114,142	6,528	62,523	66.5	63.0	5.3
1990[5]	189,164	125,840	118, 793	3,223	115,570	7,047	63,324	66.5	62.8	5.6
1991	190,925	126,346	117,718	3,269	114,449	8,628	64,578	66.2	61.7	6.8
1992	192,805	128,105	118,492	3,247	115,245	9,613	64,700	66.4	61.5	7.5
1993	194,838	129,200	120,259	3,115	117,144	8,940	65,638	66.3	61.7	6.9
1994[5]	196,814	131,056	123,060	3,409	119,651	7,996	65,758	66.6	62.5	6.1
1995	198,584	132,304	124,900	3,440	121,460	7,404	66,280	66.6	62.9	5.6
1996	200,591	133,943	126,708	3,443	123,264	7,236	66,647	66.8	63.2	5.4
1997[5]	203,133	136,297	129,558	3,399	126,159	6,739	66,837	67.1	63.8	4.9
1998[5]	205,220	137,673	131,463	3,378	128,085	6,210	67,547	67.1	64.1	4.5

[1]Not seasonally adjusted.
[2]Civilian labor force as percent of civilian noninstitutional population.
[3]Civilian employment as percent of civilian noninstitutional population.
[4]Unemployed as percent of civilian labor force.

TABLE B-50   CHANGES IN PRODUCTIVITY AND RELATED DATA, BUSINESS SECTOR, 1959–98

[PERCENT CHANGE FROM PRECEDING PERIOD., QUARTERLY DATA AT SEASONALLY ADJUSTED ANNUAL RATES]

Year or Quarter	Output per Hour of All Persons — Business Sector	Nonfarm Business Sector	Output[1] Business Sector	Nonfarm Business Sector	Hours of All Persons[2] Business Sector	Nonfarm Business Sector	Compensation per Hour[3] Business Sector	Nonfarm Business Sector	Real Compensation per Hour[4] Business Sector	Nonfarm Business Sector	Unit Labor Costs Business Sector	Nonfarm Business Sector	Implicit Price Deflator[5] Business Sector	Nonfarm Business Sector
1959	4.2	4.2	8.5	9.0	4.1	4.6	4.2	4.0	3.5	3.2	0	–0.2	0.6	1.1
1960	1.7	1.2	1.1	1.6	.1	.5	4.3	4.4	2.6	2.7	2.5	3.1	1.1	1.1
1961	3.5	3.1	1.9	1.9	4.6	–1.2	4.0	3.4	2.9	2.4	.4	.3	.9	.9
1962	4.7	4.6	6.5	6.9	1.7	2.1	4.5	4.1	3.5	3.0	.2	–.5	.9	.8
1963	3.9	3.4	4.5	4.5	.6	1.1	3.7	3.5	2.3	2.2	–.2	.1	.7	.8
1964	4.6	4.3	6.4	6.8	1.7	2.4	5.2	4.6	3.8	3.3	.3	.3	1.0	1.2
1965	3.5	3.0	7.0	7.0	3.4	3.9	3.7	3.3	2.1	1.7	.2	.3	1.7	1.5
1966	4.0	3.5	6.7	7.1	2.6	3.6	6.7	5.8	3.3	2.8	2.6	2.3	2.5	2.3
1967	2.2	1.7	1.9	1.7	–.3	–.0	5.7	5.8	2.5	2.7	3.4	4.0	2.9	3.3
1%8	3.4	3.4	4.9	5.2	1.4	1.7	8.2	7.9	3.8	3.5	4.6	4.3	3.9	3.9
1969	.4	.1	3.0	3.0	2.5	2.9	7.0	6.8	1.5	1.3	6.6	6.7	4.3	4.2
1970	2.0	1.4	–.1	–.2	–2.0	–1.6	7.0	7.2	1.9	1.4	5.7	5.7	4.4	4.5
1971	4.3	4.1	3.8	3.8	–.4	–.3	6.4	6.5	1.9	2.0	2.0	2.3	4.5	4.5
1972	3.3	3.4	6.7	6.9	3.3	3.4	6.3	6.4	3.0	3.1	2.9	2.9	3.3	2.9
1973	3.2	3.1	7.0	7.3	3.7	4.0	8.6	8.2	2.2	1.9	5.2	4.9	5.2	3.6
1974	–1.7	–1.6	–1.5	–1.5	.1	.1	9.7	9.9	4.2	–1.1	11.6	11.6	9.4	10.0
1975	3.5	2.7	–1.4	–1.7	4.3	4.3	10.3	10.1	1.0	.9	6.6	7.2	9.5	10.6
1976	1.4	3.6	6.7	7.1	3.1	3.4	1.8	8.6	2.9	2.7	5.2	4.9	5.4	5.6
1977	1.7	1.6	5.7	5.7	3.9	4.0	7.9	8.0	1.3	1.4	6.0	6.3	6.1	6.4
1978	1.1	1.3	6.1	6.4	4.9	5.0	3.9	9.1	1.3	1.4	7.7	7.6	7.3	6.9
1979	–.4	–.8	2.9	2.8	3.4	3.6	9.7	9.5	–1.5	4.3	10.1	10.1	8.6	8.6
1980	–.3	–.4	–1.2	–1.2	–.9	–.8	10.3	10.8	–2.4	–2.4	11.1	11.2	9.1	9.8
1981	1.3	1.1	2.5	1.9	.7	.7	9.5	1.7	–.8	–.6	7.6	8.5	9.3	1.6
1982	–.5	–.8	–3.1	–3.2	–2.5	–2.5	7.5	7.4	1.2	1.1	8.0	8.2	5.9	6.4
1983	3.2	4.1	4.9	6.1	1.7	1.9	4.1	4.2	.9	1.1	.9	.1	3.7	3.4
1984	2.5	1.7	8.5	7.9	5.8	6.0	4.4	4.2	.0	–.1	1.8	2.5	3.0	3.1
1985	1.6	1.0	3.9	3.6	2.1	2.5	4.9	4.6	1.3	1.0	3.2	3.6	3.0	3.4
1986	2.6	2.6	3.3	3.4	.7	.8	5.2	5.2	3.3	3.2	2.5	2.5	2.1	2.2
1987	–.1	–.2	2.9	3.0	3.0	3.2	3.9	3.8	.2	.1	1.9	4.0	2.6	2.6
1988	.7	.8	3.8	4.1	3.1	3.3	4.7	4.5	.6	.4	4.0	3.7	3.5	3.4
1989	.1	.6	3.4	3.2	2.5	2.6	2.8	2.7	–1.9	–2.0	1.9	2.1	4.1	4.2
1990	.7	.5	.8	.7	.2	.3	5.7	5.5	.3	.1	5.0	5.0	4.0	4.2
1991	.6	.7	4.7	–1.8	–2.3	–2.4	4.8	4.9	.5	.7	4.1	4.1	3.8	4.1
1992	3.4	3.1	3.2	3.0	–.2	–.1	5.2	5.1	2.1	2.1	1.7	1.9	2.4	2.4
1993	.1	.1	2.7	3.0	2.6	2.9	2.5	2.2	–.5	–.7	2.4	2.2	2.5	2.5

TABLE B-50   CONTINUED

Year or Quarter	Output per Hour of All Persons Business Sector	Output per Hour of All Persons Nonfarm Business Sector	Output[1] Business Sector	Output[1] Nonfarm Business Sector	Hours of All Persons[2] Business Sector	Hours of All Persons[2] Nonfarm Business Sector	Compensation per Hour[3] Business Sector	Compensation per Hour[3] Nonfarm Business Sector	Real Compensation per Hour[4] Business Sector	Real Compensation per Hour[4] Nonfarm Business Sector	Unit Labor Costs Business Sector	Unit Labor Costs Nonfarm Business Sector	Implicit Price Deflator[5] Business Sector	Implicit Price Deflator[5] Nonfarm Business Sector
1994	.6	.5	4.1	3.9	3.5	3.3	1.8	1.9	−.7	−.6	1.2	1.4	2.2	2.3
1995	.3	.6	2.7	3.0	2.4	2.4	2.3	2.4	−.5	−.5	2.0	1.8	2.0	2.0
1996	2.7	2.4	4.2	4.1	1.5	1.6	1.6	3.5	.7	.6	.9	1.1	1.6	1.4
1997	1.7	1.4	4.6	4.5	2.9	3.0	3.8	3.7	1.5	1.4	2.1	2.3	1.7	1.9
1993: I	4.4	−4.6	−1.2	−.8	3.4	3.9	1.8	1.1	−1.0	4.6	6.6	6.0	3.5	3.8
II	−.6	−1.1	.7	2.6	3.3	3.7	3.3	2.9	.3	−.1	4.0	4.0	2.1	1.7
III	.5	1.6	2.8	3.9	2.2	2.4	1.5	1.1	−.4	−.6	1.1	−.2	1.6	1.5
IV	3.8	2.7	7.1	6.1	3.2	3.2	1.0	1.1	−2.2	−2.1	−2.7	−1.6	2.7	2.6
1994: I	0	−.2	2.6	1.6	2.6	1.1	4.0	4.3	2.0	2.3	4.0	4.5	2.0	2.1
II	−.1	.5	6.4	6.6	6.5	6.1	−.3	.2	−2.8	−2.3	−.2	−.3	2.1	2.5
III	4.4	−1.2	1.5	1.5	3.0	3.4	.8	.5	−2.8	4.1	2.3	2.4	2.7	3.2
IV	1.2	1.8	4.6	5.0	3.3	3.1	3.2	3.5	.7	1.0	1.9	1.7	2.5	2.4
1995: I	−1.0	−.4	2.0	2.5	3.0	2.9	2.1	2.0	−5	−.6	3.1	2.5	1.9	1.9
II	.9	.9	.3	.5	−.4	−.5	3.0	2.8	−.4	−.6	2.0	1.8	1.6	1.6
III	1.3	1.8	4.4	4.9	3.1	3.1	2.9	3.1	.8	.9	1.5	1.2	1.6	1.2
IV	3.2	2.6	3.6	3.3	.4	.7	3.8	3.5	1.3	1.0	.6	.9	1.3	.9
1996: I	4.4	4.1	4.5	4.2	.1	.0	2.5	2.6	−.7	−.5	4.9	−1.5	1.9	1.7
II	3.5	3.0	6.4	6.4	2.9	3.3	5.6	5.2	1.8	1.4	2.1	2.2	1.7	1.3
III	.1	0	2.5	2.5	2.4	2.4	4.0	1.7	1.5	1.3	3.8	3.7	1.6	1.4
IV	1.5	1.2	5.1	5.0	3.5	3.7	3.4	3.3	.0	−.0	1.8	2.1	1.5	2.2
1997: I	1.0	.5	4.9	4.5	3.9	4.1	3.9	4.0	1.7	1.8	2.8	3.6	2.5	3.1
II	2.0	1.8	4.7	4.5	2.6	2.6	2.6	2.6	1.3	1.2	.6	.7	1.4	1.5
III	3.7	3.6	4.9	4.8	1.2	1.2	4.1	1.9	2.1	2.0	.4	.3	1.1	1.4
IV	.9	.9	3.6	4.0	2.7	3.0	5.3	4.9	3.1	2.8	4.4	4.0	.9	.9
1998: I	4.1	3.5	7.1	7.0	2.9	3.4	4.9	4.6	4.4	4.1	.8	1.1	.2	.6
II	.1	.3	1.7	1.7	1.7	1.5	4.1	4.0	2.0	2.0	4.0	3.7	.3	.2
III	3.1	3.0	4.3	4.2	1.1	1.2	3.8	4.1	2.0	2.2	.7	1.1	.3	.6

[1]Output refers to real gross domestic product in the sector.
[2]Hours at work of all persons engaged in the sector, including hours of proprietors and unpaid family workers. Estimates based primarily an establishment data.
[3]Wages and salaries of employees plus employers' contributions for social insurance and private benefit plans, Also includes an estimate of wages, salaries, and supplemental payments for the self–employed.
[4]Hourly compensation divided by the consumer index for all urban consumers.
[5]Current dollar output divided by the output index.
Note: Percent changes are based on original data and may differ slightly from percent changes based on indexes in Table B-49.

SOURCE: Department of Labor, Bureau of Labor Statistics,

Government Finance

FEDERAL RECEIPTS, OUTLAYS, SURPLUS OR DEFICIT, AND DEBT, SELECTED FISCAL YEARS, 1929–2000

[BILLIONS OF DOLLARS; FISCAL YEARS]

Fiscal Year or Period	Total			On Budget			Off Budget			Federal Debt (End of Period)		Addendum: Gross Domestic Product
	Receipts	Outlays	Surplus or Deficit (–)	Receipts	Outlays	Surplus or Deficit (–)	Receipts	Outlays	Surplus or Deficit (–)	Gross Federal	Held by the Public	
1929	3.9	3.1	0.7	3.9	3.1	0.7	—	—	—	16.9[1]	—	—
1933	2.0	4.6	–2.6	2.0	4.6	–2.6	—	—	—	22.5[1]	—	57.4
1939	6.3	9.1	–2.8	5.8	9.2	–3.4	0.5	–0.0	0.5	48.2	41.4	88.9
1940	6.5	9.5	–2.9	6.0	9.5	–3.5	.6	–.0	.6	50.7	42.8	96.5
1941	8.7	13.7	–4.9	8.0	13.6	–5.6	.7	.0	.7	57.5	48.2	113.9
1942	14.6	35.1	–20.5	13.7	35.1	–21.3	.9	.1	.8	79.2	67.8	144.2
1943	24.0	78.6	–54.6	22.9	78.5	–55.6	1.1	.1	1.0	142.6	127.8	180.0
1944	43.7	91.3	–47.6	42.5	91.2	–48.7	1.3	.1	1.2	204.1	184.8	209.0
1945	45.2	92.7	–47.6	43.8	92.6	–48.7	1.3	.1	1.2	260.1	235.2	221.4
1946	39.3	55.2	–15.9	38.1	55.0	–17.0	1.2	.2	1.0	271.0	241.9	222.9
1947	38.5	34.5	4.0	37.1	34.2	2.9	1.5	.3	1.2	257.1	224.3	234.9
1948	41.6	29.8	11.8	39.9	29.4	10.5	1.6	.4	1.2	252.0	216.3	256.6
1949	39.4	38.8	.6	37.7	38.4	–.7	1.7	.4	1.3	252.6	214.3	271.7
1950	39.4	42.6	–3.1	37.3	42.0	–4.7	2.1	.5	1.6	256.9	219.0	273.6
1951	51.6	45.5	6.1	48.5	44.2	4.3	3.1	1.3	1.8	255.3	214.3	321.3
1952	66.2	67.7	–1.5	62.6	66.0	–3.4	3.6	1.7	1.9	259.1	214.8	348.9
1953	69.6	76.1	–6.5	65.5	73.8	–8.3	4.1	2.3	1.8	266.0	218.4	373.1
1954	69.7	70.9	–1.2	65.1	67.9	–2.8	4.6	2.9	1.7	270.8	224.5	378.0
1955	65.5	68.4	–3.0	60.4	64.5	–4.1	5.1	4.0	1.1	274.4	226.6	395.3
1956	74.6	70.6	3.9	68.2	65.7	2.5	6.4	5.0	1.5	272.7	222.2	427.6
1957	80.0	76.6	3.4	73.2	70.6	2.6	6.8	6.0	.8	272.3	219.3	450.5
1958	79.6	82.4	–2.8	71.6	74.9	–3.3	8.0	7.5	.5	279.7	226.3	460.6
1959	79.2	92.1	–12.8	71.0	83.1	–12.1	8.3	9.0	–.7	287.5	234.7	491.8
1960	92.5	92.2	.3	81.9	81.3	.5	10.6	10.9	–.2	290.5	236.8	518.2
1961	94.4	97.7	–3.3	82.3	86.0	–3.8	12.1	11.7	.4	292.6	238.4	530.9
1962	99.7	106.8	–7.1	87.4	93.3	–5.9	12.3	13.5	–1.3	302.9	248.0	567.5
1963	106.6	111.3	–4.8	92.4	96.4	–4.0	14.2	15.0	–.8	310.3	254.0	598.3
1964	112.6	118.5	–5.9	96.2	102.8	–6.5	16.4	15.7	.6	316.1	256.8	640.0
1965	116.8	118.2	–1.4	100.1	101.7	–1.6	16.7	16.5	.2	322.3	260.8	686.7
1966	130.8	134.5	–3.7	111.7	114.8	–3.1	19.1	19.7	–.6	328.5	263.7	752.8
1967	148.8	157.5	–8.6	124.4	137.0	–12.6	24.4	20.4	4.0	340.4	266.6	811.9
1968	153.0	178.1	–25.2	128.1	155.8	–27.7	24.9	22.3	2.6	368.7	289.5	868.1
1969	186.9	183.6	3.2	157.9	158.4	–.5	29.0	25.2	3.7	365.8	278.1	947.9

TABLE B-78   CONTINUED

Fiscal Year or Period	Total			On Budget			Off Budget			Federal Debt (End of Period)		Addendum: Gross Domestic Product
	Receipts	Outlays	Surplus or Deficit (–)	Receipts	Outlays	Surplus or Deficit (–)	Receipts	Outlays	Surplus or Deficit (–)	Gross Federal	Held by the Public	
1970	192.8	195.6	–2.8	159.3	168.0	–8.7	33.5	27.6	5.9	380.9	283.2	1,009.0
1971	187.1	210.2	–23.0	151.3	177.3	–26.1	35.8	32.8	3.0	408.2	303.0	1,077.7
1972	207.3	230.7	–23.4	167.4	193.8	–26.4	39.9	36.9	3.1	435.9	322.4	1,176.9
1973	230.8	245.7	–14.9	184.7	200.1	–15.4	46.1	45.6	.5	466.3	340.9	1,306.8
1974	263.2	269.4	–6.1	209.3	217.3	–8.0	53.9	52.1	1.8	483.9	343.7	1,438.1
1975	279.1	332.3	–53.2	216.6	271.9	–55.3	62.5	60.4	2.0	541.9	394.7	1,554.5
1976	298.1	371.8	–73.7	231.7	302.2	–70.5	66.4	69.6	–3.2	629.0	477.4	1,730.4
Transition quarter	81.2	96.0	–14.7	63.2	76.6	–13.3	18.0	19.4	–1.4	643.6	495.5	454.8
1977	355.6	409.2	–53.7	278.7	328.5	–49.8	76.8	80.7	–3.9	706.4	549.1	1,971.4
1978	399.6	458.7	–59.2	314.2	369.1	–54.9	85.4	89.7	–4.3	776.6	607.1	2,212.6
1979	463.3	504.0	–40.7	365.3	404.1	–38. 7	98.0	100.0	–2.0	829.5	640.3	2,495.9
1980	517.1	590.9	–73.8	403.9	476.6	–72.7	113.2	114.3	–1.1	909.1	709.8	2,718.9
1981	599.3	678.2	–79.0	469.1	543.1	–74.0	130.2	135.2	–5.0	994.8	785.3	3,049.1
1982	617.8	745.8	–128.0	474.3	594.4	–120.1	143.5	151.4	–7.9	1,137.3	919.8	3,211.3
1983	600.6	808.4	–207.8	453.2	661.3	–208.0	147.3	147.1	.2	1,371.7	1,131.6	3,421.9
1984	666.5	851.9	–185.4	500.4	686.1	–185.7	166.1	165.8	.3	1,564.7	1,300.5	3,812.0
1985	734.1	946.4	–212.3	547.9	769.6	–221.7	186.2	176.8	9.4	1,817.5	1,499.9	4,102.1
1986	769.2	990.5	–221.2	569.0	807.0	–238.0	200.2	183.5	16.7	2,120.6	1,736.7	4,374.3
1987	854.4	1,004.1	–149.8	641.0	810.3	–169.3	213.4	193.8	19.6	2,346.1	1,888.7	4,605.1
1988	909.3	1,064.5	–155.2	667.8	861.8	–194.0	241.5	202.7	38.8	2,601.3	2,050.8	4,953.5
1989	991.2	1,143.7	–152.5	727.5	932.8	–205.2	263.7	210.9	52.8	2,868.0	2,189.9	5,351.8
1990	1,032.0	1,253.2	–221.2	750.3	1,028.1	–277.8	281.7	225.1	56.6	3,206.6	2,410.7	5,684.5
1991	1,055.0	1,324.4	–269.4	761.2	1,082.7	–321.6	293.9	241.7	52.2	3,598.5	2,688.1	5,858.8
1992	1,091.3	1,381.7	–290.4	788.9	1,129.3	–340.5	302.4	252.3	50.1	4,002.1	2,998.8	6,143.2
1993	1,154.4	1,409.4	–255.0	842.5	1,142.8	–300.4	311.9	266.6	45.3	4,351.4	3,247.5	6,475.1
1994	1,258.6	1,461.7	–203.1	923.6	1,182.4	–258.8	335.0	279.4	55.7	4,643.7	3,432. 1	6,845.7
1995	1,351.8	1,515.7	–163.9	1,000.8	–1,227.1	–226.3	351.1	288.7	62.4	4,921.0	3,603.4	7,197.7
1996	1,453.1	1,560.5	–107.5	1,085.6	1,259.6	–174.0	367.5	300.9	66.6	5,181.9	3,733.0	7,549.2
1997	1,579.3	1,601.2	–21.9	1,187.3	1,290.6	–103.3	392.0	310.6	81.4	5,369.7	3,771.1	7,996.5
1998	1,721.8	1,652.6	69.2	1,306.0	1,335.9	–29.9	415.8	316.6	99.2	5,478.7	3,719.9	8,404.5
1999[2]	1,806.3	1,727.1	79.3	1,362.3	1,404.0	–41.7	444.0	323.1	121.0	5,614.9	3,669.7	8,747.9
2000[2]	1,883.0	1,765.7	117.3	1,417.7	1,429.8	–12.2	465.3	335.9	129.5	5,711.4	3,517.8	9,105.8

[1] Not strictly comparable with later data.

[2] Estimates.

Note: Through fiscal year 1976, the fiscal year was on a July 1–June 30 basis; beginning October 1976 (fiscal year 1977), the fiscal year is as an October 1–September 30 basis. The 3-month period from July 1, 1976 through September 30, 1976 is a separate fiscal period known as the transition quarter.

Refunds of receipts are excluded from receipts and outlays.

See *Budget of the United States Government, Fiscal Year 2000*, February 1999, for additional information.

SOURCES: Department of Commerce (Bureau of Economic Analysis), Department of the Treasury, and Office of Management and Budget.

TABLE B-81	FEDERAL RECEIPTS, DEFICIT, AND DEBT, FISCAL YEAR 1994–2000

[MILLIONS OF DOLLARS; FISCAL YEARS]

	Actual					Estimates	
	1994	**1995**	**1996**	**1997**	**1998**	**1999**	**2000**
Receipts and Outlays							
Total receipts	1,258,627	1,351,830	1,453,062	1,579,292	1,721,798	1,806,334	1,882,992
Total outlays	1,461,731	1,515,729	1,560,512	1,601,232	1,652,552	1,727,071	1,765,687
Total surplus or deficit	−203,104	−163,899	−107,450	−21,940	69,246	79,263	117,305
On-budget receipts	923,601	1,000,751	1,085,570	1,187,302	1,305,999	1,362,298	1,417,678
On-budget outlays	1,182,359	1,227,065	1,259,608	1,290,606	1,335,948	1,404,015	1,429,830
On-budget surplus or deficit (−)	−258,759	−226,314	−174,038	−103,304	−29,949	−41,717	−12,152
Off-budget receipts	335,026	351,079	367,492	391,990	415,799	444,036	465,314
Off-budget outlays	279,372	288,664	300,904	310,626	316,604	323,056	335,857
Off-budget surplus or deficit	55,654	62,415	66,588	81,364	99,195	120,980	129,457
Outstanding Debt, End of Period							
Gross Federal debt	4,643,705	4,921,018	5,181,934	5,369,707	5,478,724	5,614,934	5,711,380
Held by Government accounts	1,211,588	1,317,645	1,448,967	1,598,559	1,758,846	1,945,197	2,139,550
Held by the public	3,432,117	3,603,373	3,732,968	3,771,148	3,719,878	3,669,737	3,571,830
Federal Reserve System	355,150	374,114	390,924	424,507	458,131	—	—
Other	3,076,967	3,229,259	3,342,043	3,346,641	3,261,747	—	—
Receipts: On-Budget and Off Budget	1,258,627	1,351,830	1,453,062	1,579,292	1,721,798	1,806,334	1,882,992
Individual income taxes	543,055	590,244	656,417	737,466	828,596	868,945	899,741
Corporation income taxes	140,385	157,004	171,824	182,293	188,677	182,210	189,356
Social insurance and retirement receipts	461,475	484,473	509,414	539,371	571,931	608,824	636,529
On-budget	126,450	133,394	141922	147,381	156,032	164,788	171,215
Off-budget	335,026	351,079	367,492	391,990	415,799	444,036	465,314
Excise taxes	55,225	57,484	54,014	56,924	57,673	68,075	69,902
Estate and gift taxes	15,225	14,763	17,189	19,845	24,076	25,932	26,972
Customs duties and fees	20,099	19,301	18,670	17,928	18,297	17,654	18,364
Miscellaneous receipts:							
Deposits of earnings by Federal Reserve System	18,023	23,378	20,477	19,636	24,540	26,354	25,231
All other[1]	5,141	5,183	5,057	5,829	8,118	8,340	16,897
Outlays, On-Budget and Off Budget	1,461,731	1,515,729	1,560,512	1,601,232	1,652,552	1,727,071	1,765,687
National defense	281,642	272,066	265,753	270,505	268,456	276,730	274,069
International affairs	17,083	16,434	13,496	15,228	13,109	15,474	16,102
General science, space, and technology	16,227	16,724	16,709	17,174	18,219	18,529	18,569
Energy	5,219	4,936	2,839	1,475	1,270	49	−1,995
Natural resources and environment	21,064	22,078	21,614	21,369	22,396	24,261	23,746
Agriculture	15,046	9,778	9,159	91032	12,206	21,449	15,146

Continued

TABLE B-81   CONTINUED

	Actual					Estimates	
	1994	**1995**	**1996**	**1997**	**1998**	**1999**	**2000**
Commerce and housing credit	–4,228	17,808	–10,472	14,624	1,014	452	6,352
On-budget	–5,331	–15,939	–10,292	–14,575	797	–512	4,519
Off-budget	1,103	–1,969	–180	–49	217	964	1,833
Transportation	38,066	39,350	39,565	40,767	40,332	42,640	46,435
Community and regional development	10,454	10,641	10,685	11,005	9,720	10,428	10,234
Education, training, employment and social services services	46,307	54,263	52,001	53,008	54,919	60,065	63,351
Health	107,122	115,418	119,378	123,843	131,440	143,095	152,270
Medicare	144,747	159,855	174,225	190,016	192,922	204,982	216,599
Income security	214,085	220,493	225,967	230,899	233,202	243,130	258,029
Social security	319,565	335,846	349,676	365,257	379,225	392,608	408,575
On-budget	5,693	5,476	5,807	6,885	9,156	11,292	10,354
Off-budget	313,881	330,370	343,869	358,372	370,069	381,316	398,221
Veterans benefits and services	37,584	37,890	36,985	39,313	41,781	43,526	44,024
Administration of Justice	15,256	16,216	17,549	20,173	22,832	24,467	27,529
General government	11,307	13,835	11,914	12,749	13,444	11,852	14,490
Net Interest	202,957	232,169	241,090	244,016	243,359	227,244	215,187
On-budget	232,160	265,474	277,597	285,230	299,989	279,113	271,679
Off-budget	–29,203	–33,305	–36,507	–41,214	–46,630	–51,869	–56,492
Allowances	—	—	—	—	—	3,118	2,631
Undistributed offsetting receipts	–37,772	–44,455	–37,620	49,973	47,194	40,028	–45,656
On-budget	–31,362	–38,023	–31,342	–43,490	–40,142	–32,673	–37,951
Off -budget	–6,409	–6,432	–6,278	–6,483	–7,052	–7,355	–7,705

See Note, Table B-78.

SOURCES: Department of the Treasury and Office of Management and Budget.

International Statistics

U.S. INTERNATIONAL TRANSACTIONS, 1946–98

[MILLIONS OF DOLLARS; QUARTERLY DATA SEASONALLY ADJUSTED, EXCEPT AS NOTED. CREDITS (+), DEBITS(−)]

| Year or Quarter | Goods[1] | | | Services | | | Balance on Goods and Services | Investment Income | | | Unilateral Transfers Net[3] | Balance on Current Account |
	Exports	Imports	Net	Net Military Trans-actions[2][3]	Net Travel and Trans-portation Receipts	Other Services, Net		Receipts on U.S. Assets Abroad	Payments on Foreign Assets in U.S.	Net		
1946	11,764	−5,067	6,697	−424	733	310	7,316	772	−212	560	−2,991	4,885
1947	16,097	−5,973	10,124	−358	946	145	10,857	1,102	−245	857	−2,722	8,992
1948	13,265	−7,557	5,708	−351	374	175	5,906	1,921	−437	1,484	−4,973	2,417
1949	12,213	−6,874	5,339	−410	230	208	5,367	1,831	−476	1,355	−5,849	873
1950	10,203	−9,081	1,122	−56	−120	242	1,188	2,068	−559	1,509	−4,537	−1,840
1951	14,243	−11,176	3,067	169	298	254	3,788	2,633	−583	2,050	−4,954	884
1952	13,449	−10,838	2,611	528	83	309	3,531	2,751	−555	2,196	−5,113	614
1953	12,412	−10,975	1,437	1,753	−238	307	3,259	2,736	−624	2,112	−6,657	−1,286
1954	12,929	−10,353	2,576	902	−269	305	3,514	2,929	−582	2,347	−5,642	219
1955	14,424	−11,527	2,897	−113	−297	299	2,786	3,406	−676	2,730	−5,086	430
1956	17,556	−12,803	4,753	−221	−361	447	4,618	3,837	−735	3,102	−4,990	2,730
1957	19,562	−13,291	6,271	−423	−189	482	6,141	4,180	−796	3,384	−4,763	4,762
1958	16,414	−12,952	3,462	−849	−633	486	2,466	3,790	−825	2,965	−4,647	784
1959	16,458	−15,310	1,148	−831	−821	573	69	4,132	−1,061	3,071	−4,422	−1282
1960	19,650	−14,758	4,892	−1,057	−964	639	3,508	4,616	−1,238	3,379	−4,062	2,824
1961	20,108	−14,537	5,571	−1,131	−978	732	4,195	4,999	−1,245	3,755	−4,127	3,822
1962	20,781	−16,260	4,521	−912	−1,152	912	3,370	5,618	−1,324	4,294	−4,277	3,387
1963	22,272	−17,048	5,224	−742	−1,309	1,036	4,210	6,157	−1,560	4,596	−4,392	4,414
1964	25,501	−18,700	6,801	−794	−1,146	1,161	6,022	6,824	−1,783	5,041	−4,240	6,823
1965	26,461	−21,510	4,951	−487	−1,280	1,480	4,664	7,437	−2,088	5,350	−4,583	5,431
1966	29,310	−25,493	3,817	−1,043	−1,331	−1,497	2,940	7,528	−2,481	5,047	−4,955	3,031
1967	30,666	−26,866	3,800	−1,187	−1,750	1,742	2,604	8,021	−27,477	5,274	−5,294	2,583
1968	33,626	−32,991	635	−596	−1,548	1,759	250	9,367	−3,378	5,990	−5,629	611
1969	36,414	−35,807	607	−718	−1,763	1,964	91	10,913	−4,869	6,044	−5,735	399
1970	42,469	−39,866	2,603	−641	−2,038	2,330	2,254	11,748	−5,515	6,233	−6,156	2,331
1971	43,319	−45,579	−2,260	653	−2,345	2,649	−1,303	12,707	−5,435	7,272	−7,402	−1,433
1972	49,381	−55,797	−6,416	1,072	−3,063	2,965	−5,443	14,765	−6,572	8,192	−8,544	−5,795
1973	71,410	−70,499	911	740	−3,158	3,406	1,900	21,808	−9,655	12,153	−6,913	7,140
1974	98,306	−103,811	−5,505	165	−3,184	4,231	−4,292	27,587	−12,084	15,503	−9,249[4]	1,962
1975	107,088	−98,185	8,903	1,416	−2,812	4,854	12,404	25,351	−12,564	12,787	−7,075	18,116

TABLE B-103   CONTINUED

Year or Quarter	U.S. Assets Abroad, Net [Increase/Capital Outflow (–)]				Foreign Assets in the U.S., Net [Increase/Capital Inflow (+)]			Allocations of Special Drawing Rights (SDRs)	Statistical Discrepancy	
	Total	U.S. Official Reserve Assets[2][5]	Other U.S. Government Assets[2]	U.S. Private Assets	Total	Foreign Official Assets[2]	Other Foreign Assets		Total (Sum of the Items with Sign Reversed)	Of Which: Seasonal Adjustment Discrepancy
1946	—	–623	—	—	—	—	—	—	—	—
1947	—	–3,315	—	—	—	—	—	—	—	—
1948	—	–1,736	—	—	—	—	—	—	—	—
1949	—	–266	—	—	—	—	—	—	—	—
1950	—	1,758	—	—	—	—	—	—	—	—
1951	—	–33	—	—	—	—	—	—	—	—
1952	—	–415	—	—	—	—	—	—	—	—
1953	—	1,256	—	—	—	—	—	—	—	—
1954	—	480	—	—	—	—	—	—	—	—
1955	—	182	—	—	—	—	—	—	—	—
1956	—	–869	—	—	—	—	—	—	—	—
1957	—	–1,165	—	—	—	—	—	—	—	—
1958	—	2,292	—	—	—	—	—	—	—	—
1959	—	1,035	—	—	—	—	—	—	—	—
1960	4,099	2,145	–1,100	–5,144	2,294	1,473	821	—	–1,019	—
1961	–5,538	607	–910	–5,235	2,705	765	1,939	—	–989	—
1962	4,174	1,535	–1,085	–4,623	1,911	1,270	641	—	–1,124	—
1963	–7,270	378	–1,662	–5,986	3,217	1,986	1,231	—	–360	—
1964	–9,560	171	–1,680	–8,050	3,643	1,660	1,983	—	–907	—
1965	–5,716	1,225	–1,605	–5,336	742	134	607	—	–457	—
1966	–7,321	570	–1,543	–6,347	3,661	–672	4,333	—	629	—
1967	–9,757	53	–2,423	–7,386	7,379	3,451	3,928	—	–205	—
1968	–10,977	–870	–2,274	–7,833	9,928	–774	10,703	—	438	—
1969	–11,585	–1,179	–2,200	–8,206	12,702	–1,301	14,002	—	–1,516	—
1970	–9,337	2,481	–1,589	–10,229	6,359	6,908	–550	867	–219	—
1971	–12,475	2,349	–1,884	–12,940	22,970	26,879	–3,909	717	–9,779	—
1972	14,497	–4	–1,568	–12,925	21,461	10,475	10,986	710	–1,879	—
1973	–22,874	158	–2,644	–20,388	18,388	6,026	12,362	—	–2,654	—
1974	–34,745	–1,417	366[4]	–33,643	35,341	10,546	24,796	—	–2,558	—
1975	–39,703	–849	–3,474	–35,380	17,170	7,027	10,143	—	4,417	—

Continued

TABLE B-103 CONTINUED

Year or Quarter	Goods[1]			Services			Balance on Goods and Services	Investment Income			Unilateral Transfers Net[3]	Balance on Current Account
	Exports	Imports	Net	Net Military Trans-actions[2][3]	Net Travel and Trans-portation Receipts	Other Services, Net		Receipts on U.S. Assets Abroad	Payments on Foreign Assets in U.S.	Net		
1976	114,745	−124,228	−9,483	931	−2,558	5,027	−6,082	29,375	−13,311	16,063	−5,686	4,295
1977	120,816	−151,907	−31,901	1,731	−3,565	5,680	−27,246	32,354	−14,217	18,137	−5,226	−14,335
1978	142,075	−176,002	−33,927	857	−3,573	6,879	−29,763	42,088	−21,680	20,408	−5,788	−15,143
1979	184,439	−212,007	−27,568	−1,313	−2,935	7,251	−24,565	63,834	−32,961	30,873	−6,593	−285
1980	224,250	−249,750	−25,500	−1,822	−997	8,912	−19,407	72,606	−42,532	30,073	−8,349	2,317
1981	237,044	−265,067	−28,023	−844	144	12,552	−16,172	86,529	−53,626	32,903	−11,702	5,030
1982	211,157	−247,642	−36,485	112	−992	13,209	−24,156	86,200	−.56,412	29,788	−17,075	−11,443
1983	201,799	−268,901	−67,102	−563	−4,227	14,124	−57,767	85,200	−53,700	31,500	−17,718	−43,985
1984	219,926	−332,418	−112,492	−2,547	−8,438	14,404	−109,173	104,756	−74, 036	30,720	−20,598	−98,951
1985	215,915	−338,088	−122,173	−4,390	−9,798	14,483	−121,880	93,679	−73,087	20,592	−22,700	−123,987
1986	223,344	−368,425	145,081	−5,181	−8,779	18,474	−140,566	91,186	− 79,095	12,091	−24,679	−153,154
1987	250,208	−409,765	−159,557	−3,844	−8,010	18,098	−153,313	100,511	−91,302	9,209	−23,909	−168,013
1988	320,230	−447,189	−126,959	−6,320	−3,013	20,435	−115,856	129,366	−115,722	13,644	−25,988	−128,201
1989	362,120	−477,365	−115,245	−6,749	3,551	26,245	−92,197	153,659	−138,639	15,020	−26,963	−104,139
1990	389, 307	−498,337	−109,030	−7,599	7,501	27,999	−81,129	163,324	−139,149	24,174	−34,669	−91,624
1991	416,913	−490,981	−74,068	−5,274	16,561	31,851	−30,931	141,408	−119,891	21,517	5,032	−4,383
1992	440,352	−536,458	−96,106	−1,448	19,969	38,899	−38,685	125,003	−102,462	22,541	−35,230	−51,374
1993	456,832	−589,441	−132,609	1,269	19,714	39,686	−71,939	126,702	−102,754	23,948	−38,142	−86,133
1994	502,398	−668,590	−166,192	2,495	16,305	46,479	−100,913	157,742	−141,263	16,479	−39,391	−123,825
1995	575,845	−749,574	−173,729	4,769	21,772	47,297	−99,891	203,844	−184,569	19,275	−34,638	−115,254
1996	611,983	−803,320	−191,337	4,684	24,969	53,110	−108,574	213,196	−198,960	14,236	−40,577	−134,915
1997	679,325	−877,279	−197,954	6,781	22,670	58,297	−110,206	241,787	−247,105	−5,318	−39,691	−155,215
1996: I	150,855	−193,467	−42,612	748	5,769	12,994	−23,101	51,997	−46,638	5,359	−10,473	−28,215
II	152,130	−200,965	−48,835	993	6,548	13,090	−28,204	51,801	−47,826	3,975	−8,777	−33,006
III	151,253	−202,806	−51,553	1,105	4,345	13,025	−33,078	53,058	−51,327	1,731	−9,043	−40,390
IV	157,745	−206,082	−48,337	1,838	8,307	14,001	−24,191	56,340	−53,168	3,172	−12,284	−33,303
1997: I	163,499	−213,222	−49,723	1,542	5,944	14,107	−28,130	57,581	−57,567	14	−8,874	−36,990
II	169,240	218,336	−49,096	2,191	5,711	14,679	−26,515	61,271	−60,811	460	−9,035	−35,090
III	172,302	−221,598	−49,296	1,945	5,414	14,832	−27,105	62,551	−64,095	−1,544	−9,445	−38,094
IV	174,284	−224,123	−49,839	1,103	5,600	14,677	−28,459	60,384	−64,631	−4,247	−12,337	−45,043
1998: I	171,469	−227,167	−55,698	1,527	4,416	14,748	−35,007	62,522	−64,770	−2,248	−9,480	−46,735
II	164,821	−229,264	−64,443	1,043	4,004	15,525	−43,871	61,900	−65,277	−3,377	−9,442	−56,690
III	163,560	−227,920	−64,360	1,101	2,605	14,899	−45,755	60,434	−65,894	−5,460	−10,084	−61,299

[1]Adjusted from Census data for differences in valuation, coverage, and timing; excludes military.
[2]Quarterly data are not seasonally adjusted.
[3]Includes transfers of goods and services under U.S. military grant programs.

TABLE B-103   CONTINUED

Year or Quarter	U.S. Assets Abroad, Net [Increase/Capital Outflow (–)]				Foreign Assets in the U.S., Net [Increase/Capital Inflow (+)]			Allocations of Special Drawing Rights (SDRs)	Statistical Discrepancy	
	Total	U.S. Official Reserve Assets[2][5]	Other U.S. Government Assets[2]	U.S. Private Assets	Total	Foreign Official Assets[2]	Other Foreign Assets		Total (Sum of the Items with Sign Reversed)	Of Which: Seasonal Adjustment Discrepancy
1976	–51,269	–2,558	–4,214	–44,498	38,018	17,693	20,326	—	8,955	—
1977	–34,785	–375	–3,693	–30,717	53,219	36,816	16,403	—	–4,099	—
1978	–61,130	732	–4,660	–57,202	67,036	33,678	33,358	—	9,236	—
1979	–66,054	–1,133	–3,746	–61,176	40,852	–13,665	54,516	1,139	24,349	—
1980	–86,967	–8,155	–5,162	–73,651	62,612	15,497	47,115	1,152	20,986	—
1981	–114,147	–5,175	–5,097	–103,875	86,232	4,960	81,272	1,093	21,792	—
1982	–122,335	–4,965	–6,131	–111,239	96,418	3,593	92,826	—	37,359	—
1983	–61,573	–1,196	–5,006	–55,372	88,780	5,845	82,934	—	16,779	—
1984	–36,313	–3,131	–5,489	–27,694	118,032	3,140	114,892	—	17,231	—
1985	–39,889	–3,858	–2,821	–33,211	146,383	–1,119	147,502	—	17,494	—
1986	–106,753	312	–2,022	–105,044	230,211	35,648	194,563	—	29,696	—
1987	–72,617	9,149	1,006	–82,771	248,383	45,387	202,996	—	–7,753	—
1988	–100,221	–3,912	2,967	–99,275	246,065	39,758	206,307	—	–17,644	—
1989	–168,744	–25,293	1,259	–144,710	224,390	8,503	215,887	—	48,494	—
1990	–74,011	–2,158	2,307	–74,160	140,992	33,910	107,082	—	24,643	—
1991	–57,881	5,763	2,911	–66,555	109,641	17,389	92,253	—	–47,378	—
1992	–68,774	3,901	–1,657	–71,018	168,776	40,477	128,299	—	–48,628	—
1993	–194,537	–1,379	–342	–192,817	279,671	71,753	207,918	—	999	—
1994	–171,102	5,346	–389	–176,059	304,460	39,583	264,877	—	–9,533	—
1995	–327,453	–9,742	–589	–317,122	465,449	109,768	355,681	—	–22,742	—
1996	468,801	6,668	–708	–374,761	563,357	127,344	436,013	—	–59,641	—
1997	–478,502	–1,010	174	477,666	733,441	15,817	717,624	—	–99,724	—
1996: I	–69,695	17	–210	–69,502	90,534	51,833	38,701	—	7,376	4,928
II	–60,623	–523	–377	–59,723	109,122	13,601	95,521	—	–15,493	116
III	–83,101	7,489	163	–90,753	149,361	23,432	125,929	—	–25,870	–8,779
IV	–155,381	–315	–284	–154,782	214,339	38,478	175,861	—	–25,655	3,734
1997: I	–145,139	4,480	–22	–149,597	181,735	26,949	154,786	—	394	5,812
II	–86,606	–236	–269	–86,101	149,773	–5,411	155,184	—	–28,077	685
III	–123,317	–730	436	–123,023	181,438	21,258	160,180	—	–20,027	–10,018
IV	–123,441	–4,524	29	–118,946	220,491	–26,979	247,470	—	–52,007	3,528
1998: I	–45,648	–444	–388	–44,816	95,529	11,324	84,205	—	–3,146	6,217
II	–109,787	–1,945	–433	–107,409	164,859	–10,274	175,133	—	1,618	1,474
III	–48,052	–2,026	194	–46,220	112,862	–46,370	159,232	—	–3,511	–10,760

[4]Includes extraordinary U.S. Government transactions with India.
[5]Consists of gold, special drawing rights, foreign currencies, and the U.S. reserve position in the International Monetary Fund (IMF).

SOURCE: Department of Commerce, Bureau of Economic Analysis.

TABLE B-105   U.S. INTERNATIONAL TRADE IN GOODS BY AREA, 1989–98

[BILLIONS OF DOLLARS]

Item	1989	1990	1991	1992	1993	1994	1995	1996	1997	1998 First 3 Quarters at Annual Rate[1]
Exports	362.1	389.3	416.9	440.4	456.8	502.4	575.8	612.0	679.3	666.5
Industrial countries	234.2	253.8	261.3	265.1	270.6	295.2	338.1	355.4	386.5	389.5
Canada	81.1	83.5	85.9	91.4	101.2	114.8	127.6	134.5	152.0	155.8
Japan	43.9	47.8	47.2	46.9	46.7	51.8	63.1	66.0	64.6	57.9
Western Europe[2]	98.4	111.4	116.8	114.5	111.3	115.3	132.5	138.3	153.0	158.8
Australia, New Zealand, and South Africa	10.9	11.2	11.4	12.4	11.5	13.2	15.0	16.6	16.8	17.0
Australia	8.1	8.3	8.3	8.7	8.1	9.6	10.5	11.7	11.9	12.0
Other countries, except Eastern Europe	122.2	130.6	150.4	169.5	179.8	201.7	232.0	249.3	285.1	268.9
OPEC[3]	12.7	12.7	18.4	19.7	18.7	17.1	18.3	20.3	24.2	22.5
Other[4]	109.5	117.9	132.0	149.8	161.1	184.6	213.7	229.0	261.0	246.4
Eastern Europe[2]	5.5	4.3	4.8	5.6	6.2	5.3	5.7	7.3	7.8	8.0
International organizations and unallocated	.2	.6	.4	.1	.2	.1	—	—	—	—
Imports	477.4	498.3	491.0	536.5	589.4	668.6	749.6	803.3	877.3	912.5
Industrial countries	292.5	299.9	294.3	316.3	347.8	389.8	425.4	443.2	477.4	497.6
Canada	89.9	93.1	93.0	100.9	113.3	131.1	147.1	158.7	171.0	176.1
Japan	93.5	90.4	92.3	97.4	107.2	119.1	123.5	115.2	121.7	121.3
Western Europe[2]	102.4	109.2	102.0	111.4	120.9	132.9	147.7	161.7	175.8	190.0
Australia, New Zealand, and South Africa	6.6	7.3	7.0	6.6	6.4	6.7	7.1	7.7	9.0	10.2
Australia	3.9	4.4	4.1	3.7	3.3	3.2	3.4	3.9	4.9	5.4
Other countries, except Eastern Europe	182.8	196.1	194.9	218.2	238.1	272.9	317.2	353.2	391.4	404.0
OPEC[3]	29.2	37.0	33.4	32.4	32.6	31.7	34.3	42.7	44.0	35.0
Other[4]	153.6	159.1	161.5	185.8	205.4	241.3	282.9	310.5	347.4	369.0
Eastern Europe[2]	2.1	2.3	1.8	2.0	3.5	5.8	7.0	7.0	8.5	10.9
International organizations and unallocated	—	—	—	—	—	—	—	—	—	—
Balance (excess of exports +)	−115.2	−109.0	−74.1	−96.1	−132.6	−166.2	−173.7	−191.3	−198.0	−246.0
Industrial countries	−58.2	46.1	−33.0	−51.2	−77.2	−94.6	−87.3	−87.8	−91.0	−108.1
Canada	−8.8	−9.6	−7.1	−9.5	−12.2	−16.3	−19.6	−24.2	−19.0	−20.4
Japan	−49.7	−42.6	45.0	−50.5	−60.5	−67.3	−60.3	−49.2	−57.1	−63.4
Western Europe[2]	−4.0	2.2	14.8	3.1	−9.7	−17.6	−15.2	−23.3	−22.8	−31.1
Australia, New Zealand, and South Africa	4.2	3.9	4.4	5.8	5.2	6.6	7.9	8.9	7.9	6.9
Australia	4.2	3.9	4.2	5.0	4.8	6.4	7.1	7.8	7.0	6.6

Continued

TABLE B-105   CONTINUED

Item	1989	1990	1991	1992	1993	1994	1995	1996	1997	1998 First 3 Quarters at Annual Rate[1]
Other countries, except Eastern Europe	–60.6	–65.5	–44.5	–48.7	–58.3	–71.2	–85.2	–103.9	–106.3	–135.0
OPEC[3]	–16.6	–24.3	–15.0	–12.7	–14.0	–14.6	–15.9	–22.4	–19.9	–12.5
Other[4]	–44.1	–41.2	–29.5	–36.0	–44.3	–56.6	–69.2	–81.5	–86.4	–122.6
Eastern Europe[2]	3.5	2.1	3.0	3.7	2.7	–.5	–1.3	.3	–.7	–2.9
International organizations and unallocated	.2	.6	.4	.1	.2	.1	—	—	—	—

[1]Preliminary; seasonally adjusted.

[2]The former German Democratic Republic (East Germany) included in Western Europe beginning fourth quarter 1990 and in Eastern Europe prior to that time.

[3]Organization of Petroleum Exporting Countries, consisting of Algeria, Ecuador (through 1992), Gabon (through 1994), Indonesia, Iran, Iraq, Kuwait, Libya, Nigeria, Qatar, Saudi Arabia, United Arab Emirates, and Venezuela.

[4]Latin America, other Western Hemisphere, and other countries in Asia and Africa, less members of OPEC.

Note: Data are on an international transactions basis and exclude military.

SOURCE: Department of Commerce, Bureau of Economic Analysis.

TABLE B-107 INTERNATIONAL INVESTMENT POSITION OF THE UNITED STATES AT YEAR-END, 1989–97

[BILLIONS OF DOLLARS]

Type of Investment	1989	1990	1991	1992	1993	1994	1995	1996	1997
Net International Investment Position of the United States									
With direct investment at current cost	–222.4	–206.3	–269.1	–398.2	–275.6	–351.9	–603.1	–767.1	–1,223.6
With direct investment at market value	–49.1	–166.8	–263.1	–454.6	–180.4	–232.9	–537.1	–743.7	–1,322.5
U.S. Assets Abroad									
With direct investment at current cost	2,076.0	2,180.0	2,285.1	2,325.0	2,742.5	2,901.8	3,296.8	3,767.0	4,237.3
With direct investment at market value	2,348.1	2,291.7	2,468.4	2,464.2	3,055.3	3,217.4	3,754.3	4,347.1	5,007.1
U.S. official reserve assets	168.7	174.7	159.2	147.4	164.9	163.4	176.1	160.7	134.8
Gold[1]	105.2	102.4	92.6	87.2	102.6	100.1	101.3	96.7	75.9
Special drawing rights	10.0	11.0	11.2	8.5	9.0	10.0	11.0	10.3	10.0
Reserve position in the International Monetary Fund	9.0	9.1	9.5	11.8	11.8	12.0	14.6	15.4	18.1
Foreign currencies	44.6	52.2	45.9	40.0	41.5	41.2	49.1	38.3	30.8
U.S. Government assets, other than official reserves	84.5	82.0	79.1	80.7	81.0	80.4	81.0	81.7	81.5
U.S. credits and other long-term assets	83.9	81.4	77.5	79.1	79.1	78.2	79.0	79.8	79.6
Repayable in dollars	82.4	80.0	76.3	78.0	78.1	77.5	78.3	79.1	78.9
Other	1.5	1.3	1.2	1.1	1.0	.8	.7	.7	.6
U.S. foreign currency holdings and U.S. short-term assets	.6	.6	1.6	1.6	1.9	2.2	2.0	1.9	1.9
U.S. private assets:									
With direct investment at current cost	1,822.8	1,923.3	2,046.8	2,096.8	2,496.6	2,658.0	3,039.7	3,524.6	4,021.0
With direct investment at market value	2,094.9	2,035.1	2,230.0	2,236.0	2,809.3	2,973.6	3,497.2	4,104.7	4,790.8
Direct investment abroad:									
At current cost	560.4	620.0	644.3	659.4	714.8	752.1	849.7	937.0	1,023.9
At market value	832.5	731.8	827.5	798.6	1,027.5	1,067.8	1,307.2	1,517.1	1,793.7
Foreign securities	314.3	342.3	455.8	515.1	853.5	889.7	1,054.4	1,280.2	1,446.3
Bonds	116.9	144.7	176.8	200.8	309.7	303.1	355.3	403.4	445.0
Corporate stocks	197.3	197.6	279.0	314.3	543.9	586.6	699.1	876.8	1,001.3
U.S. claims on unaffiliated foreigners reported by U.S. nonbanking concerns	234.3	265.3	256.3	254.3	242.0	323.0	367.6	450.0	562.4
U.S. claims reported by U.S. banks, not included elsewhere	713.8	695.7	690.4	668.0	686.2	693.1	768.1	857.5	998.4

TABLE B-107   CONTINUED

Type of Investment	1989	1990	1991	1992	1993	1994	1995	1996	1997
Foreign Assets in the United States									
With direct investment at current cost	2,298.4	2,386.3	2,554.3	2,723.2	3,018.2	3,253.7	3,899.9	4,534.1	5,460.9
With direct investment at market value	2,397.2	2,458.6	2,731.4	2,918.8	3,235.7	3,450.4	4,291.4	5,090.8	6,329.6
Foreign official assets in the United States	341.7	373.3	398.5	437.3	509.4	535.2	671.6	801.1	833.9
U.S. Government securities	263.6	291.2	311.2	329.3	381.7	407.2	497.8	612.7	614.4
U.S. Treasury securities	257.2	285.9	306.0	322.6	373.1	396.9	482.8	592.9	589.9
Other	6.4	5.3	5.2	6.7	8.6	10.3	15.0	19.8	24.5
Other U.S. Government liabilities	15.4	17.2	18.6	20.8	22.1	23.7	23.5	23.1	20.6
U.S. liabilities reported by U.S. banks, not included elsewhere	36.5	39.9	38.4	55.0	69.7	73.4	107.4	113.1	135.0
Other foreign official assets	26.3	24.9	30.3	32.2	35.9	31.0	43.0	52.2	63.9
Other foreign assets in the United States:									
With direct investment at current cost	1,956.7	2,013.0	2,155.7	2,285.9	2,508.7	2,718.5	3,228.3	3,733.0	4,627.0
With direct investment at market value	2,055.5	2,085.3	2,332.9	2,481.5	2,726.3	2,915.2	3,619.7	4,289.7	5,495.7
Direct investment in the United States:									
At current cost	435.9	467.3	491.9	500.5	550.9	561.2	614.3	667.0	751.8
At market value	534.7	539.6	669.1	696.2	768.4	757.9	1,005.7	1,223.7	1,620.5
U.S. Treasury securities	166.5	152.5	170.3	197.7	221.5	235.7	357.7	504.8	662.0
U.S. currency	67.1	85.9	101.3	114.8	133.7	157.2	169.5	186.8	211.6
U.S. securities other than U.S. Treasury securities	482.9	460.6	546.0	599.4	696.4	739.7	971.4	1,199.5	1,578.0
Corporate and other bonds	231.7	238.9	274.1	299.3	355.8	368.1	481.2	588.0	718.1
Corporate stocks	251.2	221.7	271.9	300.2	340.6	371.6	490.1	611.4	859.9
U.S. liabilities to unaffiliated foreigners reported by U.S. nonbanking concerns	167.1	213.4	208.9	220.7	229.0	239.8	300.4	346.7	453.6
U.S. liabilities reported by U.S. banks, not included elsewhere	637.1	633.3	637.2	652.7	677.1	784.9	815.0	828.2	970.0

[1]Valued at market price.

Note: For details regarding these data, see *Survey of Current Business*, July 1998.

SOURCE: Department of Commerce, Bureau of Economic Analysis.

TABLE B-73	BOND YIELDS AND INTEREST RATES, 1929–98

[PERCENT PER ANNUM]

Year and Month	U.S. Treasury Securities Bills (New Issues)[1] 3-Month	6-Month	Constant Maturities[2] 3-Year	10-Year	30-Year	Corporate Bonds (Moody's) Aaa	Baa	High-Grade Municipal Bonds (Standard & Poor's)	New Home Mortgage Yields[3]	Commercial Paper, 6 Months[4]	Prime Rate Charged by Banks[5]	Discount Rate Federal Reserve Bank of New York[5]	Federal Funds Rate[6]
1929	—	—	—	—	—	4.73	5.90	4.27	—	5.85	5.50–6.00	5.16	—
1933	0.515	—	—	—	—	4.49	7.76	4.71	—	1.73	1.50–4.00	2.56	—
1939	.023	—	—	—	—	3.01	4.96	2.76	—	.59	1.50	1.00	—
1940	.014	—	—	—	—	2.84	4.75	2.50	—	.56	1.50	1.00	—
1941	.103	—	—	—	—	2.77	4.33	2.10	—	.53	1.50	1.00	—
1942	.326	—	—	—	—	2.83	4.28	2.36	—	.66	1.50	1.00[7]	—
1943	.373	—	—	—	—	2.73	3.91	2.06	—	.69	1.50	1.00[7]	—
1944	.375	—	—	—	—	2.72	3.61	1.86	—	.73	1.50	1.00[7]	—
1945	.375	—	—	—	—	2.62	3.29	1.67	—	.75	1.50	1.00[7]	—
1946	.375	—	—	—	—	2.53	3.05	1.64	—	.81	1.50	1.00[7]	—
1947	.594	—	—	—	—	2.61	3.24	2.01	—	1.03	1.50–1.75	1.00	—
1948	1.040	—	—	—	—	2.82	3.47	2.40	—	1.44	1.75–2.00	1.34	—
1949	1.102	—	—	—	—	2.66	3.42	2.21	—	1.49	2.00	1.50	—
1950	1.218	—	—	—	—	2.62	3.24	1.98	—	1.45	2.07	1.59	—
1951	1.552	—	—	—	—	2.86	3.41	2.00	—	2.16	2.56	1.75	—
1952	1.766	—	—	—	—	2.96	3.52	2.19	—	2.33	3.00	1.75	—
1953	1.931	—	2.47	2.85	—	3.20	3.74	2.72	—	2.52	3.17	1.99	—
1954	.953	—	1.63	2.40	—	2.90	3.51	2.37	—	1.58	3.05	1.60	—
1955	1.753	—	2.47	2.82	—	3.06	3.53	2.53	—	2.18	3.16	1.89	1.78
1956	2.658	—	3.19	3.18	—	3.36	3.88	2.93	—	3.31	3.77	2.77	2.73
1957	3.267	—	3.98	3.65	—	3.89	4.71	3.60	—	3.81	4.20	3.12	3.11
1958	1.839	—	2.84	3.32	—	3.79	4.73	3.56	—	2.46	3.83	2.15	1.57
1959	3.405	3.832	4.46	4.33	—	4.38	5.05	3.95	—	3.97	4.48	3.36	3.30
1960	2.928	3.247	3.98	4.12	—	4.41	5.19	3.73	—	3.85	4.82	3.53	3.22
1961	2.378	2.605	3.54	3.88	—	4.35	5.08	3.46	—	2.97	4.50	3.00	1.96
1962	2.778	2.908	3.47	3.95	—	4.33	5.02	3.18	—	3.26	4.50	3.00	2.68
1963	3.157	3.253	3.67	4.00	—	4.26	4.86	3.23	5.89	3.55	4.50	3.23	3.18
1964	3.549	3.686	4.03	4.19	—	4.40	4.83	3.22	5.83	3.97	4.50	3.55	3.50
1965	3.954	4.055	4.22	4.28	—	4.49	4.87	3.27	5.81	4.38	4.54	4.04	4.07
1966	4.881	5.082	5.23	4.92	—	5.13	5.67	3.82	6.25	5.55	5.63	4.50	5.11
1967	4.321	4.630	5.03	5.07	—	5.51	6.23	3.98	6.46	5.10	5.61	4.19	4.22
1968	5.339	5.470	5.68	5.65	—	6.18	6.94	4.51	6.97	5.90	6.30	5.16	5.66
1969	6.677	6.853	7.02	6.67	—	7.03	7.81	5.81	7.81	7.83	7.96	5.87	8.20

TABLE B-73   CONTINUED

Year and Month	U.S. Treasury Securities					Corporate Bonds (Moody's)		High-Grade Municipal Bonds Standard & Poor's)	New Home Mortgage Yields[3]	Commercial Paper, 6 Months[4]	Prime Rate Charged by Banks[5]	Discount Rate Federal Reserve Bank of New York[5]	Federal Funds Rate[6]
	Bills (New Issues)[1]		Constant Maturities[2]										
	3-Month	6-Month	3-Year	10-Year	30-Year	Aaa	Baa						
1970	6.458	6.562	7.29	7.35	—	8.04	9.11	6.51	8.45	7.71	7.91	5.95	7.18
1971	4.348	4.511	5.65	6.16	—	7.39	8.56	5.70	7.74	5.11	5.72	4.88	4.66
1972	4.071	4.466	5.72	6.21	—	7.21	8.16	5.27	7.60	4.73	5.25	4.50	4.43
1973	7.041	7.178	6.95	6.84	—	7.44	8.24	5.18	7.96	8.15	8.03	6.44	8.73
1974	7.886	7.926	7.92	7.56	—	8.57	9.50	6.09	8.92	9.84	10.81	7.83	10.50
1975	5.838	6.122	7.49	7.99	—	8.83	10.61	6.89	9.00	6.32	7.86	6.25	5.82
1976	4.989	5.266	6.77	7.61	—	8.43	9.75	6.49	9.00	5.34	6.84	5.50	5.04
1977	5.265	5.510	6.69	7.42	7.75	8.02	8.97	5.56	9.02	5.61	6.83	5.46	5.54
1978	7.221	7.572	8.29	8.41	8.49	8.73	9.49	5.90	9.56	7.99	9.06	7.46	7.93
1979	10.041	10.017	9.71	9.44	9.28	9.63	10.69	6.39	10.78	10.91	12.67	10.28	11.19
1980	11.506	11.374	11.55	11.46	11.27	11.94	13.67	8.51	12.66	12.29	15.27	11.77	13.36
1981	14.029	13.776	14.44	13.91	13.45	14.17	16.04	11.23	14.70	14.76	18.87	13.42	16.38
1982	10.686	11.084	12.92	13.00	12.76	13.79	16.11	11.57	15.14	11.89	14.86	11.02	12.26
1983	8.63	8.75	10.45	11.10	11.18	12.04	13.55	9.47	12.57	8.89	10.79	8.50	9.09
1984	9.53	9.80	11.89	12.44	12.41	12.71	14.19	10.15	12.38	10.16	12.04	8.80	10.23
1985	7.48	7.66	9.64	10.62	10.79	11.37	12.72	9.18	11.55	8.01	9.93	7.69	8.10
1986	5.98	6.03	7.06	7.68	7.78	9.02	10.39	7.38	10.17	6.39	8.33	6.33	6.81
1987	5.82	6.05	7.68	8.39	8.59	9.38	10.58	7.73	9.31	6.85	8.21	5.66	6.66
1988	6.69	6.92	8.26	8.85	8.96	9.71	10.83	7.76	9.19	7.68	9.32	6.20	7.57
1989	8.12	8.04	8.55	8.49	8.45	9.26	10.18	7.24	10.13	8.80	10.87	6.93	9.21
1990	7.51	7.47	8.26	8.55	8.61	9.32	10.36	7.25	10.05	7.95	10.01	6.98	8.10
1991	5.42	5.49	6.82	7.86	8.14	8.77	9.80	6.89	9.32	5.85	8.46	5.45	5.69
1992	3.45	3.57	5.30	7.01	7.67	8.14	8.98	6.41	8.24	3.80	6.25	3.25	3.52
1993	3.02	3.14	4.44	5.87	6.59	7.22	7.93	5.63	7.20	3.30	6.00	3.00	3.02
1994	4.29	4.66	6.27	7.09	7.37	7.96	8.62	6.19	7.49	4.93	7.15	3.60	4.21
1995	5.51	5.59	6.25	6.57	6.88	7.59	8.20	5.95	7.87	5.93	8.83	5.21	5.83
1996	5.02	5.09	5.99	6.44	6.71	7.37	8.05	5.75	7.80	5.42	8.27	5.02	5.30
1997	5.07	5.18	6.10	6.35	6.61	7.26	7.86	5.55	7.71	5.62	8.44	5.00	5.46
1998	4.81	4.85	5.14	5.26	5.58	6.53	7.22	5.12	7.07	—	8.35	4.92	5.35

[1]Rate on new issues within period; bank-discount basis.

[2]Yields on the more actively traded issues adjusted to constant maturities by the Department of the Treasury.

[3]Effective rate (in the primary market) on conventional mortgages, reflecting fees and charges as well as contract rate and assuming, on the average, repayment at end of 10 years. Rates beginning January 1973 not strictly comparable with prior rates.

[4]Bank-discount basis; prior to November 1979, data are for 4–6 months paper. Series no longer published by Federal Reserve (FR). See FR release H.15 *Selected Interest Rates* dated May 12, 1997.

[5]For monthly data, high and low for the period. Prime rate for 1929–33 and 1947–48 are ranges of the rate in effect during the period.

[6]Since July 19, 1975, the daily effective rate is an average of the rates on a given day weighted by the volume of transactions at these rates. Prior to that date, the daily effective rate was the rate considered most representative of the day's transactions, usually the one at which most transactions occurred.

[7]From October 30, 1942, to April 24, 1946, a preferential rate of 0.50 percent was in effect for advances secured by Government securities maturing in 1 year or less.

TABLE B-110 FOREIGN EXCHANGE RATES, 1977–98

[CURRENCY UNITS PER U.S. DOLLAR, EXCEPT AS NOTED]

Period	Belgium (Franc)	Canada (Dollar)	France (Franc)	Germany (Mark)	Italy (Lira)	Japan (Yen)	Netherlands (Guilder)	Sweden (Krona)	Switzerland (Franc)	United Kingdom (Pound)[1]
March 1973	39.408	0.9967	4.5156	2.8132	568.17	261.90	2.8714	4.4294	3.2171	2.4724
1977	35.849	1.0633	4.9161	2.3236	882.78	268.62	2.4548	4.4802	2.4065	1.7449
1978	31.495	1.1405	4.5091	2.0097	849.13	210.39	2.1643	4.5207	1.7907	1.9184
1979	29.342	1.1713	4.2567	1.8343	831.11	219.02	2.0073	4.2893	1.6644	2.1224
1980	29.238	1.1693	4.2251	1.8175	856.21	226.63	1.9875	4.2310	1.6772	2.3246
1981	37.195	1.1990	5.4397	2.2632	1138.58	220.63	2.4999	5.0660	1.9675	2.0243
1982	45.781	1.2344	6.5794	2.4281	1354.00	249.06	2.6719	6.2839	2.0327	1.7480
1983	51.123	1.2325	7.6204	2.5539	1519.32	237.55	2.8544	7.6718	2.1007	1.5159
1984	57.752	1.2952	8.7356	2.8455	1756.11	237.46	3.2085	8.2708	2.3500	1.3368
1985	59.337	1.3659	8.9800	2.9420	1908.88	238.47	3.3185	8.6032	2.4552	1.2974
1986	44.664	1.3896	6.9257	2.1705	1491.16	168.35	2.4485	7.1273	1.7979	1.4677
1987	37.358	1.3259	6.0122	1.7981	1297.03	144.60	2.0264	6.3469	1.4918	1.6398
1988	36.785	1.2306	5.9595	1.7570	1302.39	128.17	1.9778	6.1370	1.4643	1.7813
1989	39.409	1.1842	6.3802	1.8808	1372.28	138.07	2.1219	6.4559	1.6369	1.6382
1990	33.424	1.1668	5.4467	1.6166	1198.27	145.00	1.8215	5.9231	1.3901	1.7841
1991	34.195	1.1460	5.6468	1.6610	1241.28	134.59	1.8720	6.0521	1.4356	1.7674
1992	32.148	1.2085	5.2935	1.5618	1232.17	126.78	1.7587	5.8258	1.4064	1.7663
1993	34.581	1.2902	5.6669	1.6545	1573.41	111.08	1.8585	7.7956	1.4781	1.5016
1994	33.426	1.3664	5.5459	1.6216	1611.49	102.18	1.8190	7.7161	1.3667	1.5319
1995	29.472	1.3725	4.9864	1.4321	1629.45	93.96	1.6044	7.1406	1.1812	1.5785
1996	30.970	1.3638	5.1158	1.5049	1542.76	108.78	1.6863	6.7082	1.2361	1.5607
1997	35.807	1.3849	5.8393	1.7348	1703.81	121.06	1.9525	7.6446	1.4514	1.6376
1998	36.310	1.4836	5.8995	1.7597	1736.85	130.99	1.9837	7.9522	1.4506	1.6573
1997: I	34.190	1.3593	5.5926	1.6575	1637.48	121.16	1.8630	7.3744	1.4357	1.6314
II	35.388	1.3864	5.7813	1.7148	1691.18	119.80	1.9289	7.7099	1.4460	1.6354
III	37.305	1.3850	6.0845	1.8065	1761.83	118.02	2.0340	7.8318	1.4883	1.6254
IV	36.283	1.4087	5.8886	1.7577	1722.20	125.39	1.9809	7.6499	1.4343	1.6587
1998: I	37.558	1.4298	6.0957	1.8190	1792.04	128.23	2.0505	8.0172	1.4767	1.6465
II	37.022	1.4469	6.0162	1.7944	1770.03	135.69	2.0218	7.8181	1.4934	1.6541
III	36.348	1.5136	5.9091	1.7623	1739.18	140.01	1.9874	8.0011	1.4703	1.6531
IV	34.309	1.5430	5.5758	1.6630	1645.88	119.40	1.8749	7.9753	1.3602	1.6758

TABLE B-110   CONTINUED

	Trade-Weighted Value of the U.S. Dollar							
	Nominal				Real[6]			
Period	G-10 Index (March 1973=100)[2]	Broad Index (January 1997=100)[3]	Major Currencies Index (March 1973=100)[4]	OITP Index (January 1997=100)[5]	G-10 Index (March 1973=100)[2]	Broad Index (March 1973=100)[3]	Major Currencies Index (March 1973=100)[4]	OITP Index (March 1973=100)[5]
1977	103.4	34.7	105.3	2.9	93.4	94.1	94.1	93.7
1978	92.4	33.2	96.7	3.1	84.3	88.2	86.9	91.7
1979	88.1	33.7	95.5	3.3	83.3	89.4	88.8	91.2
1980	87.4	34.8	95.3	3.7	85.1	91.5	91.8	91.0
1981	103.4	38.5	104.1	4.2	101.1	98.0	100.8	92.6
1982	116.6	44.8	114.7	5.5	112.0	107.6	109.2	104.3
1983	125.3	50.5	118.6	7.4	117.5	111.6	110.7	113.4
1984	138.2	57.5	126.3	9.7	129.0	118.2	118.0	119.3
1985	143.0	64.5	131.0	13.0	132.8	123.3	122.0	127.0
1986	112.2	60.4	107.9	16.3	103.9	108.6	99.7	132.9
1987	96.9	58.3	95.4	19.2	91.1	99.1	89.2	126.8
1988	92.7	59.0	88.8	23.3	88.5	92.4	84.1	115.8
1989	98.6	65.2	92.4	29.0	94.9	94.0	88.1	110.9
1990	89.1	70.0	88.4	39.1	86.6	91.2	85.1	108.8
1991	89.8	73.1	86.9	45.7	86.9	89.7	83.4	107.8
1992	86.6	76.3	85.4	52.9	83.6	86.8	82.3	101.2
1993	93.2	84.4	87.7	66.0	89.9	88.3	85.0	100.4
1994	91.3	90.4	86.1	80.5	88.6	86.4	84.6	95.5
1995	84.2	92.5	81.4	92.5	82.4	84.0	80.8	95.3
1996	87.3	97.4	85.2	98.2	86.4	85.9	85.8	92.5
1997	96.4	104.5	91.9	104.7	95.9	90.5	93.2	93.6
1998	98.8	116.3	96.5	125.7	98.7	98.4	98.3	105.7
1997: I	93.7	101.5	90.0	100.5	93.4	88.6	91.5	91.1
II	95.7	102.6	91.3	101.3	95.2	89.0	92.4	91.0
III	98.6	104.7	92.5	104.1	98.0	90.6	93.8	92.8
IV	97.5	109.1	93.6	112.9	97.0	93.9	95.0	99.3
1998: I	100.3	115.1	95.9	123.9	100.0	98.2	97.5	106.4
II	100.3	115.7	97.3	122.9	99.9	98.2	99.0	104.3
III	100.2	119.1	99.1	128.3	100.2	100.7	101.2	107.5
IV	94.5	115.1	93.7	127.7	94.8	96.5	95.7	104.8

[1]Value is U.S. dollars per pound.
[2]G-10 comprises the countries shown in this table. Discontinued after December 1998.
[3]The broad index is a weighted average of the foreign exchange value of the dollar against the currencies of a broad group of U.S. trading partners.
[4]Subset of the broad index. Includes G-10 countries plus Spain, Ireland, Austria, Finland, Portugal, and Australia.
[5]Subset of the broad index. Includes other important U.S. trading partners (OITP) whose currencies are not heavily traded outside their home markets.
[6]Adjusted for changes in the consumer price index.
Note: Certified noon buying rates in New York.
For a discussion of the newly introduced multilateral trade-weighted indexes for the U.S. dollar, see Federal Reserve *Bulletin*, October 1998.

SOURCE: Board of Governors of the Federal Reserve System.